Ethics in Consumer Choice

Nina Langen

Ethics in Consumer Choice

An Empirical Analysis based on the Example of Coffee

Foreword by Prof. Dr. Monika Hartmann

Springer Gabler

Nina Langen
Bonn, Germany

Dissertation der Landwirtschaftlichen Fakultät der Rheinischen Friedrich-Wilhelms-Universität Bonn, 2012

D 98

ISBN 978-3-658-00758-4
ISBN 978-3-658-00759-1 (eBook)
DOI 10.1007/978-3-658-00759-1

The Deutsche Nationalbibliothek lists this publication in the Deutsche Nationalbibliografie; detailed bibliographic data are available in the Internet at http://dnb.d-nb.de.

Library of Congress Control Number: 2012955241

Springer Gabler

Printed on acid-free paper

Springer Gabler is a brand of Springer DE.
Springer DE is part of Springer Science+Business Media.
www.springer-gabler.de

Foreword

Individuals have a multitude of possibilities by means of their decisions to influence ecological, social and economic developments at the regional, national and global level. Purchasing products that meet ecological or social requirements or making donations are some examples of ethical consumer behaviour. However, what influences individuals to take into consideration ethical criteria when making a purchase decision and do these factors differ depending on the kind of product and product attributes? How may we explain that in surveys carried out in Germany and in many other countries, most of the respondents indicate that ethical aspects play a role in their purchase decision whereas this is not reflected in the corresponding behaviour of the respondents? Do those who make donations have a different motivation than those who integrate ethical criteria into their purchase decision?

In her dissertation, "Ethics in Consumer Choice – An Empirical Analysis based on the Example of Coffee" Dr. Langen addresses this question as well as other interesting and relevant issues regarding "ethics in consumer decisions". Her dissertation investigates the question as to whether consumers in Germany differentiate between various forms of ethical behaviour. In the context of her analysis, the author considers not only the purchase of products certified by a Fair Trade label, an eco-label or a cause-related marketing label, but also donations as a form of ethical behaviour. The author first ascertains to what extent products and product attributes certified as ethical and sustainable are perceived to be relevant by consumers and which factors significantly influence the perception of these attributes and the purchase decision process. In addition, her dissertation aims to gain insights into whether the investigated forms of ethical behaviour can be classified as complementary or substitutional. The author examines whether the various consumer segments can be identified according to their different preferences for alternative forms of ethical behaviour. On the basis of a comprehensive theoretical and empirical analysis and a complex methodological mixture adapted to the individual surveys, interesting findings on the determinants of ethical behaviour are presented. These findings are highly relevant for future scientific studies in the field of consumer research as well as for decision makers in politics and industry whose goal is the promotion of ethical consumption.

The findings contained in this study are based on analyses carried out by Dr. Langen with a high degree of diligence and expertise. She offers the reader many new insights into the influence of ethical aspects on consumer behaviour with regard to food products. I hope that the work of Dr. Langen receives the great recognition and broad resonance in research and practice that it certainly deserves.

Prof. Dr. Monika Hartmann

Acknowledgement

Many people have supported me in one or the other way during the course of this dissertation. I would like to thank them all. If "gratitude is the memory of the heart" (J.B. Massieu), then my memory of the heart is much larger than these acknowledgements.

I am indebted to Prof. Monika Hartmann for being my first supervisor, for supporting me during the course of the thesis, for providing me with the freedom to develop my own research agenda and for the valuable experiences she facilitated during my time at the department for agricultural and food market research. I also greatly appreciate Prof. Thomas Kutsch's willingness to take over the co-reference of this thesis. It is not the first time that he has accompanied and supported my career! I would also like to express my gratitude to Prof. Karin Holm-Müller for taking over the chair of my dissertation defence.

The Robert Bosch Foundation provided me with an extraordinary scholarship which I gratefully acknowledge. This financial support enabled me not only to conduct the three different experimental consumer studies. Much more importantly, it gave me independence during the first years of my PhD studies, which I highly appreciate and without which I never would have started this long-term project. In this regard I am grateful to all those institutions that supported my passion to attend and present my research findings at conferences throughout the world.

Part of this research has been conducted during my time as a junior researcher at the Center for Development Research (ZEF B). I would like to thank the many colleagues, especially Dr. Andrea Doerr, due to whom this time has been a unique one. I am particular thankful for the support of Prof. Frohberg and Prof. Hiemenz, who, together with other colleagues, provided useful comments at the first stages of my research. Besides that I very much appreciate the steady support of Dr. Manske.

I would like to thank my colleagues Dr. Sabine Täuber, Dr. Ruth Delzeit and Dr. Carola Grebitus from the Institute for Food and Resource Economics for many lunch time discussions, self-supported working groups and exchanges of information and ideas at different stages of my work. I am indebted to Hugo Storm and Dr. Sören Scholz for excellent assistance in relation to the choice experimental study. I am especially thankful for the intellectual and emotional support of my office made Gesa Maschkowski, my friends in the "E-Team" and the members of TRANSDISS.

I wish to thank all those not personally known study participants who participated in my studies; without them this research would have never been possible! Besides, the choice experimental study would not have been feasible without the help of the marketing and market analysis seminar participants in the winter term 2007/2008. They spent much time with me in the field. Thank you all!

I would like to thank my co-authors for their contributions to the papers. In particular I would like to thank Vera Roidl for the possibility to apply the Information Display Matrix.

I am grateful to Ann DeVoy, Ursula Tröger and Christoph Quodbach for intensive English proof-reading.

I also would like to express my sincere thanks to my friends and my family. They were not only an inspiration but also at times a much needed distraction from the thesis and altogether a source of constant support. I would like to thank my grandmother for her willingness to take care of all our animals during the week-time and my parents for their continuous motivation and assistance, especially that they provided me so much freedom to do what I like.

Finally, I would like to thank Heiko Buschbell for his help and modelling assistance with SAS and the choice sets, but even more for his ceaseless support and encouragement.

Nina Langen

Abstract

Ethics in Consumer Choice - An Empirical Analysis based on the Example of Coffee

Individuals are confronted with the difficulty of making choices throughout their lives. The desire to behave ethically can be one motive for a certain choice. People's wish to support philanthropic, sustainable, ecological and social issues can lead to different forms of ethical behaviour, such as the purchase of products with ethical characteristics and charitable giving. In the market place, it can be observed that a recent aspect of consumer demand in western countries is the growing interest in products which have certain ethical features. Market shares of these goods are growing but still small. At the same time volumes of charitable giving are stagnating at a high level in Germany. Due to budget constraints the financial means of households for ethical behaviour are limited.

Against this background, the objective of the thesis is to elaborate differences and similarities of forms of ethical behaviour in general and to analyse whether German consumers differentiate between different types of ethical behaviour in particular.

Accordingly, the thesis is divided into four parts. In part A, an introduction to the topic is given. This is followed by part B entitled 'ethics and consumers' choice' as this discusses first, the foundations of consumers' decision making and approaches to measure consumer preferences and second, provides an overview and a comparison of ethical consumption, Fair Trade, charitable giving to form a basis for the empirical studies. The empirical studies follow in part C, entitled 'empirical studies based on the example of coffee'. In this section, five papers present the results of three empirical studies with sample sizes from n = 112 to n = 484 conducted in 2008 and 2009. Each of the papers addresses different sub-questions of the overall research question. At the end of the thesis, the major results are summarised in part D and the findings from the theoretical part and the empirical studies are brought together in a synthesis.

One of the most relevant outcomes is that all five papers reveal that consumers in Germany have well-defined preferences for the different forms of ethical behaviour and can be distinguished accordingly. Most of the study participants regard the different possibilities of ethical behaviour as complements. However, consumers could also be identified who regard e.g. charitable giving and the purchase of CrM products as substitutes. Accordingly, market segmentation is required to address the different consumer groups appropriately to prevent substitution of the different means of ethical behaviour. The determinants of ethical behaviour identified in the papers, such as a positive attitude towards charitable organisations, can be used for that purpose. Another prominent result is that consumers' stated preferences for ethical product features are reflected in their product information search process and their product choice. The combination of stated and revealed preference methods applied in the studies is therefore appropriate to model ethical behaviour and to arrive at conclusions which are in line with actual market figures.

The dissertation is characterised by its intensive combination of theoretical and empirical research. It furthermore contributes to the literature as the method triangulation applied in the different surveys reveals previously unknown relationships between different kinds of ethical behaviour, such as ethical consumption and charitable giving, as well as between different forms of ethical products. Choice experiment, latent class analysis, the information display matrix and item-based attitude assessment allowed the comparison of stated and revealed preferences as well as an analysis of the relevance of ethical product features within the context of different product and process attributes. The dissertation provides insights into a research field which is becoming more and more relevant and improves the understanding of consumers' assessment and the interdependencies of the possibilities of ethical behaviour. This allows the development of recommendations for consumer policy makers, business and NGOs concerned with the ethics of consumer choices as well as future research on ethical behaviour in general and ethical consumption in particular.

Keywords: Consumer Behaviour, Ethical Consumption, Charitable Giving, Fair Trade, Cause-related Marketing, Organic Products, Choice Modelling, Latent Class Approach, Information Display Matrix

Deutsche Kurzfassung

Ethics in Consumer Choice - An Empirical Analysis based on the Example of Coffee

Menschen treffen täglich Entscheidungen. Der Wunsch, diese mit den persönlichen ethischen Grundsätzen in Einklang zu bringen kann dabei ein Motiv für eine bestimmte Wahl sein. Je nachdem, ob Individuen philanthropische, nachhaltige, ökologische oder soziale Ziele unterstützen möchten fällt das ethische Verhalten anders aus; neben ehrenamtlichem Engagement sind monetäre Spenden an Entwicklungshilfeorganisationen und der Kauf von Produkten mit ethischen und sozialen Prozessattributen einige Möglichkeiten. Als Beispiel für ethische Produkte können Fair Trade und biologisch zertifizierte Nahrungsmittel genannt werden. Beides sind Nischenprodukte deren Marktanteile jedoch ansteigen. Solche Produkte mit ethischem oder nachhaltigem Zusatznutzen für Konsument und Dritte finden sich in Deutschland vermehrt in den Einkaufstätten, während das Spendenvolumen für gemeinnützige Zwecke in Deutschland auf hohem Niveau stagniert. Aufgrund von Budgetrestriktionen sind die finanziellen Mittel, die den Haushalten für ethisches Handeln zur Verfügung stehen begrenzt.

Das Ziel der Dissertation ist daher, die Unterschiede und Gemeinsamkeiten der verschiedenen Formen ethischen Handelns aufzuzeigen und die Frage zu beantworten, ob Verbraucher in Deutschland zwischen verschiedenen Ausprägungen ethischen Handelns unterschieden.

Die Arbeit gliedert sich entsprechend in vier Teile. Der Erste führt in die Thematik ein. Im zweiten Teil B werden als Grundlage für die empirischen Studien das Entscheidungsverhalten von Konsumenten sowie Ansätze und Methoden zur Präferenzmessung beschrieben und diskutiert sowie ein Überblick und ein Vergleich von ethischem Konsum, Fair Trade und wohltätigen Spenden gegeben. Die empirischen Studien werden im dritten Teil der Arbeit, empirical studies based on the example of coffee benannt, vorgestellt. Die Ergebnisse der drei in 2008 und 2009 durchgeführten Untersuchungen mit Stichprobengrößen von n = 112 bis n = 484 werden in fünf Artikeln beschrieben. Jeder der Aufsätze behandelt einzelne Aspekte der Hauptfragestellung. Am Ende der Dissertation werden die wichtigsten Ergebnisse zusammengefasst und die Schlüsse des theoretischen Teils B und des empirischen Teils C zu einer Synthese, D, gebracht.

Alle fünf Artikel zeigen, dass Konsumenten in Deutschland ausgeprägte Präferenzen für verschiedene Formen ethischen Verhaltens besitzen und entsprechend unterschieden werden können. Die meisten Studienteilnehmer betrachten die unterschiedlichen Möglichkeiten ethischen Verhaltens als komplementär. Es konnten jedoch auch Konsumenten identifiziert werden, die beispielsweise Spenden und den Kauf von CrM Produkten als Substitute ansehen. Dies macht eine Marktsegmentierung erforderlich, wenn eine Substitution der verschiedenen Formen ethischen Verhaltens verhindert werden soll. Die in den empirischen Studien identifizierten Determinanten ethischen Verhaltens, wie z.B. eine positive Einstellung Spendenorganisationen gegenüber, können dazu herangezogen werden. Ein anderes bedeutendes Ergebnis ist, dass die von Konsumenten im Interview geäußerten Präferenzen sich in den aufgedeckten Vorlieben und Entscheidungen widerspiegeln. Die genutzte Methodenkombination zur Ermittlung von erklärten (stated preference) und aufgedeckten (revealed preference) Präferenzen eignet sich daher, ethisches Verhalten abzubilden das dem realem Marktgeschehen nahekommt.

Die Dissertation zeichnet sich durch intensive Verknüpfung theoretischer und empirischer Arbeit aus. Eine Besonderheit ist die Vielzahl an verwendeten und kombinierten Methoden. Dies erlaubt Einblicke in das bis dato nicht untersuchte Verhältnis der verschiedenen Formen ethischen Verhaltens wie beispielsweise Spenden und ethischem Konsum sowie in die von Konsumenten gesehenen Unterschiede zwischen verschiedenen ethischen Produkten. Die Nutzung von Auswahlexperiment, Latent Class Analyse, Betrachtung des Informationssuchverhaltens und Einstellungsermittlungen mittels Itembatterien erlaubt nicht nur einen Vergleich zwischen erklärten und aufgedeckten Präferenzen, sondern offenbart auch die Relevanz der betrachteten ethischen Produkt- und Prozessattribute innerhalb der Kaufentscheidung von Konsumenten in Deutschland. Die Arbeit liefert wertvolle Einblicke in ein immer relevanter werdendes Forschungsfeld und trägt zum Verständnis der Wechselwirkungen der verschiedenen Möglichkeiten ethischen Konsumentenhandelns bei. Dies ermöglicht es, Empfehlungen für politische und unternehmerische Entscheider sowie NGOs auszusprechen für die ethische Aspekte des Konsumentenverhaltens von Relevanz sind. Dies gilt ebenso für weitere Forschungsvorhaben die ethisches Verhalten im Allgemeinen und ethischen Konsum im Besonderen untersuchen.

Table of Contents

List of Figures

Part A

Part B

Chapter 2

Chapter 4

Part C

Chapter 6

Chapter 7

List of Tables

Part B

Chapter 3

Chapter 4

Part C

Chapter 5

Chapter 6

Chapter 7

Acronyms and Abbreviations

AIC	Akaike Information Criterion
AWA	Allensbacher Markt- und Werbeträgeranalyse
BIC	Bayesian Information Criterion
BMU	Bundesministeriums für Umwelt, Naturschutz und Reaktorsicherheit
BÖLW	Bund Ökologische Lebensmittelwirtschaft
BRC	British Retail Consortium
c. p.	Ceteris Paribus
CE	Choice Experiments
COSA	Committee on Sustainability Assessment
CrM	Cause-related Marketing
DAC	Development Assistance Committee
DCA	Discrete-Choice-Analysis
EBA	Elimination by aspects
EED	Evangelischer Entwicklungsdienst
EFTA	European Fair Trade Association
FINE	A discussion forum for **F**LO, **I**FAT, **N**EWS and **E**FTA
F.O.B.	Free On Board
FLO	Fairtrade Labelling Organizations International
FSC	Forest Stewardship Council
FT	Fair Trade
GDP	Gross Domestic Product
GfK	Gesellschaft für Konsumforschung, GfK Gruppe
GTZ	German Development Cooperation Agency
IDM	Information Display Matrix
IFAT	International Fair Trade Association
IFOAM	International Federation of Organic Agriculture Movements

IIA	Independence of Irrelevant Alternatives
IID	Independent and Identically Distributed
ISEAL	International Social and Environmental Accreditation and Labelling Alliance
LCA	Latent Class Analysis
LCDCA	Latent Class Discrete Choice Analysis
LDC	Least Developed Countries
MNL	Multinominal Logit Model
MRS	Marginal rate of substitution
NGO	Non-governmental organisation
NEWS	Network of European World Shops
OECD	Organisation for Economic Co-operation and Developmment
POS	Point of Sale
RUM	Random Utility Model
SAS	Statistical Analysis System
SOR	Stimulus-Organism-Response
StBA	Statistisches Bundesamt / German Federal Statistical Office
UN	United Nations
WTP	Willingness to Pay
ZMP	Zentrale Markt- und Preisberichtstelle für Erzeugnisse der Land-, Forst- und Ernährungswirtschaft GmbH

A What this Dissertation is about: Relevance, questions and approaches to arrive at the Ethics in Consumer Choice

The following introduction provides the reader with an overview of the reasons and questions which have led to this dissertation. It describes the motivations to conduct the research on the ethics in consumer choice, explains and presents the goal and research questions as well as suitable methods to arrive at the answers to these questions. Thus, the introduction presents a comprehensive picture of the thesis.

1 Introduction

1.1 Motivation of the study

Individuals' possibilities to behave ethically

Individuals are confronted with the difficulty of making choices throughout their lives. They are faced with competing lifestyles, alternative products to buy, different foods to eat. One motive for a certain choice can be the desire to behave ethically. The wish to support philanthropic, sustainable, ecological and social issues can lead to different forms of ethical behaviour. Individuals can choose the classical way by doing voluntary work or donating money to charitable organisations engaged e.g. in developmental aid. But they can also do this by purchasing products with ethical and social process attributes (add-ons). If the product purchase is based on an individual's sense of responsibility towards society and personal concerns for one or several ethical issues, this is what is referred to as ethical consumption in the literature (see e.g. DE PELSMACKER et al. 2005a, p. 363; HARRISON et al. 2005, p. 2; TALLONTIRE et al. 2001, p. 6; 21). Ethical issues related to products and therefore consumption can be manifold, e.g. social and environmental concerns such as health issues, labour standards, social justice, animal welfare and sustainable production methods. They coexist with 'traditional' consumers' decision-making criteria, such as price and quality (HARRISON et al. 2005, p. 2). Hence, concerned consumers have the choice between different forms of ethical behaviour such as a purchase of a product with ethical characteristics and/or a donation to charity (see Figure 1).

Research reveals that a recent aspect of consumer demand in western countries is the growing interest in products which have certain ethical features (see e.g. CARRIGAN and ATTALA 2001; GRACIA et al. 2009; MAIETTA 2003; NIELSEN 2008a; b; VANTOMME et al. 2006; VITELL et al. 2001). Products that contribute to sustainable economics, social and environmental development through their attributes (e.g. organic products) or the consequences of their production process e.g. for the producers (as in Fair Trade products) are called ethical products. The purchase of such goods enables consumers to express their values through the market. These ethical products have become more and more popular, as is revealed by the increase of ethical consumption over the last three decades (HARRISON et al. 2005, p. 3).[1] Up to five forms of ethical consumption can be distinguished (see chapter 4.1.1). In the context of this thesis, three forms of ethical consumption will be considered: the positive ethical purchase behaviour of Fair Trade, organic and Cause-related Marketing products. Some of these will be compared to another form of ethical behaviour: charitable giving.

Classical 'ethical' products are Fair Trade and certified organic goods (DE PELSMACKER et al. 2005a, p. 363; SHAW and CLARKE 1999, p. 112). Fair Trade is an approach that aims at alleviating poverty and improving the livelihoods of small producers by the payment of so-called fair and sustainable, guaranteed minimum contract prices, by implementing social and environmental standards in all areas related to the production process of the traded goods and by improving market access and providing stability in trading relationships (GIOVANNUCCI and KOEKOEK 2003, p. 38). Hence, Fair Trade products concern ethical issues such as, for instance, working conditions, child labour and stable and higher prices for disadvantaged producers in developing countries, all of which are guaranteed by the Fairtrade Labelling Organizations International (FLO) (CARLSSON et al. 2007; OZCAGLAR-TOULOUSE et al. 2006). Organic certification focuses on people and animal welfare issues and environmental sustainability (e.g. prevention of soil degradation, no use of chemical fertilisers) (IFOAM 2011a; b). Accordingly, organic labels act as a signal of process-related production characteristics of food (BRIGGEMAN and LUSK 2011, p. 2). Even though the routes and main foci are different, some argue that in the last few years organic and Fair Trade certification have assimilated (see Figure 1) (BYERS et al. 2008, p. 6f.) and that especially customers in large-scale supermarkets are not familiar with the difference between these two certification schemes (GIOVANNUCCI and KOEKOEK 2003, p. 21).

In addition to those established areas that link consumers' purchase decisions to personal concerns, consumers increasingly have the opportunity to buy products whereby the purchase

[1] The increase of ethical products is not only driven by consumer demand but is also a result of explicit marketing of e.g. supermarkets offering their own 'ethical' brands or companies offering the possibility to donate to charity through the purchase of food (ADAMS and RAISBOROUGH 2010, p. 257; CSCP 2008, p. 1). The development of products which meet the new consumer demand is furthermore facilitated by NGOs which set standards, certification programmes and registered labels in the early 1990s in western countries addressing consumers' concerns with respect to environment, health and social issues and made trust building possible (ISEAL 2008a; b).

leads to target-oriented donations to classical charity organisations. The donation (indicated in terms of the money spent or the things done or achieved for the good cause) is promoted on the product by label. In the following, goods of this type will be called **Cause-related Marketing (CrM) products**.

Similarities and differences of the possibilities of ethical behaviour

CrM food campaigns in Germany often support environmental or health issues[2] and are similar to a donation to the respective charitable organisations. On one hand, ROBERTS (1996) and others consider CrM to be comparable to Fair Trade in the sense that it is a tool consumers use to express their social concerns; on the other hand, EIKENBERRY (2009) distinguishes CrM from Fair Trade. While she acknowledges the latter to be seriously aimed at promoting ethical consumption, she regards the former primarily as a marketing tool. Accordingly, unlike Fair Trade and organic production, CrM is sometimes suspected to be a green-washing strategy of companies. Moreover, in contrast to organic or Fair Trade certification, the product consumers buy in a CrM promotion is not produced according to special rules. It could be just a conventional product with the add-on of the donation to the good cause. Nevertheless, organic, Fair Trade and CrM products are to some extent similar. They allow consumers to express their concerns about environmental and social issues such as the reduction of pesticide use, fair producer prices in developing countries, schooling for poor children, etc. to improve the environment or the welfare of people in developing countries via a purchase in a supermarket without additional transaction costs. Transaction costs are often related to other forms of ethical behaviour such as giving donations to charity.

CrM campaigns reveal that the two approaches, namely **ethical consumption and charitable giving behaviour**, are closer regarding their characteristics and tools than e.g. the original Fair Trade slogan „trade not aid" suggests. For example, Fair Trade has many properties of a development project as funds and the operating criteria emanate from the North and it is interventionist in the sense that producers have to organise themselves in co-operations and unions, democratic structures have to be built up, child labour is restricted, etc. (PAUL 2005, p. 123). Fair Trade has furthermore several features that resemble more a gift than a market exchange of goods, e.g. the long-term partnership between cooperatives and traders instead of a one-time interaction (FISHER 2007, p. 80). The long-term partnership of the charity

[2] See 'Krombacher Regenwald Projekt' or 'Dallmayr Ethiopia' and their cooperation with 'Menschen für Menschen' which plant five trees in Ethiopia per sold coffee package of Dallmayr Ethiopia for environmental issues and Volvic's partnership with Unicef to provide clean drinking water in Ethiopia for health issues.

organisation Bread for the World and the German Fair Trade labelling initiative Transfair can be mentioned as examples for the proximity of the two tools. They have been cooperating for more than 30 years (BROT FÜR DIE WELT 2009). Furthermore, both approaches, i.e. ethical consumption as well as giving to charity, are – along with free trade, economic growth and governmental transfers – discussed as a means to reach one of the primary United Nations Millennium Goals: eradicating extreme poverty[3] and hunger and cutting world poverty in half, between 1990 and 2015 (UN 2011). The similarity between donations to charity and the purchase of ethical products can furthermore be approached by focussing on the determinants that push consumers into action. Here altruism can be mentioned as common denominator of both kinds of ethical behaviour. On the one hand, donations can be defined as a form of social participation and a contribution to welfare production which is understood as altruistic behaviour (PRILLER and SOMMERFELD 2005, p. 9). On the other hand, altruism has been used to explain the voluntary provision of public goods. The environmental and social quality of products is a public goods aspect. Accordingly, altruism can be reflected in a purchase of e.g. an eco-labelled organic product (LOUREIRO et al. 2001, p. 405). Another connective element of donations and ethical purchase behaviour is the willingness of individuals to give (for whatever reason).

At the same time, the discussed forms of ethical behaviour are different with respect to the fact that the purchase of e.g. Fair Trade products is an indirect form of aid whereas giving to charitable organisations is a direct form[4]. Besides, people do not receive a 'product'[5] for their money when they give to charity. Furthermore, while the purchase of aliments (food) is a habitual purchase decision, charitable giving, in contrast, is characterised by higher involvement so that it can be regarded as a more extensive choice decision. The comparison of donation habits and ethical purchase decisions is difficult as these 'things' are not 'sold' in the same shop. Therefore, they are not part of one choice set[6] in a narrower context but rather in the broader sense. Accordingly, donations are not a perfect alternative to the purchase of an ethical product but at least a possible substitute.

To sum up, there are differences between charitable giving and ethical consumption as well as common features e.g. regarding the major foci (see Figure 1). Furthermore, there are

[3] For an introduction into forms and trends of poverty and into ways of measuring it, see WORLD BANK (2008).
[4] CrM products have an intermediate position as direct funds for charity are generated.
[5] The warm-glow feeling can possibly be considered to be a 'product'.
[6] The idea of the so-called choice set is that it consists of all "entities over which the individual's preferences are defined" (PUDNEY 1989, p. 8).

differences as well as similarities between the described forms of ethical consumption which will be further discussed in the following chapters. Due to the parallels, ethical consumption patterns (Fair Trade, organic, CrM) and donations to charity are linked in this dissertation as forms of ethical behaviour.

Figure 1: Examples of foci of donations to developmental charity organisations, Fair Trade, organic production and CrM campaigns and how they merge

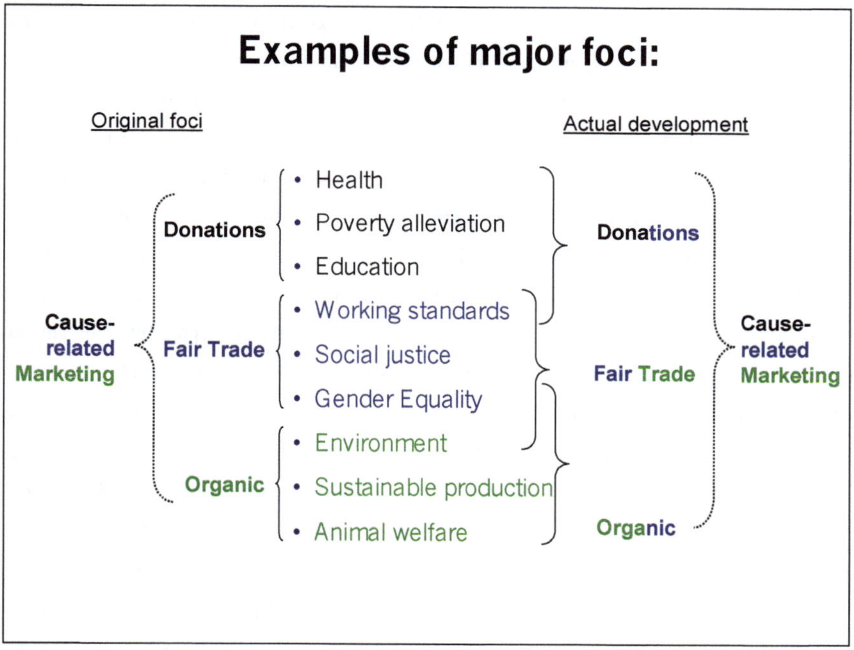

Note: For the foci of developmental charity organisations, see e.g. the project areas of the charity organisation MENSCHEN FÜR MENSCHEN (2011). For the foci of Fair Trade, see the generic and product standards of FLO (2009b). For the foci of organic standards, see IFOAM (2011a; b). For examples of the different foci of CrM campaigns, see e.g. VOLVIC (2011) (building of wells for the provision of drinking water in African countries) and DALLMAYR (2011) (plantation of trees to prevent soil degradation in Ethiopia).

Source: author's illustration.

Why is the similarity of the forms of ethical behaviour important?

The development of the sales of Fair Trade products show that German consumers are willing to pay a price premium for products of marginalised producers in developing countries as well as for organic goods. People in Germany are also willing to donate to charity organisations that support people in developing countries. But, for the moment, German consumers are buying fewer Fair Trade products (market share in 2010: < 2 %) and fewer organic products (market share in 2009: 3.4 %) than contributing to the Third Sector (see Figure 2) (TRANSFAIR 2011; BÖLW 2011, p. 21). Nevertheless, while consumer expenditures for the niche market of Fair Trade and organic certified as well as CrM products are growing (OLOKO 2008, p. 3; TRANSFAIR 2011), the amount of donations given directly to charitable organisations have stagnated in nominal terms on a high level since 2005 (SOMMERFELD 2008, p. 9; TNS INFRATEST 2009). Furthermore, a survey of NIELSEN (2008, p. 4) shows that European consumers claim to be more interested in contributing to environmental and social causes through their purchase of ethical products (59 %) than by means of charitable giving (11 %, rest: do not know). And, as EIKENBERRY (2009, p. 53) notes, there are studies showing that consumers think a purchase of CrM products is a donation and that by means of their purchase decision for an ethical product consumers "believe they have already done their philanthropic share". This would imply that there is a substitution relationship between donations and ethical consumption. As due to budget restrictions households' financial means available for ethical behaviour are limited, it is conceivable that one possibility of ethical behaviour goes at the expense of the other. Thus, if there exists a substitutional relationship between donations on the one hand and Fair Trade or CrM purchases on the other hand and given the goal to achieve the highest return for the good cause, the most efficient mean should be favoured. In contrast, if the different forms of ethical behaviour are complementary, because e.g. the Fair Trade system is able to address another target group than the charity system and the returns for Fair Trade producers complement the funds collected by charity, the question of systems efficiency is circumstantial. Nevertheless, research has shown consumers are interested in "not only *how* their food is produced but also *who* benefits from their food purchase" (BRIGGEMAN and LUSK 2011, p. 1). This means the distribution of profits across the actors of the supply chain and especially the benefits for the producers is of relevance for consumers (see also CHANG and LUSK 2009, p. 484). This holds even if there is no competition between ethical consumption and charitable giving. Accordingly, the expectations of consumers regarding the efficiency of the different systems are important. [7]

---

[7] There seems to be an efficiency gap between Fair Trade and charity organisations (STEINRÜCKEN 2004). The costs for organisation and administration in the Swiss Fair Trade organisation Max Havelaar Foundation Switzerland were 10 percent points higher than the ones of Bread for the World in 2002. Possible reasons, pointed out by STEINRÜCKEN (2004, p. 347), might be the existence of scale effects in large (in terms of gift volume) charity organisations like Bread for the World[7]. The margin retailer's gain by selling Fair Trade products is part of the efficiency discussion (see chapter 4.2.4). And the question 'how much of the higher retail price of ethical products consumers accept to not reach the ethical goal but the retailer?' is also part of it. It is possible that studies focussing only on the issue of efficiency, like the one of STEINRÜCKEN (2004), miss

Figure 2: Support of sustainable and ethical issues in 2008 in Germany

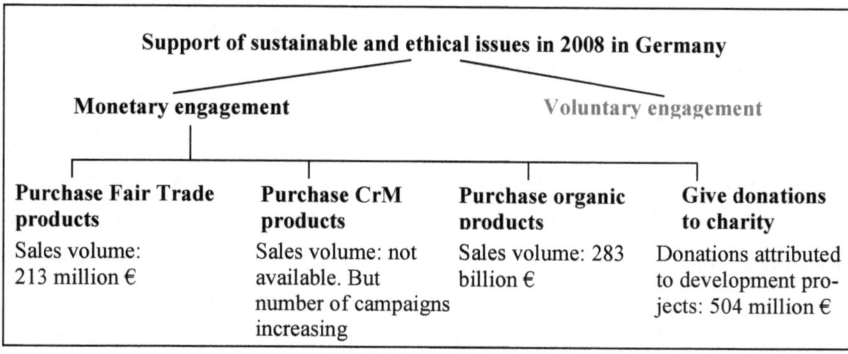

Source: author's illustration. Sales volume Fair Trade labelled products by Transfair (2009). Sales volume organic certified products by ZMP (2009). Donations attributed to development projects without emergency aid by TNS Infratest (2008a). Number of CrM campaigns: see Table 1 in chapter 9 (Oloko 2008, p. 5).

1.2 Goal of the thesis and methodological approach

This thesis aims to contribute to and deepen the general understanding of consumers' attitudes and perception of different forms of ethical behaviour and their implications for consumers' choices. The considered forms of individuals' choices for and within ethical behaviour are the consumption of certain ethical products and charitable giving. The central research question addressed is "**Do consumers differentiate between different types of ethical behaviour?**"

The following sub-research questions are closely linked to this. First, this dissertation explores to which extent ethical and sustainable product and process attributes are relevant and important for consumers during their food-purchase decision. The second sub-research question is whether Fair Trade, organic and CrM are perceived to be (almost) the same or do German consumers distinguish between these 'labels'? The distinction can be made not only with respect to the convenience of the different modes of ethical behaviour but also with regard to the impact consumers' engagement has on the needy people for which consumers care and act ethically. Therefore, it is asked whether classical monetary donations to charity

important components of Fair Trade in comparison to other forms of ethical behaviour, such as monetary donations to charitable organisations. With regard to the efficiency of the Fair Trade chain, only a few studies exist. This is not surprising if we consider the difficulties in obtaining information from FLO, Transfer or Gepa. People working in the Fair Trade movement are not willing to provide information which might be critical in the sense that they reveal difficulties, for example, with inefficiency, information asymmetries or the implementation of their own goals. Rapunzel and the Evangelischer Entwicklungsdienst told the author that they do not like to support such research studies because they fear that drawbacks of the movement might be revealed. And negative publicity is not what they want.

are affected and possibly reduced by the increased demand for Fair Trade, organic and CrM products, i.e. does the rise in Fair Trade, organic and CrM products occur at the expense of donations? To analyse these issues this thesis examines whether those consumers who are engaged in ethical consumption also have strong preferences for charitable giving to developmental organisations or whether these different forms of altruistic behaviour attract different consumer groups. In the latter case, it can be assumed that consumers distinguish between the different forms of ethical behaviour and thus ethical consumption can be seen as complementary to donations. In the former case, they might be substitutes which raises the question regarding the efficiency of the different forms of altruistic spending. Though this latter aspect will not be subject of the thesis, this research will analyse whether consumers care at all about the donation amount reaching the producers which can be a first indicator and proxy for the relevance of the efficiency of donation/CrM and Fair Trade systems and distinguish in their purchase decision between high and low donation amounts and therefore more and less efficient support systems.[8] Hence, the third goal of the present study is to find out whether consumers place emphasis on the amount of money reaching the marginalised producer in the case of Fair Trade or the indicated cause in the case of CrM as well as on the transparent labelling of this on the product. In addition, consumers' willingness to pay (WTP) for different amounts directly reaching the recipient will be investigated.

The goal is to derive insights into German consumers' assessment and distinction between different types of ethical behaviour, namely the purchase of Fair Trade, organic and CrM products as well as monetary donations to charity, and how this influences consumers' choices. Accordingly, this research explores the key factors driving consumer preferences as well as deterring consumers from ethical behaviour. Distinct consumer segments will be determined according to their preferences for the different forms of ethical behaviour. This will be critical for understanding the reasons for growth and/or stagnation and for predicting how the different forms of ethical behaviour will further develop. Furthermore, marketing recommendations for the facilitation and development of ethical behaviour will be derived.

---

[8] At present, there is no information provided on Fair Trade products regarding the amount of the price premium paid by consumers that actually reaches the producer. Although CrM campaigns frequently indicate the effect the purchase of one unit of a product has for the cause, the information is often given only as project-specific donations in form of their own currencies like e.g. hours of schooling, square meters of rainforest saved from destruction or trees which are planted in a project. The monetary value of these actions is often not indicated which implies that also those labels lack transparency for the consumer as it is difficult to know the costs of e.g. a schooling hour (see OLOKO 2008).

Concerning the methodologies applied, this thesis takes into account insights from various disciplines to investigate consumers' decision making regarding ethical food choices. For this purpose, experimental settings are designed to be as close to reality as possible. The majority of studies related to the consumption of Fair Trade products, for instance, employ either an economic approach focussing on consumer preferences and measurement of WTP, or a psychological and social approach that considers attitudes and values. The separate examination of the classical economic approach and its assumption of exclusively selfish action is not able to incorporate social relations or diversity in preferences. Therefore, this approach fails in the presence of other-related preferences and altruistic action (BOULANGER 2007, p. 17; WALLENBORN 2007, p. 60). The psychological approach focusses on values and attitudes, but does not seem able to provide a comprehensive picture of ethical behaviour as other important factors, such as product prices and consumers' income, are neglected. Hence, this thesis considers different approaches to ethical consumption. In particular, key aspects of the existing theoretical models, such as egoistic motives, altruism and the influence of peers on consumers' decision making, are incorporated in the empirical models.

Against this background a triangulation of methods seems appropriate. Consequently, three complementary consumer studies were undertaken, each focussing on a particular aspect of the central research question and addressing it with an adequate methodological approach. The results are described in five papers presented in part C of the dissertation.

1.3 Organisation of the thesis

The thesis is divided into four parts. In part A, an introduction to the topic is given. This is followed by part B entitled 'ethics and consumers' choice' as this first, discusses the foundations of consumers' decision making and approaches to measure consumer preferences to form a basis for the empirical studies and second, provides an overview and a comparison of ethical consumption, Fair Trade, charitable giving. The empirical studies follow in part C, entitled 'empirical studies based on the example of coffee'. In this section, five papers present the results of three empirical studies with sample sizes from n = 112 to n = 484 conducted in 2008 and 2009. Each of the papers addresses different sub-questions of the overall research question. The major results are summarised in part D and the findings from the theoretical part and the empirical studies are brought together in a synthesis.

To be more precise, **chapter 2** presents models of consumer choice which were the basis for the survey questionnaires, and provides deeper insights into consumers' decision making with emphasis on the stages of consumers' decision making process. Moreover, the concepts of utility, preferences and choice are introduced and different decision making strategies are discussed. This chapter provides the theoretical background for the papers presented in chapter 5 and 6.

Chapter 3 focusses on the method of preference measurement applied in the paper presented in chapter 6, which are choice experiments. The theoretical framework of Discrete Choice Analysis (DCA) is explained as well as the features of the multinomial logit model (MNL). The traditional model for choice analysis is the MNL which is limited by one strong assumption: homogenous preferences. As consumers might contribute to charity or buy Fair Trade products for various reasons, preferences are expected to vary across individuals. Therefore, particular consideration is given to latent class discrete choice analysis as this takes heterogeneous preferences into account and allows for consumer segmentation based on choice data. This chapter also provides insights into the design of a choice experiment as this is not part of the paper presented in chapter 6.

To give the reader a more widespread picture of those forms of ethical behaviour analysed in the thesis, in **chapter 4** an overview of the possibilities of ethical behaviour is given. The phenomenon of ethical consumption, starting with approaches to consumption, insights into research areas followed by an overview with respect to market relevance and trends is described in section 4.1. The similarities and differences between ethical, sustainable and Fair Trade consumption are pointed out at the end of chapter 4.1. An extensive review of the Fair Trade movement, its principles, impact, limitations and similarities as well as differences to charity is presented in the subsequent paragraph (section 4.2).[9] Section 4.3 provides insights into donors' characteristics and motivations for charitable giving in general and with a focus on Germany. As the papers presented in chapters 7, 8 and 9 deal with CrM, its foundations, critical success factors as well as consumer expectations and attitudes towards CrM, CrM is not further highlighted in the thesis aside from in the papers.

The results of the three consumer studies conducted in 2008 and 2009 are presented in five papers in **part C** of the dissertation. Each of the five papers starts with an introduction to the specific research question, proceeds with a theoretical part or an explanation of the particular model applied in the paper, a presentation of results, major findings, conclusions and discussions at the end of the paper.

---

[9] As Fair Trade is more than just a form of ethical consumption, e.g. also a certification scheme with implications for producers, it is necessary to discuss Fair Trade in a separate subsection of chapter 4 and not only as a sub-item of the ethical consumption section.

Product evaluation depends on cognitive processes and information processing (e.g. HONG and WYER 1989). As a multiplicity of labels and information on a product confuses 83 % of the German consumers and makes them insecure (BMU 2008, p. 45), the question arises as to which product attributes and labels consumers perceive and which are not considered, e.g. due to information overload. Accordingly, the **first paper 'Relevance of Fair Trade, organic production and Cause-related Marketing for product choice – An analysis based on the Information Display Matrix'**, which has been accepted for publication pending revision at Ecological Economics and was co-authored with Vera Roidl and Monika Hartmann, presented in **chapter 5**, examines the relevance of ethical and organic production in the context of different product and process attributes, such as taste and brand, for consumers' information search using the Information Display Matrix (IDM) with the example of coffee choice. As the discrepancy between market shares of ethical products and consumers stated preferences for these products in surveys is immense, the goal of this study is to assess the relevance of ethical product features without gaining socially desirable answers. The IDM is an adequate instrument for this. According to the assumption of diminishing marginal utility, consumers search for the most relevant information first (FOSCHT and SWOBODA 2004, p. 82; SOLOMON et al. 2006, p. 267). Therefore, from the stage in which an attribute has been looked at, a conclusion can be drawn as to the relevance of the respective attribute. The eight attributes tested were selected representing different coffee characteristics found at the point of sale during extensive market investigations of existing coffee packages (price, brand, country of origin, taste, health issue) as well as those attributes whose relevance is tested in this dissertation (organic and Fair Trade production, the indication of a donation amount going directly to the producer). In addition to examining the importance of the different product characteristics, consumers' information search pattern is analysed. The search pattern gives information about consumers' search strategies. Consumers can apply several different search strategies which are explained in chapter 2.3. As a main assumption of the theory underlying choice experiments is that consumers apply compensatory search patterns, it is useful to investigate the search process for ethical products. The main determinants for the active information search on specific attributes (e.g. price and ethical attributes) are identified based on several logit models. In addition, the study examines whether supplementary information about ethical issues related to the product or its production process influences this process. The survey was conducted in 2009 with 214 participants.

As the relevance of ethical attributes in an environment of different product attributes such as brand and taste was tested in study 1, the second study concentrates on the issue of efficiency as well as the relationship between Fair Trade, organic and donations to charity to gain deeper insights into the subtle differences between these forms of ethical behaviour. The **paper** presented in **chapter 6 'Are ethical consumption and charitable giving substitutes or not? Insights into consumers coffee choice',** which has been published in Food Quality and Preferences, analyses whether the rise in Fair Trade, organic and CrM products occurs at the expense of donations and whether those two developments are linked. It further investigates whether Fair Trade, organic and CrM are perceived to be (almost) the same or whether consumers distinguish between those 'labels'. Third, the determinants for consumers' WTP for the different forms of support are identified. To analyse these issues a survey with 484 participants was conducted in 2008. In this study, hypothetical choice experiments and face-to-face interviews were carried out. A latent class model for discrete choice analysis was used to discriminate between consumer segments with well distinguished preferences and WTP measures for the modes of ethical consumption as well as for different donation amounts. While there are some studies on WTP for Fair Trade products in economic literature (e.g. DE PELSMACKER et al. 2005a; b) up to now there has been no economic assessment of consumers' preferences regarding Fair Trade, donations to charity in form of CrM and the efficiency of the respective systems.

Chapter 7 consists of the **third paper 'Acceptance and critical success factors of Cause-related Marketing in Germany – Evidence from a consumer survey'** of which an earlier version was presented at the Corporate Responsibility Research Conference in 2010 together with Dilani Saverimuthu, Carola Grebitus and Monika Hartmann. The study deals with the acceptance and critical success factors of CrM in Germany. Although CrM is increasingly applied, little is known about German consumers' attitudes, knowledge and perception of CrM campaigns and critical factors influencing consumers' purchase intention. These issues are highlighted in this paper. Based on a consumer survey with 217 participants conducted in 2009, paper 3 focuses on the role of the cause-brand-fit and corporations' credibility for German consumers' willingness to switch to a CrM promoted product. Based on a factor and a cluster analysis, marketing recommendations for enterprises on how to effectively address different consumer segments regarding the CrM products are derived. In this regard, four groups of consumers are identified that differ in their attitudes towards CrM products.

Consumers in Germany ask for and place considerable value on sustainability issues. At the same time, consumers mistrust companies and they suspect that they use communications in the sustainability area only as a marketing tool (HAVAS MEDIA 2009, p. 1f.).[10] In the light of this, **paper four 'Is Cause-related Marketing Green-Washing?'** presented in **chapter 8** assesses whether consumers perceive CrM to be green-washing. An earlier version of this paper was presented at the 11th Biennial ISEE Conference in 2010 (co-authors are Carola Grebitus and Monika Hartmann). So far, only few studies have examined the effect of CrM activities on consumers' attitudes and purchase behaviour in general. Therefore, in this survey written questionnaires were used to acquire information on 112 consumers' purchase behaviour, their overall evaluation of CrM and whether they suspect CrM to be a form of green-washing. Furthermore, it is investigated whether consumers differentiate between CrM and traditional donations or the purchase of Fair Trade products. The influence of these attitudes on consumers' willingness to pay for CrM products is assessed via a contingent valuation task. For this purpose, the meaning of the term green-washing, the implication of accusing CrM to be green-washing and previous research on the issue is explained. Ordered logit models as well as cluster analysis are applied.

As it became evident that green-washing is usually mentioned when there are complaints about a lack of transparency within CrM promotions, the question **'Is there need for more transparency and efficiency in cause-related marketing?'** is addressed in the **fifth paper** presented in **chapter 9**, co-authored with Carola Grebitus and Monika Hartmann and published in the International Journal on Food System Dynamics. This is relevant as the rising popularity of ethical consumption has motivated firms to increasingly implement CrM campaigns in Germany. But research reveals that especially German consumers are sceptical with regard to the amount of money spent for the good 'cause' by the enterprises. This can be explained by little information provided by CrM campaigns to consumers. As a consequence, the lack of information and the information asymmetry can reduce consumers' willingness to purchase CrM products. Therefore, this study analyses whether the efficiency of a CrM campaign and transparent communication about the distribution of profits are important for consumers. Consumers' trust in the efficiency of CrM promotions, i.e. to which extent they

[10] This is not astonishing when considering the results of a recent study of TERRACHOICE (2010, p. 6) which reports that since 2009 the number of 'greener products' has gone up by 73 % and that out of these 4,744 so-called green, natural, or eco-friendly products in the US and Canada 95 % have been storied with misleading, meaningless and even false claims. Especially when fake-labels are created labelling is no longer a solution to the problem of adverse selection and information asymmetry but rather part of the problem. With regard to CrM, in the literature it is often claimed that in order to maintain the success of CrM, it is of great importance to avoid the impression that it is green-washing (see e.g. VARADARAJAN and MENON 1988). In addition, statements such as the one of Illy that companies engaged in ethical and sustainable production issues, such as Fair Trade, are only motivated by marketing goals and not the topic as such (KORT 2010) influence consumers. Consequently, it is necessary to deal with the green-washing issue.

expect and perceive CrM to be efficient in distributing the donation amount indicated on the CrM product, and consumers' requests regarding this issue are determined. The 112 survey participants filled in written questionnaires regarding their purchase behaviour and attitudes towards CrM. For the data analysis ordered logit models were applied.

The dissertation concludes with a **synthesis** of part B and C **in part D** in which the main findings of the thesis are summarised, the limitations of the study are discussed and recommendations for future research are provided.

1.4 References

ADAMS, M. and RAISBOROUGH, J. (2010): Making a difference: ethical consumption and the everyday. *The British Journal of Sociology*, 61 (2): 256-274.

BMU (2008): *Umweltbewusstsein in Deutschland 2008: Ergebnisse einer repräsentativen Bevölkerungsumfrage*. Available from: http://www.umweltdaten.de/publikationen/fpdf-l/3678.pdf, [accessed 2008-12-18].

BÖLW (2011): *Zahlen, Daten, Fakten: Die Biobranche 2011*. Available from: http://www.boelw.de/uploads/media/pdf/Dokumentation/Zahlen__Daten__Fakten/ZDF2011.pdf, [accessed 2011-03-09].

BOULANGER, P. - M. (2007): What's wrong with consumption for sustainable development. In: Zaccai, E. (Ed.): *Sustainable Consumption, Ecology and Fair Trade*. London: Routledge: 17-32.

BRIGGEMAN, B. C. and LUSK, J. L. (2011): Preferences for fairness and equity in the food system. *European Review of Agricultural Economics*, 38 (1): 1-29.

BROT FÜR DIE WELT (2009): *Fairer Handel: Seit 30 Jahren Lobbyarbeit*. Available from: http://www.brot-fuer-die-welt.de/kampagnen/index.php, [accessed 2009-01-10].

BYERS, A., GIOVANNUCCI, D. and LIU, P. (2008): Value-adding standards in the North American food market. Trade opportunities in certified products for developing countries. *FAO Commodities and Trade Technical Paper*, 11.

CARLSSON, F., FRYKBLOM, P. and LAGERKVIST, C. J. (2007): Consumer willingness to pay for farm animal welfare: mobile abattoirs versus transportation to slaughter. *European Review of Agricultural Economics*, 34 (3): 321-344.

CARRIGAN, M. and ATTALLA, A. (2001): The myth of the ethical consumer – do ethics matter in purchase behaviour? *Journal of Consumer Marketing*, 18 (7): 560-576.

CHANG, J. B. and LUSK, J. J. (2009): Fairness and food choice. *Food Policy*, 34 (6): 483-491.

CSCP (2008): *Konzeptpapier: Nachhaltiger Konsum.* Konzeptpapier im Rahmen der Themenreihe „Nachhaltiger Konsum“ für das Deutsche Global Compact Netzwerk (DGCN) in 2008. Available from: http://www.scp-centre.org/fileadmin/cscp/Project_Files/DGCN_Files/Konzeptpapier_nachhaltiger_Konsum_DGCN_CSCP_2008.pdf, [accessed 2008-12-04].

DALLMAYR (2011): *Mit Kaffeegenuss Bäume in Äthiopien pflanzen.* Available from: http://www.dallmayr-ethiopia.de, [accessed 2011-06-27].

DE PELSMACKER, P., DRIESEN, L. and RAYP, G. (2005a): Do consumers care about ethics? Willingness to pay for Fair-Trade Coffee. *The Journal of Consumer Affairs*, 39 (2): 363-385.

DE PELSMACKER, P., JANSSENS, W. and MIELANTS, C. (2005b): Consumer values and fair-trade beliefs, attitudes and buying behaviour. *International Review on Public and Nonprofit Marketing*, 2 (2): 50-69.

EIKENBERRY, A. M. (2009): The Hidden Cost of Cause Marketing. *Stanford Social Innovation Review*, Summer 2009: 51-55.

FISHER, C. (2007): Selling Coffee, or Selling Out?: Evaluating Different Ways to Analyze the Fair-Trade System. *Culture and Agriculture*, 29 (2): 78-88.

FLO (2009b): *Product standards.* Available from: http://www.fairtrade.net/standards.html, [accessed 09-01-20].

FOSCHT, T. and SWOBODA, B. (2004): *Käuferverhalten.* Wiesbaden: Gabler.

GIOVANNUCCI, D. and KOEKOEK, F. J. (2003): T*he state of sustainable coffee. A study of twelve major markets.* Washington, DC: World Bank.

GRACIA, A., LOUREIRO, M.L. and NAYGA, R. M. (2009): Consumers' valuation of nutritional information: A choice experiment study. *Food Quality and Preference*, 20 (7): 463-471.

HARRISON, R., NEWHOLM, T. and SHAW, D. (2005): Defining the Ethical Consumer. In: Harrison, R., Newholm, T. and Shaw, D. (Eds.): *The Ethical Consumer*, London: Sage: 1-10.

HAVAS MEDIA (2009): *Sustainable Future 09: German Factsheet.* Available from: http://www.havasmedia.com/staticfiles/Germany%20Factsheet.pdf, [accessed 2010-02-18].

IFOAM (2011a): *The Principles of Organic Agriculture.* Available from: http://www.ifoam.org/about_ifoam/principles/index.html, [accessed 2011-03-09].

IFOAM (2011b): *Definition of Organic Agriculture*. Available from: http://www.ifoam.org/growing_organic/definitions/doa/index.html, [accessed 2011-03-09].

ISEAL (2008a): *Monitoring and Evaluating Impacts*. Available from: http://www.isealalliance.org/index.cfm?fuseaction=Page.viewPage&pageld=493&parentID=490, [accessed 2008-06-17].

ISEAL (2008b): *What we do*. Available from: http://www.isealalliance.org/index.cfm?fuseaction=Page.viewPage&pageld=490, [accessed 2008-06-17].

KORT, K. (2010): Wir machen keine Geschäfte mit der Nachhaltigkeit. *Handelsblatt*, 27.02.2010. Available from: http://www.handelsblatt.com/unternehmen/mittelstand_aktuell/_b=2512570,_p=43,_t=ftprint,doc_page=0,fp=false,isPdf=1;printpdf, [accessed 2010-03-05].

LOUREIRO, M., MCCLUSKEY, J. J. and MITTELHAMMER, R. C. (2001): Assessing Consumer Preferences for Organic, Eco-labeled, and Regular Apples. *Journal of Agricultural and Resource Economics*, 26 (2): 404-416.

MAIETTA, O. W. (2003): *The hedonic price of Fair Trade coffee for the Italian consumer*. Paper presented at the International Conference: Agricultural policy reform and the WTO: where are we heading? Capri (Italy), June 23-26, 2003.

MENDOZA, R. und BASTIAENSEN, J. (2003): Fair trade and the coffee crisis in the Nicaraguan Segovias. *Small Enterprise Development*, 14 (2): 36-46.

MENSCHEN FÜR MENSCHEN (2011): *Projekte*. Available from: http://www.menschenfuermenschen.de/#mainmenu/projekte/, [accessed 2011-06-23].

NIELSEN (2008): *Corporate Ethics and Fair Trading: A Nielsen Global Consumer Report*. Available from: http://www.nielsen.com/solutions/CSR_Fairtrade_global_report October08.pdf, [accessed 2009-01-02].

OLOKO, S. (2008): *Cause related Marketing - Der Status Quo in Deutschland*. Berlin.

OZCAGLAR-TOULOUSE, N., SHIU, E. and SHAW, D. (2006): In search of fair trade: ethical consumer decision making in France. *International Journal of Consumer Studies*, 30 (5): 502-514.

PAUL, E. (2005): Evaluating Fair Trade as a development project: methodological considerations. *Development in Practice*, 15 (2): 134-150.

PRILLER, E. and SOMMERFELD, J. (2005): Wer spendet in Deutschland? Eine sozialstrukturelle Analyse. *WZB Discussion Paper*. Wissenschaftszentrum Berlin für Sozialforschung (WZB).

PUDNEY, S. (1989): *Modelling Individual Choice: The Econometrics of Corners, Kinks and Holes*. Cornwall: T. J. Press.

ROBERTS, J. A. (1996): Will the real socially responsible consumer please step forward? *Business Horizons*, 39 (1): 79-83.

SHAW, D. and CLARKE, I. (1999): Belief formation in ethical consumer groups: an exploratory study. *Marketing Intelligence & Planning*, 17 (2): 109-119.

SOLOMON, M. R., BAMOSSY, G., ASKEGAARD, S. and HOGG, M. K. (2006): *Consumer behaviour. A European perspective*. Harlow: Prentice Hall.

SOMMERFELD, J. (2008): Die Bedeutung des Spenden- und Gemeinnützigkeitsrechts in der Praxis - Eine Analyse von Experteninterviews. *Presented at WZB und DZI Tagung: „Motive, gesellschaftliche Rahmenbedingungen und Einflussfaktoren auf das Spendenverhalten"*, 13. 10.2008, Berlin.

STECKLOW, S. and WHITE E. (2004): What Price Virtue? At Some Retailers, 'Fair Trade' Carries A Very High Cost: Stores Charge Big Markups On Goods Intended to Help Farmers in Poor Countries. *The Wall Street Journal*, June 08, 2004. Available from: http://www.globalexchange.org/campaigns/fairtrade/coffee/2064.html, [accessed 2007-04-17].

STEINRÜCKEN, T. (2004): Fairer Handel durch Sozialsiegel? Ökonomische Analyse eines alternativen Handelskonzepts. *List Forum für Wirtschafts- und Finanzpolitik*, 30 (4): 339-356.

TALLONTIRE, A., RENTSENDORJ, E. and BLOWFIELD, M. (2001): Ethical Consumers and Ethical Trade: A Review of Current Literature, Policy Series 12. Chatham, UK: Natural Resources Institute.

TERRACHOICE (2010): *The sins of greenwashing*. http://sinsofgreenwashing.org/findings/greenwashing-report-2010/, 2011-04-20.

TNS INFRATEST (2008a): *14 Jahre Deutscher Spendenmonitor: Fakten und Trends im Zeitverlauf*.

TNS INFRATEST (2009): *15 Jahre Deutscher Spendenmonitor: Fakten und Trends im Zeitverlauf*.

TRANSFAIR (2009): *50 Prozent Plus für Fairtrade*. Available from: http://www.transfair.org/presse/detailseite-presse/article/45/50-prozent-p.html, [accessed 2009-04-23].

TRANSFAIR (2011): *Absatz Fair Trade Produkte im Einzelnen*. Available from: http://www.transfair.org/produkte/absatz-fairtrade-produkte.html, [accessed 2011-03-09].

UN (2011): *Goal 1: Eradicate extreme poverty & hunger*. Available from: http://www.un.org/millenniumgoals/poverty.shtml, [accessed 2011-05-09].

VANTOMME, D., GEUENS, M., DEHOUWER, J. and DE PELSMACKER, P. (2006): Explicit and Implicit Determinants of Fair-Trade Buying Behavior. *Advances in Consumer Research*, 33: 699-703.

VARADARAJAN, P.R. and MENON, A. (1988): Cause-related Marketing: A Coalignment of Marketing Strategy and Corporate Philanthropy. *Journal of Marketing*, 52: 58-74.

VITELL, S. J., SINGHAPAKDI, A. and THOMAS, J. (2001): Consumer ethics: an application and empirical testing of the Hunt-Vitell theory of ethics. *Journal of Consumer Marketing*, 18 (2): 153-178.

VOLVIC (2011): *Herzlich Willkommen bei der Trinkwasserinitiative*. Available from: http://www.volvic.de/unicef/, [accessed 2011-06-27].

WALLENBORN, G. (2007): How to attribute power to consumers? When epostemology and politics converge. In: Zaccai, E. (Ed.): *Sustainable Consumption, Ecology and Fair Trade*. Oxon: Routledge: 57-69.

WORLDBANK (2008): *Understanding Poverty* Available from: http://web.worldbank.org/WBSITE/EXTERNAL/TOPICS/EXTPOVERTY/0,,contentMDK:20153855~menuPK:373757~pagePK:148956~piPK:216618~theSitePK:336992,00.html [accessed 2008-10-10].

ZEHNER, D. C. (2002): An Economic Assessment of "Fair Trade" in Coffee. *Chazen Web Journal of International Business*, Fall 2002: 1-24.

ZEPEDA, L. and DEAL, D. (2009): Organic and local food consumer behaviour: Alphabet Theory. *International Journal of Consumer Studies*, 33 (6): 697-705.

ZMP (2009): *Wie hoch sind die Bio-Anteile wirklich*? Vortrag am 19. Februar 2009, Biofach, Nürnberg, Germany.

B Ethics and Consumers' Choice

This thesis is about the ethics in consumer choice. Ethics is a branch of philosophy addressing questions about actions raising a claim on morality. It is about the relationship between moral action and judgements. Values and customs of persons are studied. The main areas of questions that ethics as science deals with are happiness, freedom, good and evil. Ethics has been applied to various fields of life such as economics, business, politics, environment, etc. (PIEPER 1994, p. 17ff.; 100ff.). Morality is either used descriptively "to refer to some codes of conduct put forward by a society or, some other group, such as a religion, or accepted by an individual for her own behaviour" or "normatively to refer to a code of conduct that, given specified conditions, would be put forward by all rational persons" (GERT 2011). Importantly, "morality is a human creation that changes through time" (HARRIS 1999). Insofar, moral concepts refer to interpersonal relations and are a form of social-ethics while environmental-ethics deal with the relationship between individuals and the environment (KUTSCH 2002, p. 10). The purchase of Fair Trade products as well as charity can therefore be regarded as socially-ethically motivated (KUTSCH 2001, p. 174) while the purchase of organic products fits more into the concept of environmental-ethics. Accordingly, these two to some extent interrelated branches of ethics are relevant for the questions discussed in this dissertation.

2 Consumers' decision making

Consumers' decision making is a topic under investigation in different disciplines such as economics, political science, sociology or psychology. Furthermore, it is researched from the two poles of normative questions, such as the logic of decision making and the nature of rationality, on the one hand, and descriptive analysis of peoples beliefs and preferences, on the other hand (JUNGERMANN et al. 2005, p. 5; KAHNEMAN and TVERSKY 2008a). In economics, rational choice theory (see e.g. DIEKMANN and VOSS 2004) and behavioural economics (see e.g. PELZMANN 2000) exist to explain humans' decision making. The key topics of behavioural economics are the study of information processing including the information processing approach[11] which endorses bounded rationality (BETTMAN et al. 1998, p. 187) and heuristics (see e.g. GIGERENZER and TODD 1999 as well as the keyword 'adaptive

[11] For further information, see chapter 5.

toolbox'[12]), framing effects, and Prospect Theory[13] (see e.g. KAHNEMAN and TVERSKY 1979; THALER 2008).

The construct of preferences is regarded as a good indicator for purchase behaviour as each purchase decision is a preference decision and as such a statement towards the appraisal of the product attributes and their ability to fulfil individual consumers' demand (HAHN 1997, p. 8; TROMMSDORFF 2004, p. 490). Accordingly, preferences are a central determinant of purchase decisions (HILLIG 2006, p. 11), and hence consumers' choice. Therefore, the emphasis of this chapter lies on the concepts of preferences and the link to utility and choice. The chapter starts with the description of purchase decision models, and then focuses on preferences before decision making strategies are discussed in detail at the end of the chapter. The presentation of the decision making strategies provides background information for the study presented in chapter 5 which analyses experimentally the relevance of ethical and sustainable product features during consumers' information search process. [14]

2.1 The decision making process – Total and partial models of choice

The choice process involved in consumer purchase decisions has received a large amount of interest. As a result there are many models and theories to explain consumers' purchase behaviour. They differ with regard to the idea of man they are based on as well as with respect to the level of complexity. Microeconomic as well as behavioural science offer approaches to represent preferences and consumers' purchase choices. The most famous models in microeconomics are the neoclassical model[15], Samuelson's revealed preference theory and the Lancaster approach. SAMUELSON's revealed preference theory (1937; 1948) applies the relative utility terminus preference and regards observable purchase decisions as preference expressions (see chapter 2.2). The LANCASTER approach (1966, p. 133f.) extents this view by assuming that individuals do not evaluate goods in a holistic way but as a bundle of utility providing attributes. Not the good per se (coffee, milk) but the properties or attributes or characteristics of the good (caffeine content, protein content) provide utility to the consumer. The advantage of the Lancaster model is that it can be shown that consumer preferences for

[12] The adaptive toolbox of GIGERENZER and TODD (1999) is a metaphor depicting how bounded rationality can be integrated in the human mind (MARTIGNON 2001, p. 148).

[13] Prospect Theory describes decision making under risk. It is based on the findings that in risky situations preferences often violate the assumptions of expected utility theory (KAHNEMAN and TVERSKY 1979).

[14] For an overview of consumers purchase behaviour, see e.g. KOTLER et al. (2007, pp. 305-355).

[15] Because of the strict assumptions of the neoclassical household theory, such as product homogeneity, perfect information etc., this model is not appropriate for marketing issues, such as product differentiation (HAHN 1997, p. 18; MEFFERT 1993, p. 147f.).

goods differ according to the product attributes (HAHN 1997, p. 11ff.; TROMMSDORFF 2004, p. 490). The discrete choice approach (see chapters 3 and 6) relies on this assumption. [16]

Most of the non-microeconomic models and theories can be grouped into one of the three types of research approaches: behavioural approaches, neo-behavioural approaches and cognitive approaches.

Behavioural approaches concentrate on the observable and measurable variables of the purchase decision making. Observable are, on the one hand, the stimulus (S) affecting the individual (e.g. an attractive product) and, on the other hand, the response (R) to the stimulus (e.g. the purchase of the product). Non-observable psychological processes within the consumer are not taken into account and regarded as a black box. The purchase (R) is interpreted as a reaction to observable stimuli (S). These models are so-called black box models or SR models. Black box models regard e.g. marketing instruments such as the marketing budget for and the price of a product as input variable and the sales volume of a product as output.

Neo-behavioural approaches in contrast place emphasis on the processes which are executed in the organism (O), the individual itself. For this purpose latent constructs, such as attitudes[17] the individual holds, are used to explain the non-observable processes in the organism. These models are called Stimulus-Organism-Response (SOR) models. They try to explain what happens inside the black box of the organism. For that purpose intrapersonal and interpersonal variables are used. Intrapersonal variables are activating processes (such as emotions, motives, preferences, and attitudes), and cognitive processes (such as perception, learning). Interpersonal variables are cultural influences, social classes and peer groups. Depending on the object of purchase, different variables interact and determine the purchase (MEFFERT 1993, p. 144ff.). And, depending on the theoretic foundations of an explanatory model, e.g. economy, psychology or sociology, the focus and therefore the factors and determinants influencing the purchase decision differ (LENSCH 2009, p. 75).

Cognitive approaches extend the neo-behavioural concept by including cognitive, motivational and emotional processes to account for the individual information processing of humans (MEFFERT 1992, p. 24ff.).

---

[16] For the limitations of the approach developed by Lacaster as a "new approach to consumer theory", see HENDLER (1975). HENDLER (1975, p. 199) states that the approach is an "important special case of consumer choice rather than a general model of consumer demand".

[17] Attitudes are regarded as latent or underlying variables that guide and influence behaviour (FISHBEIN and AJZEN 1975, p. 8).

SOR models can be summarised as structural models as they try to structure and order the external and internal factors and stimuli influencing the decision. Two kinds of structural models can be distinguished: total models and partial models. Total models try to incorporate all relevant variables influencing consumers' decision making while partial models concentrate on specific aspects of the decision making (MEFFERT 1992, p. 28). In the following the two total and two partial models that are most widely used (FOSCHT and SWOBODA 2007, p. 25) and relevant for this dissertation are explained in detail.[18] They are relevant insofar as the questions posed to study participants covered many of the relevant aspects and determinants of the total models described and all of the constructs of the Theory of Planned Behaviour (see the appendices in chapters 5, 6 and 8).

The model of BLACKWELL, MINIARD and ENGEL

The total model developed by BLACKWELL, MINIARD and ENGEL (2001) relates the variables influencing consumers' decision making in a unique manner (see Figure 1). It consists of three main components: the decision making process, the information process and the judgement process. The decision making process starts with the awareness of a problem which is activated by different stimuli affecting the individual such as marketing stimuli and e.g. those arising from family influences (input and influencing factors in Figure 1). In this phase, the consumer recognises a problem or need (e.g. I am thirsty) or responds to a marketing stimulus (e.g. the consumer passes a coffee store and is attracted by the aroma of coffee). A stimulated customer then needs to decide how much information (if any) is necessary to arrive at a decision. If the need is strong and there is a product or service that meets the need close to hand, then a purchase decision is likely to be made there and then.

The information search succeeds the first phase if no direct solution for the problem is available. Information is selected until the expected utility of the additional information is higher than the costs related to the information search. A shopper can obtain information from several sources such as family[19], friends and neighbours, so-called commercial sources such

[18] Other famous multidimensional models are the FISHBEIN model (1967) which exists in many modifications as well as the TROMMSDORFF model (1975) (BERNDT 1996, p. 64ff.; MEFFERT 1993, p. 152f.). The FISHBEIN model (1967) is based on the SOR model and incorporates attitudinal and social influences trying to explain the formation of behavioural intention, which is seen as the direct predecessor of evident behaviour. The TROMMSDORFF model (1975) is a compositional model using rating scales to assess attitudes (BERNDT 1996, p. 64ff.). Sociological models focus on the influence of social groups, such as families, on individuals' purchase decisions (MEFFERT 1993, p. 160).
For an overview of other models not described in this thesis, see also HAHN (1997, p. 10; 16); HELM and STEINER (2007, p. 33); KROEBER-RIEL and WEINBERG (2003, p. 50; 70); MEFFERT (1993, p. 143ff.).

[19] For the influence of family on individuals' choices, see e.g. KUTSCH (2005, p. 26ff.).

as advertising, salespeople, retailers, packaging and point-of-sale displays, public sources such as newspapers, radio, television, and consumer organisations as well as his/her own experiences with the product. The usefulness and influence of these sources of information vary by product and by customer.

In the evaluation stage, the shopper decides between the available alternative products, brands and services according to the personal preferences which are related to attitudes, personality, lifestyle, etc. of the consumer. These interpersonal variables are affected by norms and values. An important determinant of the degree of evaluation is whether the consumer feels 'involved' in the product. In this context, involvement refers to the degree of perceived relevance and personal importance that accompanies the choice. Where a purchase is 'highly involving', the customer is likely to carry out extensive assessment. So-called high involvement purchases are characterised by high expenditure or high personal risk – for example, making investments. In contrast, low involvement purchases (e.g. choosing some coffee for daily use in the supermarket) are presumed to have very simple evaluation processes.

The final phase is the post-purchase evaluation of the decision. It is common for consumers to experience concerns after making a purchase decision. This arises from a concept that is known as 'cognitive dissonance'. The customer, having bought a product, may feel that an alternative would have been preferable. In this case the shopper will not repurchase, but is likely to switch brands next time (KOTLER et al. 2007, p. 335ff.).

The BLACKWELL, MINIARD and ENGEL (2001) model of consumer choice is primarily focussed on extensive purchase decision making but as simplification is also possible, e.g. by modification or skipping of some phases, limited and habitual decisions are also explainable (FOSCHT and SWOBODA 2007, p. 25). It is important to note that the decision making process part of the BLACKWELL, MINIARD and ENGEL (2001) model of consumer choice is used as 'the' schema to illustrate consumers' decision making process (see e.g. HELM and STEINER 2008, p. 33; KOTLER et al. 2007, p. 335ff.).

Figure 1: Blackwell, Miniard and Engel model of consumer choice

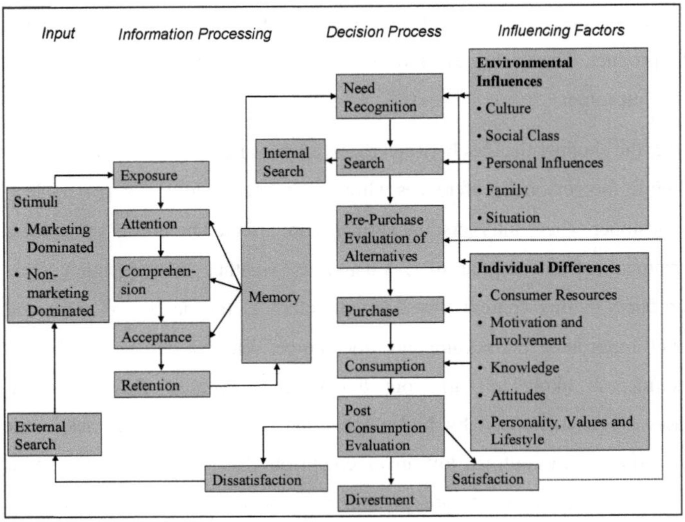

Source: BLACKWELL, MINIARD and ENGEL (2001, p. 83).

The model of HOWARD and SHETH

The second total model discussed in this thesis is the model of HOWARD and SHETH (1968). It is referred to as the most cited and most often used total model in the marketing literature (FOSCHT and SWOBODA 2007, p. 26). This integrative model incorporates most of the aspects of consumer behaviour and in particular the dynamics of purchase behaviour over time. It gets around the limitations of the phase model of BLACKWELL, MINIARD and ENGEL by using different constellations of the variables included in the model. The model resembles a SOR schema. It consists of four major elements: stimulus input variables, response variables, hypothetical constructs, and exogenous variables (see Figure 2). The central box consists of "various internal variables and processes, which taken together, show the state of the buyer" (HOWARD and SHETH 1968, p. 470). The variables within the central box are hypothetical constructs and non-observable. The hypothetical constructs are classified into two types: learning constructs (specific and non-specific motives, brand-potential of the evoked set, decision mediators, and predisposition towards brands, inhibitors and satisfaction with the purchase of the brand) and perceptual constructs (sensitivity to information, perceptual bias, search for information) (HOWARD and SHETH 1968, p. 472ff.). The values of the hypothetical constructs are "inferred from relations among the output intervening variables" (HOWARD and SHETH 1968, p. 470). Stimuli from the social environment of the consumer as well as the brand marketing, such as price, influence the central box. The information cues of the brand emanate from the product itself or are symbolic as they e.g. arise from advertising. If provided and stored information differs, the consumer starts his search process depending on the personal attitudes towards the brand or the information source. For a detailed description of the variables, see HOWARD and SHETH (1968). As a result of the interaction of inputs and the internal state of the consumer, the outputs vary. Furthermore, the internal state of the consumer is influenced by seven external variables which appear as ellipses at the top of Figure 2.

Figure 2: Howard and Sheth model of buyer behaviour

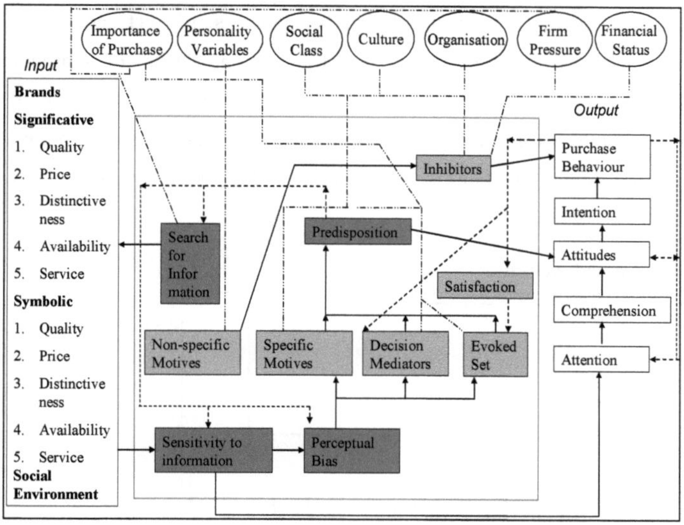

Note: exogenous variables in ellipses. In the rectangular light grey box: hypothetical constructs. Out of these in light grey: learning constructs. In dark grey: perceptual constructs.

Source: HOWARD and SHETH (1968, p. 471).

While the didactic value of these total models is enormous, they can hardly be used in applied research due to their complexity and difficulties in variable specification. Partial models are preferable for the analysis of specific situations and markets (FOSCHT and SWOBODA 2007, p. 28).

The Theory of Reasoned Action and the Theory of Planned Behaviour

The two partial models discussed in this dissertation are the Theory of Reasoned Action by FISHBEIN and AJZEN (1975) and the Theory of Planned Behaviour by AJZEN (1991) as both are used in the context of ethical consumption and charitable giving (see the respective chapters of the dissertation). They originate from social psychology. In particular the Theory of Planned Behaviour has been applied to aspects of ethical consumer behaviour and ethical purchase (see e.g. SHAW and SHIU 2002) as well as green consumerism (see e.g. KALAFATIS et al. 1999). Both models concentrate on the relationship of attitude and behaviour and aim to predict a person's behaviour by means of the three components (in the case of the Theory of Reasoned Action) attitudes, subjective norms, and behavioural intention (the Theory of Planned Behaviour adds perceived behavioural control as fourth component).

According to the Theory of Reasoned Action (see Figure 3) a person's attitudes, subjective norms and behavioural intentions determine their actual behaviour; they are assumed to be reflected in a consumer's choice. It is assumed that behaviour is a direct function of intentions, which are indeed influenced by norms and attitudes. The Theory of Reasoned Action assumes that if consumers evaluate a suggested behaviour as positive (attitude), and if they think their significant others wanted them to perform the behaviour (subjective norm), this results in a higher motivation (intention) and they are more likely to behave accordingly (AJZEN 1991; MADDEN et al. 1992).

Figure 3: Theory of Reasoned Action

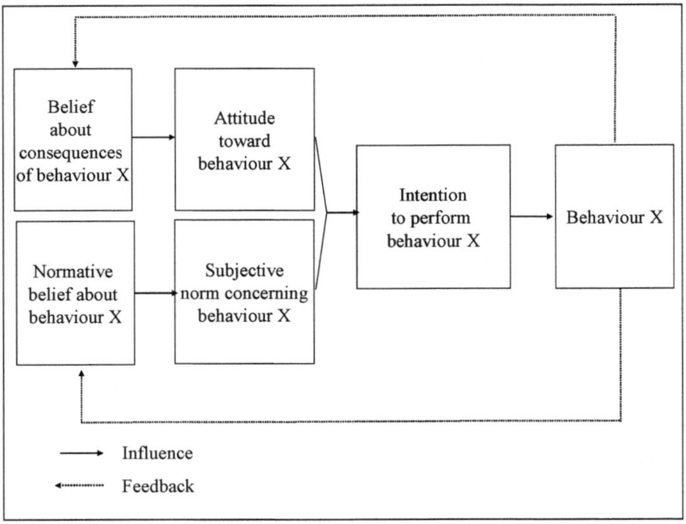

Source: FISHBEIN and AJZEN (1975, p. 16).

The Theory of Planned Behaviour (see Figure 4) extents the Theory of Reasoned Action by means of including a measure of individuals' perceived behavioural control. The extension accounts for the limitations in the Theory of Reasoned Action which arise mainly "in dealing with behaviours over which people have incomplete volitional control" (AJZEN 1991, p. 181). This is, for example, the case when the time between intention and behaviour is long and unpredictable events happen and change the intention. The perceived behavioural control influences not only the intention but also the behaviour directly. The perceived behavioural control is understood as a person's judgement of how well he/she can accomplish actions required to deal with future situations (AJZEN 1991, p. 184)[20]. The Theory of Planned Behaviour shows that consumer (purchase) behaviour is not only influenced by values and beliefs but also by social pressure which follow from the motivation to comply with the social norms (WISWEDE 2000, p. 31f.).

Figure 4: Theory of Planned Behaviour

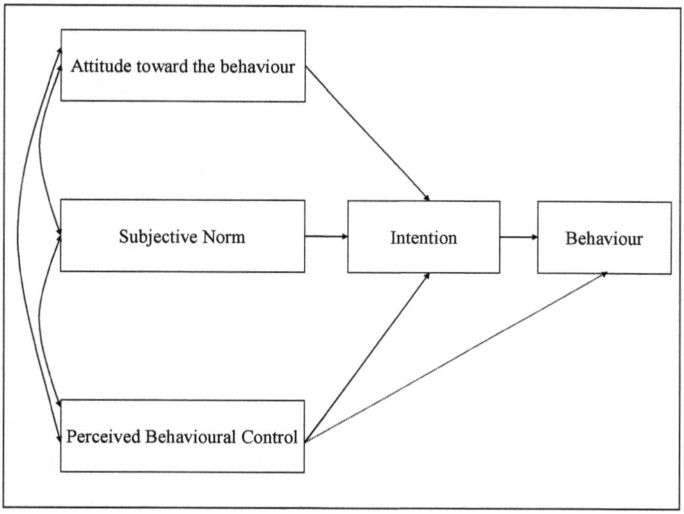

Source: AJZEN (1991, p. 182).

Types of purchase decisions

Especially for the two total models described earlier it is important that the following types of purchase decisions can be differentiated: extensive (also called rational behaviour), habitual, limited and impulsive (also called spontaneous) purchase decisions as well as socially dependent purchase behaviour. Hybrid forms are possible (MEFFERT 1993, p. 141ff.; FELSER 2007, p. 63).

[20] An example of a question revealing respondents' perceived behavioural control that was posed in the study presented in chapter 6 is: "By means of donating to charity I can make a difference".

Extensive decisions require a comparatively higher cognitive involvement than habitual decisions. The identification of the relevant decision criteria and the evaluation of the alternatives are more complex in extensive decision making than in any other type. The purchase of food can be rational (FELSER 2007, p. 63), e.g. when the consumer assesses all different types of coffee packages available under certain principles.

A typical example for **habitual** decision making is the choice of always the same product brand in the store without taking into account new available product alternatives; the behaviour is stable.

Limited decisions are close to habitual decisions. But here at least a few product alternatives form a choice set out of which the final product is chosen. In this case heuristics and rules-of-thumbs are applied due to the limited information available.

Impulsive or **spontaneous** decisions are a result of a stimulus right at the point of sale, without information processing, the formation of decision criteria and the consideration of alternatives, e.g. when the consumer decides to purchase a certain coffee just in front of the coffee shelf.

Socially dependant decision making arises when the presence or absence of e.g. a friend who is known for his/her preferences for a certain brand influences the decision (MEFFERT 1992, p. 40ff.).

To sum up, the plurality of models of consumer choice is due to the fact that consumer decision making is a fundamental part of consumer behaviour, but, at the same time, the way consumers assess and choose products varies widely and depends strongly on dimensions such as the personal circumstances but also the degree of risk which is related to the decision (which is e.g. high in extensive purchase decisions). We can maintain that a decision making process is composed of a series of stages the sequence of which depends on different influencing variables.

2.2 Preferences, utility and choice

Preferences, utility and choice are probably the most important terms for the description of the decision making process. Utility describes the subjective and evaluative absolute value a decision maker associates with an option (I like coffee) while preference is a relative measure of preferring one option over another (I prefer coffee (option A) to tea (option B) at a certain point of time) (BÖCKER 1986, p. 556; JUNGERMANN et al. 2005, p. 49ff). Preferences in this definition[21] are personal, depend on the attributes of the products available in the market, are time constrained as well as context dependent and therefore relative (HAHN 1997, p. 6; HELM and STEINER 2008, p. 42). The utility individuals associate with a consequence or an option is expressed in evaluative judgements and can be captured in terms of utility measures. Under certain circumstances (e.g. symmetry, transitivity conditions etc. see e.g. JUNGERMANN et al. 2005, p. 54f.) preferences can be translated in utility measures. Utility measures are figures representing the preference relation. E.g. ordinal utility measures $U(A)=10$, $U(B)=2$ can be assigned to the two alternatives A and B representing the preference relations (DIEKMANN and VOSS 2004, p. 16). The choice is the final decision of the individual to take an option.

The construct of utility is therefore a measure of the individual need satisfaction. The net utility of a product is the difference between subjective utility and costs of the product. Utility is for that reason an upstream construct of preference and a preference is the basis for the choice of an option. In contrast to utility, preferences are observable (GENSLER 2003, p. 11; JUNGERMANN et al. 2005, p. 49ff.). It is not supposed that the utility of an option is always consciously assessed before a preference can be noticed and the same holds for preferences which are not always clear before a choice is taken. The reason is that the types of purchase decisions (habitual, spontaneous etc.) influence the choice (JUNGERMANN et al. 2005, p. 49ff.).

The following paragraph briefly summarises the microeconomic view on preferences and utility. There are two main assumptions concerning the nature of preferences in microeconomics. First: completeness. An individual is always able to specify whether product A is preferred to B, B is preferred to A or whether A and B are equally attractive. Second: transitivity. If A is preferred to B, and B is preferred to C, then A is preferred to C. This implies that an individual's choices are internally consistent (VARIAN 1991, p. 32f.). A choice is regarded as internally consistent if it can be explained "as the choosing of 'most preferred' alternative with respect to a postulated preference relation" (SEN 1977, p. 323). Given these assumptions, it is possible to show that individuals are able to rank in order all possible products from the least to the most desirable. This ranking is called utility[22]. If A is preferred to B, then the utility assigned to A exceeds the utility assigned to B: $U(A)>U(B)$.

---

[21] The term 'preferences' is not used in a uniform way in marketing literature. In particular, the separation from other forms of subjective evaluations is insufficient (HILLIG 2006, p. 14f.).

[22] For a review of the development of the concept of utility, see BÖHM and HALLER (2008).

Graphically, indifference curves are used to illustrate consumers' preferences. An indifference curve shows a set of consumption bundles among which the individual is indifferent, which means each point on the indifference curve provides the consumer with the same level of utility, see Figure 5 (VARIAN 1991, p. 50).[23] The negative of the slope of the indifference curve at any point is called the marginal rate of substitution (*MRS*) and reflects the law of diminishing marginal utility. The *MRS* can be used to estimate consumers' willingness to pay for products and product attributes (see chapter 6) (VARIAN 1991, p. 45ff.).

Indifference curves are used to construct utility functions (e.g. Cobb-Douglas utility function) which allow ranking different options by allocating a utility measure to each (VARIAN 1991, p. 50f.) (see Figure 5). For further insights into the properties of preferences and utility functions, see BÖHM and HALLER (2008).

Figure 5: Indifference curves and utility function

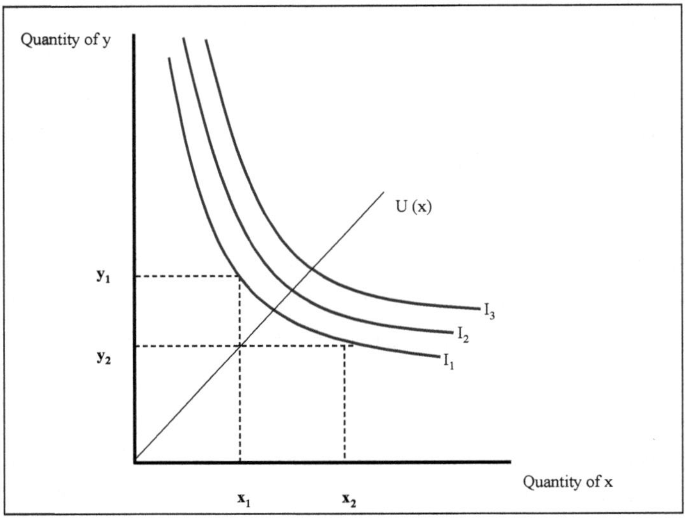

Source: VARIAN (1991, p. 54).

Standard economic assumptions regarding preferences

A common assumption in microeconomics is that "each individual has stable and coherent preferences" (RABIN 1998, p. 11). The underlying reasons for the personal preferences remain unclear (JACKSON and MICHAELIS 2003, p. 22f.). It is furthermore assumed that

[23] Indifferent curves of perfect substitutes, perfect complements or neutral goods can be found in VARIAN (1991, p. 37ff.).

"people know their preferences" (FREEMAN 2003, p. 8) and that individuals have the computational capacity or ability to identify the alternative which provides them maximal utility value, and that individuals choose accordingly (PAYNE et al. 1999, p. 245). Rational choice theory postulates a rational decision maker chooses an alternative after a process of reflection in which three questions are answered: what is feasible, what is desirable and "what is the best alternative according to the notion of desirability given the feasible constraints" (RUBINSTEIN 1998, p. 7). Economic theory defines a choice as a 'rational' choice if it is characterised by internal consistency. In addition to the concept of value maximisation and the assumption of stable preferences, rational choice theory is based on the principle of the independence of irrelevant alternatives (IIA) (BOSSERT 1993, p. 552; PETERS and WAKKER 1991, p. 1788; RUBINSTEIN 1998, p. 7ff.).

This IIA principle postulates that consumers' preference between alternatives does not depend on the absence or presence of other options in a choice set (MEYER and KAHN 1991, p. 91). Thus, the relative desirability of x compared to y is independent of the existence or non-existence of a third alternative z (for an extensive review, see KAHNEMAN and TVERSKY 2008b). The IIA assumption is often illustrated using the example of red and blue busses in the context of a choice of transportation mode between busses and cars. This is a typical problem of line extension where the company wants to increase the bus ridership by offering two different bus colours (red and blue) instead of only one (red) (ORME and HEFT 1999, p. 7). In the first scenario all busses are red. It is assumed that consumers choose between a red bus and a car with equal probability of 0.5 (odds ration equal to 1). Now some of the red busses are painted blue. Suppose the colour of a bus is not a relevant attribute influencing the choice between bus and car as a mode of transportation. Then the probability of choosing a car is still 0.5 after some of the red busses have been painted blue; for the red and blue bus it is 0.25 each. But IIA implies that the odds ratio between bus and car is the same which means the new probabilities are 0.33 for the car, 0.33 for the red bus and 0.33 for the blue bus. This shows that the IIA property presumes not only constant cross-elasticities but also constant substitution rates so that in a scenario a given product takes the "share from the other products in proportion to their shares" (SAWTOOTH 2001, p. 12). The IIA property requires shifts in choices to be proportional to changes in utilities. This leads to the conclusion that in case of close substitutes the IIA axiom fails. Especially in aggregate choice data, arising from aggregation over heterogeneous utility functions, this assumption is often violated (BETTMAN et al. 1998, p. 207; LOUVIERE 1994, p. 242; PAYNE et al. 1993, p. 55).

TVERSKY and SIMONSON (2008) show that the IIA principle is equivalent to the assumption of utility maximisation. This means decision makers are ranking choices according to their preferences and choose from this order the most preferred alternative which promises the highest possible expectable utility.

The following presentation of this connection follows TVERSKY and SIMONSON (2008, p. 519ff.). $T = \{x, y, z, ...\}$ is a finite set which includes all alternatives under study. The choice between alternatives is described by the choice function C that links with any offered set $S \subset T$ a nonempty subset of S, denominate $C(S)$. The subset consists of the alternatives selected by the decision maker. $C(S)$ includes a single alternative if there are no ties. If ties are possible, $C(S)$ consists of the elements of S which are tied for first rank. If there now exists a function v which assigns a real value to each x in T so that $x \in C(S)$ if $v(x) \geq v(y)$ for all $y \in S$ this choice function C satisfies value maximisation. Value maximisation means that the order of the alternatives is independent of the choice set in which the alternatives are presented to the decision maker. Especially if x is preferred to y in a binary choice, it is also favoured in a multiple non-binary choice. Besides, if $x \in C(S)$ and $x \in R \subset S$ then $x \in C(R)$. This means, a non-preferred alternative cannot turn into a preferred one when new alternatives are added to the choice set. For that reason the principle of value maximisation captures the concept of independence of irrelevant alternatives.

There are a series of contexts (e.g. extremeness aversion), which according to TVERSKY and SIMONSON (2008, p. 521), violate the principle of values maximisation. The example given by LEIBENSTEIN (1954, p. 140 in FRANTZ 2007, p. 3) can also be briefly mentioned: in certain areas, such as decisions about family size, the maximisation of an economic catalogue seems to be an inadequate assumption. Nevertheless, the supposition of maximising behaviour could be a first approximation under particular circumstances, namely if economic considerations are the basic determinants of behaviour (FRANTZ 2007).

When rational choice fails

Traditionally, decisions under uncertainty have been modelled using the expected utility framework. In the beginning of this chapter it was said that utility is a measure of satisfaction. Expected utility is defined as the mean utility achieved under risk. However, the use of the expected utility framework to explain decision making *under risk* is debilitated by experimental evidence that its core assumptions are often violated in practice (SCHOEMAKER 1982). Much of psychological and behavioural research (e.g. ETZIONI 1986; FRANTZ 2007;

McFadden 1999; Payne et al. 1999; Rabin 1998; Thaler 2008; Simonson and Tversky 1993) into decision making suggests that the stable preference assumption of rational choice theory and value maximisation are not able to explain all kinds of human decision making. Instead of behaving rationally individuals' decision making is influenced by e.g. their previous experiences, bounded rationality[24] and limited cognitive resources. Moreover, as prospect theory says, people evaluate losses and gains differently. This implies that decisions can be influenced by the *framing* of choices as well as their anticipated values (Kahneman and Tversky 1979, Simonson and Tversky 1993, Tversky and Kahneman 2008). Furthermore, individuals make decisions based on reference points rather than absolute values[25].

In fact, many studies suggest that preferences are context dependent which means that the IIA assumption does not hold true and that the choice for one option is not only influenced by the characteristics of the chosen option but also the characteristics of the other options in the choice set. Simonson and Tversky (1993) distinguish in their framework of *context dependent* preferences the background context which is defined by prior alternatives and the local context which is defined by the actual choice set. This implies that people do not have an extensive preference order but use the actual context to find the most attractive alternative. This means personal needs and preferences vary depending on purchase situation and cause of purchase (e.g coffee for daily use versus coffee for state occasion). This is according to Tversky and Simonson (2008, p. 521) one reason for the failure of rational choice theory in explaining choices.

Moreover, in literature the question is posed whether the advantageousness of product alternatives is assessed with or without consideration of restrictive purchase factors such as individuals' budget constraint. Accordingly *unconstrained* and *constrained* preferences are differentiated. When preferences are formed in a process in which constraints are taken into account, individuals compare the net-utility provided by the different products available. Accordingly, constraint preferences are formed by the relative preferability of a product (Hahn 1997, p. 6; Helm and Steiner 2008, p. 28). However, preferences can be formed outside of real purchase decisions (Hillig 2006, p. 14f.).

We also must not forget that the shapes of preferences curves differ "from individual to individual, alternative to alternative and at different points of time" (Hensher et al. 2005,

---

[24] For an overview of modelling bounded rationality, see Rubinstein (1998).
[25] For the value function according to prospect theory, see Jungermann et al. (2005, p 67).

p. 4). But there is a clear agreement about at least the temporary validity of preferences which are an indicator of the advantages of one alternative in comparison to another (HENSHER et al. 2005, p. 4).[26]

Another discussion is about the question as to whether preferences are *constructed* rather than *revealed* in the elicitation process (see e.g. PAYNE et al. 1999; PAYNE et al. 1992; SLOVIC 2008). This implies that preferences can be created by others than the consistent expected utility calculation (PAYNE et al. 1992; TVERSKY and SIMONSON 2008, p. 526). SEN (1977, p. 324) assumes that choice "may reflect a compromise among a variety of considerations of which personal welfare may be just one".

To sum up, the construction of preferences influencing factors are amongst the context of the choice, the elicitation methods and the problem framing social preferences and fair allocation, biases in judgement as well as anchoring effects (RABIN 1998; TVERSKY and SIMONSON 1993).[27] Therefore, people apply a variety of heuristic procedures to achieve outcomes that are 'good enough' rather than truly optimal (CONLISK 1996). Moreover, individuals live in social groups and these reference groups may influence the consumption decisions of an individual (LEIBENSTEIN 1975, p. 5 in ALBANESE 2007, p. 196). In this context, it is important that decisions are not taken in a social vacuum but that social factors influence decision making (TETLOCK 1985 in PAYNE et al. 1993, p. 3). Accordingly, the embedding of emotional humans in social contexts is important for the goal of minimising negative emotions as the decision maker may have to justify his decision to others or him/herself (BETTMAN et al. 1998, p. 193). This implies that other-regarding preferences and concerns for the well-being of others cannot be ignored in social interactions (FEHR and SCHMIDT 2005, p. 1)[28]. BETTMAN et al. (1998, p. 193) argue that depending on the situation special subsets of these goals are relevant. The selection between different decision making strategies can therefore be described as a trade-off between first, the effort which is needed to use each strategy and second, each strategy's ability to generate a perfect response (JOHNSON et al. 1988, p. 19).

[26] Therefore, choice experiments, as conducted in the survey presented in chapter 6, are appropriate to assess the research questions of this thesis.

[27] For an elaborate review, see RABIN (1998) and SLOVIC (2008). Sociologists also work with a different idea of man than that known as 'homo oeconomicus' and characterised as egoistic, with stable preferences and fully informed. They use the RREEMM (resourceful, restricted, expecting, evaluating, maximising man). Full information and stable and egoistic preferences are no longer assumed but emotional, altruistic and norm guided preferences are admitted (MAYERL 2008, p. 155f.). For further insight into this, see MAYERL (2008).

[28] BRIGGEMAN and LUSK (2011, p. 1; 3) show that consumers care about the livelihood of producers which can be categorised as other-related behaviour.

This overview reveals that at least two schools of thought regarding the nature of preferences exist: the microeconomics tradition which is based on the assumption of existing and stable preferences and the constructive processing approach of behavioural decision theory supposing that preferences are constructed based upon task and context of the preference elicitation or choice (e.g. HOEFFLER and ARIELY 1999, p. 113ff.; MCFADDEN 1999; RABIN 1998). According to HOEFFLER and ARIELY (1999, p. 115f.), marketing is moving towards the constructive approach even though neither the one nor the other approach provides a complete explanation for the preference formation process. What HOEFFLER and ARIELY (1999, p. 116) state and investigate in their research is that consumers have some kind of preferences (a favoured combination of product attributes) which change or stabilize over time due to increased experience. This means both – stable and constructed preferences – are possible at different times. Moreover, the modern rational choice theory goes beyond the homo economics model and is no longer restricted to the above-mentioned concepts but also includes the influence of social contexts, altruistic behaviour and non-material interest (DIEKMANN and VOSS 2004, p. 13). Furthermore, there are possibilities to relax e.g. the IIA as described in detail in chapter 3.1.3.

Consequently, preferences are included in models, such as the total and partial models introduced in the first part of this chapter, explaining consumer decision making starting with an extern stimulus (such as advertisement) or an intern stimulus (such as the feeling of hunger) activating an individual consumer need which should be met via a certain product holding specific characteristics. Information stored, searched or provided influences how the consumer perceives intrinsic and extrinsic product attributes. Emotions, attitudes, involvement, knowledge etc. also influence the organisms' actions and are often included in decision making models. Preferences for a product then lead to a certain purchase probability but not necessarily to a purchase (see e.g. ESCH et al. 2008; HAHN 1997, p. 8ff.; HELM and STEINER 2008, p. 39; KROEBER-RIEL and WEINBERG 2003, p. 171ff.). Today, it is common sense that decision making is not always rational and consumers rely on decision rules (SOLOMON 2009, p. 381f.). These are explained in the following section.

The design as well as the analysis of the choice experimental study presented in chapter 6 is influenced by the total and partial choice process models presented in this chapter as well as the microeconomic assumptions about the nature of preferences and utility. Questions were asked regarding e.g. personal attitudes towards donations, Fair Trade, etc. which were supplemented by questions focussing on the attitudes of the respondents' friends towards these issues. Social influences as well as personal characteristics are captured by this and integrated in the model applied in chapter 6. At the same time, e.g. the marginal rate of substitution was estimated for Fair Trade and organic production as well as donations; a microeconomic concept. The study presented in chapter 5 was constructed to assess the extent to which preferences for ethical product features are influenced by information.

2.3 Decision making strategies

Four primary aspects of choice processing can be used to describe, characterise and distinguish different decision making strategies consumers apply under the constraints of limited computational capacities, knowledge and time (BETTMAN et al. 1998, p. 189ff.; MARTIGNON 2001, p. 147f.).

These four characteristics are first, the type and amount of information which is processed as information which is not taken into account cannot be processed and is therefore irrelevant for the heuristic applied for the decision by the respondent. Second, the selectivity or consistency in information processing which means whether the information processed differs from one attribute/alternative to another. Third, the pattern of information request and processing: if a person considers first all attribute levels of a single attribute of a good before looking at a second attribute or the contrary, when the individual considers first all attributes of one alternative before investigating the second alternative. And fourth, the degree to which a strategy is compensatory which means that a poor value of an attribute can be compensated by a good value of another attribute of the same alternative. This means explicit trade-offs between attributes are required for a compensatory strategy. Accordingly, in a non-compensatory decision making strategy poor attribute values cannot be compensated by good values of another attribute of the alternative. This issue might be critical for the validity of the respective method as e.g. rational decision theory assumes that decisions are based on compensatory strategies so that values and beliefs are traded off (FRISCH and CLEMEN 1994, p. 51; PAYNE et al. 1993, p. 75).

The decision making strategies most often discussed in research are the following eight: weighted adding strategy, the lexicographic strategy, the satisficing strategy, the elimination by aspects (EBA) strategy, the equal weight strategy, the majority of confirming dimensions strategy, frequency of good and bad features strategy, the componential context model strategy also known as economic screening rule model. They range from accurate strategies such as the weighted adding strategy to more heuristic[29] strategies that process information in a more non-compensatory and selective way such as the EBA strategy (BETTMAN et al. 1998, p. 189).

The following description of the eight above-mentioned decision strategies is based on BETTMAN et al. (1998, p. 191) and PAYNE et al. (1988, p. 536f.). A decision strategy is called a *weighted adding strategy* if a person assigns a subjective value to each attribute level of one option and then multiplies the personal importance weight and the attributes value and sums up all the attributes. The overall values for the alternatives are compared and the alternative with the highest value is selected by the individual. Based on the four aspects of choice processing this strategy is extensive, consistent (not selective), alternative-based and compensatory. It involves implicit trade-offs and the computational effort is quite high.

When the alternative with the best level on the most important attribute is chosen the decision strategy is called *lexicographic*. The strategy is limited, consistent across alternatives, attribute-based, and non-compensatory.

In a *satisficing* decision strategy all alternatives are considered by the individual in the order they appear in the choice set. It is looked at whether the attribute levels meet certain personally predetermined cut-off levels. If not, the alternative is immediately rejected and the next option considered. The first alternative that passes the cut-off value for all attributes is considered. The order in which the alternatives are presented and considered therefore influences the choice. Depending on the values of cutoffs and attribute levels the satisficing strategy's extent of processing varies. Furthermore, this strategy is selective, alternative-based and non-compensatory.

The *EBA* strategy is a combination of the lexicographic and the satisficing strategy. The option that does not meet a certain minimum cut-off level for the most important attribute is removed. This elimination process is repeated until one option remains. The consumer choice is characterised here as a latent elimination process (GILBRIDE and ALLENBY 2006, p. 495). This EBA model accounts for the effect of similarity in choice and the violations of the IIA assumption (PAYNE et al. 1993, p. 55). The strategy is attribute-based and non-compensatory. The extensiveness and selectivity of processing varies depending on the exact pattern of elimination of options.

---

[29] For a review of the development of the meaning of the term heuristic see GOLDSTEIN and GIGERENZER (2002) and FREDERICK (2002). In this thesis, it is understood that a heuristic is designed to simplify choice (FREDERICK 2002, p. 548).

The *equal weight* strategy is a variation, simplification and a special case of the weighted adding strategy. All options and all attribute levels are considered but the information on attribute weights is ignored and unit weights are assumed. The strategy is extensive, consistent (not selective), alternative-based and compensatory.

The sixth strategy to be mentioned here is the *majority of confirming dimensions* strategy. Here a pairwise alternative comparison is carried out. In this case, two alternatives are compared and the option with a majority of better attributes is then compared with a third option from the choice set until all alternatives are evaluated and one option is left over. The strategy is extensive, consistent, attribute-based and compensatory.

The *frequency of good and/or bad features* strategy reflects that consumers develop cut-offs for determining good and bad features in order to separate good and poor alternatives. Many possibilities are thinkable. The strategy is therefore sometimes compensatory and sometimes not. At any rate, it is alternative-based. The underlying idea is that the magnitude of the outcome may be less important for a person than the impression that the outcome is a gain or a loss.

The *componential context mode* strategy is also known as the economic screening rule model as well as the two-stage screening rule model. We talk about it when people use a combination of strategies for decision making. Typically some alternatives are eliminated in the first phase and the remaining alternatives are then analysed more precisely in a second phase. This means EBA is often applied in the initial phase to reduce the choice set and then a compensative strategy such as weighted adding is used to select one option among the remaining ones (PAYNE et al. 1988, p. 536f.; BETTMAN et al. 1998, p. 191). For the description of further decision making strategies see RIEDL et al. (2008).

According to GILBRIDE and ALLENBY (2006, p. 506) little research has been undertaken to compare the different choice rules due to difficulties in estimating them. Another challenge is that the strategies are often applied subconsciously so that the decision maker is not aware that he uses a special rule or heuristic. In addition, choices are often made intuitively (FREDERICK 2002, p. 549f.).

BETTMAN et al. (1998) developed an integrated framework for constructive choice processes combining the accuracy-effort approach PAYNE et al. developed in 1993 (p. 70ff.) and the perceptual framework associated with KAHNEMAN and TVERSKY (1979). BETTMAN et al. (1998) analyse situations where accuracy and effort goals predominate or where it is relevant to minimize negative emotions. Hereby they identify weaknesses of the strategies. For example, the EBA does not include possible computational errors because individual processing skills depend on e.g. socio-demographic factors as well as prior knowledge and expertise (PAYNE et al. 1993, p. 3). Furthermore, they state that time pressure[30] may have an influence on the strategy selection when it imposes an effort constraint. With respect to trade-offs, BETTMAN et al. (1998, p. 197) found that attribute-based choice processing minimises trade-offs whereas alternative-based processing forwards trade-offs. One important finding is that problem-focused coping involves more information processing but avoidant behaviours are associated with emotion-focused coping. But, because it is not possible to easily assess the amount of emotion which characterises a decision, this is a vague distinction. All in all, BETTMAN et al. (1998, p. 199ff.) identify six main sub-aspects in problem difficulties which are: problem size, time pressure, attribute correlation, completeness of information, information format, and comparable versus non-comparable choice. Regarding problem size it can be said that the higher the number of alternatives, the higher the probability that a non-compensatory strategy is used. With respect to the number of attributes, an increase in size increases selectivity but does not change individuals' decision strategies[31]. With respect to time pressure, BETTMAN et al. (1998, p. 200) found that under severe time pressure people switch to attribute-based processing and lexicographic and EBA strategies. These heuristics are are more robust under time pressure than e.g. the weighted adding strategy. Furthermore, time pressure influences consumers in such a way that they assess negative information more intensively[32]. One interesting finding concerning the interactions between consumer knowledge and decision making is that attributes, which are not very likely to be selected in the beginning, become more attractive because of added attribute information (BETTMAN et al. 1998, p. 204).[33] Regarding information depth OLSEN and JACOBY (1972, p. 169) found that study participants used only limited amounts of information available to arrive at the purchase decision. In their study only 4 to 7 of the n = 12 to 15 (of five different products such as shampoo and ground coffee) product attributes were used to make the decision. JACOBY et al. (1977, p. 214) arrived at similar results. With respect to content, JACOBY et al. (1977, p. 210) state that in several studies brand name and price were the most important attributes considered. It is interesting to note that in the research of JACOBY et al. (1977, p. 214)

[30] Acceleration and selection are not only an alteration of information, but also adaption strategies to time pressure (WEENIG and MAARLEVELD 2002, p. 690).

[31] In the study presented in chapter 5, three alternatives were available. Due to this small number of options, it could be assumed that respondents use compensatory strategies.

[32] In the study presented in chapter 5, some form of time pressure has been implemented as the number of cards which can be turned over and looked at was limited to 11.

[33] In the study presented in chapter 5, this is confirmed.

consumers were more satisfied with their final choice and tended to regard less information when the information of the brand name was considered. One explanation JACOBY et al. (1977, p. 214) give is that the more familiar consumers feel with a brand, the less they need information on other product characteristics. The explanation JACOBY et al. (1977, p. 215) have for the importance of the price information is convincing: compared to much of the other information, such as net weight, product prices change from one purchase occasion to the next. This hold true for food prices in Germany in general and for coffee in particular which often serves as loss-leader price (DER SPIEGEL 1996).

To sum up, in complex product choice situations consumers apply different decision making strategies such as simplifying heuristics and non-compensatory strategies (PAYNE et al. 1993, p. 2). By using rules for searching for information, stopping the information search and making the decision, these decisions become fast, frugal and computationally cheap (GIGERENZER and SELTEN 2001, p. 9). But, as BETTMAN and KAKKAR (1977) show, the organisation of the task environment strongly influences consumers' information processing. For example, the way coffee is presented in the supermarket shelves (by brand or by taste etc.) has an influence on consumers' decision making (BETTMAN and KAKKAR 1977, p. 234).

2.4 References

AJZEN, I. (1991): The theory of planned behavior. *Organizational Behavior and Human Decision Processes*, 50 (1): 179-211.

ALBANESE, P. (2007): Leibenstein´s theory of consumption behaviour. In: Frantz, R. (Ed.): *Renaissance in Behavioral Economics: Essays in honor of Harvey Leibenstein*. London et al.: Routledge: 194-210.

BERNDT, R. (1996): *Marketing 1: Käuferverhalten, Marktforschung und Marketing-Prognosen*. Berlin: Springer.

BETTMAN, J. R. and KAKKAR, P. (1977): Effects of Information Presentation Format on Consumer Information Acquisition Strategies. *The Journal of Consumer Research*, 3 (4): 233-240.

BETTMAN, J. R., LUCE, M. F. and PAYNE, J. W. (1998): Constructive Consumer Choice Processes. *The Journal of Consumer Research*, 25 (3): 187-217.

BLACKWELL, R., MINIARD, P. and ENGEL, J. (2001): *Consumer Behaviour*. 9th ed. Mason, Ohio: Thomson South-West.

BÖCKER, F. (1986): Präferenzforschung als Mittel marktorientierter Unternehmensführung. *Schmalenbachs Zeitschrift für betriebswirtschaftliche Forschung*, 38 (7-8): 543-574.

BÖHM, V. and HALLER, H. (2008): Demand Theory. In: Durlauf, S. N. and Blume, L. E. (Eds.): *The New Palgrave Dictionary of Economics*. 2nd ed., Palgrave Macmillan, The New Palgrave Dictionary of Economics Online. Available from: http://www.dictionaryofeconomics.com/article?id=pde2008_D000069, [accessed 2011-06-24].

BOSSERT, W. (1993): Rational choice and two-person bargaining solutions. *Journal of Mathematical Economics*, 23: 549-563.

BRIGGEMAN, B. C. and LUSK, J. L. (2011): Preferences for fairness and equity in the food system. *European Review of Agricultural Economics*, 38 (1): 1-29.

CONLISK, J. (1996): Why bounded rationality? *Journal of Economic Literature* 34, 669-700.

DER SPIEGEL (1996): *Hoch die Tasse*. 51/1996: 81. Available from: http://wissen.spiegel.de/wissen/image/show.html?did=9133905&aref=image017/SP1996/051/SP199605100860086.pdf&thumb=false, [accessed 2010-01-20].

DIEKMANN, A. and VOSS, T. (2004): Die Theorie rationalen Handelns. Stand und Perspektive. In: Diekmann, A. and Ziegler, R. (Eds.): Rational-*Choice-Theorie in den Sozialwissenschaften: Anwendungen und Probleme*. München: Oldenbourg: 13-32.

ESCH, F. R., MÖLL, T., ELGER, C. E., NEUHAUS, C. and WEBER, B. (2008): Wirkung von Markenemotionen: Neuromarketing als neuer verhaltenswissenschaftlicher Zugang, *Marketing ZFP*, 30 (2): 109-127.

ETZIONI, A. (1986): Socio-Economics: A Proposal for a New Interdisciplinary Field. *Journal of Social Behavior and Personality*, 1 (4): 475-482.

FEHR, E. and SCHMIDT, K. M. (2005): *The Economics of Fairness, Reciprocity and Altruism - Experimental Evidence and New Theories*. Chapter written for the Handbook of Reciprocity, Gift-Giving and Altruism. Munich Discussion Paper No. 2005-20. Available from: http://epub.ub.uni-muenchen.de/726/1/Fehr-Schmidt_Handbook_2005-Munichecon.pdf, [accessed 2010-01-20].

FELSER, G. (2007): *Werbe- und Konsumentenpsychologie*. 3rd ed. Heidelberg: Spektrum.

FISHBEIN, M. and AJZEN, I. (1975): *Belief, Attitude, Intention, and Behavior: An Introduction to Theory and Research*. Reading, MA: Addison-Wesley.

FOSCHT, T. and SWOBODA, B. (2007): *Käuferverhalten*. 3rd. ed. Wiesbaden: Gabler.

FRANTZ, R. (2007): *Renaissance in Behavioral Economics: Essays in honor of Harvey Leibenstein*. London et al.: Routledge.

FREDERICK, S. (2002): Automated Choice Heuristics. In: Gilovich, T., Griffin, D. and Kahneman, D. (Eds.): *Heuristics and Biases: The psychology of intuitive judgement*. Cambridge [et al.]: Cambridge University Press: 548-558.

FREEMAN, A. M. III. (2003): *The Measurement of Environmental and Resource Values: Theory and Methods*. Washington, DC: Resources for the Future.

FRISCH, D. and CLEMEN, R. T. (1994): Beyond Expected Utility: Rethinking Behavioral Decision Research. *Psychological Bulletin*, 116 (1): 46-54.

GENSLER, S. (2003): Heterogenität in der Präferenzanalyse: ein Vergleich von hierarchischen Bayes-Modellen und Finite-Mixture-Modellen. In: Albers et al. (Eds.): *Beiträge zur betriebswirtschaftlichen Forschung*, 107. Dissertation. Universität Frankfurt/Main. Wiesbaden: Deutscher Universitäts-Verlag.

GIGERENZER, G. and SELTEN, R. (2001): Rethinking Rationality. In: Gigerenzer, G. and Selten, R. (Eds.): *Bounded Rationality: The adaptive toolbox*. Cambridge, Mass. [et al.]: MIT Press: 1-12.

GIGERENZER, G. and TODD, P. M. (1999): Fast and Frugal Heuristics: The Adaptive Toolbox. In: Gigerenzer, G., Todd, P. M. and the ABC research group (Eds.): *Simple Heuristics that make us smart*. New York: Oxford University Press: 3-36.

GILBRIDE, T. J. and ALLENBY, G. M. (2006): Estimating Heterogeneous EBA and Economic Screening Rule Choice Models. *Marketing Science*, 25: 494-509.

GOLDSTEIN, D. G. and GIGERENZER, G. (2002): Models of Ecological Rationality: The Recognition Heuristic. *Psychological Review*, 109: 75-90.

HAHN, C. (1997): Conjoint- und Discrete Choice-Analyse als Verfahren zur Abbildung von Präferenzstrukturen und Produktauswahlentscheidungen: Ein theoretischer und computergestützter empirischer Vergleich. In: Barrmeyer, M.-C. and Caspers, F.W. (Eds.): *Betriebswirtschaftliche Schriftenreihe*. Dissertation. University of Münster. Münster: LIT Verlag.

HELM, R. and STEINER, M. (2008): *Präferenzmessung: Methodengestützte Entwicklung zielgruppenspezifischer Produktinnovationen*. Stuttgart: Kohlhammer.

HENDLER, R. (1975): Lancaster's New Approach to Consumer Demand and Its Limitations. *The American Economic Review*, 65 (1): 194-199.

HENSHER, D. A., ROSE, J. and GREEN, W. (2005): *Applied Choice Analysis: A Primer*. Cambridge: Cambridge University Press.

HILLIG, T. (2006): *Verfahrensvarianten der Conjoint Analyse zu Prognose von Kaufentscheidungen – Eine Monte-Carlo-Simulation*. Dissertation. TU Berlin, 2004. Wiesbaden: Deutscher Universitätsverlag. Gabler Edition Wissenschaft.

HOEFFLER, S. and ARIELY, D. (1999): Constructing Stable Preferences: A Look Into Dimensions of Experience and Their Impact on Preference Stability. *Journal of Consumer Psychology*, 8 (2): 113-139.

HOWARD, J. A. and SHETH, J. N. (1968): A theory of buyer behavior. In: Kassarjian, H. H. and Robertson, T. S. (Eds.): *Perspectives in Consumer Behavior*, Illinois: 467-487. Available from: http://www.jagsheth.net/docs/A%20Theory%20of%20Buyer%20Behavior2.pdf, [accessed 2010-12-28].

JACKSON, T. and MICHAELIS, L. (2003): *Policies for Sustainable Consumption: A report to the Sustainable Development Commission.* Available from: http://www.sd-commission.org.uk/publications/downloads/030917%20Policies%20for%20sustainable%20consumption%20_SDC%20report_.pdf, [accessed 2010-12-28].

JACOBY, J., SZYBILLO, G. J. and BUSATO-SCHACH, J. (1977): Information Acquisition Behaviour in Brand Choice Situations. *Journal of Consumer Research*, 3 (4): 209-216.

JOHNSON, E. J., PAYNE, J. W. and BETTMAN, J. R. (1988): Information Displays and Preference Reversals. *Organizational Behaviour and Human Decision Processes*, 42: 2-21.

JUNGERMANN, H., PFISTER, H.-R. and FISCHER, K. (2005): *Die Psychologie der Entscheidung: Eine Einführung*. 2nd ed. München: Spektrum Akademischer Verlag.

KAHNEMAN, D. and TVERSKY, A. (1979): Prospect Theory: An Analysis of Decision under Risk. *Econometrica*, 47 (2): 263-292.

KAHNEMANN, D. and TVERSKY, A. (2008a): Choice, Values, and Frames. In: Kahnemann, D. and Tversky, A. (Eds.): *Choice, Values, and Frames*. 8th ed. Cambridge: Cambridge University Press: 1-16.

KAHNEMANN, D. and TVERSKY, A. (2008b): *Choice, Values, and Frames*. 8th ed. Cambridge: Cambridge University Press.

KALAFATIS, S. P., POLLARD, M., EAST, R. and TSOGAS, M. H. (1999): Green marketing and Ajzen's theory of planned behaviour: a cross-market examination. *Journal of Consumer Marketing*, 16 (5): 441-460.

KOTLER, P., ARMSTRONG, G., SAUNDERS, J. and WONG, V. (2007): *Grundlagen des Marketing*. 4th ed. Munich: Pearson Studium.

KROEBER-RIEL, W. and WEINBERG, P. (2003): *Konsumentenverhalten*. 8th ed. München: Vahlen.

KUTSCH, T. (2005): Soziologische Aspekte – Lebenstile. In: Stehle, P. and Matissek, R. (Eds.): *Ernährung, Süßwaren und Lebensstil - Eine interdisziplinäre Betrachtung*. 1. Bonner Forum Ernährungswissenschaft. Berlin: Verlag Dr. Köster: 14-34.

LANCESTER, K. J. (1966): A new approach to consumer theory. *Journal of Political Economy*, 74: 132-157.

LEIBENSTEIN, H. (1954): *A Theory of Economic Demographic Development*. Princeton NJ: Princeton University Press.

LEIBENSTEIN, H. (1975): The Economic Theory of Fertility Decline. *Quarterly Journal of Economics*, 89: 1-131.

LENSCH, A. K. (2009): *Auswirkungen gesundheitsbezogener Ernährungsinformationen auf die Kaufentscheidung: Analyse am Beispiel funktioneller Lebensmittel mit Folsäure*. Dissertation. University of Bonn. Hamburg: Verlag Dr. Kovač.

LOUVIERE, J. J. (1994): Conjoint Analysis. In: Bagozzi, R. P. (Ed.): *Advanced Methods of Marketing Research*. Cambridge, Mass.: Blackwell: 223-259.

MADDEN, T. J., SCHOLDER ELLEN, P. and AJZEN, I. (1992): A comparison of the theory of planned behavior and the theory of reasoned action. *Personality and Social Psychology Bulletin,* 18 (1): 3-9.

MARTIGNON, L. (2001): Comparing Fast and Frugal Heuristics and Optimal Models, In: Gigerenzer, G. and Selten, R. (Eds.): *Bounded Rationality: The adaptive toolbox*. Cambridge, Mass. [et al.]: MIT Press: 147-172.

MAYERL, J. (2008): *Kognitive Grundlagen sozialen Verhaltens. Theoretische und statistische Analysen zur Modellierung von Einstellungs-Verhaltens-Beziehungen*. Dissertation. University of Stuttgart.

MCFADDEN, D. (1999): Rationality for economists? *Journal of Risk and Uncertainty*, 19 (1-3): 73-105.

MEFFERT, H. (1992): *Marketingforschung und Käuferverhalten*. 2nd ed. Wiesbaden: Gabler.

MEFFERT, H. (1993): *Marketing: Grundlagen der Absatzpolitik*. Wiesbaden: Gabler.

MEYER, R. J. and KAHN, B. E. (1991): Probabilistic Models of Consumer Choice Behavior. In: Robertson, T. S. and Kassarjian, H. H. (Eds.): *Handbook of Consumer Behavior*. Englewood Cliffs, NJ: Prentice-Hall: 85-123.

OLSON, J. C. and JACOBY, J. (1972): Cue Utilization in the quality perception process. *Proceedings of the Third Annual Conference of the Association for Consumer Research*: 167-179.

ORME, B. K. and HEFT, M. A. (1999): Predicting actual sales with CBC: How capturing heterogeneity improves results. *Proceedings of the Sawtooth Software Conference*: 183-200.

PAYNE, J .W., BETTMAN, J. R. and JOHNSON, E. J. (1988): Adaptive strategy selection in decision making. *Journal of Experimental Psychology: Learning, Memory, and Cognition*, 14 (3): 534–552.

PAYNE, J. W., BETTMAN, J. R. and JOHNSON, E. J. (1992): Behavioral decision research: a constructive processing perspective. *Annual Review of Psychology*, 42: 87-131.

PAYNE, J. W., BETTMAN, J. R. and JOHNSON, E. J. (1993): *The adaptive decision maker*. Cambridge: Cambridge University Press.

PAYNE, J. W., BETTMAN, J. R. and SCHKADE, D. A. (1999): Measuring Constructed Preferences: Towards a Building Code. *Journal of Risk and Uncertainty*, 19 (1-3): 243-270.

PELZMANN, L. (2000): *Wirtschaftspsychologie*. 3th ed. Springer: Wien.

PETERS, H. and WAKKER, P. (1991): Independence of Irrelevant Alternatives and Revealed Group Preferences. *Econometrica*, 59 (6): 1787-1801.

RABIN, R. (1998): Psychology and Economics. *Journal of Economic Literature*, 36 (1): 11-46.

RIEDL, R., BRANDSTÄTTER, E. and ROITHMAYR, F. (2008): Identifying decision strategies: A process- and outcome-based classification method. *Behavior Research Methods*, 40 (3): 795-807.

RUBINSTEIN, A. (1998): *Modeling Bounded Rationality*. The MIT Press: Cambridge, Massachusetts.

SAMUELSON, P. A. (1938): A Note on the Pure Theory of Consumer's Behaviour. *Economica*, 5 (17): 61-71.

SAMUELSON, P. A. (1948): Consumption Theory in Terms of Revealed Preference. *Economica*, 15 (69): 243-253.

SAWTOOTH (2001): Choice-based Conjoint (CBC) Technical Paper. In: Sawtooth Software (Ed.): *Technical Paper Series*.

SCHOEMAKER, P. J. H. (1982): The expected utility model: its variants, purposes, evidence and limitations. *Journal of Economic Literature*, 20: 529–563.

SEN, A. K. (1977): Rational Fools: A Critique of the Behavioral Foundations of Economic Theory. *Philosophy and Public Affairs*, 6 (4): 317-344.

SHAW, D. and SHIU, E. (2002): An assessment of ethical obligation and self-identity in ethical consumer decision-making: a structural equation modelling approach. *International Journal of Consumer Studies*, 26 (4): 286-293.

SIMONSON, I. and TVERSKY, A. (1993): Choice in Context: Tradeoff Contrast and Extremeness Aversion. *Journal of Marketing Research*, 29 (3): 281-295.

SLOVIC, P. (2008): The construction of preference. In: Kahneman, D. and Tversky, A. (Eds): *Choices, Values and Frames*. 8th ed. Cambridge: Cambridge University Press: 489-502.

SOLOMON, M. R. (2009): *Consumer Behavior - Buying, Having and Being*. New Jersey: Pearson Prentice Hall.

TETLOCK, P. E. (1985): The neglected social context of judgment and choice. *Research in Organisational Behaviour*, 7: 297-332.

THALER, R. H. (2008): Toward a Positive Theory of Consumer Choice. In: Kahnemann, D. and Tversky, A. (Eds.): *Choice, Values, and Frames*. 8th ed. Cambridge: Cambridge University Press: 269-287.

TROMMSDORFF, V. (1975): *Die Messung von Produktimages für das Marketing: Grundlagen und Operationalisierung*. Köln: Heymann.

TROMMSDORFF, V. (2004): Nutzen und Einstellung. Über ein (?) Konstrukt der Theorie des Konsumentenverhaltens. In: Gröppel-Klein, A. (Ed.): *Konsumentenverhaltensforschung im 21. Jahrhundert*. Wiesbaden: Gabler: 479-500.

TVERSKY, A. and KAHNEMAN, D. (2008): Rational Choice and the Framing of Decisions. In: Kahnemann, D. and Tversky, A. (Eds.): *Choice, Values, and Frames*. 8th ed. Cambridge: Cambridge University Press: 209-223.

TVERSKY, A. and SIMONSON, I. (1993): Context-Dependant Preferences. *Management Science*, 39 (10): 1179-1189.

TVERSKY, A. and SIMONSON, I. (2008): Context-Dependant Preferences. In: Kahneman, D. and Tversky, A. (Eds.): *Choices, Values and Frames*. 8th ed. Cambridge: Cambridge University Press: 518-527.

VARIAN, H. R. (1991): *Grundzüge der Mikroökonomik*. München: R. Oldenbourg Verlag.

WEENIG, M. W. H. and MAARLEVELD, M. (2002): The impact of time constraint on information search strategies in complex choice tasks. *Journal of Economic Psychology*, 23, 689-702.

WISWEDE, G. (2000): Konsumsoziologie - Eine vergessene Disziplin. In: Rosenkranz, D. and Schneider, N. F. (Eds.): *Konsum: soziologische, ökonomische und psychologische Perspektiven*. Opladen: Leske und Budrich: 23-72.

3 Measuring preferences

After the exhibition of the nature of preferences in the previous chapter now the question is answered how consumers' preferences can be approached and measured.

The method with which preferences should be measured can only be determined after the research object is specified and the study participants are defined (HELM and STEINER 2008, p. 205). Regarding the methods, it can be roughly differentiated between stated and revealed preference methods as well as between compositional, decompositional and hybrid approaches. Furthermore, a distinction between individual and aggregate utility functions, compensatory versus non-compensatory decision processes can be made (HELM and STEINER 2008, p. 206f.). In this thesis three different methods are applied to reveal consumer preferences besides the stated preferences which are assessed via direct questions in questionnaires. The first is the IDM. The IDM allows the researcher to map the multi-attribute nature of the information search process. First, the acquisition frequency and the viewing time can be measured both representing the attention a test person is giving to a product attribute. Second, the direction and the variability of the search and therefore the search patterns are monitored. Third, the search over time as well as the attention which shows the time dynamics are measured (WILLEMSEN et al. 2005). Preferences can be derived from this. As the IDM is in detail described in chapter 5, the reader is refered to this.

The second method used is the contingent valuation method which is mostly applied in the context of public goods. It was applied to reveal preferences in the study described in chapter 8. For deeper insights into this method, see e.g. CARSON and HANEMAN (2005), MITCHELL and CARSON (1989) and PORTNEY (1994).

In the survey described in chapter 6, a choice experiment was conducted. In the following, the focus will lay on the choice-based approach of preference measurement which is able to model hypothetical decisions on non-aggregate level which is appropriate for the purpose of this thesis.

3.1 Discrete choice analysis

Choice Experiments (CE) are a flexible approach to record preference data from individuals in artificial but at the same time realistic situations (ADAMOWICZ et al. 1998; p. 6f.). Realistic in the sense, that a situation is created where an individual is asked to compare alternatives on the basis of their attributes and come to a decision between the alternatives (ADAMOWICZ et al. 1998; p. 7). This may affect both the response rate and the external validity positively

(VRIENS et al. 1998, p. 239). Hypothetical because, as ALFNES and STEINE (2005, p. 3) explain, the combination of the product attributes for which consumers' preferences are investigated may be new and accordingly the products are not yet available in the retail. This is the case in study 2 where CE are applied.

Discrete Choice Experiments (DCE) are an attribute-based survey method to reveal consumer preferences and measure utility (AMAYA-AMAYA et al. 2008, p. 13). DCE are a decompositional[34] multi-cue approach that allows estimating the relevance of different product attributes in comparison and in relation to other important product characteristics. Estimating the determinants of consumers WTP for the product attributes in question is possible. In CE respondents are asked to choose their most preferred alternative from a set of hypothetical scenarios called choice sets or profile or treatment combination. The choice sets are composed by at least two different alternatives (e.g. coffee A, coffee B) that vary in at least one attribute (e.g. price, taste, etc.). An attribute is a characteristic of the good which is manipulated by the researcher. An attribute is an independent variable and formed out of one or more attribute levels (e.g. price A, B, C). So, an alternative is a combination of different attribute levels. For making a real choice decision a test person needs at least two alternatives to be available from which one is 'not to make a choice', the so-called opt-out option.

The utility parameters can be interpreted as elasticities. These elasticities indicate in which direction the choice probability of a stimulus changes if the attribute level of the stimulus changes. If e.g. the choice probability is one and the test person definitely takes the stimulus then the elasticity is zero (GENSLER 2003, p. 63f.).

Advantages of CE mentioned by ADAMOWICZ et al. (1998, p. 7) are that the researcher is able to control for the stimuli in contrast to an observational study and that due to the chance of controlling the design matrix statistical efficiency increases. Furthermore, the applied attribute ranges can be wider compared to real market products/situations and therefore more robust models are obtained. Other advantages are: choice based conjoint approaches allow for analysing choice-set composition effects and the use of "a none-of-the-alternatives option" which is needed to predict the demand (VRIENS et al. 1998, p. 240). Two disadvantages of choice-based approaches are that they are compared to ratings-based conjoint analysis less informative (VRIENS et al. 1998, p. 239) and they lack because of its hypothetical nature some

[34] Decompositional means that based on the identified overall utility (the choice) it can be referred to the relevance of the individual product attributes tested (BROCKE and HOLLING 2007, p. 500; WEIBER and ROSENDAHL 1997, p. 107).

incentive compatibility which might lead to biased estimates (ALFNES and STEINE 2005, p. 2; CARLSSON et al. 2007, p. 327).

Recent examples of studies using hypothetical choice experiments are in the field of food demand ABIDOYE et al. (2011), MENAPACE et al. (2011) and LOUREIRO and UMBERGER (2007).

3.1.1 Theoretical framework of Discrete Choice Analysis

DCE are based on many elements of standard economic theory of consumer behaviour; e.g. the rational decision maker holds stable preferences and faces a maximisation problem in which the individual chooses the alternative that maximises individuals' utility taking the budget constraints into account. But, there are three important extensions: goods are not regarded as homogenous (a coffee is not a coffee) and utility is not only a question of quantity. It is assumed that the attributes (e.g. caffein content or brand or price) of the commodity under valuation (e.g. coffee) and their levels (e.g. high or low caffein content, high or low price) determine the utility (value) of the respective alternative (and not the commodity per se) which is known as the LANCASTER (1966) approach. Furthermore, DC theory deals with a choice between a finite set of mutually exclusive alternatives as the individual chooses each time only one alternative of the choice set. Accordingly, products are not regarded as infinitely divisible. And, while in classic consumer theory it is assumed that consumers' behaviour is deterministic in DC analysis it is assumed to be intrinsically probabilistic and hence random (AMAYA-AMAYA et al. 2008, p. 13f). The idea behind random utility theory is that researchers are not able to fully assess the utility individuals connect with a good. Therefore the random utility model $U_{ni} = V_{ni} + \varepsilon_{ni}$ is composed of an observable, deterministic utility component $V_{ni} = f(X_{ni}, \beta)$ which is a function of the vector of product attributes and respondent characteristics and an unobservable, random component ε_{ni}. The unobservable component is modelled as random error component which occurs due to unobserved attributes affecting the choice or measurement errors. The key assumption is that individual n will choose alternative i if and only if that alternative maximises their utility[35] among all J alternatives which are included in the choice set C_n. That is:

[35] Expected utility maximisation requires individuals to process all germane information and to trade off beliefs and values (PAYNE et al. 1993, p. 75).

$y_{ni} = f(U_{ni}) = \begin{cases} 1 if U_{ni} = \max_j \{U_{ij}\} \\ 0 \end{cases} \forall j \neq i \in C_n$ where y_{ni} is a choice indicator equal to 1 if alternative i is chosen, and 0 otherwise.

Alternative i is only chosen if the following expression holds:

$(V_{ni} + \varepsilon_{ni}) > (V_{nj} + \varepsilon_{nj}) \cdot \forall j \neq i \in C_n$ and rearranged: $(V_{ni} - V_{nj}) > (\varepsilon_{nj} - \varepsilon_{nj})$. As the researcher does not observe $(\varepsilon_{nj} - \varepsilon_{nj})$ the whole expression cannot be exactly determined. Therefore, statements about choice outcomes can only be formulated in form of probability of occurrence. The probability that an individual chooses alternative i that is described by the attributes X_n equals the probability that the differences between the random utility of any other alternative j and the chosen alternative i is less than the differences between the systematic utility levels of alternatives i and j for all J alternatives in the choice set C_n (AMAYA-AMAYA et al. 2008, p. 15; MCFADDEN 1974, p. 107f.).

To sum up, the random utility theory (MCFADDEN 1974) as well as LANCASTER's (1966) idea that the utility a products provides is constituted by the attributes of the respective good, are the theoretical basis for DCA (LOUVIERE 1994). The idea is that individuals reveal their utilities by their choices they make in a revealed preference experiment. Moreover, it is assumed that respondents consider all information available and choose the alternative which provides them with the highest utility. DCE can be used to model the probability that one alternative is chosen by a respondent as a function of the attributes and attribute levels as well as socioeconomic characteristics of the respondent[36]. Besides, WTP measures can be derived if price is one of the attributes and significant (HOLMES and ADAMOWICZ 2003, p. 179).

3.1.2 The multinomial logit model and its limitations

The most prominent discrete choice model is the multinomial logit model (MNL) firstly applied by MCFADDEN (1974) which is solved by maximising the log-likelihood function (HOLMES and ADAMOWICZ 2003, p. 191f.; VRIENS et al. 1998, p. 238). One reason for the popularity of MNL is its straightforwardness (PUDNEY 1989, p. 117). Other reasons are, according to LOUVIERE et al. (2006, p. 15), the simplicity in estimation and the easy to use estimation software. Besides the MNL nested MNL, latent class discrete choice models,

---

36 The socioeconomic characteristics act as an indicator of unobserved attributes. But it must be realised that socioeconomic characteristics "per se are not sources of utility of an alternative" (HENSHER et al. 2005, p. 480).

binary probit models as well as mixed logit or generalised extreme value models are applied (see e.g. HAAIJER and WEDEL 2003; TRAIN 2003).

The MNL is limited by two strong assumptions. One restrictive assumption of the MNL is the postulation that the error terms are independent and identically distributed (IID) which implies the IIA assumption (VRIENS et al. 1998, p. 239) (see chapter 2.2). The IID assumption implies that the variances (connected with the part of a random utility expression describing each alternative) "are identical and that these unobserved effects are not correlated between pairs of alternatives" (LOUVIERE et al. 2006, p. 15). The violation of the IID assumption potentially causes serious problems of under- or overestimation of choice shares (biased estimation of model parameters), elasticities and can result in a misrepresentation of the substitution patterns among the choice alternatives, statistically inferior model fit, and lead as a consequence to distorted policy implications (LOUVIERE et al. 2006, p. 15).

The second is the assumption of homogenous preferences. This implies that the preference structure is assumed to be homogenous over respondents. That means, the deterministic part of utility is assumed not to differ across individuals, and the variance of the random component is supposed to be IID. To that effect the β is equal for all individuals. Moreover, it implicates that individual specific variables such as age or education level can not vary in a conditional logit model. It is obvious that this IID assumption results in limited substitution possibilities (LOUVIERE et al. 2006, p. 105). Besides, if preference heterogeneity exists, aggregate models "underestimate the standards errors of the models parameters" (NATTER and FEUERSTEIN 2002, p. 450). Then MNL estimates are biased and inefficient (VRIENS et al. 1998, p. 239). To sum up, in the case of preference heterogeneity the aggregation of individual results instead of analysing them on the individual level leads to misunderstanding. CE are in their original form, due to the IID assumption, not able to model differences between customers (GENSLER 2003, p. 78f.; HILLIG 2006, p. 83f.).

Several authors state consumers' individual preferences are heterogeneous as individuals perceive and estimate different alternatives between which they choose in very different ways (e.g. ANDREONI and MILER 2002; BÖCKENHOLT 2002; CICIA et al. 2002; JOHNSON 1997). If they were not, any kind of product differentiation would not work. Furthermore, several studies (see JOHNSON 1997; HUBER and ORME 1997; ORME and HEFT 1999) provide evidence that prediction of market shares and study results can be improved by capturing heterogeneity. ORME and HEFT (1999, p. 183) show that latent class models that account for heterogeneity by modelling utilities at group level do better predict actual sales than aggregate models.

Especially for the case of concerned Fair Trade consumers, OZCAGLAR-TOULOUSE et al. (2006, p. 510) found that ethical consumers do not act as a homogenous group. CICIA et al. (2002, p. 212) showed that consumers of organic oil can very good be differentiated from conventional consumers but that socio-demografics are not appropriate for differentiation between consumer groups. Due to these findings, the incorporation of heterogeneity improves consumer models (NATTER and FEURSTEIN 2002, p. 450). With regard to the research questions of this thesis, it can be presumed that consumers contribute to charity and buy ethical products for various reasons. Therefore, preferences are expected to differ across individuals. Without understanding the form and extent of heterogeneity in preference it would be difficult to infer anything about the relationship between different forms of ethical behaviour. Hence, in the study presented in chapter 6 a latent class choice model is applied (see 3.1.3) which allows for heterogeneous preferences.

3.1.3 The latent class choice model

The aggregate analysis of CE data via MNL presented so far assumes that there is only random variability among interviewees which is not distinguishable from the response error. Therefore, this aggregate model, estimating a single set of regression coefficients across all observations, is not appropriate if there are distinct segments or groups of respondents who are comparatively similar but “differ from group-to-group” (SAWTOOTH 2004, p. 15; WEDEL and KAMAKURA 2003, p. 106). BOXALL and ADAMOWICZ (2002, p. 426), ORME and HEFT (1999, p. 9), as well as SAWTOOTH (2004, p. 1; 15) show that preference heterogeneity can be captured by the use of latent class (LC) modelling and that furthermore independence of irrelevant alternatives have not to be presumed. Hence, random utility models, based on latent class or finite mixture modelling, are applied to analyse experimental consumer data and to model discrete choices (e.g. SCARPA and THIENE 2005).

LC analysis assumes that within the basic population different groups or segments can be distinguished having different needs and values[37] and hence may show different preference structures. LC models allow separating the sample in several internally homogenous subgroups (having internal similar utilities and preferences) with divergent preferences. Utilities are estimated separately for each segment instead of aggregate, average parts worth

[37] It is widely accepted that consumption activities are influenced by a person’s set of values. Many services and products are purchased because consumers believe that these goods help to reach a value-related goal. A value can be defined as “a belief that some condition is preferable to its opposite” (SOLOMON 2009, p. 173). Furthermore, values are identified to be more effective in profiling consumers and segmenting markets than demographics (DORAN 2009).

utilities (BÖCKENHOLT 2002, p. 179; CROON 2002, p. 137). Thereby, within the segments the preference shares become more extreme because of the greater variance of the utilities and LC models better fit the data. The extremer utilities led the simulations "behave more like first choice models within each segment" which makes the simulation resistant to IIA problems (ORME and HEFT 1999, p. 9). Hence, LC analysis is able to reduce the negative effects of the IIA assumption in logit analysis by finding groups of people with similar utilities and preferences (BOXALL and ADAMOWICZ 2002, p. 426; SAWTOOTH 2004, p. 1; 15).[38] Besides, the model fit of LC models is good by just using main effects (SAWTOOTH 2004). In addition, LC models allow for including different variable scale types (nominal, ordinal, continuous and/or count data) and covariates in the same analysis (MAGIDSON and VERMUNT 2004). Conditional independence is the only restriction imposed on the characteristics of the observable variables within each latent class and the relationships between the latent classes (BÖCKENHOLT 2002, p. 163). The field of application is correspondingly manifold (BÖCKENHOLT 2002, p. 163). VRIENS et al. recommend already in 1998 (p. 246) the use of LC conjoint models if one wants to study consumers' preference structure.

LC models belong to the class of Finite Mixture Models[39]. Finite Mixture Models are on segment level superior to cluster analysis in identifying segments of consumers. Beyond this the model is based on probabilistic theory and therefore based on statistics. For segmenting consumers inference statistic tests can be used. The estimated utility parameters are stable if there are sufficient degrees of freedom. One restriction of this method is that the individual utility parameters are a linear combination of the segment utility parameters (GENSLER 2003, p. 108; STEINER and BAUMGARTNER 2003, p. 15). According to WEDEL and KAMAKURA (2003), latent class models are besides mixture regression models the most powerful possibility for market segmentation analysis. For an overview of studies combining latent class analysis and market segmentation, see WEDEL and KAMAKURA (2003, p. 21).

To sum up, LC analysis allows the simultaneous determination and description of both, product choice and group membership, as well as separating the sample in several internally homogenous subgroups mapping the heterogeneity in the population (BOXALL and ADAMOWICZ 2002, p. 423). Therefore, LC models are a sophisticated way to account for

[38] Another possibility to avoid the failings of the IIA assumption is to add interaction terms, cross elasticities or other complex terms to aggregate logit models. Such models might become very complex and, as ORME and HEFT (1999, p. 16) state, have too many terms in relation to all observations and risk so to become over-fitting. Other models, besides latent class models, relaxing the IIA are mixed logits, multinomial probits, and nested logit models (AMAYA-AMAYA et al. 2008; HOLMES and ADAMOWICZ 2003, p. 202).

[39] For an overview over finite mixture models, see e.g. DILLON and KUMAR (1994).

preference heterogeneity among consumers on group level without requiring many hypotheses about the distribution of preferences (GREENE and HENSHER 2003, p. 682; MILON and SCROGIN 2006, p. 167).

LC choice models assess individual choice behaviour as a function of observable attributes of the choices, on one hand, and of latent heterogeneity in the characteristics of the respondents, on the other hand (BOXALL and ADAMOWICZ 2002, p. 423; GREENE and HENSHER 2003, p. 682). In a simultaneous process the LC choice model estimates utility parameters of the different attributes and the probability of the affiliation of the respondents to different segments. For the maximisation of both, the choice and the class membership probabilities a MNL is applied (GREEN 2003).

The following presentation of the latent class model follows BOXALL and ADAMOWICZ (2002, p. 424ff.), GREEN and HENSHER (2003, p. 682ff.), KAMAKURA et al. (1994, p. 453ff.), MILON and SCROGIN (2006, p. 167f.), RUTO et al. (2008, p. 91f.) and SWAIT (1994, p. 79ff.). The LC model is specified as a random utility model $U_{ni} = V_{ni} + \varepsilon_{ni}$ which is composed of an observable, deterministic utility component $V_{ni} = f(X_{ni})$ and an unobservable, random component ε_{ni}. In addition, the LC choice model assumes that consumers are heterogeneous and that the population consists of S segments or classes. An individual n has to choose his or her preferred alternative i among a set of C alternatives of a coffee, the so-called choice set, in each of the T_n choice situations[40]. If individual n belongs to latent segment $s \in S$, then the utility function of the preferred alternative $i \in C$ can be given as:

(1) $U_{nit|s} = \beta_s X_{nit} + \varepsilon_{nit|s}$.

Formally, the utility U_{int} individual n receives from choosing alternative i consists of the observable additive component $\beta_s X_{nit}$ with β_s as class specific preference parameter vector, X_{nit} as the column vector of the alternative specific attributes and the individual specific factors and $\varepsilon_{\text{int}|s}$ representing the unobservable random component which is the unobserved heterogeneity for alternative i and individual n belonging to class s .

[40] The T_n repeated choices made by individual n are assumed to be independent of each other given class membership (KAMAKURA and RUSSEL 1989, p. 381). This is congruent to the assumption of local independence and means that within a segment the variables are assumed to be independent (MAGIDSON et al. 2003, p. 2f.; VERMUNT and MAGIDSON 2005a, p. 13).

As basis of the individual choice a random utility framework is assumed. This implys that under the postulation that decision-makers are utility maximisers and conditional on segment membership, the choice of alternative i at choice occasion t out of T (n) choice occasions is observed if and only if the utility gained from the chosen alternative i is equal to or greater than the utilities of choosing another alternative out of all alternatives C.

(2) $U_{nit|s} \geq U_{njt|s} \quad \forall j \neq i; \; i, j \in C_n$.

The utilities are random variables. Therefore, only probabilistic statements concerning the choice of an alternative can be made after the density function describing the random component in equation (2) is specified. Here, the error term $\varepsilon_{\text{int}|s}$ is assumed as IID following an extreme value Type I distribution (also known as Gumbel distribution). As equation (1) shows that parameters are class specific, the joint logic probability or the likelihood of a choice i made by individual n is conditional on the segment s individual n belongs to and results as:

(3) $$P_{nit|s} = \prod_{t=1}^{Ti} \frac{\exp(\mu_s \beta_s X_{nit})}{\sum_{j=1}^{J} \exp(\mu_s \beta_s X_{njt})}.$$

In equations (1) and (3) X_{nit} is a vector of observable attributes affiliated with alternative i and individual n observed making a choice on occasion t. β_s is a segment specific vector of taste parameters. The differences in the β_s vectors between classes allow this approach to capture preference heterogeneity for the coffee attributes between groups of consumers. The scale parameters μ_s for the s th segment's utility function are assumed to equal 1.

The unobservable individual's segment membership likelihood function M^* classifies coffee buyers into one of the S latent segments. Segment membership is influenced by latent general attitudes and perceptions, the so-called psychometric constructs and observable socioeconomic characteristics, and can be summarized in the following two equations:

(4) $M^*_{ns} = \Gamma_{ps} P^*_n + \Gamma_s S_n + \zeta_{ns}$.

(5) $P^*_n = \beta_P P_n + \zeta_{nP}$.

Where M^*_{ns} refers to the membership likelihood function for individual n belonging into segment s, P^*_n is a vector of the latent psychometric construct and P_n is a vector of the observable indicators of this construct held by individual n. S_n constitutes the vector of the observable socioeconomic characteristics of individual n, Γ and β_p are parameter vectors to be estimated, the error terms are, again assumed to be IID extreme value type I distributed across segments and individuals, represented by ζ vectors. In the classical latent variable approach the observed variables are related to the latent variables. According to BOXALL and ADAMOWICZ (2002) a vector labelled Z_n as covariates can be used as a proxy for individual motivating factors influencing the coffee choice. This vector Z_n consists of both, the observable indicators of the latent psychometric constructs P_n and of the observable socioeconomic characteristics S_n. Note that individual specific variables do not vary over alternatives. The equation for the membership likelihood function for individual n and segment s results in

(6) $M^*_{ns} = \lambda_s Z_n + \zeta_{ns}$, with $s = 1,...,S$ and λ_s as a vector of class specific parameters. These class-specific parameters express the influence of the covariates on the probability of belonging to a certain segment.

Expressing the probability of individual n belonging to segment s in the form of MNL we arrive at

$$(7)\ P_{ns} = \frac{\exp(\alpha\lambda_s Z_n)}{\sum_{s=1}^{S}\exp(\alpha\lambda_s Z_n)}.$$

Here individual-specific characteristics Z_n and not the product attributes X_{ni} create choice probabilities. A positive λ means that the associated individual descriptor variable Z_n increases the prior probability that individual n belongs to segment s. The α scale factor represents the scale across the segment membership function and is as such not identifiable and therefore set equal to 1. The probability P is defined as $0 \le P(s) \le 1$, summing up across all latent segments S (to be determined) to 1.

When equation (3), which provides the conditional (on membership of a particular segment s) choice probability, is combined with (7), which provides the segment membership probability, the unconditional joint probability P_{nis} that individual n belongs to segment s and chooses alternative i at choice occasion t is given by $P_{\text{ints}} = P_{ns} P_{\text{int|s}}$.

Hence, the marginal probability that a randomly chosen respondent n chooses $i \in C_n$ yield the expression

$$(8)\ P_{ni} = \sum_{s=1}^{S} P_{ns} P_{nit|s}\,.$$

Substituting the equations for the conditional choice equation (3) and the membership equation (7) probabilities we arrive at

$$(9)\ P_{ni} = \sum_{s=1}^{S} \left[\left(\frac{\exp(\alpha\lambda_s Z_n)}{\sum_{s=1}^{S} \exp(\alpha\lambda_s Z_n)} \right) * \left(\prod_{t(n)}^{T(n)} \frac{\exp(\mu_s \beta_s X_{nit})}{\sum_{j=1}^{J} \exp(\mu_s \beta_s X_{njt})} \right) \right].$$

Equation (9) allows choice attribute data and individual consumer characteristics to simultaneously explain choice behaviour. The two types of scale parameters μ and α are according to SWAIT (1994, p. 81) and BOXALL and ADAMOWICZ (2002, p. 426) in general only identifiable under conditions where the segment specific utility parameters are set to be equal. But such an assumption of parameter equality cross segments would be contrary to the spirit of the LC choice model. Therefore, the scale factors in (9) are set equal to 1. One important feature of the LC choice model arising from equation (9) is that the LC choice model works without the IIA assumption. This is because membership in the segments is probabilistic (BOXALL and ADAMOWICZ 2002, p. 426). When α =0, $\beta_s = \beta$ and $\mu_s = \mu$ for each segment, this means we impose taste homogeneity and homogenous preferences over all segments and thus the LC choice Model in (9) reduces to a MNL model (BOXALL and ADAMOWICZ 2002, p. 427; SWAIT 1994, p. 81). To obtain the parameters λ_s and β_s the sample log-likelihood function $L = \sum_n \sum_{i \in C} I_i \ln P_{\text{int}}$ is maximised using maximum likelihood[41], with I_i being an indicator variable for the observed choice. The estimated group specific parameters can be used to calculate the marginal rate of substitution (MRS) in equation (10) between the coffee attribute in question and the marginal utility of income/money. This MRS can be a measure for the WTP for the product attribute level under consideration (RUTO et al. 2008, p. 91f.).

$$(10)\ MRS(k,€) = -\hat{\beta}_{ks} / \hat{\beta}_{€s}\,.$$

[41] The Latent Gold Choice software package used to run the LC choice model uses the EM and the Newton-Raphson algorithm to find the maximum likelihood estimates (VERMUNT and MAGIDSON 2005a, p. 35ff.).

3.2 Designing a choice experiment

As CE are extensive cognitive tasks for respondents and the design of the experiments impacts in the one or the other way choice behaviour, the design stage is very important (STREET et al. 2008, p. 48). The key steps and its crucial aspects in designing a CE are therefore summarised in Table 1.

Table 1: Steps of choice modelling

Step	Crucial aspects
Problem definition	Formulation of the decision problem and relevant alternatives considered by individuals
Selection of attributes	Identification of important attributes via focus groups discussions, pilot surveys or literature reviews. Monetary costs are included as they allow the estimation of WTP
Assignment of attribute levels	Attribute levels should be based on focus groups discussions, pilot surveys or literature reviews
Development of the experimental design	Combination of the levels of attributes into a number of alternative scenarios/profiles which are presented to the respondents via statistical designs. Complete factorial designs: often very large as e.g. the full factorial design of 3 attributes and 3 levels each are 27 options. Advantage: allows estimation of full effects (main effects plus interactions). Fractional factorial designs reduce the number of scenario combinations from e.g. 27 to 9 options
Construction of the choice sets	The by the experimental design identified profiles are grouped into choice sets
Estimation procedure	OLS regression; maximum likelihood estimation procedures such as logit, probit, ordered logit, conditional logit, nested logit models

Source: Adapted from AMAYA-AMAYA et al. (2008, p. 17); HANLEY et al. (2001, p. 437).

LOUVIERE et al. (2006, p. 101) identify four design principles for CE: (1) identification of the relevant problem and related factors/attributes, (2) precision, meaning that the statistical efficiency of the experiments allows a precise estimation of the parameters of interest, (3) cognitive complexity should not exceed respondents' capacity and (4) market realism which refers to the degree to which the actual decision environment is mirrored. These design objectives have to be taken into account when the following design stages (analogue to stages 1-5 in Table 1) are passed through: After the decision problem and the in this context relevant alternatives considered by individuals making the decision are defined by the researcher, the relevant attributes of the alternatives and their respective attribute values referred to as levels are identified. This could be done by e.g. the use of focus groups or literature reviews. At this stage it is important to find a balance between a choice task close to reality with attributes and levels actually found in the market as well as new and hypothetical attribute (levels). Furthermore, the amounts of levels assigned to each of the attributes have to be determined. This decision, whether two or more levels are used, have implications for on the one hand researchers' ability to detect non linear effects of the marginal utility of attributes as well as of utility relationships[42] as well as on the size of the experimental design which increases exponentially with the number of levels. The latter is important as individuals confronted with the CE have only limited capability to perform either a certain amount of choice sets or make the decision between a certain numbers of alternatives in a single choice set (AMAYA-AMAYA et al. 2008, p. 18). This means, the choice complexity has a negative influence on choice consistency and hence on the quality of results (DESHAZO and FERMO 2002, p. 141). Therefore, and based on her own study BROCKE (2006, p. 186f.) concludes that the number of attributes kept in a discrete choice study should be as small as possible. If there are too many combinations of the attribute levels, the choice sets are drawn from the set of all possible choice sets according to statistical design principles (HOLMES and ADAMOWICZ 2003, p. 177; AMAYA-AMAYA et al. 2008, p. 18ff.). Pre-testing is another possibility to deal with the issue of choice set complexity (DESHAZO and FERMO 2002, p. 141).

Besides, the presentation format of the choices (non-visual versus visual illustration of attributes) is an issue researchers have to decide on (ARENTZE et al. 2003, p. 229). While non-visual presentations in e.g. table format could lead to a very much constructed choice environment a visual presentation in form of e.g. a picture of the product in question could also have certain impact on consumers' choice, e.g. if the presented colour of the presented coffee package is disliked by the respondent.

As especially the choice of the experimental design (stage 4) is of crucial importance the respective relevant issues are highlighted in the following.

The choice sets are created e.g. using the software package SAS and the Kuhfeld macros (see KUHFELD 2005) taken the properties of a good design into account. These properties of a good design are according to HUBER and ZWERINA (1996, p. 309ff.): level balance, orthogonality, minimal overlap and utility balance. Level balance is satisfied when the levels of each attribute appear with the same frequency. Orthogonality is reached when the levels of each

[42] See e.g. AMAYA-AMAYA et al. (2008, p. 18).

attribute vary independently of one another. Minimal overlap is fulfilled when the alternatives within each choice set have non-overlapping attribute levels. Utility balance is achieved when the utilities of alternatives within choices sets are the same. For a deeper discussion of these features, see e.g. HUBER and ZWERINA (1996); LOUVIERE et al. 2006; RYAN et al. (2008, p. 75ff.).

In this context the researcher should think about which 'main' and 'interaction' effects he wants to measure (LOUVIERE et al. 2006, p. 94ff.). The main effects are the "difference between the average (mean) response to each attribute level and the overall average (or "grand mean") (HOLMES and ADAMOWICZ 2003, p. 180). Including interaction effect between individual specific variables and alternative specific attributes offers some "insight into heterogeneity of consumers" (HOLMES and ADAMOWICZ 2003, p. 202) and allows for estimating complementarity and substitutability. For example, the interaction of price and age creates information on the marginal utility of money. The creation of interactions assumes that the researcher has already an idea which variables lead to heterogeneity (HOLMES and ADAMOWICZ 2003, p. 202). Furthermore, interaction affects can be measured between two or more attributes and refers to the situation that the marginal utility of one attribute depends on the characteristics of another attribute. So can, for example the marginal utility of price be influenced by the quality level of a product (LOUVIERE et al. 2006, p. 87).

A high efficiency of the experimental design can be obtained by creating independent, uncorrelated profiles. To arrive at independent and uncorrelated profiles the attribute levels need to be independent between and within alternatives. Such a design is called L^{mn} factorial design in the case of labelled experiments where m refers to the number of alternatives in each choice set and n refers to the number of attributes and L refers to the number of attribute levels. In an unlabeled experiment it is L^{m}. If the full factorial design (in which every level of every attribute is combined with each level of all other attributes) is not applicable because it would be too large (then it is not appropriate to present all possible combinations to the respondents) a fractional design can be applied (AMAYA-AMAYA et al. 2008, p. 19; HOLMES and ADAMOWICZ 2003, p. 180; LOUVIERE 1988, p. 35; LOUVIERE et al. 2006, p. 89). There is no congruence about which design method reveals the best combination of choice sets in a fractional design. Some researches are in favour of orthogonal designs resulting in uncorrelated attributes of the alternatives while others prefer efficient designs which are sometimes not orthogonal (AMAYA-AMAYA et al. 2008, p. 19f.). Another concept is that of respondent efficiency (LOUVIERE 2001, p. 29f.). This will be established by respondents' familiarity with the product under investigation, the motivation to participate in the choice experiment, the clarity of the communication of the experiment as well as the amount of choice sets, alternatives, attributes and attributes levels included in the choice task. The higher the complexity of the experiment and the less familiar participants are with the choice task the more will a bad respondent efficiency offset the gains arising from a high statistical efficiency (AMAYA-AMAYA et al. 2008, p. 20). The effect of the number of choice sets and the question how many choice sets are too many has been investigated by several researcher (e.g. CARLSSON and MARTINSSON 2008; DESHAZO and FERMO 2002; HENSHER 2006). Results were not consistent. Consequently, the researcher has to decide on the trade-off between feasibility and statistical goals each time he designs a choice experiment.

The choice alternatives can be generic/unlabelled or branded/alternative specific. A generic alternative is for example coffee A versus coffee B instead of Dallmayr coffee versus Tempelmanns coffee in a branded choice set (HOLMES and ADAMOWICZ 2003, p. 186). The in chapter 6 presented CE is a based on a generic choice model. One reason is that the prediction of market shares becomes more difficult the less familiar respondents are with the brands in a branded model (NATTER and FEURSTEIN 2002, p. 456). This implies that the brand effect possibly dominates all other attributes and that respondents do not consider a trade-off between the other attributes because their decision is alternative-based. In that case deeper insights into the relationship and the marginal rates of substitution between the attributes which are not the brand attribute, such as Fair Trade versus donation, cannot be inferred (AMAYA-AMAYA et al. 2008, p. 22). The second reason is that according to HENSHER et al. (2005, p. 113), one benefit of generic or unlabeled experiments is that it is easier to meet the IIA assumption as a label assigned to an alternative acts as "an attribute for that alternative".

Another important point researches have to handle is the coding of attributes with qualitative levels in discrete CE. When dummy coding is applied the effect of the *L*th level of the *L*-1 levels of an attribute which is transformed into dummy variables is perfectly correlated with the intercept/constant term in the regression. This implies that the estimated coefficients β are correlated with the intercept β_0 and thus an identification problem occurs as it is not possible to separate the utility associated with the *L*-1 level from other parts of utility included in the constant. Effects coding allows identifying effects which are uncorrelated with the intercept (BECH and GYRD-HANSEN 2005, p. 1082).

For a deeper insight into the different issues to take into account when designing a CE, see e.g. AMAYA-AMAYA et al. (2008); HENSHER et al. (2005); LOUVIERE et al. (2006).

3.3 References

ABIDOYE, B. O., BULUT, H., LAWRENCE, J. D., MENNECKE, B. and TOWNSEND, A. M. (2011): U.S. Consumers' Valuation of Quality Attributes in Beef Products. *Journal of Agricultural and Applied Economics*, 43 (1): 1-12.

ADAMOWICZ, W. L., LOUVIERE, J. J. and SWAIT, J. (1998): *Introduction to Attribute-Based Stated Choice Methods, Final Report to Resource Valuation Branch*, Damage Assessment Center, NOAA, U.S. Department of Commerce.

ALFNES, F. and STEINE, G. (2005): None-of-these bias in stated choice experiments. Paper prepared for presentation at the *XIth International Congress of European Association of Agricultural Economists,* Copenhagen, Denmark, August 24-27, 2005.

AMAYA-AMAYA, M., GERARD, K., and RYAN, M. (2008): Discrete Choice Experiments in a nutshell. In: Ryan, G. and Amaya-Amaya, M. (Eds.): *Using Discrete Choice Experiments to Value Health and Health Care*. Dordrecht: Springer: 13-46.

ANDREONI, J. and MILLER. J. (2002): Giving According to GARP: An Experimental Test of the Consistency of Preferences for Altruism. *Econometrica*, 70 (2): 737-753.

ARENTZE, T., BORGERS, A., TIMMERMANS, H. and DELMISTRO, R. (2003): Transport Stated Choice Responses: Effects of Task Complexity, Presentation Format and Literacy. Transportation Research Part E: *Logistics and Transportation Review*, 39 (3): 229-244.

BECH, M. and GYRD-HANSEN, D. (2005): Effects coding in discrete choice experiments. *Health economics*, 14 (10): 1079-1083.

BÖCKENHOLT, U. (2002): Comparison and Choice: Analyzing Discrete Preference Data by Latent Class Scaling Models. In: Hagenaars, J. A. and McCutcheon, A. L. (Eds.): *Applied Latent Class Analysis*. Cambridge: Cambridge University Press: 163-182.

BOXALL, P. C. and ADAMOWICZ, W. L. (2002): Understanding Heterogeneous Preferences in Random Utility Models: A Latent Class Approach. *Environmental and Resource Economics,* 23 (4): 421-446.

BROCKE, M. (2006): *Präferenzmessung durch die Discrete Choice-Analyse: Effekte der Aufgabenkomplexität*. Diss. Universität Münster, Wiesbaden: Deutscher Universitätsverlag.

BROCKE, M. and HOLLING, H. (2007): Messung des Markenwerts mit der Conjoint-Analyse. In: Florack, A., Scarabis, M. and Primosch, E. (Eds.): *Psychologie der Markenführung*. München: Vahlen: 499-512.

CARLSSON, F., FRYKBLOM, P. and LAGERKVIST, C. J. (2007): Consumer willingness to pay for farm animal welfare: mobile abattoirs versus transportation to slaughter. *European Review of Agricultural Economics*, 34 (3): 321-344.

CARLSSON, F. and MARTINSSON, P. (2008): How Much is Too Much? *Environmental Resource Economics*, 40 (2): 165-176.

CARSON, R. T. and HANEMANN, M. W. (2005): Contingent Valuation. In: Mäler, K.-G. and Vincent, J. R. (Eds.): *Handbook of Environmental Economics*, Volume 2. Amsterdam: North-Holland: 821-936.

CICIA, G., DEL GIUDICE, T. and SCARPA, R. (2002): Consumers' perception of quality in organic food: A random utility model under preference heterogeneity and choice correlation from rank-orderings. *British Food Journal*, 104 (3/4/5): 200-213.

CROON, M. (2002): Ordering the Classes. In: Hagenaars, J. A. and McCutcheon, A. L. (Eds.): *Applied Latent Class Analysis*. Cambridge: Cambridge University Press: 137-162.

DESHAZO, J.R. and FERMO, G. (2002): Designing Choice Sets for Stated Preference Methods: The Effects of Complexity on Choice Consistency. *Journal of Environmental Economics and Management*, 44: 123-143.

DILLON, W. R. and KUMAR, A. (1994): Latent Structure and Other Mixture Models in Marketing: An Integrative survey and Overview. In: Bagozzi, R. P. (Ed.): *Advanced Methods of Marketing Research*. Cambridge, Mass.: Blackwell: 295-351.

DORAN, C. J. (2009): The Role of Personal Values in Fair Trade Consumption. *Journal of Business Ethics*, 84 (4): 549-563.

GENSLER, S. (2003): Heterogenität in der Präferenzanalyse: ein Vergleich von hierarchischen Bayes-Modellen und Finite-Mixture-Modellen. In: Albers et al. (Eds.): *Beiträge zur betriebswirtschaftlichen Forschung*, 107. Dissertation. Universität Frankfurt/Main. Wiesbaden: Deutscher Universitäts-Verlag.

GREENE, W. H. (2003): *Econometric Analysis*. New Jersey: Upper Saddle River, Prentice Hall.

GREENE, W. H. and HENSHER, D. A. (2003): A latent class model for discrete choice analysis: contrasts with mixed logit. *Transportation Research Part B*, 37: 681–698.

HAAIJER, R. and WEDEL, M. (2003): Conjoint Choice Experiments: General Characteristics and Alternative Model Specifications. In: Gustafson, A., Herrmann, A. and Huber, F.

(Eds.): *Conjoint Measurement: Methods and Applications*, 3rd. ed., Heidelberg: Springer: 371-412.

HANLEY, N., MOURATO, S. and WRIGHT, R. E. (2001): Choice Modelling approaches: A superior alternative for environmental valuation? *Journal of economic surveys*, 15 (3): 435-462.

HELM, R. and STEINER, M. (2008): *Präferenzmessung: Methodengestützte Entwicklung zielgruppenspezifischer Produktinnovationen*. Stuttgart: Kohlhammer.

HENSHER, D. A., ROSE, J. M. and GREENE, W. H. (2005): *Applied choice analysis: a primer*. Cambridge: Cambridge University Press.

HENSHER, D. A. (2006): Revealing differences in willingness to pay due to dimensionality of stated choice designs: an initial assessment. *Environmental and Resource Economics*, 34: 7-44.

HILLIG, T. (2006): *Verfahrensvarianten der Conjoint-analyse zur Prognose von Kaufentscheidungen: Eine Monte-Carlo-Simulation*. Dissertation, University of Berlin, 2004, Wiesbaden: Deutscher Universitätsverlag.

HOLMES, T. P. and ADAMOWICZ, W. L. (2003): Attribute-Based Methods. In: Champ, P. A., Boyle, K. J. and Brown, T. C. (Eds.): *A Primer on Nonmarket Valuation*. Dordrecht: Kluwer: 171-219.

HUBER, J. and ORME, B. K. (1997): Dealing with product similarity in conjoint simulations. *Proceedings of the Sawtooth Software Conference*, February 1999. Sequim, WA: 253-266.

HUBER, J. and ZWERINA, K. (1996): The Importance of Utility Balance in Efficient Choice Designs. *Journal of Marketing Research*, 22: 307-317.

JOHNSON, R. M. (1997): Individual Utilities from Choice Data: A New Method. *Sawtooth Software research paper series*.

KAMAKURA, W. A. and RUSSELL, G. J. (1989): A Probabilistic Choice Model for Market Segmentation and Elasticity Structuring. *Journal of Marketing Research*, 26 (4): 379–390.

KAMAKURA, W. A., WEDEL, M. and AGRAWAL, J. (1994): Concomitant variable latent class models for conjoint analysis. *International Journal of Research in Marketing*, 11 (5): 451–464.

KUHFELD, W. F. (2005): Marketing Research Methods in SAS – Experimental Design, Choice, Conjoint, and Graphical Techniques. SAS 9.1 Edition, TS-722.

LANCESTER, K. J. (1966): A new approach to consumer theory. *Journal of Political Economy*, 74: 132-157.

LOUREIRO, M. L. and UMBERGER, W. J. (2007): A choice experiment model for beef: What US consumer responses tell us about relative preferences for food safety, country-of-origin labeling and traceability. *Food Policy*, 32: 496–514.

LOUVIERE, J. J. (1988): *Analyzing Decision Making: Metric Conjoint Analysis*. Newbury Park: Sage Publications.

LOUVIERE, J. J. (1994): Conjoint Analysis. In: Bagozzi, R. P. (Ed.): *Advanced Methods of Marketing Research*. Cambridge, Mass.: Blackwell: 223-260.

LOUVIERE, J. J. (2001): Choice Experiments: an Overview of Concepts and Issues. In: Bennett, J. and Blamey, R. (Eds.): *The choice modelling approach to environmental valuation*. Cheltenham: Elgar: 13-36.

LOUVIERE, J., HENSHER, D. and SWAIT, J. D. (2006): *Stated Choice Methods: Analysis and Application*. 4th edition, Cambridge: Cambridge University Press.

MAGIDSON, J., EAGLE, T. and VERMUNT, J. K. (2003): New developments in latent class choice modeling. *Proceedings of the Sawtooth Software Conference 2003*.

MAGIDSON, J. and VERMUNT, J.K. (2004): Latent class models. In: Kaplan, D. (Ed.): The *Sage Handbook of Quantitative Methodology for the Social Sciences*. Thousand Oakes: Sage Publications. Chapter 10: 175-198.

MCFADDEN, D. (1974): Conditional logit analysis of qualitative choice behaviour. In: Zarembka, P. (Ed.): *Frontiers in Econometrics*. New York: Academic Press: 105-142.

MENAPACE, L., COLSON, G., GREBITUS, C. and FACENDOLA, M. (2011): Consumers' preferences for geographical origin labels: evidence from the Canadian olive oil market. *European Review of Agricultural Economics*, doi:10.1093/erae/jbq051.

MILON, J. W. and SCROGIN, D. (2006): Latent preferences and valuation of wetland ecosystem restoration. *Ecological Economics*, 56: 162–175.

MITCHELL, R. C. and CARSON, R. T. (1989): *Using surveys to value public goods: The contingent valuation method.* Washington, D.C.: Resources for the Future.

NATTER, M. and FEURSTEIN, M. (2002): Real world performance of choice-based conjoint models. *European Journal of Operational Research*, 137: 448-456.

ORME, B. K. and HEFT, M. A. (1999): Predicting actual sales with CBC: How capturing heterogeneity improves results. *Proceedings of the Sawtooth Software Conference*: 183-200.

OZCAGLAR-TOULOUSE, N., SHIU, E. and SHAW, D. (2006): In search of fair trade: ethical consumer decision making in France. *International Journal of Consumer Studies*, 30 (5): 502-514.

PAYNE, J. W., BETTMAN, J. R. and JOHNSON, E. J. (1992): Behavioral Decision Research: a constructive processing perspective. *Annual Review of Psychology*, 43: 87-131.

PAYNE, J. W., BETTMAN, J. R. and JOHNSON, E. J. (1993): *The adaptive decision maker*. Cambridge [et al.]: Cambridge University Press.

PORTNEY, P. R. (1994): The Contingent Valuation Debate: Why Economists Should Care. The *Journal of Economic Perspectives*, 8 (4): 3-17.

PUDNEY, S. (1989): *Modelling Individual Choice: The Econometrics of Corners, Kinks and Holes*. Cornwall: T. J. Press.

RUTO, E., GARROD, G. and SCARPA, R. (2008): Valuing animal genetic resources: a choice modeling application to indigenous cattle in Kenya. *Agricultural Economics*, 38 (1): 89-98.

RYAN, M., WATSON, V. and GERARD, K. (2008): Practical issues in conducting a discrete choice experiment. In: Ryan, G. and Amaya-Amaya, M. (Eds.): *Using Discrete Choice Experiments to Value Health and Health Care*. Dordrecht: Springer: 73-97.

SAWTOOTH (2004): The CBC Latent Class Technical Paper. Version 3. In: Sawtooth Software (Eds.): *Technical Paper Series*.

SCARPA, R. and THIENE, M. (2005): Destination Choice Models for Rock Climbing in the Northeastern Alps: A Latent-Class Approach Based on Intensity of Preferences. *Land Economics*, 81 (3): 426-444.

SOLOMON, M. R. (2009): *Consumer Behavior - Buying, Having and Being*. New Jersey: Pearson Prentice Hall.

STEINER, W. J. and BAUMGARTNER, B. (2003): Conjoint-Analyse und Marktsegmentierung. *Regensburger Diskussionsbeiträge zur Wirtschaftswissenschaft*, 382.

STREET, D. J., BURGESS, L., VINEY, R. and LOUVIERE, J. (2008): Designing discrete choice experiments for health care. In: Ryan, M., Gerard, K. and Amaya-Amaya, M. (Eds.): *Using Discrete Choice Experiments to Value Health and Health Care*. Dordrecht: Springer: 47-72.

SWAIT, J. (1994): A structural equation model of latent segmentation and product choice for cross-sectional revealed preference choice data. *Journal of Retailing and Consumer Services*, 1 (2): 77–89.

TRAIN, K. E. (2003): *Discrete Choice Methods with simulation.* Cambridge: Cambridge University Press.

VERMUNT, J. K. and MAGIDSON, J. (2005a): *Latent GOLD® Choice 4.0 User's Manual.*

VRIENS, M., OPPEWAL, H. and WEDEL, M. (1998): Ratings-based versus choice-based latent class conjoint models – An empirical comparison. *Journal of the Market Research Society*, 40 (3): 237-248.

WEDEL, M. and KAMAKURA, W. (2003): *Market Segmentation - Conceptual and Methodological Foundations*. 2nd ed. Boston [et al.]: Kluwer.

WEIBER, R. and ROSENDAHL, T. (1997): Anwendungsprobleme der Conjoint-Analyse. *Marketing ZFP*, 2: 107-118.

WILLEMSEN, M. C., JOHNSON, E. J. and BÖCKENHOLT, U. (2005): Process tracing for dummies: Solutions for design, analysis and presentation. *Society for Judgment and Decision making (SJDM) annual meeting,* Toronto 12.11.2005. Available from: http://www.mouselabweb.org/downloads/jdm2005.pdf, 20.06.2010, [accessed 2009-04-06].

4 Possibilities of ethical behaviour

In this chapter, three possibilities of ethical behaviour are described in detail. First, ethical consumption is analysed by identifying factors playing an important role for its rise. In addition, previous research with a special emphasis on WTP studies is summarised before WTP measures are derived in the study described in chapter 6. As an attitude-behaviour gap is likely with regard to studies on ethical behaviour, reasons for this gap and possibilities of avoidance are discussed and taken into account in the design of the surveys described in chapters 5 to 9. The market relevance of ethical consumption in its form of positive purchasing is analysed especially for Germany. Space is also allocated to critique towards the somewhat enthusiastic undertone of research regarding ethical consumption. The question regarding the links and missing links between ethical, sustainable and Fair Trade consumption closes the chapter on ethical consumption.

In the second part, the Fair Trade movement and the underlying morality of Fair Trade are discussed. The function of standards and labels are explained before the international Fair Trade standard and competing coffee standards are presented. The literature review provides an overview of the discussed topics in Fair Trade studies, especially regarding the impact on Fair Trade producers' livelihood. Findings from impact studies are useful in the discussion of the shortcomings of Fair Trade and the similarities and the differences between Fair Trade and aid respectively.

The third part delivers insights into individuals' motivations to give to charity including the theoretical foundations, donors' characteristics and the 'market' for charitable giving in Germany.

In contrast to Fair Trade, the organic movement and market in Germany and Europe has been the subject of many empirical and theoretical studies, therefore no extra chapter is devoted to this topic. Cause-related Marketing is not presented in this chapter either because it is explained in detail in chapters 7, 8 and 9.

> "Choice lies at the centre of the idea of consumerism" GABRIEL and LANG (1995, p. 27).
>
> "Consumers are still searching for an object of desire. But consumption is not only the satisfaction of one's own needs but simultaneously the demonstration of philosophy of life." CARBONARO (2009).
>
> "Die Menschen erkennen sich in ihren Waren wieder." MARCUSE (2008, p. 29).
>
> "Im Lifestyle-Kapitalismus ist der Stil eines Menschen, seine Identität, unmittelbar verbunden mit den Dingen, die er konsumiert" MISIK (2007, p. 8). Und: „Es ist die Bedeutung der Güter, die die Kunden konsumieren" MISIK (2007, p. 9).

4.1 The phenomenon of ethical consumption

While all human societies have been engaged in consumption as such, the contemplation of consumers as social actors is linked to the development of the capitalist societies of the 19th and 20th century, which is characterised by the distinction of production and consumption as well as the advent of advertising (KJARNES 2007, p. 46; TRENTMANN 2006, p. 2). The food sector is only one of different consumption sectors; others include energy or mobility (WALLENBORN 2007, p. 58). As consumption is discussed in many disciplines (e.g. consumer research, psychology, sociology, economics etc.), each of these asking slightly different questions, the methodological approaches to analyse food consumption also differ. They can be divided into two groups: one reducing individuals' consumption decisions to the individual material needs (see the microeconomic approach described in chapter 2 that perceives consumers as individuals who behave rationally and seek to maximise their well-being) and the other taking into account the context in which the individual is making his decision (see the Theory of Reasoned Action and the Theory of Planned Behaviour described in chapter 2).

In the discussion of consumption it shall be also considered that a consumer is merely an abstraction and only one part of the individual. The individual has a variety of social responsibilities as a worker, citizen, spectator, and consumer, etc. Accordingly, consumption choices combine aspects of the individual not directly related to consumption, e.g. knowledge, spirituality, and habitual action (DEVINNEY et al. 2010, p. 187; GABRIEL and LANG 1995, p. 3; WALLENBORN 2007, p. 58). Consequently, the individual should not be divided into the different roles but researched within his complex interactions and as a whole. Contemporary theories of consumption consider this and go beyond the ideas of the classical microeconomic approach. They try to determine the influence of social structures, norms, contexts and situations on consumers' decision making[43].

Approaching consumption

Consumption can be approached from the following angles: First, consumption is part of daily, mostly unconsidered and habitualised routines which are formerly acquired best solutions to demand (SCHULTZ and STIEß 2008). In this sense, sociologists and anthropologists describe the *needs-based* approach to consumer behaviour (e.g. KIM et al. 2002) relating consumers' well-being to the satisfaction of needs. Maslow's hierarchy of needs is the best-known expression of this approach. This form of consumption is also called *ordinary consumption* or *consumption as habit* (e.g. SHOVE and WARDE 1997; KHARE and INMAN 2006). The key lesson JACKSON and MICHAELIS (2003, p. 32) drew from this research field is that ordinary consumption decisions are restricted/controlled by an extensive set of influences which include historical, social and political components.

When the basic material needs are fulfilled, goods are consumed that allow individuals to position themselves socially with respect to their group. This means goods are not only valued for what they can do but also for what they represent to individuals and to others. There is evidence that consumerism can take the role of religion and thus aims at giving individuals a sense of self. Thus, referring to Maslow's hierarchy of needs, it can be presumed that in affluent societies basic physical needs are fulfilled and consumers "turn to higher-order concerns that include the need to know and self-actualisation" (HARRISON et al. 2005, p. 5). Self-actualisation is achieved in modern societies through a combination of hedonistic and ethical consumption (HARRISON et al. 2005, p. 5). Accordingly, *status-seeking* behaviour (e.g. BOURDIEU 1984) as well as consumption paying attention to the *symbolic role* of consumer goods is described (JACKSON and MICHAELIS 2003, p. 33).

To sum up, consumption can be regarded as embedded in a system of everyday life organisation. It is assumed that consumption responds to individual as well as societal demands and reflects contextual and structural conditions. In addition, consumption mirrors and reveals personal style, attitudes, taste, targets, and status as well as reference groups.

[43] As this issue is very much related to lifestyle research which is too broad to discuss here. For deeper insights into sociological aspects of lifestyle research with emphasis on the characteristics of western consumer societies, such as the importance of leisure time, consumption as a value and area of life as well as institutionalised critique on consumption, the interested reader is referred to KUTSCH (2005).

Hence, consumption that goes beyond the fulfilment of the personal material needs can be only explained by considering the context of the individual and the decision.

Only over the last few decades, though, awareness has increased that consumption entails ecological, environmental and human costs (FRAJ and MARTINEZ 2007, p. 26; HARRISON et al. 2005, p. 3).

Reasons for the increased awareness of the effects of consumption

One of the major reasons for the increased awareness of the topic is that achieving sustainable development is one of the UN millennium goals (UN 2011). Hence, sustainable consumption has been on the political agenda at least since the United Nations Environmental Programme (UNEP) initiated a sustainable consumption programme in 1998 to achieve more sustainable production and consumption patterns (UNEP 2009). Already at the World Summit for Social Development Copenhagen in 1995 it was stated in the Copenhagen Declaration on Social Development that "...the major cause of the continued deterioration of the global environment is the unsustainable pattern of consumption and production, particularly in industrialised countries, which is a matter of grave concern, aggravating poverty and imbalances" (UN 1995).

Externalities of consumption also gain in importance in society[44], in enterprises (cf. Corporate Social Responsibility or CSR or e.g. the 'day of sustainability the REWE (2008) organised in 2008), in politics[45], in the mass media (see articles in Wirtschaftswoche such as STEINKIRCHNER et al. 2007; in Süddeutsche such as MAKOWSKY 2007 and THE ECONOMIST 2006), and also in social media such as web logs (e.g. HÖGE 2008). Movies, such as 'We Feed the World – Essen global" presented first in 2005 awakened especially Europeans to start thinking about their responsibility for inequalities, hunger and unsustainable food production practices in the world. Furthermore, there are buyer's guides claiming to help consumers to change the world via consumption (BUSSE 2006; GRIMM 2006). The Co-operative Bank's Ethical Consumerism Report have been published in Great Britain since 2000 (e.g. VICKERY 2005; THE CO-OPERATIVE BANK 2010) and the Otto Group Trendstudie (TRENDBÜRO 2007; 2009) in Germany. The increasing relevance can be referred to the huge spectrum of

44 STEHR (2007) even talks about the moralisation of markets.

45 Sustainable consumption patterns are mentioned in article 4 of the agenda 21 in Rio 1992, Oslo 1994 and Johannesburg 2002. Examples of political engagement are furthermore the establishment of the 'Rat für Nachhaltige Entwicklung' by the German government in 2001 and the OECD report on good practices on promoting sustainable consumption in OECD countries published in 2008.

externalities of consumption so that the topic exhibits many interfaces to other topics such as CSR, product stewardship and ethical marketing (CSCP 2008, p. 3).

All in all, this has initiated a new way of thinking in society in favour of a special kind of consumption that tries to minimise potential negative externalities of consumption: **ethical consumption**.

Definition of ethical consumption

Ethical consumption includes all kinds of personal consumption choices in which a concern for a particular ethical issue – be it e.g. preferences for social justice and human rights, combatting against inequalities in the relationship between North and South, the environment and animal welfare – coexists with traditional decision making criteria such as quality and price. In short: ethical purchase behaviour is a 'traditional consumption' plus a concern (HARRISON et al. 2005, p. 2; VICKERY 2005, p. 7). When a consumer purchases the cheapest good that is satisfies his needs, this is referred to as 'traditional' purchasing.[46] Accordingly, an ethical consumers considers not only his own needs and preferences but also the effect the purchase decision has on public welfare, "on the external world around them" (HARRISON et al. 2005, p. 2). This implies that such a concerned consumer feels responsible towards society (AHAUS et al. 2009, p. 4; TALLONTIRE et al. 2001, p. 5) and expresses these feelings by means his purchase behaviour (DE PELSMACKER 2005b, p. 51; TALLONTIRE et al. 2001, p. 5) which is then a result of people's individual and moral beliefs (AUGER et al. 2007, p. 207). This means, the ethical consumer[47] makes a more direct link between what he consumes and the social and environmental question itself (VERMEIR and VERBEKE 2006, p. 170).[48] Especially the choice of food is seen as an interrelation between the private sphere and public areas, the individual and the collective (KJARNES 2007, p. 44). Therefore, apart from the satisfaction of a need consumption can be regarded as a way of showing membership in a social group as well as a

[46] Ethical consumption which is not focussed on profit maximisation in the sense of buying the cheapest product under c. p. conditions seems to be irrational from the neoclassical economic point of view (NICHOLLS and OPAL 2005, p. 13).

[47] CCN (2010) calls individuals who make choices based on ethical, social, economic and ecological considerations a consumer citizen.

[48] This means in an extreme case and definition, no matter which concern the consumer bears in mind when choosing a product, the choice can be only called ethical if no self-centred goal lead to the choice. To give one example: A person purchases organic products. If the person cares about the use of pesticides and the possible environmental effect they may have on e.g. wildlife and soils and if this influences the decision the purchase can be called ethical. If, in contrast, the primary concern is one's own health the purchase is not a fully ethical one, according to a strict definition like the one of HARRISON et al. (2005, p. 2) that resembles altruistic behaviour. A similar deliberation can be found in WALLENBORN (2007, p. 57). There, the difficulty is discussed of how to define whether a consumer is to be called 'green': because of his or her actions (buying organic food) or attitudes (e.g. against air pollution). People buying organic products can do it for their own purpose, such as health or for altruistic purposes, such as animal welfare.

consumption of signs individuals need to define themselves (see e.g. WALLENBORN 2007, p. 66f.).

Products that contribute to sustainable economics, social and environmental development though their attributes (organic products) or the consequences of their production process (Fair Trade products) are called ethical and sustainable products in many studies as well as in this thesis.

If we follow this concept, ethical consumerism becomes apparent in various fields of everyday-life such as the food people eat (organic, Fair Trade), the products people buycott (energy efficient appliances), the means of transport (public) people choose, the origin of clothes they wear or the use of second-hand items or the aim of investments (for renewable energy shares).

Accordingly, different forms of ethical consumption can be distinguished.

Forms of ethical consumption

TALLONTIRE et al. (2001, p. 5ff.) as well as MICHELETTI (2006, p. 23) both distinguish between three types of ethical consumerism for which they use slightly different terms: (1) consumer action (discursive political consumerism in MICHELETTI), (2) positive and (3) negative ethical purchase behaviour (positive and negative political consumerism in MICHELETTI), respectively. Discursive political consumerism focusses on the interactions and exchanges between consumers and producers and how they change the market (DENEGRI-KNOTT et al. 2006, p. 960). It has many faces, e.g. a range of communicative efforts can be focussed on business and the public about corporate policy and practice in order to engage in a dialogue with the market actors (MICHELETTI 2006, p. 23). The purchase of Fair Trade and organic goods is an example of positive purchase behaviour. Boycotts of certain goods or brands such as Nestlé and Shell are examples of negative ethical purchase behaviour (FRIEDMAN 1999, p. 52; KLEIN et al. 2004, p. 92). [49] The number of people participating in boycott activities as well as buycotts (see 4.1.2) is increasing according to STOLLE and MICHELETTI (2003, p. 4).

HARRISON et al. (2005, p. 2f.) developed a slightly different typology of ethical consumer purchasing practices according to how the consumer tries to influence the seller or the product as such. In addition to boycotts and positive buying, they identify a third category they call

[49] Buying or boycotting products based on ethical or political values is discussed within the theory of consumer votes (SHAW 2007).

"fully screened" which refers to comparative ethical ratings across the whole product area such as consumer purchasing guides. The fourth category HARRISON et al. (2005, p. 2f.) introduce is called "relationship purchasing". Consumers' activities to educate sellers about consumers' ethical needs with regard to the products they want to buy belong in this category. Community supported agriculture farms in the US, UK, Switzerland and Japan are given as examples. From the authors point of view this can be summarised under the above-mentioned first type of ethical consumption: consumer action/discursive political consumerism. The fifth type of ethical consumer practise is called 'anti-consumerism or sustainable consumerism'. Here consumers avoid unsustainable products such as cars or practise do-it-yourself alternatives such as mending clothes.

Plurality of terms

Upon examination of the pertinent literature it becomes obvious that there is no succinct definition of ethical consumption. Some authors emphasise the differences to traditional consumption (HARRISON et al. 2005; VICKERY 2005), while others look at the foundation in consumer movements such as Fair Trade (TALLONTIRE et al. 2001), categorise different forms of ethical consumption (TALLONTIRE et al. 2001; MICHELETTI 2006) or focus on the consumers' motivation to consume certain products instead of others (HARRISON et al. 2005; AUGER et al. 2007). Moreover, many different terms regarding forms of consumption that take into account environmental, ethical and other non-selfish motives have been coined to describe the phenomenon. All definitions have in common the idea of making a difference – regarding various ethical aspects – through consumption. The terms used range from socially responsible, political over ecological and green to concerned and sustainable to ethical consumption (DE PELSMACKER et al. 2003, p. 2; MICHELETTI et al. 2004, p. xiv). GOODMAN (2004, p. 891; 900) refers to reflexive and conscious consumers. These terms sometimes have slightly different connotations but are often used as synonyms. Many researchers (e.g. HAYES 2006, p. 449) use the term ethical consumer in their research without implying any particular theory of consumption but just to describe those consumers who deliberately support e.g. Fair Trade by purchase, NGOs by activism or charitable giving.

As the review of ethics in marketing conducted by ÖBERSEDER and SCHLEGELMILCH (2010) reveals, research on questions of ethics and consumer behaviour has only appeared on a large scale in the past ten years. Since then, ethical, political, ecological, green and sustainable consumption has been the subject of numerous studies on consumerism (e.g. BABAKUS et al. 2004; CARRIGAN et al. 2004; CLARKE et al. 2007; D'AUTON and HILTON 2001; DE

PELSMACKER et al. 2005a, b; FRAJ and MARTINEZ 2007; HARRISON et al. 2005; HILTON 2003; JACKSON and MICHAELIS 2003; KUTSCH 2002; NEWHOLM and SHAW 2007; OZCAGLAR-TOULOUSE et al. 2006; TRENTMANN 2006; SCHOENHEIT 2007; SCHULZ 2008; SHAW and SHIU 2003; SHAW 2007; SHAW et al. 2006; STRONG 1996).

Reasons for ethical consumption

There are different approaches to explain the *reasons* for ethical consumption. On the one hand, there are the above-mentioned approaches which focus more on the individual, such as the needs-based approach, ordinary consumption and status-seeking behaviour. NEWHOLM (2000 in HARRISON et al. 2005, p. 5) introduces a further aspect and states that consumers express their ethics via consumption choices because consumption becomes a prominent time-consuming activity. On the other hand, there are more global approaches such as the concept of risk society by BECK (1999). BECK (1999) considers the augmentation of human derived risks. These are stated to force consumers to consider more and more the consequences of their way of life as a reason for consumer politicisation. As a consequence consumption becomes a form of political dispute (see BECK 1999 and GIDDENS 1990). MICHELETTI (2003, in ADAMS and RAISBOROUGH 2010, p. 257) even goes so far as to say that conscious consumption is becoming *the* mean through which people can take responsibility and participate in solving ecological and human problems arising from the production process of goods. In addition, other external factors are discussed such as the globalisation of markets which is accompanied by a weakening of national governments and the rise of multinational brands and companies on the one hand and an increased effectiveness of market campaigning of groups resulting in a shift of market power to consumers together with the growth of a wider corporate responsibility movement on the other hand (HARRISON et al. 2005, p. 5).[50]

Figure 6 presents the nature, forms and similar terms of ethical consumption as elaborated in the previous paragraph.

[50] See also NEWHOLM and SHAW (2007, p. 254).

Figure 6: Ethical consumption: nature, similar terms and forms

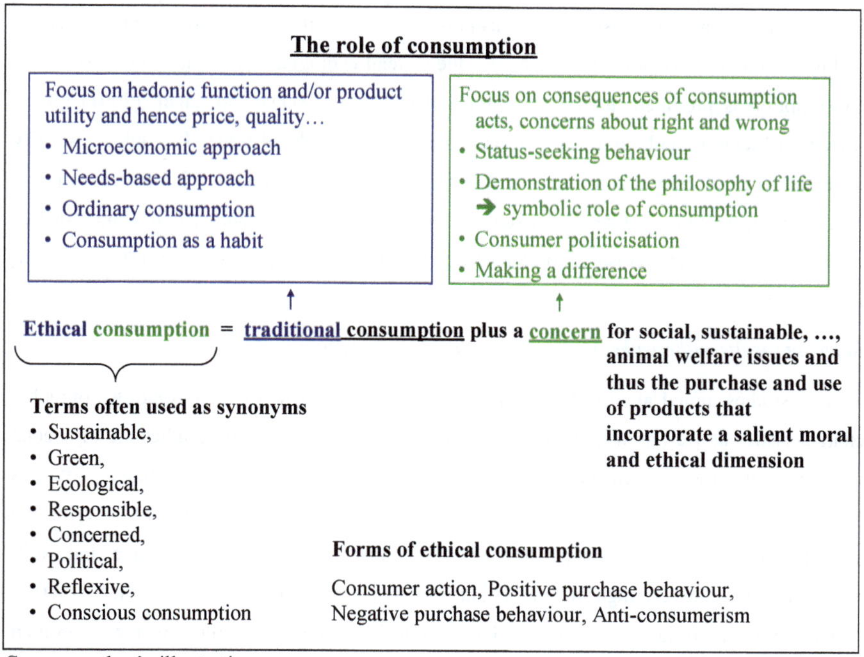

Source: author's illustration.

4.1.1 Research areas of ethical consumption

Topics of research

Ethical consumption is analysed from different perspectives, and surveys in this field focus on different issues. Some ask whether it is just another marketing claim (KORT 2010). Others comprehend it as social movement (e.g. BARNETT et al. 2005) or a form of consumer activism (GABRIEL and LANG 1995, p. 152ff.), pose the question what the ethics of ethical consumption are (e.g. BARNETT et al. 2005), and discuss it from the perspective of the three dimensions of sustainability (HANSEN and SCHRADER 2001). Some studies try to find the reasons for ethical decision making and behaviour (e.g. SHAW and SHIU 2002; 2003.) as well as the increase of ethical consumption (STRONG 1996), search the possible foundation in consumer movements – TALLONTIRE et al. (2001) consider ethical consumerism to be a phenomenon based on ethical trade movements like the Fair Trade and organic movement and like Forest Stewardship Council which trades goods produced in sustainable managed forests – whereas others demonstrate market potentials for ethical products (CARRIGAN et al. 2004), investigate individuals' tolerance for unethical consumer behaviour (BABAKUS et al. 2004), and link the ethical consumer to theories of consumer empowerment (SHAW et al. 2006; SHAW 2007). An overview of research on sustainable consumption, on how it is linked to everyday decision making, and on frameworks such as the social-ecological approach to sustainable consumption is provided in SCHULTZ and STIEß (2008). TALLONTIRE et al. (2001) give a review of literature and surveys on ethical consumers and ethical trade. The authors specify different types of ethical consumers and explore their stimulus and WTP a premium price. Furthermore, they take a look at the reasons for the change of consumer behaviour, such as healthy eating, vegetarianism, moral correctness and self preservation (TALLONTIRE et al. 2001, p. 3).

Relevant results with respect to drivers of ethical consumption

Several studies aimed at identifying ethical consumers in terms of their socio-demographic characteristics as well as with respect to attitudes and values. As those studies are of special interest for this thesis, their main results will be briefly summarised. For instance, ROBERTS (1996), CARRIGAN and ATTALA (2001) and TALLONTIRE et al. (2001, p. 5ff.) describe the ethical consumer as a person of 30 years and older, educated above average and well-informed with relatively high income. A survey carried out by the VERBRAUCHER INITIATIVE (2007) arrive at similar results for the German Fair Trade consumer: more women than men (41 % versus 33 %, rest: don't know/no answer), and families with comparatively high income (50 % have an available monthly income above 2500 €) purchase Fair Trade products.

In particular, the gender question is frequently discussed in the context of social and environmental concerns. Research reveals that there is a gender gap in environmental attitudes and behaviour; women are more affected and have higher levels of social and environmental concerns than men. For example, mostly females have previously bought Fair Trade products (see e.g. BLEND and VAN RAVENSMAAY 1999; LOUREIRO and LOTADE 2005; TALLONTIRE et al. 2001). Other studies, however, concluded that ethical purchasing is not influenced by gender (e.g. CARRIGAN and ATTALLA 2001; ROBERTS 1996; SIKULA and COSTA 1994; TSALIKIS and ORTIZ-BUONAFINA 1990). De PELSMACKER et al. (2007, p. 111) report on studies regarding other socio-demographic variables and show contradicting results: Some confirm an influence of education, age and income on the purchase decision, others not. This is one of the reasons why several authors stress that rather than socio-demographic variables, psychological variables such as values, attitudes, beliefs and norms as well as altruistic behaviour influence consumers' choice in the direction of ethical concerns (see e.g. CHATZIDAKIS et al. 2007; FRAJ and MARTINEZ 2007; GRANKVIST et al. 2007; LUSK et al.

2007; ROBERTS 1996; ROBINSON and SMITH 2002; SHAW and SHIU 2003; UMBERGER et al. 2009; VERMEIR and VERBEKE 2006, VITELL et al. 2001). VERMEIR and VERBEKE (2006, p. 184ff.) find that in addition attitudes, social norms involvement, and the perceived availability of sustainable products is important for consumers' purchase decision. Another important result is that consumers are not a homogenous group.[51] Accordingly, VERMEIR and VERBEKE (2006, p. 186) recommend that marketing departments address different groups of consumers specifically.

FRAJ and MARTINEZ (2007) test to which extent environmental attitudes can be used as meaningful causal variables to approach ecological behaviour. They apply a three-dimensional approach and address emotional, conative as well as cognitive components by means of factor analysis and structural equation modelling. Environmental attitudes are identified as the main significant factor influencing ecological behaviour.

GRANKVIST et al. (2007) investigate the role of values for the construction of preferences for organic and Fair Trade products and find that the impact depends very much on the type of label. Another important finding is that Fair Trade and organic labels increase the attractiveness of a product but not automatically its purchase probability. Especially price mark-ups were identified as barrier (e.g. GRANKVIST et al. 2007, p. 169).

Also SHAW and SHIU (2003) model ethical consumers' decision making by paying attention to values. They use structural equation modelling techniques as well as reliability analysis to identify important factors that influence consumers' choice for ethical products. SHAW and SHIU (2003, p. 1487f.) extend the original framework of the Theory of Reasoned Action and the Theory of Planned Behaviour by including a measure of ethical obligation and self-identity. The reasons SHAW and SHIU (2003, p. 1487f.) give for these two measures are that ethical consumers make ethical choices because the ethical issues have become an essential component of their self identity. Earlier research had already shown that a measure of ethical obligation is able to predict behaviour. The findings resulting from structural equation modelling are convincing as the latent constructs of subjective norms, internal ethics, internal reflection, external control, and behavioural control were able to predict behavioural intention to a great extent (SHAW and SHIU 2003, p. 1493ff). CHATZIDAKIS et al. (2007) also use the Theory of Planned Behaviour and link it to the Neutralisation Theory of SYKES and MATZA

[51] A result confirmed by the findings of the choice-experimental study described in chapter 6.

(1957)[52] to explain why the gap between the consumers' stated ethical consumption intentions and their real behaviour is very large. They find that personal values and beliefs are of much more crucial importance for ethical decision making than universal values or social norms (CHATZIDAKIS et al. 2007, p. 96). This means, the research conducted by SHAW and SHIU (2003) and CHATZIDAKIS et al. (2007) suggests that ethical behaviour can be modelled by means of an (extended) Theory of Planned Behaviour.

LUSK et al. (2007) apply choice experiments to reveal consumer preferences for environmentally certified meat. They incorporate attributes with a public good dimension into individuals' utility function and find that more altruistic consumers are willing to pay more for organic meat than less altruistic respondents and free riders.

The results of the above-mentioned studies show that attitudes, norms, values, self identity, altruism and socio-demographics are important factors for explaining the relevance of ethics in consumers' choice. Accordingly, the surveys and analysis presented in part C entail variables with respect to e.g. consumers' attitudes, ethical oblication and socio-demographics.

4.1.1.1 Consumers' willingness to pay

The important question related to eliciting WTP data is whether the data is valid. In marketing research, two different elicitation methods are used: revealed-preference and stated-preferences data (see e.g. SHOGREN et al. 2001). Stated preference data provides WTP measures of individuals while revealed preference data, such as scanner data, is mostly limited to aggregate information. However, to reveal stated preferences consumers answer hypothetical questions and are not forced to e.g. purchase the product they are asked to evaluate. Accordingly, stated preferences might be hypothetical and not reflect actual purchase behaviour. In experimental economics, so-called incentive compatible methods have been discussed. Elicitation methods that provide an incentive for people to truthfully reveal their preferences are called incentive compatible. Some types of auction mechanisms, such as the Vickrey auction and the Becker-DeGroot-Marschak mechanism, but also non-hypothetical choice experiments can be mentioned in this regard. Incentive compatability in this context means that for respondents it is best to reveal their exact WTP (KAAS and RUPRECHT 2006, p. 37f.) and not to provide a higher WTP due to social desirability.

---

[52] The Neutralisation Theory describes a mechanism which facilitates behaviour that either breaks socially accepted norms or is in violation of expressed attitudes. By neutralising, individuals reduce the impact their norm violating actions might have on their social relationships and self-concept (SYKES and MATZA 1957).

Studies reporting that consumers claim to be willing to pay considerably more for ethical products are numerous (e.g. LOUREIRO et al. 2002; DE PELSMACKER et al. 2005a, b; MAIETTA 2003; BOUGHERARA and COMBRIS 2009; BECCHETTI and ROSATI 2007 for European consumers and BLEND and VAN RAVENSWAAY 1999 for US consumers). The majority of the studies operationalise ethical consumption via single aspects of the whole concept and use Fair Trade and organic products as examples to assess and reveal consumer preferences for ethical consumption[53].

Most of the research regarding consumers' WTP price premiums for ethical products relies on stated preferences collected through questionnaires (e.g. BLEND and VAN RAVENSWAAY 1999 use the example of organic apples; BUXEL and SCHULZ 2010; GFK 2008c; TRENDBÜRO 2009) and hypothetical survey techniques such as choice experiments and experimental auctions. For example, conjoint analysis is applied by BASU and HICKS (2008) (at the example of Fair Trade coffee in Germany and the U.S.), by CONNER and MABAYA (2006) (at the example of organic and Fair Trade chocolate in the U.S.) and by DE PELSMACKER et al. (2005a) (at the example of Fair Trade coffee in Belgium). The contingent valuation method is applied by LOUREIRO and LOTADE (2005) (at the example of Fair Trade and organic coffee in the United States). The price premium consumers are willing to pay for Fair Trade products lies between 10 % in the case of Fair Trade coffee in the survey of DE PELSMACKER et al. (2005a) and 3.4 % in LOUREIRO and LOTADES' (2005) coffee study.

For Germany, three stated preferences surveys with a focus on ethical products are available. GFK'S (2008c) study indicates that German consumers' WTP for organic/environmental labels and Fair Trade labels differs: while 10.3 % stated to be willing to pay up to 5 % more for Fair Trade products 16.7 % stated to be willing to pay a 5 % higher price for organic products. However, more people stated to be willing to pay between 10 % and 20 % more for Fair Trade than for organic goods. All in all, 29.5 % stated to accept at least a 5 % higher price for Fair Trade products whereas 33.5 % stated to accept this premium for organic products. Another recent study regarding ethical consumption in Germany is the Otto Group Trendstudie (TRENDBÜRO 2009). 90 % of the respondents participating in this telephone survey claim to be interested in ethical consumption while only 67 % claim to have purchased

[53] For example, the title of a survey by ARNOT et al. (2006) is "Do ethical consumers care about price? A revealed preference analysis of Fair Trade coffee purchases", a title of a paper of VON ZIEHLBERG and VON ALVENSLEBEN (1998) is „Die Bedeutung ethischer Motive beim Kauf von Lebensmitteln am Beispiel fair gehandelten Kaffees“. Therefore, it is not surprisingly that in the context of Fair Trade ethical consumers, a "consommé" acteur or the responsible consumer are often discussed (PIROTTE 2007, p. 128; RUWET 2007, p. 144ff.).

ethical products at least sometimes. The same holds true for another recent study in Germany: BUXEL and SCHULZ's (2010) look into the acceptance and usage of labels on food. More than 60 % of the respondents indicate that they pay very much attention to Fair Trade and organic labels which are regarded as trustworthy and preferred when the price is the same. Even if the price of organic and Fair Trade products is up to 5 % higher than a conventional product consumers claim to be willing to pay this price premium. However, there is an inconsistency in BUXEL and SCHULZ (2010) findings: only 41 % state to have seen the Fair Trade label on products before. In contrast, the publicity of the German Biosiegel is at 90 % significantly higher. TRENDBÜRO (2009) conducts market segmentation via socio-demographics and finds differences regarding the WTP a premium for ethical products across the different segments. Women, elderly and higher educated consumers stated to be willing to pay considerably more than younger and less educated people (TRENDBÜRO 2009, p. 35). Respondents' compliance to the importance of fair products produced without child labour is, at more than 90 % on average, enormous (TRENDBÜRO 2009, p. 36). An interesting finding is that the younger generation, i.e. consumers aged 16 to 27, the so-called network children, has comparatively little interest in ethical consumption but delegates responsibility to companies and business from which they expect socially responsible behaviour (TRENDBÜRO 2009, p. 38).

Significantly fewer studies examine consumers' revealed preferences with regard to ethical aspects of goods. For example, ANDERSON and HANSEN (2004) investigate ethical consumption regarding eco-labelled plywood in a real market experiment. BJØRNER et al. (2004) use GfK shopping diary data on toilet paper. The Becker-DeGroot–Marschak mechanism was applied to experimental auctions by BOUGHERARA and COMBRIS (2009) (to the choice of orange juice in France) as well as by TAGBATA and SIRIEIX (2008) (using the example of organic and Fair Trade chocolate in France). ARNOT et al. (2006) show via a real market experiment with coffee in a university café bar that price premiums for ethical products identified by stated preference studies are not just artefacts of hypothetical settings but really do exist. In their experimental choice setting Fair Trade coffee drinkers were less price sensitive than non Fair Trade coffee drinkers and Fair Trade coffee exhibits lower own-price elasticity than comparable conventional coffee.

4.1.1.2 The attitude-behaviour gap

Several studies reveal that individuals overstate their willingness to behave ethically (e.g. AUGER et al. 2007; CARRIGAN and ATTALLA 2001; CHATZIDAKIS et al. 2007; DE PELSMACKER et al. 2005a; DEVINNEY et al. 2010; VERMIER and VERBEKE 2006). This means that people state to be interested in or even concerned about ecological and social issues related to food production such as animal welfare, environmental sustainability, fair producer wages etc., but that these stated preferences and stated awareness are not reflected in their purchase decisions and in how they act (CARRIGAN and ATTALLA 2001; VERMEIR and VERBEKE 2006).

Three major groups of reasons for the attitude behaviour gap can be identified: ability-related factors, external conditions constraining consumers' lifestyle changes towards their private sustainable consumption and social desirability (see Figure 7).

As illustrated in Figure 7, bounded rationality, information overload, limited cognitive capacities as well as scarce knowledge and consciousness regarding ethical issues related to the production of goods might lead to a subjective perception of uncertainty and are, in addition to restricted financial resources, possible ability-related factors that hinder consumers to act according to their preferences stated in surveys (see e.g. SCHOENHEIT 2009, p. 29). Furthermore, external conditions, such as a wide distribution and availability of ethical products in the mass market, might hinder the development of ethical consumption (see e.g. SEVENONEMEDIA 2009, p. 18). Situational factors, such as promotions and behaviour which is based on habits, can also be categorised as external influencing reasons (VERMEIR and VERBEKE 2006, p. 173). Other market-related barriers given as explanations are high prices acting as external contraints, and market characteristics such as the classification of a product as an essential or luxury good (KJARNES 2007, p. 43; TALLONTIRE et al. 2001, p. 17f.). Socially desirable answers are another important source for the attitude-behaviour gap with regard to ethical consumption. When individuals try to present themselves in a positive light regardless their actual behaviour and true feelings, this behaviour is called social desirability and respective answers are socially desirable answers. This means in a socially desirable answer individuals underreport those activities they perceive to be socially undesirable and overreport those habits said to be socially desirable and accepted (RANDALL and FERNANDES 1991, p. 806). Social desirability has been identified as one of the most widespread sources of bias influencing the validity of survey research findings as well as those of experiments (NEDERHOF 1985, p. 263). According to RANDALL and FERNANDES (1991) especially in ethics research, social desirability is prominent. As DEVINNEY et al. (2010, p. 56) put it aptly, the estimates of the relevance of ethical issues for buying decisions vary significantly conditional on the methodology used and the source of analysis. Especially simple rating scales such as the Likert scale used in surveys as well as semi-structured group responses are often susceptible to socially desirable answers which then lead to an overstatement of the importance of ethical issues for the individual purchase decision. The question is to which extent the research method is able to reveal the true preferences and behaviour, or even force consumers to do so. This is called an incentive compatibility issue.

Figure 7: Major reasons for the attitude-behaviour gap with regard to ethical consumption

- **Ability-related factors**
  - Knowledge and consciousness regarding ethical issues related to the product
  - Bounded rationality
  - Information overload
  - Cognitive capacity
  - Financial resources
- **External conditions**
  - Market related barriers, e.g. distribution, available alternatives
  - Situational factors, e.g. promotions, behaviour based on habit
  - Product characteristics, e.g. luxury good
- **Socially desirable answers**
  - Method of data acquisition, e.g. incentive compatible

Note: Ability-related factors are interrelated.

Source: author's illustration.

Furthermore, it is possible that consumers are sceptical towards companies' authenticity and truthfulness and therefore not willing to buy ethical products. This problem as well as the above-mentioned personal constraints could be resolved by consumer empowerment. This could be attained by providing more information, also in form of labelling, and education (THØGERSEN 2005). According to CARRIGAN and ATTALA (2001) as well as WEATHERELL et al. (2003) market shares of Fair Trade, organic and local food are still small due to the fact that availability, quality, convenience and brand familiarity are the most important purchase criteria while ethical factors are only relevant and considered by a minority of consumers characterised by a specific profile. This is confirmed by studies 1 and 2 of this thesis. And possibly the most important explanation is that the consumers' choices are, in the context of a broader choice decision, influenced by different attitudes and therefore more complex than when the consumer reflects about one single question in a survey environment (VERMEIR and VERBEKE 2006, p. 173).

4.1.2 Market relevance of sustainable consumption and trends

A considerable raise in the popularity of ethical consumption can be derived from the sales figures of Fair Trade and organic products. Both are increasingly consumed in industrialised countries. The largest market for Fair Trade products is the United States of America (BYERS et al. 2008, p. 12.). Major European markets are the UK, Switzerland, Italy, the Netherlands and Germany which accounted for about 80 % of the European Fair Trade sales in 2001 and 2002 (KRIER 2005). The overall sales volume of Fair Trade products amounted to 2.65 billion € in 2007 (KRIER 2008, p. 8). Even though sales volumes for Fair Trade and organic products are increasing at double rates worldwide and also in Germany (BYERS et al. 2008; ÖKOLANDBAU.DE 2006, p. 2; RIPPIN 2009, p. 3; TRANSFAIR 2010; ZMP 2007, p. 18) market shares[54] are low. The market shares for organic products depend very much on the kind of product and are very different. For example, the market shares of organic baby food around 59 % (ZMP 2007, p. 19) while it is on average 3.4 % in Germany (BÖLW 2011, p. 8)[55].

In the following the German market for Fair Trade products, and two recent trends, LOHAS and Carrotmobs, are briefly described to provide the reader with an impression of the ongoing changes with regard to ethical consumption in Germany. As especially the organic movement and market in Germany and Europe has, in contrast to the topics described here, been subject of many empirical (e.g. MICHELSEN et al. 1999; BAKER et al. 2004; PADEL and MIDMORE 2005) and theoretical studies (e.g. MANN 2003) the interested reader is referred to these for further information. For the market relevance of CrM products, see papers 3, 4, 5.

The German market for Fair Trade products

In Germany, national trade statistics do not deliver data on volumes and sales of certified products because they do not distinguish between conventional and certified products that are traded. Another problem is the lack of harmonisation of standards which makes it difficult for official agencies to track trade and production figures. In general, data of exporters, import organisations, certifiers or certification NGOs are not always reliable. In the case of Fair Trade sales and trade data is collected by FLO and Forum Fairer Handel (BYERS et al. 2008, p. 8f.; GIOVANNUCCI and KOEKOEK 2003, p. 28). Furthermore, most of the Fair Trade

[54] These positive market shares can be interpreted as revealed consumer preferences.

[55] For further information about the market for organic products in Germany, see BÖLW (2011), RIPPIN (2009), and ZMP (2007).

products sold in Germany bear the international FLO Fair Trade label. Thus, FLO has a dominant position in the market for Fair Trade sales data. [56]

As can be seen in Figure 8, in recent years Fair Trade food sales in Germany have grown at a double digit rate, currently representing about 1 % of all food sales. The overall sales volume of Fair Trade products with the certification label is 340 Mio. € in 2010 (TRANSFAIR 2011). Around 70 % of all Fair Trade products sold in Germany are also certified organic. Coffee is the front runner of the Fair Trade products in Germany: it has more than 50 % share of sales (LZ NET 2007); with a market share of 1.3 % in 2009 (TRANSFAIR 2011). The number of products also increased; 1,000 Fair Trade labelled products were available in around 30,000 stores in Germany in 2008 (SEVENONEMEDIA 2009, p. 18).

Figure 8: Sales volume Fair Trade products in Germany [million €]

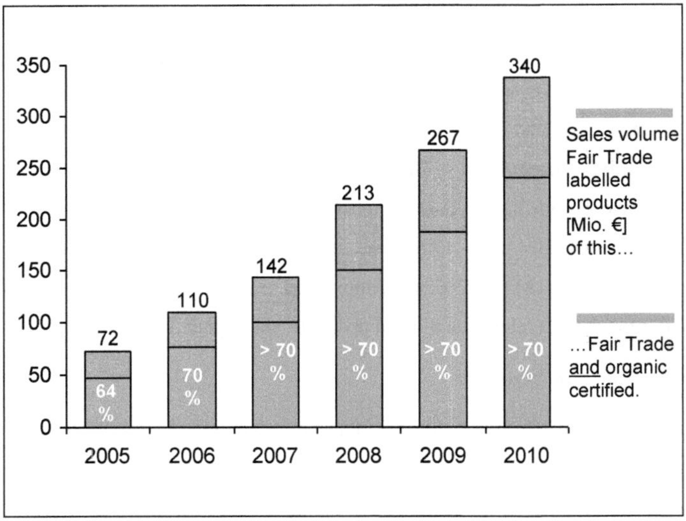

Source: author's illustration based on FORUM FAIRER HANDEL (2006; 2007; 2008a; 2009); TRANSFAIR (2011).

The most important factors discussed with regard to the increase in sales are the distribution and labelling of Fair Trade products. Only products sufficiently available in stores where consumers usually shop will be purchased by the majority of consumers. To offer Fair Trade products in large distribution channels and mass distribution centres, a label is needed

[56] Data availability and publicity of the international label are the reasons for the concentration on the FLO certification scheme within this thesis.

guaranteeing products' Fair Trade character to consumers (RENARD 2003, p. 90) (see also 4.2.3). In Germany the national Fair Trade label, Transfair, was launched in 1993. Since then Fair Trade products have been sold in the broader retail and conventional supermarkets. Up to then it was only available in world shops, churches etc. (FORUM FAIRER HANDEL 2007). 2006 again was a turning point with respect to the distribution and availability of Fair Trade products in Germany. Multinational food companies such as Tchibo and discounters such as Lidl are increasingly attracted by Fair Trade products. In 2006 the discounter Lidl introduced a Fair Trade product range at a comparatively low price level. The market share of discounter in Germany is large. Consequently, the sales volume of Fair Trade products is increasing in Germany as shown above (LZ NET 2007).

LOHAS

An important new consumer trend has become popular under the acronym LOHAS. This stands for 'Lifestyle of Health and Sustainability' and describes a lifestyle as well as a consumer type who supports personal health issues and sustainability by means of a directed product selection (NIELSEN 2008a). It denotes that consumers' purchase and consumption decisions are more and more driven by not only (altruistic) sustainable and ethical aspects but also by (personal egoistic) health issues. This resembles the definition of ethical consumption. Accordingly, the LOHAS trend can be regarded as a form of ethical consumption. This trend has been highly discussed, described and researched in business, marketing research, public media, policy as well as academic literature in the last four years (AWA 2008; BMU 2008; ERNST and YOUNG 2007; GFK 2008d; GRIMM 2006; HOLTHOFF-STENGER 2008a; b; HONKANEN et al. 2006; IRI 2007; NIELSEN 2008a; SCHULZ 2008; SEVEN ONE MEDIA 2009; STRATUM 2008; VICKERY 2005; WENZEL et al. 2007). AWA (2008) describes the consumption behaviour as quality, innovation, brand and information oriented, with preferences for organic, regional and fair traded products. Consumers are critical with respect to production and trade impacts and demand companies to act in a socially responsible way. Ecology turns from a political topic to a maxim leading private action. Figures regarding the relevance and dimension of LOHAS differ from study to study. HUBERT BURDA MEDIA (2007) estimates that 4 Mio. Germans can be regarded as LOHAS; this would be 5.6 % of the German population. AWA (2008) mentions higher figures: 12 % of all Germans older than 14 years are identified as LOHAS. ERNST and YOUNG (2007) differentiate between three scenarios with market shares of 10 % to 30 % in case of a boom. A typical LOHAS is female, older than 50 years, in a good economic situation and holding a university degree (AWA 2008). Thus, this short introduction shows that LOHAS seem not to be different from the ethical consumer described in the previous chapters. Nevertheless, the acronym highlights the egoistic health aspect more than ethical consumption does.

Another Trend: Carrotmobs

In chapter 4.1 buying or boycotting products based on ethical or political values was identified as a form of ethical consumption. The number of people participating in boycott activities as well as buycotts is increasing, according to STOLLE and MICHELETTI (2003, p. 4). Buycotts can be described as the 'flip side' and counterpart of consumer boycotts (FRIEDMAN 1996, p. 440). In the case of buycotts consumers buy services or products of selected companies to reward them for actions which are in line with consumers' values and goals (FRIEDMAN 1996, p. 440). In a boycott, consumers and business share a common goal for which they get involved. One major driving force for a buycotts is the expected participation of others which proved to be affecting individuals' willingness to participate in a boycott (KLEIN et al. 2004, p. 98; WATHIEU et al. 2002, p. 300). Consumers assuming that others will also engage in a buycott action will be stimulated to become active themselves as the outcome of one's own buycotting is then presumed to be greater (WATHIEU et al. 2002, p. 300).

Since 2008 a new type of consumer buycott has been observable, especially in the big cities of Europe, the US but also in Australia and Latin America. Engaged people team up with each other and organise by choice a so-called Carrotmob (CM).[57] They define the goal of the CM (e.g. reduction of CO_2 emissions in the shop in which the CM takes place), ask potential shop owners whether they are willing to participate and how much of the total revenue on the day of CM the shop owner is willing to invest in his own shop in order to achieve the goal of the CM. The organising team then advertises the event so that in exchange for the shop owners' promise of investment in the goal, a huge number of new customers purchases products at the day of the CM. This engagement takes place in more informal networks, and tends to be local and sporadic. For a deeper insight in the CM movement, see LANGEN and HARTMANN (2011).

4.1.3 Challenging ethical consumption

While most of the research on ethical consumption has a positive undertone and purports to show that there is a demand for ethical products among the average customers, DEVINNEY et al. (2010, p. 2) question what they call "the myth of the ethical consumer". Their major criticism is that most of the research that indicates positive consumer purchase intentions (e.g.

[57] Up until August 2010, 92 of those CM took place all over the world.

HARRISON et al. 2005) is limited to the perspective of what they call the believers.[58] This is accompanied by the question to which degree it is possible to "generalize from a niche market to a mass market" (DEVINNEY et al. 2010, p. 3). DEVINNEY et al. (2010, p. 6) do not deny that ethical consumption occurs and that individuals bring their values and beliefs into the purchasing decision but they think that these beliefs and values are only one of many other aspects of consumers' purchase decisions. Furthermore, they show that other-related behaviour exists but that it is very specific, which means that within the context of some choices consumers behave in an ethically responsible way and within others they do not. Thus, from an ethical purchase decision of one good no conclusions should be drawn concerning the ethical purchase decision of another good (DEVINNEY et al. 2010, p. 8).

DEVINNEY et al. (2010, p. 3) state that the increasing availability of ethical and sustainable products is not consumer driven but market driven by the companies themselves sourcing e.g. more Fair Trade products.

Another aspect ZACCAI (2007, p. 9) remarks on is that for the moment ethical consumption is not being analysed "with coherent objectives from the social, environmental and economic perspectives" and that the objectives are not all defined yet. Accordingly, it is still under-researched and unclear as to which way consumer behaviour models work in the socio-cultural environment that ethical consumerism is embodied in (DEVINNEY et al. 2010, p. 2). To illustrate the lack of coherence of models of consumer behaviour used to represent ethical consumer behaviour and to show that explicit models of what motivates consumers to act in a certain way determine the researchers' search for the ethical consumer, DEVINNEY et al. (2010, p. 48ff.; 55) compare two simple meta-models of social consumer behaviour. They refer to the first as a 'linear model of social consumption' whereas the second is denoted a 'recursive model of social consumption'. The difference between these two is that the linear model has a distinct beginning and a distinct end whereas in the recursive model neither the starting point nor the end point is fixed. The starting point of the linear model are fundamental values which impact beliefs and attitudes which in turn influence intentions which turn into the consumers' action as an end point. Information and knowledge as well as external influences and context affect all components of the model. It resembles the Theory of Reasoned Action model without the feedback loops. In contrast, the recursive model is a

58 The statements of TRENDBÜRO (2009) can be an example for this. TRENDBÜRO (2009, p. 24; p. 32f.) state that ethical consumers want to use their purchasing power to support a sustainable business and economy and state further that for ethical consumers the importance of organic products will increase especially because consumers associate organic products with health and well-being. But what about the non-ethical consumers?

strong simplification of the model of Howard and Sheth as well as the one of Blackwell, Miniard and Engel. Complex interactions between values, beliefs and attitudes, intentions, external influences, context, information and knowledge and action are possible but the different model components (exogenous and endogenous influences) are not clearly identifiable in the recursive model. The major weakness of this linear model is that nothing explains how the values are formed and that the context of the choice is faded out. According to DEVINNEY et al. (2010, p. 49), the linear model is the basis for management and business ethics literature. This has implications for the research process and the results of research: if e.g. the context of the decision is not taken into account and e.g. the role of society in forming values is ignored, how can then market research arrive at empirically sound results? Therefore, DEVINNEY et al. (2010) are not only sceptical as to whether consumer research working with simple linear models of consumer behaviour is able to provide insights into the complex ethical decision making of consumers. They think the attempt is futile.

4.1.4 The (missing) link between ethical, sustainable and Fair Trade consumption

The previous sections have shown that ethical consumption can be divided into different types as it is constituted by a diversity of objects and practices. Definitions resemble each other but they are distinguishable in specific points. Moreover, as mentioned in the introduction, Fair Trade and organic certified products are regarded as classical ethical products so that the purchase of such labelled products is perceived as ethical purchase behaviour, especially positive ethical purchase behaviour, and the consumption of these goods is called ethical consumption. While the focus of the two labelling schemes is different (see the introductory paragraphs), ethical consumption is often modelled by the use and purchase of organic as well as Fair Trade products (see the paragraph on the research areas of ethical consumption). This shows that there is a link between ethics and sustainability. Therefore, this paragraph looks at the relationship between ethics and sustainability, with a special emphasis on ethical and Fair Trade products as well as organic and Fair Trade production to point out some more common aspects and some more separative elements and differences.

The link between ethical and sustainable consumption

There are many definitions of sustainable consumption[59] (JACKSON and MICHAELIS 2003) but the one defined at the Oslo Symposium of Sustainable Consumption 1994 is most often used (UNESCO n.d.):

"sustainable consumption is the use of goods and services that respond to basic needs and bring a better quality of life, while minimising the use of natural resources, toxic materials and emissions of waste and pollutants over the life cycle, so as not to jeopardise the needs of future generations" (IISD 2005).

This definition links production and consumption which are seen as two sides of the same coin with respect to sustainability and sustainable development and takes into account that product design and marketing influence consumers' decisions as well as consumers influencing production through their consumption choices. Within this framework, different fields of consumption (from broader fields of mobility, tourism and nutrition to water usage, waste management and the reduction of emissions) are investigated. In the UNEP, several key issues of sustainability, such as the improvement of resource efficiency, the increase in use of renewable energy sources, minimisation of waste, etc. are summarised under the umbrella term of sustainable consumption which is close to the definition of sustainability first given in the Brundtland Report. It is obvious that the definition is idealistic and describes a normative concept which assumes simple relationships between demand and supply as well as the fact that profit is sometimes easier to generate with unsustainable production/consumption (UNESCO n.d.; SCHOENHEIT 2009, p. 21). Another important shortcoming raised by UNESCO (n.d.) is that personal lifestyle choice is over-emphasised in comparison to the important role of governments. UNESCO (n.d.) proposes therefore a wider definition:

"Sustainable consumption integrates a range of social, economic and political practices at the individual, household, community, business and government levels that support and encourage: 1. reducing the direct environmental burden of producing, using and disposing goods and services; 2. meeting basic needs for key consumption goods and services, such as food, water, health, education and shelter; 3. maximising opportunities for sustainable livelihoods in the South; 4. consuming goods and services that contribute positively to the health and well-being of women and children; 5. increasing the development and adoption of energy and water efficient appliances, public transport and other demand-side measures; 6. the production and sale of new goods and services adapted to global environmental constraints; 7. lifestyles that place greater value on social cohesion, local traditions and non-material values. "

This definition shows more precisely what *sustainable* consumption means, where the multitude of terms such as conscious consumption originates from and which kind of

[59] See e.g. the International Declaration on Cleaner Production 1998, UNEP in UNEP (n.d., p. 2).

consumption can be labelled sustainable: *efficient* consumption which means that services and resources in the production process are used efficiently (point 1), *different* consumption which means that the patterns of consumption have to change (point 4, 6), *conscious* consumption which focusses on the improvement of life quality (point 3, 7) (see also CSCP 2008, p. 1). It can be maintained that UNEP (n.d.) calls sustainable consumption a type of consumption that addresses equity, social issues and green issues. This goes further than *green* consumption. Sustainable consumption is in this definition not separable from *ethical* consumption as defined by DE PELSMACKER (2005b); HARRISON et al. (2005) and the other above-mentioned researchers.

This is due to the fact that sustainable consumption generally is regarded as a sub-form of ethical consumption (PONTE 2004, p. 8). Therefore, the terms are not used as synonyms within this thesis. This interrelation between ethics and sustainability becomes evident when arguing whether a choice question can be discussed only from the sustainability aspect or whether ethics is needed to come to a final assessment. Thus, THOMPSON (2007) gives examples of how society discusses the question of e.g. sustainable agricultural production and shows that once there is consent about the amount of sustainability that should be achieved in agricultural production a range of ethical questions have to be posed and then trade-offs between these have to be made. Therefore, THOMPSON (2007, p. 64) concludes that sustainability is a crucial element for ethics. Ethics is regarded a form of social investigation, and sustainability is one of a number of goals that this investigation should address. BOULANGER (2007, p. 17) also understands sustainability as an ethical problem as each individual's way of life keeps other individuals from living their lives in a decent way. This becomes a question of justice and therefore of ethics (BOULANGER 2007, p. 17f.).

The link between ethical and Fair Trade

The distinction between Fair Trade and ethical trade given by TALLONTIRE (2002) as well as SMITH and BARRIENTOS (2005) is based on the different foci of the two and the purposes they address. As SMITH and BARRIENTOS (2005, p. 191) maintain, the differences become obvious in the context of global value chain analysis. From that point of view, Fair Trade focuses on terms of trade between small-scale producers and buyers while the foucs of ethical trade is on labour practices and working conditions in global value chains and mainstream production ensuring that minimum international standards are met (SMITH and BARRIENTOS 2005, p. 191). Ethical trade "affects only the criteria for producers entering and selling within the chain" and not the trading relations within the chain (SMITH and BARRIENTOS 2005, p. 192).

This means the type of value chain relations and the forms of governance of Fair Trade and ethical trade are different. Fair Trade is characterised by a civic coordination of alternative trading organisations and small-scale producers, whereas ethical trade faces an industrial organisation between medium- and large-scale producers as well as retailers and brands (SMITH and BARRIENTOS 2005, p. 193).

TALLONTIRE (2002, p. 13) makes her differentiation not with respect to value chain analysis but more from the contents of the movements and comes to a similar assessment. She says the term ethical trade is used in relation to supply chain management of multinational retailers and brands to ensure that human rights standards for workers are complied with. If, furthermore, the focus of a trading partnership is not on small-scale farmers in poor countries, TALLONTIRE (2002) refers to this as ethical trade.

TALLONTIRE (2002, p. 13) and also SMITH and BARRIENTOS (2005, p. 190; 193) admit that due to the expansion of Fair Trade and ethical trade, the issues which in former times were separate are now more and more overlapping. Therefore, TALLONTIRE (2002, p. 13) fears that some consumers may not see the small difference she states and thus consider ethical labels from companies and brands and Fair Trade labels to be similar.

The link between Fair Trade and sustainability

The Fair Trade system, as a mixture of economic, environmental and social goals related to the supply chain of goods, is supposed to be "very much within the spirit of sustainability thinking" (CRANE and MATTEN 2004, p. 335). The fair price should cover production cost in general and the costs of sustainable production in particular. The Fair Trade certification standard consists of generic and product specific standards accounting for the three pillars of sustainability: economy, sociality and environment[60]. The chapters of the generic standard are named accordingly (FLO 2009c).

PONTE (2004, p. 1) tries to answer the question as to whether certification systems and standards are able to address and solve the challenges resulting from the economic, social and environmental dimensions of sustainability. He compares four different coffee certification systems which focus more or less on sustainability aspects. He concludes that the impact of the certification system on economic sustainability results mostly from the level of the offered price premium and its difference to the actual market price. All in all, the effect on income is determined by the extra income minus the costs of accomplishing the standard minus the

[60] See CRANE and MATTEN (2004, p. 22ff.) for a comprehensive definition of sustainability.

certification costs. Costs arising from matching the standard are the extra costs of production (possibly changing farming practices which have impact on yields and quality) and possibly changing labour costs (no child labour any longer, higher labour costs in mixed cultivation than in plantations) (PONTE 2004, p. 28ff.). These costs differ from standard to standard. PONTE (2004, p. 31ff.) shows that the impact of Fair Trade certification is mainly on the social and economic dimension of sustainability. For example, better market access and credit worthiness or paying in advance can reduce risk for cooperatives and farmers. Another important social benefit results from the projects the community finances out of the Fair Trade premium[61]. CONNER and MABAYA (2006, p. 11) also highlight the positive long-term effects of Fair Trade producers arising from the use of sustainable practices and the social and human capacity building. To sum up, from a theoretical perspective Fair Trade is able to address the issue of sustainability (PAUL 2005, p. 149).

The link between organic and Fair Trade production

PADEL et al. (2009, p. 246ff.) show that since the beginning of the organic movement fairness issues, such as equity, respect, justice, and transparency, are in addition to sustainability, naturalness and system thinking core principles of organic agriculture. In contrast, concerning the issue of ecological sustainability, the Fair Trade standard is not as strict in its environmental rules and regulations as organic labelling standards are: e.g. pesticides are not totally forbidden but their use/application should be reduced to a minimum. Nevertheless, according to RICE (2001, p. 41) Fair Trade and organic products are linked since the alternative trade organisations initiating the Fair Trade movement were based on philosophies of social justice and/or environmental well-being. However, it can be maintained that in the Fair Trade certification scheme ecological issues tend to be incorporated indirectly.

BROWNE et al. (2000, p. 71f.) regard Northern consumers' pressure for sustainability to encompass both social and environmental sustainability issues, with the latter also being closely linked to organics, as crucial for the ongoing mixture of ethical, organic and concerned consumption. According to them, consumers' expectations are the reasons that ethical, organic and environmentally sustainable trading are beginning to overlap. BROWNE et al. (2000) raise the question as to whether it is possible to look at so-called ethical issues without also looking at the environment and are therefore in line with the argumentation of THOMPSON (2007). Nevertheless, there might remain a trade-off for consumers when they are

[61] For further benefits, see PONTE (2004, p. 31f.).

confronted in the supermarket with the choice between a Fair Trade product and an organic one. The following example highlights this possible trade-off consumers have to make with regard to sustainability issues and Fair Trade products. Fair Trade products from developing countries are intended to strengthen producers in the South which should result in social sustainability. But with regard to their CO_2 footprint (see e.g. the CO_2 emissions of air-freighted food) the environmental sustainability of Fair Trade products is at least questionable (CSCP 2008, p. 8).

This short abstract of the interrelation between ethics, sustainability, organic and Fair Trade production shows that the links are today more pronounced than the separating elements. Nevertheless, it can be distinguished between these terms, issues and labelling schemes.

4.2 Fair Trade

In the previous chapter it became apparent that fair traded products are without doubt a paramount important type of ethical products. They have recently been the object of theoretical (e.g. BECCHETTI and ADRIANI 2004; GOODMAN 2004) and empirical studies (e.g. DE FERRAN and GRUNERT 2007; LOUREIRO and LOTADE 2005). As Fair Trade has a very special view on globalisation, trade and producers in the South, which results in assumptions about how to interact with small-scale producers, this chapter looks in detail at the Fair Trade movement, its morality as well as the topics discussed in literature. Finally, the chapter compares Fair Trade with donations.

4.2.1 The morality of Fair Trade

The Fair Trade movement describes the situation producers in the South are confronted with in a globalised trade system as follows: poor, small-scale, marginalised, disadvantaged and unorganised producers struggle against low market prices, the overwhelming power of multinational corporations, and a high dependency on middlemen such as buyers, brokers, retailers and wholesalers (PIEPEL et al. 2000, p. 281; OSMUNDSVÅG 2007, p. 167f.). The farmers are characterised by their lack of access to information, financial services, and technology.

The morality of Fair Trade can be illustrated by classifying researchers' opinions about and their definition of Fair Trade: on the one hand, Fair Trade is thought as an instrument seeking greater equity in international trade to overcome producers' vulnerability and to create economic self-sufficiency. Hence, Fair Trade is development and a business instrument and promotes development through trade (LE MARE 2008, p. 1924; TALLONTIRE 2002, p. 12). It is a particular trade channel which is part of the capitalist system of free trade (BECCHETTI and

ADRIANI 2004; OSMUNDSVÅG 2007, p. 167). On the other hand, the marketing efforts of Fair Trade "seek to influence cultural and political values in such a way that consumers and corporations in the North will have to respond to them by incorporating the welfare of Southern workers and ecosystems into their purchasing decisions" (LINTON 2005, p. 600). In the same way, GOODMAN (2004, p. 891) describes Fair Trade as a "form of alternative development [which] has become the moral business of latte drinkers and other reflexive consumers in Europe and the US". GOODMAN (2004, p. 891) perceives Fair Trade "to attempt to reconnect producers and consumers economically, politically, and psychologically through the creation of a transnational moral economy". Accordingly, for NICHOLLS and OPAL (2005, p. 13) Fair Trade is neither about charity nor about not-for-profit but a means of empowerment of producers and consumers and therefore a form of political and ethical consumption. SAGE (2003, p. 49) takes this idea further and says that morality is one of the important features of food networks. This morality can be interpreted within the discussion of 'ethics of care' (see SMITH 2005) in the sense that consumers care about 'here', 'now', 'there' and 'then', which means consumers care about producers' livelihoods (GOODMAN 2004, p. 903). This resembles a partnership; a voluntary and mutual arrangement between actors of society (BITZER et al. 2008, p. 271). Moral connections and responsibility along the whole commodity chain allow Fair Trade, in the eyes of GOODMAN (2004, p. 903), to become "as much ethical as it is political".

4.2.2 From a decentralised movement to an international label

Fair Trade began as a decentralized movement of an interest group (KRIER 2005, p. 20; LOUREIRO and LOTADE 2005, p. 130) and emerged in the late 1940s[62] as an alternative and integrated market system/commodity chain parallel to the conventional market channels. In the early integrated commodity chain, mainly artisan products and coffee from Southern countries were sold in special stores managed by non-governmental organisations and volunteers. In 1988 Max Havelaar started selling Fair Trade products in the conventional market to catch a bigger consumer audience. For this purpose some Fair Trade labels, such as Max Havelaar in the Netherlands and Transfair in Germany, were established. In 1997, the Fairtrade Labelling Organizations International (FLO) was formed as an umbrella organisation of 20 national Fair Trade labelling initiatives to allow "the movement to speak with one voice" to meet the challenges of the diversified and growing Fair Trade market

[62] GRIMES (2005, p. 238) as well as MOORE (2004, p. 73) see the beginning of the Fair Trade movement in the Mennonite church in the US in the late 1940s. It came to Europe in the 1950s when Oxfam started selling products from Chinese refugees in small stores (GRIMES 2005, p. 238)[62].

(GIOVANNUCCI and KOEKOEK 2003, p. 40). FLO is a coordinating organisation, which harmonises standards and norms (see 4.2.3) of the different alternative trade movements and organises the inspection and certification processes.[63] An international label for Fair Trade products exists since 2002 and guarantees the compliance of the process and trade conditions (FLO 2011). The FLO standard is based on the commonly used definition of Fair Trade, a definition as agreed by FLO, WFTO, NEWS! and EFTA: "Fair Trade is a trading partnership, based on dialogue, transparency and respect, that seek greater equity in international trade. It contributes to sustainable development by offering better trading conditions to, and securing the rights of, marginalized producers and workers – especially in the South. Fair Trade Organizations, backed by consumers, are engaged actively in supporting producers, awareness raising and in campaigning for changes in the rules and practice of conventional international trade" (EFTA 2011).

The national initiatives are FLO members. The Fair Trade movement is composed of producers, retailers, certification agencies, NGOs and consumers acting worldwide (e.g. FLO and IFAT) and locally (e.g. Transfair in Germany). It can be described as a global network using the strategy: trade not aid (CHAMBOLLE and PORET 2007, p. 1).[64] In Germany, 110 firms (worldwide 1483 in 2005) sell Fair Trade products; one of them is Gepa, the largest retailer of Fair Trade products in Europe (TRANSFAIR 2007, FLO 2007c).

Today, Fair Trade is a social movement as well as a special trade channel which has a double purpose: supporting poor producers in the South in improving their living conditions and empowering Southern, disadvantaged marginalised producers (it is therefore a kind of development intervention) and changing conventional trade relations (hence it is an alternative form of trade and therefore business) (PAUL 2005, p. 134).

Empowerment as well as the establishment of a different kind of trade system is intented to be reached by (i) facilitating market access for small producer products, (ii) direct and sustainable partnerships between Fair Trade sellers in the North and producers in the South providing market access for marginalised producers from the South to markets in the North and, at the same time, provide marginalised farmers with a better negotiating position with market partners, (iii) knowledge transfer, such as market information, which leads to capacity

[63] While in the beginning only small-scale farmers produced Fair Trade products, today plantation workers and their interests are also integrated into the FLO regime – due to the fact that some products like bananas and soccer balls are not produced by small-scale farmers (RENARD 2005, p. 424).

[64] Other key Fair Trade organisations include the International Fair Trade Association (IFAT), which is the global network of the Fair Trade organisations with members in over 60 countries, the European Fair Trade Association (EFTA), a network of Fair Trade associations in European countries, the Network of European World Shops (NEWS) and a discussion forum for FLO, IFAT, NEWS and EFTA called FINE. IFAT is a member of the umbrella organisation FINE. The Fair Trade organisations follow certain rules such as transparency and accountability (see IFAT 2011, p. 2).

building on the level of producers and cooperatives, (iv) the provision of micro-credit services, (v) the payment of fixed minimum prices which, on the one hand, stabilises family income and, on the other hand, makes it predictable, (vi) price premiums which are paid in the Fair Trade system for social development, superior labour rights and the improvement of gender equality in the local producer communities (BITZER et al. 2008, p. 272; DANKERS 2003, p. 23; MURADIAN and PELUPESSY 2005, p. 2033f.; PAUL 2005, p. 134; RAYNOLDS et al. 2007, p. 154 ; RENARD 2005, p. 423). This is what should, from the Fair Trade perspective, ensure stable and fair trading conditions for marginalised producers in developing countries (OZCAGLAR-TOULOUSE et al. 2006, p. 502).[65]

The insights into the morality as well the evolution of the Fair Trade movement show the demands the Fair Trade movement aims to meet. It is not just about providing income opportunities for producers in the South but to build up what GOODMAN (2004, p. 891) calls "ethical production-consumption links" by politicising consumption. LE MARE (2008, p. 1927) calls this the wish to change the "power relationships along the supply chain" by empowering consumers so that they make ethical purchase and consumption decisions and to empower producers so that "they can capture more of the values of" their products. Thus, Fair Trade products are not only a combination of physical product characteristics but also a bundle of environmental and social values such as empowerment (BECCHETTI and ROSATI 2007, p. 820).

Accordingly, consumers' reasons for supporting Fair Trade can be different. In this respect, Fair Trade is very similar to donations. There, too, the reasons for giving to charity are very diverse.

In this dissertation, Fair Trade is understood as one form of ethical consumption and Fair Trade products are food products which are allowed to bear the international Fair Trade label since their production process follows the FLO standard.

4.2.3 Social and environmental standards and labelling

There are numerous social and environmental standards systems as well as voluntary codes of conduct developed by NGOs with a focus on environmental sustainability and social justice. The number of private and voluntary certification programmes and standards has increased especially in the last few years. Reasons are changing consumer needs, the increased

[65] According to BITZER et al. (2008, p. 280), this last point in particular is lacking in many coffee trading partnerships.

importance of health and safety as well as overproduction and a resulting decline in commodity prices. Traditionally product differentiation was achieved by means of taste, price, and packaging; product differentiation is now also based on the production process. As standards in general entail the possibility of product differentiation and upgrading, social and environmental standards provide a distinction based on the production process and can be used as competitive strategy (BITZER et al. 2008, p. 278; BYERS et al. 2008, p. 2f.).

In this chapter the function of standards and labels are discussed. This is followed by a description of the FLO Fair Trade standards. As the research object of the studies is coffee, special emphasis is given to standards in the coffee chain before a short comparison of different standards is provided.

The function of standards and labels

Social, environmental or health issues related to the production process of a good cannot be controlled by the consumer. These product attributes are therefore called credence goods (RENARD 2003, p. 95). According to information economics the main goal of certification and labelling is to overcome the information asymmetries/distortion between the consumer and the producer or supplier of commodities with important credence attributes and to reduce the costs of the information search with regard to products' credence attributes (HADFIELD and THOMSON 1998, p. 566ff.; LELAND 1979, p. 1330; TEISL and ROE 1998, p. 141). Information asymmetries possibly result in the problem of adverse selection described first by AKERLOF (1970, p. 500) which in turn may lead to market collapse (TEISL and ROE 1998, p. 141). In the case of credence attributes, labelling guarantees special production conditions and labels fulfil the role of trust building (RENARD 2003, p. 94).[66] Labelling allows consumers to make choices better in line with their preferences while firms producing goods with desired product attributes gain market shares and can maximise rents if they can use credible labels. Fair competition is therefore ensured (GOLAN et al. 2001, p. 118). To fulfil these functions the requirements for a label are manifold, e.g. a label must be clear and represent what it is standing for (RENARD 2003, p. 94). Furthermore, independent certification organs are necessary. The type of information involved, the level and distribution of benefits as well as the cost of information provision impact the appropriate level of governments' intervention in labelling decisions from the one extreme, establishing mandatory laws, over supporting voluntary labelling to the other extreme, not intervening at all. Therefore, the economics of

[66] In addition, labelling constitutes a network and produces identity (RENARD 2003, p. 94).

labelling (for an extensive review see GOLAN et al. 2001) should be considered from case to case.

The Fair Trade standard

Fair Trade is a voluntary certification scheme (TALLONTIRE 2002, p. 13). Until now, no single legal standard has existed for fairly traded products comparable with the German Biosiegel[67]. Most of the so-called Fair Trade products are certified according to the standards set by the FLO. The Fair Trade standards need to be maintained by producers, their organisations and the traders who trade with Fair Trade products (CONNER and MABAYA 2006, p. 2f.; FLO 2007a, p. 7).

FLO has established product standards (which include Fair Trade minimum prices and premiums) and a framework of generic standards which distinguishes between smallholder production (here achieving a minimum price is most important for the producer) and plantation (for workers fair wages and decent working conditions are relevant). This framework is complemented with product specific criteria. The standards include: labour standards and trade standards. Environmental criteria are included in crop specific standards. Currently, product specific standards exist for almonds, bananas, coffee, cocoa, dried fruit, fresh fruit and fresh vegetables, fruit juices, herbs and spices, honey, nuts and oil seeds, quinoa, rice, cane sugar, tea, wine grapes, flowers and plants, seed cotton, sport balls (FLO 2009b).

The **pricing** is done in different ways according to the product concerned. The goal is to base the minimum price on the estimated costs of sustainable production (BYERS et al. 2008, p. 41). For example, for coffee the minimum price varies according to the type of coffee (Arabica or Robusta/washed or non-washed) and the country of origin (see Table 2). In times when the market price, which is for Arabica coffees determined by the price of the second position C futures contract at the InterContinental Exchange, is higher than the FLO minimum price this higher market price and the Fair Trade additional premium are paid. Hence, the 'fair' price consists of at least the guaranteed minimum price and a price premium. The price premium is earmarked for economic, social and community projects/investments which are decided upon by the community (BYERS et al. 2008, p. 41; RENARD 2005, p. 424). The organic premium is intended to cover the expenses due to the different production methods

67 Standards are also not available for CrM.

and lower yields. To become part of the FLO system producers are expected to be democratically organised and to take on responsible management (RENARD 2005, p. 424).

For further information on the accreditation and certification process and the pros and cons, see www.fairtrade.net and DANKERS (2003, p. 31).

Table 2: FLO Pricing for Fair Trade coffee for small farmers' organisations

Prices [US $ cents] per pound F.O.B. port of origin	Fair Trade minimum price		Organic Differential	Fair Trade premium
Type of coffee	Central America, Africa, Asia	South America, Caribbean Area	All regions	All regions
Washed Arabica	121	119	20	10
Non-washed Arabica	115	115	20	10
Washed Robusta	105	105	20	10
Non-washed Robusta	101	101	20	10

Source: FLO (2007b).

Differences between certification schemes with a focus on coffee

Four types of voluntary certification schemes can be differentiated according to their standard setting party. First-party certifications are forms of in-house corporate self-regulation motivated to a certain extent by self-interest. Accordingly, legitimacy is limited. Second-party certifications include industry associations to enhance the rigor and transparency of procedures. But credibility concerns remain. Especially in the coffee sector private company standards (first- and second-party certification) for sustainable and quality coffee production have emerged and were established by coffee roasters and distributors to address consumer concerns for sustainable and ethical production, to protect against possible negative publicity and to capture a share of the growing market for sustainable coffee. Starbucks and Nestlé (its brand Nespresso) are two companies that are very important for the coffee market with private coffee standards (BYERS et al. 2008, p. 45). The standard of Starbucks is called C.A.F.E. which stands for Coffee and Farmers Equity Practices. It covers a set of environmental and basic social standards in line with Starbucks' quality requirements. Nespresso did not create a certification scheme but a so-called Nespresso´s AAA Sustainable Quality Program® (BYERS et al. 2008, p. 45). The Sustainable Agriculture Initiative Platform was established by multinational food companies in 2002. They are given as an example of a second-party certification scheme in the coffee value chain by MURADIAN and PELUPESSY

(2005, p. 2032f.). But, in contrast to the finding of MURADIAN and PELUPESSY (2005, p. 2032f.), the SUSTAINABLE AGRICULTURE INITIATIVE PLATFORM (2011) no longer wants to establish its own standard but go a step backwards: it aims at developing principles and practices for sustainable production. Third-party certification schemes are set by NGOs; Fair Trade according to the FLO rules is an example. Fourth-party regulatory systems are set up by multilateral or government bodies. An example is the Common Code for the Coffee Community, also known by its abbreviation 4C. The 4C initiative was launched in 2003 with support of the German Development Cooperation Agency (GTZ) and aims to establish a multi-stakeholder certification scheme with the participation of the major players in the coffee industry such as Nestlé (MURADIAN and PELUPESSY 2005, p. 2032ff.; RAYNOLDS et al. 2007, p. 151). In 2007, 3.5 % of the worldwide traded coffee was produced according to 4C (EPO 2008). 4C encourages good management and agricultural methods as well as social and environmental standards on a basic level. These standards are not certified or monitored by independent third-party organisations nor are they designed for the (economic) needs of producers and workers in developing countries but for the corporate needs of the respective company. Therefore, they fulfil not one core criterion of the pillar of economic sustainability, sustainable production, according to the concept of sustainability. Until 2008, no independent study had been carried out analysing the costs and benefits of the Starbucks certification scheme or Nespressos'quality program (BYERS et al. 2008, p. 45). [68]

With regard to the coffee sector, third-party certification is the most important of all voluntary regulatory systems (MURADIAN and PELUPESSY 2005, p. 2033). Other important third-party certification schemes besides Fair Trade are organic certification, shade grown/bird friendly, Utz Kapeh and Rainforest Alliance (MURADIAN and PELUPESSY 2005). The last three certification schemes are more recent (they were established in 1997, 2002 and 1996 respectively) than Fair Trade and organic certification (Demeter has existed since the 1920s, other organic standards since the 1970s) (see BITZER et al. 2008, p. 273 for a timeline of the others; FLO 2009a for Fair Trade). These certification standards have in common that they specify production processes, the form of market coordination, participation issues as well as social responsibility and environmental sustainability. Another similarity is that all twelve partnerships in the coffee chain, such as 4C, Utz Kapeh and Rainforest Alliance, analysed by BITZER et al. (2008) are in their current form Northern-based models in which actors from

[68] But in spite of these critical points, both will have a huge impact on coffee producers due to the fact that both companies sell a great part of the coffee that is consumed worldwide.

industrialised countries are overrepresented whereas Southern actors frequently lack considerable participation. This result is in line with the findings of VANDERHOFF BOERSMA (2002, p. 12; 20), the founder of the Fair Trade organisation Max Havelaar, who acknowledged that on the whole "the Fair Trade system has not been very democratic and [...] (that) the producers did not participate in the important decision making process" (p. 12).

Nevertheless, they differ considerably, e.g. with respect to monitoring bodies, the specifications of social, ecological production as well as trading and producer prices as RAYNOLDS et al. (2007, p. 152f; 155ff.) and BITZER et al. (2008, p. 276f.) demonstrate. Fair Trade has in comparison with the other five third-party certification systems in the coffee sector the broadest and strongest NGO base (RAYNOLDS et al. 2007, p. 151). It is the only initiative for which coffee is only produced by small-scale farmers organised in democratic organisations. Another uniqueness of Fair Trade is the payment of the guaranteed minimum price as well as social and organic premiums. The social premium is used to fund social services in the coffee communities, for ecological efforts and quality improvements. Unlike the other standards, Fair Trade specifies rules for coffee importers: they have to keep long-term contracts/commercial relationships and grant pre-financing of the harvest if required. Less importance is given to ecological issues. Here Fair Trade only includes basic environmental criteria while organic certification is the strictest[69]. In general, it can be said the first sustainability initiatives have the strictest rules while the newcomer standards are in many regards lower (BITZER et al. 2008, p. 278).

In the last few years, multiple certifications, especially in the field of coffee, have been increasingly observable. In particular, organic and Fair Trade certification overlap (BYERS et al. 2008, p. 6f.). The majority of both, Fair Trade and organic coffees, carry at least one other certification (BYERS et al. 2008, p. 46). Due to the above-described plurality of guidelines, standards and actors, and limited calculative capacity as well as bounded rationality it can be presumed that consumers are not fully informed about the differences and the subtle intricacies between the existing labels. This can lead to a situation in which consumers substitute the one by the other certification

4.2.4 Research areas of Fair Trade

Many studies and articles deal with Fair Trade but focus on different aspects. Fair Trade within the discourse of and in comparison with free markets has been a topic of discussion in

[69] PONTE (2004) and RENARD (2005) provide a more in-depth overview of the features and characteristics of these third-party certification schemes.

a number of surveys (BOOTH and WHETSTONE 2007; LINDSEY 2003; PARRISH et al. 2005; RICE 2010; SIDWELL 2008), as well as fairer markets (GRIMES 2005; HAYES 2006; LECLAIR 2003; MOORE 2004; RAYNOLDS et al. 2007; RICE 2001). The question as to whether Fair Trade is able to improve justice has also been discussed (GALTIER and DIAZ PEDREGAL 2010). Others position Fair Trade in the debate of alternative development and social responsibility (LITTRELL and DICKSON 1999; ZACCAI 2007) and ethical consumption (BARNET et al. 2005; BECCHETI and ROSATI 2005; 2007; GOODMAN 2004; NICHOLLS and OPAL 2005). In this context there is a huge amount of literature on consumers' valuation and assessment of Fair Trade, their WTP for and their knowledge about Fair Trade (see the respective chapter on ethical consumption). Literature reviews are also provided on producers' decision making with regard to participation in Fair Trade (STEINRÜCKEN 2002), their knowledge regarding the meaning of Fair Trade (DANKERS 2003) as well as the impact of Fair Trade on producers' livelihood.

In the following section, special attention is paid to the distribution of Fair Trade products in the mainstream, the distribution of benefits along the supply chain and the findings of case studies regarding the impact and outcomes of Fair Trade certification on Fair Trade producers' livelihood. The first issue is relevant background information to better classify the marketing implications resulting from the analysis conducted in the choice experimental study described in chapter 6. The second is strongly related to the first as other companies, which were regarded as an enemy in the early stages of the Fair Trade movement, enter the Fair Trade supply chain when the distribution of Fair Trade products is enlarged. Furthermore, the question of efficiency is addressed throughout this dissertation. The third is important as a basis for the comparison of Fair Trade with charitable giving. As it is often said that Fair Trade is in its principles and outcomes different from charitable giving, the question is raised as to which extent Fair Trade certification can meet its own objectives.

4.2.4.1 The distribution of Fair Trade products in the mainstream

The distribution of Fair Trade products in large mainstream channels such as supermarkets and the discounters and its implications on the Fair Trade commodity have been extensively discussed in literature (see e.g. COWE and WILLIAMS 2000; DOHERTY and TRANCHELL 2008; LE MARE 2008; RANSOM 2005; RAYNOLDS 2009; REDFERN and SNEDKER 2002; SMITH and BARRIENTOS 2005; TALLONTIRE 2002; ZANASI and PALUAN 2007).

Opportunities for increased distribution such as rising sales volumes (e.g. COWE and WILLIAMS 2000) and risks such as the erosion of the label's identity are weighed up in the discussion.

To start with the opportunities, REDFERN and SNEDKER (2002, p. 2f.) recommend and support the expansion into the mainstream to scale up and improve the ability to influence markets. They define mainstream as selling Fair Trade products in conventional supermarkets and discounters and supporting the application of Fair Trade values and practices by conventional firms. There are several routes for Fair Trade products to enter the mainstream market: Branded Fair Trade products from 100 % Fair Trade companies such as Gepa in Germany, The Day Chocolate Company and Cafedirect in Great Britain, can be sold in conventional supermarkets. All products from these companies carry the Fair Trade mark. Another possibility for retailers is to launch their own Fair Trade products such as Lidl ('Fairglobe') or Starbucks and to only sell these. Between these poles there is a range of other possibilities to enter the mainstream (see e.g. DOHERTY and TRANCHELL 2008, p. 9). SMITH and BARRIENTOS (2005, p. 197) also stress the benefits resulting from an increased availability of Fair Trade products in supermarkets; when more consumers are given the opportunity to buy Fair Trade products, the number of Fair Trade producers and workers in developing countries who benefit from the participation in Fair Trade can increase.

Reservations are expressed regarding the new partners entering the Fair Trade supply chain. According to TALLONTIRE (2002, p. 21), the cooperation with mainstream retailers goes against the aim of Fair Trade to change trading relationships. A similar concern is voiced by RANSOM (2005) who points out that awarding the Fair Trade label to large corporations may demonstrate inconsistent behaviour; on the one hand, they are a major cause of the trade conditions producers in the South struggle with and, on the other hand, they want to adorn themselves with borrowed plumes of Fair Trade. This is what has been criticized by parts of the Fair Trade community (in particular the worldshops) in Germany when the German discounter Lidl started selling Fair Trade products under their own label 'Fairglobe' in 2006. At that point in time, Lidl was not known for employee-friendly working conditions but was accused of exploiting their staff. Some viewed in the contradiction between the Fair Trade requirements for producers and the working conditions in the retail outlets in Germany as a lack of credibility (DER SPIEGEL 2006). Furthermore, RANSOM (2005) also gives voice to the concern that in 2003 some supermarkets in Great Britain were accused of overcharging for Fair Trade products. It was claimed that the supermarkets kept much of the price premium by consumers for themselves which is not the point of the premium.

4.2.4.2 Who benefits from higher retail prices of Fair Trade products?

One important critique inspiring this thesis is that the Fair Trade movement and especially FLO and its system are inefficient (the question of efficacy is not linked to this topic as it may be that studies focussing only on the issue of efficiency oversee important components of Fair Trade in comparison to donations). BOOTH and WHETSTONE (2007, p. 7) argue that around 40 % of the fee wholesalers pay to use the Fair Trade label is not used to conduct educational activities, licensing and product development but to cover the expenses of the organisation itself. BOOTH and WHETSTONE (2007, p. 7) claim that consumers are aware that such a high proportion of their paid price premium (wholesalers pass the cost of labelling use directly to the consumer) is spent on marketing and is not used to directly help the poor. As mentioned in the introduction of the thesis, STEINRÜCKEN (2004) points out the efficiency gap between the Max Havelaar Foundation Switzerland and the charity organisation Bread for the World, whereby the latter works more efficiently than the former. To the author's knowledge there is no study available providing figures with respect to the efficiency with which 1 € additionally spent for a Fair Trade coffee in a supermarket reaches the producer. Accordingly, the first approximation is given in Table 3. Table 3 shows different Fair Trade coffees sold by the most important Fair Trade brand Gepa in Germany in 2007. The information on prices, country of origin, etc. were found on the homepage of Gepa. The highest price paid for a Fair Trade coffee is for washed Arabica. Even though not all coffees under investigation are 100 % Arabica and it is not known whether the coffee was washed or not, this price is taken as the maximum price which has been paid since June 2006 to Fair Trade coffee producers. The organic premium which is paid for organic coffees is also taken into account. The table reveals that a) there is a slight difference between the average price per 100 g Fair Trade coffee due to the labelling of country of origin and coffee blends (which are cheaper) and b) that the Fair Trade minimum price producers receive for their coffee is a maximum of 20 % of the price consumers pay for a Fair Trade coffee in the supermarket. In March 2007 the average retail price for coffee was 0.73 / 100 g (DEUTSCHER KAFFEEVERBAND 2007, p. 19). The difference between the average Gepa Fair Trade coffee price and the average retail price (which also contains the Fair Trade coffees but can be neglected due to the small market shares of Fair Trade and organic coffees) amounts to 0.55 € / 100 g. This implies that around 50 % of the money paid additionally for the[70] Fair Trade Gepa coffee goes to the producer.

[70] The five studies presented in section C discuss German consumers' assumptions regarding how much money from each additionally spent Euro for ethical products is actually spent on the cause/reaches the producer.

Three articles and studies deal with the distribution of benefits along the Fair Trade supply chain focussing on the role of retailers and on how much profit they make by selling Fair Trade products. STECKLOW and WHITE (2004) find that supermarket chains gain more from Fair Trade than the producers: Sainsbury´s, for example, sells Fair Trade Bananas at a price four times higher than conventional ones. The producers received 0.16 US $, the retailer 0.55 US $ and Sainsbury's 2 US $. MENDOZA and BASTIAENSEN (2003) compare Nestlé's and Cafédirect´s coffee chain finding that only 0.04 € of the 0.34 € that Fair Trade coffee costs more at the retail price go to the producer. The identified reasons were advertising costs and licences. ZEHNER (2002) compared Starbucks Fair Trade and conventional coffee detecting that 43 % of the higher price go to the producers while 39 % were Starbucks margins. The margin retailers' gain by selling Fair Trade products is part of the efficiency discussion.

Table 3: Maximum percentage of Fair Trade retail price reaching the Fair Trade producer in Germany in 2007

Part A								Part B		Part C
Name	Organic	Coffee type	Country of origin	Blend	Volume [g]	Price [€]	Price per 100 g [€]	Fair Trade minimum price for washed Arabica per 100g including Fair Trade premium [€] [a]	Organic premium per 100g [€]	Percentage of retail price reaching the producer [%]
Café Columbia	yes	100 % Arabica	Colombia	no	250	3.49	1.40	0.23	0.04	0.19
Café Monte de Oro	no	100 % Arabica	Costa Rica	no	250	3.29	1.32	0.23	0.00	0.18
Café Orgánico	yes	n.s.	Mexico	no	500	6.79	1.36	0.23	0.04	0.20
Café Orgánico	yes	100 % Arabica	Mexico	no	250	3.49	1.40	0.23	0.04	0.19
Nicaragua Kaffee Öko	yes	100 % Arabica	Nicaragua	no	250	3.49	1.40	0.23	0.04	0.19
						Sum	6.86	0.23		
						Average	**1.37**	0.23		0.17
Bio Café Esperanza	yes	100 % Arabica	n.s.	yes	250	3.19	1.28	0.23	0.04	0.21
Bio Café Sereno	yes	100 % Arabica	n.s.	yes	250	3.69	1.48	0.23	0.04	0.18
Café Aha	no	Arabica + Robusta	n.s.	yes	500	5.49	1.10	0.21	0.00	0.19
Café Aymara Öko	yes	100 % Arabica	n.s.	yes	500	6.49	1.30	0.21	0.04	0.19
Café Camino	no	100 % Arabica	n.s.	yes	250	2.99	1.20	0.21	0.00	0.17
CaféPlus	yes	n.s.	n.s.	yes	250	3.49	1.40	0.21	0.04	0.18
Milde Mischung	no	100 % Arabica	n.s.	yes	500	5.99	1.20	0.21	0.00	0.17
						Sum	8.94	0.21		
						Average	**1.28**	0.21		0.16

n.s.: not specified.

[a] Assumption: one pound = 453g.

Source : author's compilation. For German Fair Trade coffees (Part A of the table): author's market observation, http://www.gepa.de/htdocs/vertrieb/agenda_kaffee.html#, 16.06.2007. Source for Fair Trade minimum prices (Part B of the table): FLO (2007b, p. 5). Fair Trade Prices of FLO for coffee since 01.06.07. Price for washed Arabica per pound FOB port of origin: 1.21 US $. With exchange rate of 2006: 1 € = 1.2556 $. This leads to a price of 0.9637 € / per pound washed Arabica FOB port of origin. One pound is equal to 453 g. Therefore, the price for 100 g washed Arabica FOB port of origin is 0.21 €. Source Part C: author' calculation.

4.2.4.3 Impact of certification at the producer level – The findings of case studies

In the introduction, it was mentioned that Fair Trade seeks to influence several aspects of development, including the development of market relations and access, economic, and institutional development, social and sustainable development, poverty reduction as well as gender equality. This chapter focuses on the impact on producers' livelihood. For the impact on organisations as well as consumers, see e.g. BECCHETTI et al. (2003, p. 3)[71]. The impact on sustainability was discussed in 4.1.4. and 4.2.3.

Measuring the impact of Fair Trade is, according to TALLONTIRE (2002), one of the challenges the Fair Trade movement faces. Up to now only few independent scientific studies on the impacts of Fair Trade on the producers have been available (PAUL 2005, p. 135). Moreover, mostly case studies have been used to assess the impact on Fair Trade certification at the producer level. The first initiative for developing indicators measuring costs and benefits of certification at the farm level was established by the Committee on Sustainability Assessment (COSA) in 2007. 500 pilot projects in Africa and Latin America are assessed (COSA 2007). In addition, the International Social and Environmental Accreditation and Labelling Alliance (ISEAL Alliance[72]) is assisting with the development of a 'Code of Good Practice for Measuring the Impacts of Standards Systems'. The code will be an international reference for how environmental and social standards systems can consistently evaluate the impacts of their effort (ISEAL 2008a).

The broad study literature regarding the impact of Fair Trade on the above-mentioned aspects of development has been reviewed by DANKERS (2003), TALLONTIRE (2002), BECCHETTI and COSTANTINO (2006) and LE MARE (2008). It became evident that the outcomes of the studies were diverse and complex (see also MURRAY et al. 2006, p. 1; VALKILA 2009, p. 3018). Among other reasons, this is due to the difficulty in measuring the impact and benefits of Fair Trade on poverty alleviation because tracing back material and nonmaterial benefits to single causes, such as the participation in the Fair Trade network, possibly overlaps with the participation in organic production (RAYNOLDS 2002, p. 1937f.).

---

[71] BECCHETTI et al. (2003, p. 3) showed that Fair Trade products are able to generate a Pareto improvement for both ethically concerned and not concerned consumers. Furthermore, their findings indicate that additional positive welfare effects arise in northern markets when other market actors imitate the ethical concept of Fair Trade sellers.

[72] ISEAL Alliance was founded in 2000 by FLO, Forest Stewardship Council (FSC), International Federation of Organic Agriculture Movements (IFOAM), International Organic Accreditation Service (IOAS), Marine Aquarium Council (MAC), Marine Stewardship Council (MSC), Rainforest Alliance, Social Accountability International (SAI) (ISEAL 2008b).

Most of the reviewed studies in LE MARE (2008, p. 1925; 1937) found that Fair Trade has a significant impact on economic and social aspects of development at the level of the individual producer as well as at the level of organisations. LE MARE (2008, p. 1925) systematised the possible effects of participation in the Fair Trade network on producers and distinguished six impact areas. First, market related benefits such as the provision of credit and market information and the improvement of the supplier's competence. Second, institutional benefits which result from the development of local, sustainable institutions with improved institutional capacity. These institutions help the producers to diversify their investments and activities as well as to improve the product quality and market access. Third, economic and poverty benefits which include not only increased income but also income security, higher food consumption, lower child mortality and more schooling. Fourth, social development benefits such as an increase in confidence, self-esteem and social capital as well as the development of new business skills. Fifth, benefits regarding gender equality and sixth, sustainable development benefits. The implementation of gender issues, such as gender equality and women's empowerment, was hardly achieved through Fair Trade networks. LE MARE (2008, p. 1935) mentions nine studies (see e.g. LYON 2007, p. 109; RICE 2010) which identify a lack of gender equality within Fair Trade societies and networks. For example, incomes or workload are not equally distributed between men and women in Fair Trade communities (LE MARE 2008, p. 1935) and men are overrepresented (UTTING-CHAMORRO 2005, p. 595).

According to the review of LE MARE (2008, p. 1925), the last two areas (gender and sustainability) have shown little evidence of success and the self-set targets are seldom reached at the level of the individual producer. However, Fair Trade has significantly increased assets and helped individuals to escape poverty. Furthermore, Fair Trade has increased the capacity to diversify and improve livelihoods.

Different studies (e.g. DANKERS 2003, p. 63; GIOVANNUCCI and KOEKOEK 2003, p. 32ff.; BACON 2005; RONCHI 2002b) found that especially with regard to the fostering of sustainable commercial organisations, Fair Trade networks are successful. Other valuable features include, from the perspective of coffee producers, better self-organisation and capacity building skills which lead to an improved bargaining position, superior credit worthiness, better market access and market information as well as quality improvements. In particular, the last point of vulnerability reduction shows the indirect effects Fair Trade certification can have.

The most obvious potential benefit of Fair Trade is the pricing scheme. The guaranteed minimum price directly increases income and many studies have found that price risks are reduced which in turn increases resilience to external shocks and reduces farmers' livelihood vulnerability (BACON 2005, p. 506; LYON 2007, p. 103; RAYNOLDS 2002, p. 18). The effect of the price premium (which is e.g. used to finance educational projects) on producers' living standard is higher than the effect of the minimum price and longer term (DANKERS 2003, p. 64). BECCHETTI and CONSTATINO (2006) found that Fair Trade improved producers' livelihood; the farmers had relatively higher expenditures for food, a higher dietary quality, their children faced a lower mortality and a higher level of schooling. One interesting finding across all studies is that the Fair Trade price premium and its effect on income generation is only one of the positive impacts of the Fair Trade system (DANKERS 2003, p. 63). Nevertheless, the impact of the price premium on improving farmers' income is still marginal; the demand side and the small market share of Fair Trade have been identified as the restricting factor (KLEINERT 2000, p. 106). Up to now, Fair Trade has remained a niche market and the demand for Fair Trade products is lower than the supply. As a result only a low fraction of the total Fair Trade certified production – figures deviate between 42 % (BECCHETTI and COSTANTINO 2006, p. 5) and 20 % (RENARD 2005, p. 427) – can be sold under Fair Trade conditions and the label (DANKERS 2003, p. 64; BACON 2005, p. 507; MURADIAN and PELUPESSY 2005, p. 2033; LIEBIG and SAUTTER 2000, p. 184). Accordingly, Fair Trade producers highly rely and are therefore dependant on the sympathy of consumers and their WTP a premium for the respective products (OSMUNDSVÅG 2007, p. 179).

VALKILA (2009, p. 3023) had a closer look at the issue of short-term pre-financing as well as at advance payments for poor coffee farmers and found that Fair Trade performed worse than conventional, mainstream markets. With respect to working conditions, Valkila (2009, p. 3024) found that in Nicaragua Fair Trade organic coffee production was not superior to the working conditions on coffee farms in general. And regarding the potential to assist marginalised producers to overcome the poverty trap, VALKILA (2009) also paints a less positive picture. His results show that Fair Trade organic production raises the income of the researched small-scale coffee farmers in Nicaragua only "when low-intensity organic farming is an alternative to low-intensity conventional farming" (VALKILA 2009, p. 3018). As yields of low-intensity organic farming are small, most of the farmers remained in poverty. In the case of higher intensive farming, the economic benefits of Fair Trade organic production mainly depend on prices in the conventional market.

UTTING-CHAMORRO (2005, p. 584) found the impact of Fair Trade on social development (e.g. growing confidence and self-respect) to be limited due to wider societal problems such as a lack of governmental support for small-scale farmers or volatile commodity. In order to overcome the shortcomings, UTTING-CHAMORRO (2005, p. 597) proposes that Fair Trade organisations, NGOs and other social organisations work more closely together. This would integrate Fair Trade into the broader environment of traditional development activities as they are supported by charity organisations and NGOs. But this solution would mean that social problems would be privatised to a certain extent, i.e. not discussed and solved by policy makers.

An important point DANKERS (2003, p. 64) raises is that knowledge regarding the Fair Trade principles is limited especially in large cooperatives. This might be a problem with regard to one primary goal of Fair Trade – the democratic control of the business by its members. According to DANKERS (2003, p. 64) knowledge is more pronounced when organic and Fair Trade production are present because certification controls are more individual and the farmers are more aware of the labelling requirements.

To conclude, this review of impact studies is in line with the findings of PIEPEL et al. (2000, p. 279) as well as RAYNOLDS' (2002, p. 9; 14) exploration of existing Fair Trade coffee literature up to 2002. These authors found that especially the case studies reveal that the extent to which Fair Trade has a positive impact on farmers' livelihood and can be considered successful is very much dependant on 1) national and global policies, 2) the organisation and qualities of the Fair Trade organisations (here duration, intensity and amount of marketing support for the Fair Trade goods should be mentioned), and 3) the individual characteristics of the producers, such as ideological commitment. Accordingly, proof is lacking that Fair Trade is of immediate net benefit to the poor in general (BOOTH and WHETSTONE 2007, p. 2). It is therefore questionable whether Fair Trade business relationships are able to bring about sustainable changes (PIEPEL et al. 2000, p. 279). Therefore, PIEPEL et al. (2000, p. 279f.) regard Fair Trade as a complement and not as an alternative to classical developmental aid which is provided by e.g. church organisations or NGOs.

4.2.5 Shortcomings and limitations of Fair Trade [73]

The review of impact studies has demonstrated that Fair Trade is, under certain circumstances, able to create different benefits for farmers but that these benefits are not

[73] For the critique on CrM, see the respective papers in the thesis.

obtained by merely participating in the Fair Trade network. In fact, there are many (possible) limitations of Fair Trade. In addition to the impact on producers and producer organisations, several shortcomings and limitations of Fair Trade are discussed in the literature. Here different argumentation lines are found: economic (e.g. the allocation effect of price premiums and how social standards might lead to market distortions) versus sociology (e.g. the question whether actors have equal rights).

From an economic point of view, the question as to whether Fair Trade supports and subsidises inefficient or sub-standard small-scale producers is of importance (LECLAIR 2002, p. 955; LE MARE 2008, p. 1928; RAYNOLDS 2002, p. 17). The voluntary price premiums can act as incentive to stay in the market of these products instead of looking for other economic prospects and for different, conventional distribution channels. This means that voluntary price premiums might prevent the price from fulfilling its allocation role and regulating supply and demand. Overproduction as well as a lack of diversification might be the results (PIEPEL et al. 2000, p. 292f.). Studies (see e.g. RONCHI 2006, p. 50) have tried to debilitate this critique and show that certification helps Fair Trade producers to become more efficient and better able to compete with more powerful companies.

Another criticism is that labels which are based on social standards might have protectionist effects and hinder developing countries from exporting in industrialised countries (OSMUNDSVÅG 2007, p. 179).

Furthermore, the question of dependency is still hanging in the air: Do the desired long-term trading partnerships create dependency and stand in contradiction to the creation of self-sufficient producer groups (TALLONTIRE 2002, p. 14)? In this context, dependency on the market partner in the industrialised country should be considered as well as the economic dependence on agricultural products which results from Fair Trade's focus on these products. In particular, the price premium causes artificially increased commodity prices which motivate producers to produce the respective products.

Another question concerns who is allowed to participate in Fair Trade and who is excluded from the possible benefits. This query is often not answered in favour of the most vulnerable groups. Often the poorest lack access to required assets like social capital, hence, the requirements for participating (e.g. organisation in groups or the implementation of certain quality standards) cannot be fulfilled. Therefore, the poorest are in fact often excluded from Fair Trade (NICHOLLS and OPAL 2005, p. 214). Because of the small market sales, selective support of producers who have the chance to participate in the Fair Trade system takes place which LECLAIR (2002, p. 955) considers to be a strong injustice. Distributional equity is not given and those outside the system are disadvantaged.

Other points Fair Trade is criticised for are that the rules, norms and values of the Fair Trade scheme are grounded in Northern cultures which have different priorities and experiences than Southern Fair Trade producers or consumers. Furthermore, it is claimed that the South is not equally represented in the FLO system (DE REGIL 2007, p. 16; LE MARE 2008, p. 1924). The ongoing professionalisation and centralisation as well as the fact that especially in the FLO decision making process, regional assemblies play only a consultative role are reasons why, voices critical of the work of FLO can be heard (RENARD 2005, p. 425). Furthermore, LIEBIG and SAUTTER (2000, p. 184) criticise that the Fair Trade movement concentrates on the realisation of individual moral beliefs such as compassion, helpfulness, and solidarity principles instead of elaborating a concept of trade and development highlighting the regulatory framework of political and trade action.

4.2.6 Similarities and differences between Fair Trade and aid[74]

The paragraph on impact studies revealed that Fair Trade does not necessarily achieve its self-imposed goals. But if the advantages of Fair Trade, which are expected by consumers, do not exist without doubt, the question about similarities and differences between Fair Trade and charitable giving can be posed. This question is also of interest as the Fair Trade movement places emphasis on the declaration that Fair Trade is not aid (see e.g. GOODMAN 2004, p. 903).[75] The description of Fair Trade in UTTING-CHAMORRO (2005, p. 585) is therefore exemplary for a large part of the movement:

> "Fair trade is an 'alternative trade' initiative promoting a different approach both to the conventional global trading system (free trade) and to development systems (protectionism and development aid) through the central philosophy of 'trade-not-aid'. It is a non-charity concept that 'challenges the orthodoxy of business practices . . . not simply by campaigning but by offering this alternative working model as an example".

The underlying idea is that trade is a better method than aid to help poor countries to develop (OSMUNDSVÅG 2007, p. 169). At the same time, Fair Trade "is driven by many of the same motivations" which are found behind charity (OSMUNDSVÅG 2007, p. 169; see also PAUL

[74] For a comparison with free trade scenarios, see MASELAND and DE VAAL (2002) and PARRISH et al. (2005). For example, PARRISH et al. (2005) state that Fair Trade and free trade interventions are less contradicting as usually assumed and that a comparison of both can only be meaningful if it is based on the same market conditions. They base this statement on their findings from a field study in Tanzania.

[75] The slogan 'trade not aid' is well known (CHAMBOLLE and PORET 2007, p. 1; OSMUNDSVÅG 2007, p. 169).

2005, p. 123). It has, furthermore, characteristics of a gift e.g. as traders are by prefinancing more engaged in the trading relationship than it is the case in conventional trading systems (Fisher 2007, p. 80). And also as OSMUNDSVÅG (2007, p. 169) points out, producer empowerment can no longer be considered to be the core difference between aid and Fair Trade in the 21th century since many charity organisations also emphasise their objective to promote empowerment by their aid (OSMUNDSVÅG 2007, p. 169). And as TALLONTIRE (2002, p. 12) says: Fair Trade is a development, and at the same time, a business instrument.

The central objective of today's aid programmes is poverty reduction (and no longer development typically construed as GDP growth) (COLLIER and DOLLAR 2004, p. F245; MOSLEY et al. 2004, p. F217). Economic growth is still an important means for poverty reduction but nowadays it is interpreted as pro-poor (OECD 2007a, p. 11; MOSLEY et al. 2004, p. F217). There is a large donor community: World Bank, OECD, governmental aid agencies, NGOs. Accordingly, there is a plurality of kinds of aid: grants, capital subscriptions, export credits, loans or other long-term capital, development lending capital, etc. (OECD 2007d). Furthermore, the sector of destination such as education, health, trade policy, agriculture and multisector such as environmental purposes, etc.[76] can be distinguished. Correspondingly, not all aid has an impact on growth and, more generally, each type of aid has other impacts (RADELET et al. 2005).

The OECD Development Assistance Committee (DAC)[77] developed several guidelines on poverty reduction, aid effectiveness, sustainable development, strengthening trade capacity for development, on gender equality and empowerment, capacity building, etc. to advise and assist its members in the accomplishment of their development co-operation programmes (DAC 2007a). DAC and its guidelines are important for the aid discussion because the 23 members of DAC provide more than 90% of the world's total public development assistance and World Bank and the United Nations cooperate with DAC (OECD 2007a, p. 2).

In 2005 DAC members spent in total 106.777 million US \$[78] for development assistance (OECD 2007b). Major purposes (according to the total DAC members' amount of assistance) in 2005 were social and administrative infrastructure (30.5 %), action relating to debt

---

[76] The OECD classification by sector of destination is available at http://www.oecd.org/document/21/0,3343,en_2825_495602_1914325_1_1_1_1,00.html, [accessed 07-11-13].

[77] DAC (2007b) describes itself as "a key forum of major bilateral donors [which] (...) work together to increase the effectiveness of their common efforts to support sustainable development".

[78] Between 2000 and 2005, the monetary amount of development assistance was considerable lower: 2000: 53 billion, 2001: 52 billion, 2002: 58 billion, 2003: 69 billion, 2004: 79 billion US \$ (DAC 2007c).

(27.5 %), economic infrastructure (10.6) and humanitarian aid (100 %) (OECD 2007c). Today three predominating views on aid can be distinguished (RADELET et al. 2005). First, 'aid has no effect on growth, and may actually undermine growth' (see e.g. BOONE 1996, p. 289; Gibson et al. 2001, p. 2f.). Second, 'aid has a positive relationship with growth on average (although not in every country), but with diminishing returns' (see e.g. DALGAARD and HANSEN and SCHRADER (2001, p. 17). Third, 'aid has a conditional relationship with growth, helping to accelerate growth only under certain circumstances' (COLLIER and DOLLAR 2004, p. F267; RADELET et al. 2005 which give a good overview of the state of the art). After a certain kind of aid pessimism in the mid-1990s, recent studies show that aid is effective in poverty reduction conditionally on diverse circumstances (COLLIER and DOLLAR (2004, p. F267). For instance, GUILLAUMONT and LAAJAJA (2006, p. 1) ascertained that aid is able to reduce the harmful effects of vulnerability on growth. One reason is aid has a stabilising impact, regardless of whether the aid is pro-cyclical or contra-cyclical in relation to exogenous flows like exports. This effect is strongest in LDC which are highly vulnerable (GUILLAUMONT 2007, p. 18). Two positive effects of aid on poverty reduction should be mentioned: aid improves growth (which is an important factor of poverty reduction) and makes the growth stable which is especially important for poor people (GUILLAUMONT 2007, p. 19). Aid can have an impact on the developing countries as a whole when it directly increases public resources (COLLIER and DOLLAR 2004, p. F263) or on a regional or family level. This depends on the donor and its goals. Not surprisingly, there is a huge debate on how to best allocate aid for poverty reduction, which criteria should be taken into account, how aid affects the risk of conflict, the important of good governance and corruption, etc. (COLLIER and DOLLAR 2004, p. F245ff.). Nevertheless, mostly the allocation of the "aid budget is a political process" (COLLIER and DOLLAR 2004, p. F267). According to this, the priorities of the donors have changed. For example, since 1995 donors have given more advertence to corruption (COLLIER and DOLLAR 2004, p. F263). Interestingly COLLIER and DOLLAR (2004, p. F263) state that there is no "systematic research on the effects of aid on popular participation". This can be an indication that participation and democratic processes are not as important for the donor community as it is for Fair Trade actors. Nevertheless, the studies of COLLIER (1999, 2000) and RODRIK (1999) emphasise the positive effect democracy has on growth rate, the success of aid projects and wages (COLLIER and DOLLAR 2004, p. F264).

This overview illustrates that in terms of volume Fair Trade (see chapter 4.1.2) is less important than aid. Nevertheless, the question as to whether Fair Trade is superior to aid or other trade initiatives in terms of cost effectiveness is still an open one (TALLONTIRE 2002, p. 17). The following paragraph is a first trial to approach this question.

The economics of the systems

The efficiency of Fair Trade can be analysed from different perspectives, such as philanthropy (LECLAIR 2003) and trade theory (MASELAND and DE VAAL 2002). Furthermore, the understanding of efficiency can vary from paper to paper as HAYES (2006, p. 447) indicates. HAYES (2006, p. 447) observes that researchers who use economic theory for the assessment of Fair Trade define the term 'efficiency' either as the optimal allocation of given resources or technical efficiency in production. To analyse the economics of the systems, simplification is common. A complete assessment of the different aspects of Fair Trade, as discussed in the chapter reviewing the impact studies, is not carried out. Most of the simplification concerns the pricing issue of Fair Trade.

HAYES (2006, p. 465) emphasises that the Fair Trade price premium acts as and is equivalent to a contribution and therefore a donation to the local Fair Trade organisation. Therefore, the question can be raised as to "the effectiveness of Fair Trade organisations relative to donor agencies" which are both alternative channels for poverty alleviation and welfare changes (HAYES 2006, p. 465).

Similarly, LECLEAR (2002) and MASELAND and DE VAAL (2002) define and reduce Fair Trade for analytical purposes as the payment of a price premium over the market price even though their analytic perspectives differ. HAYES (2006), however, manages to analyse Fair Trade without including the payment of a price premium by only deriving the economic benefit of Fair Trade from the improved competition for labour and the long-term access to credit and product markets. For his analysis of the economic efficiency of Fair Trade, HAYES (2006) used the theory of competitive equilibrium and Keynes' concept of involuntary unemployment. HAYES (2006, p. 465) argues that the understanding of the labour supply decision of Fair Trade farmers is a trade-off between market and inferior domestic work and not a trade-off between labour and leisure (see LECLAIR 2002). In this context, HAYES (2006, p. 454ff.) uses the theory of employer monopsony based on the key assumption that the number of employers in a given market is fixed to identify the economic effect of Fair Trade organisations in local markets. From this perspective Fair Trade can be understood as an alternative private sector solution against employer monopsony when independent producers or workers are not able to form labour unions. Fair Trade enables producer groups to compete in the product market. Fair Trade then leads to the elimination of monopoly rents in local markets. HAYES (2006, p. 447; 466) concludes that Fair Trade is under this assumption economically efficient and improves welfare in any imaginable situation and when there is aggregate involuntary redundancy. Fair Trade thus compensates for a lack of competition in the markets, faced by the households, by strengthening competition for labour.

LECLAIR (2002, p. 954) shows that the support of marginalised farmers by means of Fair Trade product purchases is inferior to direct payments to the farmers, if the impacts of Fair Trade on livelihoods are restricted to the price premium. He concludes that donations in form of direct cash payments increase the farmers' income to the same particular level as subsidisation through sales promotion without reducing the time for household activities which he calls leisure time. For his analysis of the labour supply, he assumes that households face a trade-off between work and leisure. Furthermore, he assumes that the Fair Trade premium places a premium on work and not on leisure. Finally, he assumes that a household would derive the same welfare from a lump-sum donation which is equivalent to the income effect of the price premium. According to these assumptions, price subsidies in form of Fair Trade premiums involve a social cost of inefficient allocation and are therefore not efficient (LECLAIR 2002, p. 955).

At least two of the assumptions can be discussed controversially and if they are rejected the analysis leads to a different result. First, the effect of the price premium: why should a household face such an indifference curve (indicating the level of utility a household derives from leisure and income) that the price premium acts as an incentive to work more and increase household income instead of working as much is needed in order to reach the same income level as before? This would increase leisure which can be used for e.g. schooling which is an investment in the future. Second, how can LECLAIR (2002) be sure that the welfare derived from a donation is the same as that derived from the payment of a higher price? Welfare from a producer's perspective might not only be understood in terms of economic welfare. The feelings and self-respect resulting from a donation and a higher price for work might be different. The work of LECLAIR (2002) places rigid assumptions on the form of the household's indifference curve as well as the position and shift of the budget line as is clarified in the following graphs in Figure 9.

Figure 9: Subsidisation versus direct payments: the effect on leisure

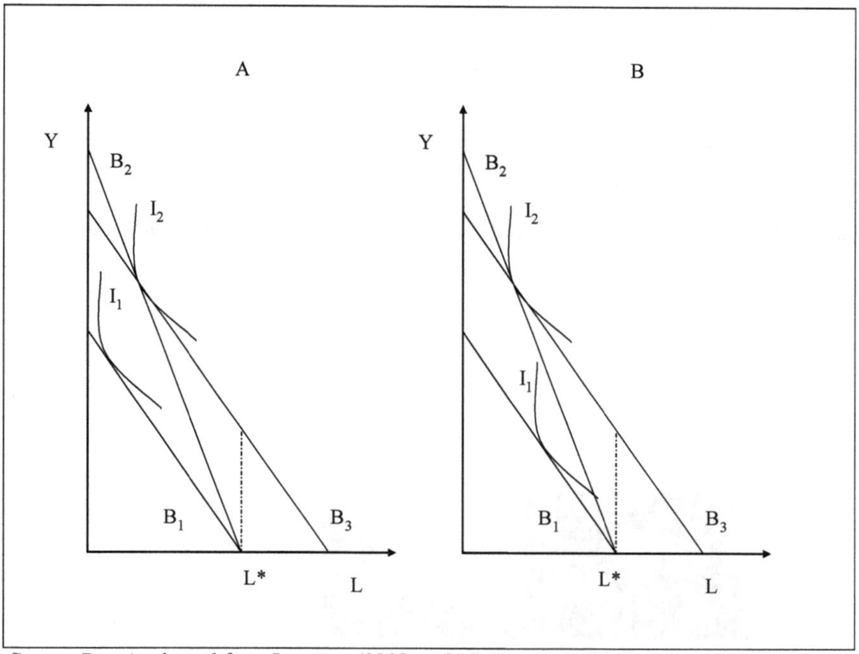

Source: Part A adopted from LECLAIR (2002, p. 954); Part B: author's illustration.

In part A of Figure 9 a household derives utility from leisure L and income Y along the budget line B_1. The budget line will shift to B_3 when a lump-sum donation is given to the household. A price increase due to the Fair Trade premium will shift the budget line along the vertical axis leading to relatively more income, more leisure and less labour. In part B of Figure 9 the same increase in income leads to less leisure and more labour because the household in part B faces a different indifference curve I_1 than the household in part A. L* indicates the point where the household decides to not work but only use the approximately 16 hours a day which are not used for eating and sleeping for leisure. This point indicates the absence of any labour. In both parts of Figure 9, a donation produces a positive income which leads to budget line B_3. From a producer's perspective the question as to whether a price increase due to Fair Trade certification is superior or not to a lump-sum donation cannot be answered without making generalisations and assumptions about the indifference curves. Therefore, research analysing different producers' preferences should be undertaken.

The use of a farm-household model[79], which in a modified form is used by LECLAIR (2002), and a simple comparison of a price support versus direct payments, reveal that direct payments (donations) are superior to price stabilisation (Fair Trade). (Here again Fair Trade impacts are reduced to the income effect of the price premium.) Assuming the household income is equal to the revenue of the sold products, the donation amount has to be equivalent to the amount of money resulting from the higher prices, as is shown in Figure 10.

Figure 10: Price support versus direct payments: the effect on quantity and costs

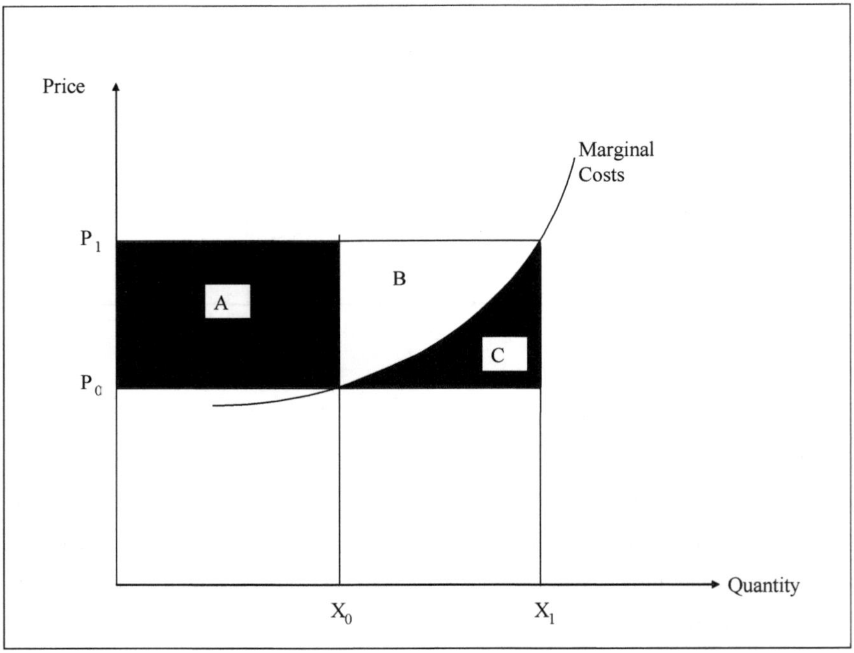

Source: author's illustration.

To increase income, direct payments to an amount of A and B are needed. Assuming that a household produces at the intercept of marginal cost and market price it would produce quantity x_0 at price p_0 in the reference situation. After a price increase to p_1 the household produces x_1 at p_1. Because the extended production is accompanied by increased production costs in the amount of C, the donation equivalent to the price support would be A and B and C. This means by purchasing Fair Trade products, consumers increase not only producers'

[79] See also KOESTER (1992, p. 83ff.) for the relationship between income, working time, leisure time and transformation curve.

income but also their supply. Accordingly, a part of the price premium goes in form of payments for production inputs away from the Fair Trade producers' income.

Other differences

Other differences between Fair Trade and aid can be found regarding the target group, the obligations of producers connected with the help, the feelings of producers, the benefits for the donor/the consumer of a Fair Trade product, as well as complementary and substitution effects on the macro and micro level[80]. LECLAIR's (2002, p. 955) comparison of Fair Trade and aid programmes shows that aid is mainly spread out over whole populations whereas Fair Trade is concentrated on specific (producer) groups. But, in this point LECLAIR (2002) ignores that charity organisations with a focus on developmental issues have developed special programmes for specific countries, groups of persons and individual purposes (e.g. water security, health insurance, women, etc.). Therefore, this difference can hardly be considered (if it ever was) a distinguishing feature. A distinct difference between Fair Trade production and donations is that, in contrast to recipients of charity, Fair Trade producers perform up-front services (e.g. guarantee production without child labour) and receive the higher product price for their work while the recipients of charity are neither active beforehand nor afterwards. It may also be that producers attach an intrinsic weight to the money earned by selling products under the Fair Trade certification scheme compared to money received from donations. From a consumer perspective, the two systems differ as in the case of Fair Trade the consumer receives a commodity and the 'warm glow' while a donation to a charitable organisation only creates a 'warm glow' (LECLAIR 2002, p. 954). LECLAIR (2002) states furthermore that traditional production methods in developing countries are preserved by Fair Trade and not by aid. This preservation is perceived as a value as such.

This section shows that the question as to whether Fair Trade is efficient as such and more efficient than donations in particular depends on the reference system and the specific assumptions which are made. In some cases, both forms of ethical behaviour supplement each other. Charitable organisations also use donations e.g. for financing the certification costs of Fair Trade producer groups to assist them to overcome the aid dependency mentioned in SUWA-EISENMANN and VERDIER (2007, p. 485) by facilitating market access.

[80] For a deeper insight into this, see SUWA-EISENMANN and VERDIER (2007).

4.3 Charitable Giving

Charitable giving can be defined as "the voluntary one-way transfer of economic goods to individuals or organizations outside the family unit" (REECE 1979, p. 142). Donations are not only voluntary[81] but also free from consideration (HEIDBÜCHEL 2000, p. 4). Many forms of donations are possible ranging from the transfer of money, such as a small amount of money given in church's offertory box, neighbourly help where time and services are provided, a donation of food and clothes or a blood donation for common welfare oriented purposes (HEIDBÜCHEL 2000, p. 4). Other kind of donations include sponsorships to foundations, membership fees, church tax, donations from companies (also sponsoring) and endowments after death.

In the year 2000 WEBB et al. (2000, p. 300) still maintained that only "little is known about individuals' charitable attitudes". This is observable even though experts in many disciplines, such as researchers, politicians and charity practitioners, are interested knowing more about charitable attitudes[82]. Scientists need the information to be able to develop an adequate theory of charitable giving and donation behaviour, politicians require the information to base their decisions about taxation of NGOs and resource allocation to social challenges and nonprofit practitioners depend on the measures of attitudes to address donors in an efficient way (WEBB et al. 2000, p. 300).

A distinction between habitual and spontaneous or impulse donations can be made (MEULEMANN and BECKERS 2003, p. 39). In the special case of monetary donations, MAYERL (2006, p. 2) defines continuous donation fees as well as single donations not related to specific events, such as catastrophes or wars, as habitual donations. On the other hand, impulse donations are defined as one-time donations made in response to catastrophes and other unique events.[83]

4.3.1 Motivations for charitable giving

Generally spoken, it can be differentiated between studies concentrating on single aspects of charitable giving and those trying to explain charitable giving and donation motives based on

[81] In Germany parts of lottery and civil penalties earnings are given to the social sector. But civil penalties and lottery earnings cannot be regarded as donations of private people because they do not meet the criteria of voluntariness. They amount to about 2 billion € each in Germany (WEBER and BUDDEMEIER 2008).

[82] For an overview of attitudes and attitude change, see e.g. OLSON and ZANNA (1993); WEBB et al. (2000, p. 307).

[83] In survey 2 presented in chapter 6 of this thesis, no distinction is made between spontaneous and habitual donations to organisations for developmental aid.

broader theories, such as the theory of pro-social behaviour and altruism. The latter will be presented in the following while the former will presented at the end of the chapter.

4.3.1.1 Theoretical foundations

HEIDBÜCHEL (2000, p. 12f.) shows that because of different usage of the term altruism the distinction between altruism, other-related behaviour, other-regarding preferences and pro-social behaviour[84] is not always clear. They are often used as synonyms. Other relevant aspects discussed in the research on social behaviour are norms of social responsibility, inequity aversion, reciprocity as well as emotions and empathy (HEIDBÜCHEL 2000, p. 46f.; FEHR and SCHMIDT 2006, p. 649). Giving can furthermore be a result of sympathy, feelings of commitment, the belief in moral values[85], private benefits of the donor[86] such as prestige, the feeling of being good and generous and drawing a benefit out of one's own act of charity, pride in one's self-sacrifice or the membership in a group as a result of giving (ROSE-ACKERMAN 1996, p. 714). Accordingly ROSE-ACKERMAN (1996, p. 714) concludes that there are many underlying motivations for people to give and that these "are inextricably linked".[87]

These different approaches to explain preferences and motivations for charity will be highlighted and distinguished in the following section.

Pro-social behaviour can be categorised in direct and indirect activities. The immediate focus of direct pro-social activities is on a needy person. If pro-social behaviour is not aimed directly at the needy person but through a mediator, such as a charity organisation, this is

---

[84] For an overview of the theories of social behaviour, altruism and other-regarding preferences see e.g. FEHR and SCHMIDT (2006); HEIDBÜCHEL (2000) and RUSHTON and SORRENTINO (1981).

[85] A value can be defined as "a belief that some condition is preferable to its opposite" (SOLOMON 2009, p. 173). It is widely accepted that consumption activities are influenced by a person's set of values. Many services and products are purchased because consumers believe that these goods help to reach a value-related goal (SOLOMON 2009, p. 173). Different types of values can be distinguished: cultural values such as happiness or security, consumption-specific values like prompt service and convenient shopping, and product-specific values, for instance, durability and ease of use. There are values which can be considered universal values (health, freedom, wisdom, world peace). Their relative importance for individuals can vary. Besides these differences between individuals it is possible to define sets of core values exclusively defining a country like America. Among countries values systems differ (SOLOMON 2009, p. 176).
The three best known research approaches dealing with values are: The Rokeach Values Survey, The List of Values and The Means-End Chain Model. The Rokeach Values Survey is not widely used by marketing researchers because more and more small clusters of consumption microculture with different core values arise (SOLOMON 2009, p. 177). For a distinction between values, motivations and personal goals, see JOLIBERT and BAUMGARTNER (1997).

[86] The term donor comprises private persons, companies, organisations as well as members of voluntary organisations (HEIDBÜCHEL 2000, p. 8f.).

[87] As there are different reasons for giving, there are also different funding strategies to motivate people to give: emphasis on the donor's faith if religious beliefs are the reason, stressing the efficiency of the organisation if commitment is dominating, providing individual and touching stories if sympathy is the important motivation to give and the solicitation by friends and neighbours to address a person's individual welfare and to let them feel good ROSE-ACKERMAN (1996, p. 714).

referred to as an indirect activity[88]. Charitable donations are a form of indirect pro-social behaviour (HEIDBÜCHEL 2000, p. 14f.). But in contrast to support and help (which involve more physical commitment, travail, and expenditure of time) or intervention (i.e. personal commitment along with physical and social risks) donations are primarily about giving and waiving as well as the transfer of scare commodities such as money or in-kind contributions (see HEIDBÜCHEL 2000).

SEN (1977, p. 326ff.) distinguishes between sympathy and commitment which for him are two different concepts: sympathy exists if the dolour of others makes a person sorrowful; commitment is indicated by the feeling that something is wrong and the wish to change this but not by the feeling of personal compassion. Sympathy based behaviour is therefore to a certain extent egoistic, while commitment is not. SEN (1977, p. 327) finds a second difference between sympathy and commitment: sympathy links similar things (the welfare of different people) while commitment links different things, namely choice with "anticipated levels of welfare". For an example, see SEN (1977, p. 332).

Cooperative behaviour in e.g. family contexts leads to a situation in which an individual benefits from the influence of others. There are examples of e.g. blood donation in which individuals behave selflessly in the interest of other people. If an individual relates a certain weight with outcomes of other people, this is referred to as altruism. Empathy and social norms, such as fairness[89], reciprocity and social responsibility, are related to altruism. Congruently learning through punishment or reward is able to enhance altruistic behaviour. Charitable donations are related to altruism in economic psychology.

Three theories of other-regarding preferences

Three theories of other-regarding preferences can be distinguished to model and to consider non-purely self-oriented behaviour: First, models of social preferences. Second, models of interdependent preferences and third, models of intention-based reciprocity.

The model of social preferences assumes that an individual's utility function not only relies on one's own material payoff, but possibly also on the allocation of resources within the reference group. This means people's preferences are created by their own and other people's consumption levels and that an individual's utility is maximised with respect to income restrictions. Given these social preferences, all individuals are assumed to behave rationally.

---

[88] Charitable organisations (religious, non-profit, beneficent) collect money, clothes, blood etc. and use it for supporting needy persons, the solution of current problems and the administration costs of the organisation.

[89] For a theory of fairness, competition and cooperation, see FEHR and SCHMIDT (1999).

The first to try to integrate the meaning which the welfare of others has for the individual into the personal utility function was BECKER (1974). BECKER (1974, p. 1063; 1090) was also the first to introduce social interactions into the modern theory of consumer demand. He developed the so-called 'rotten-kid' theorem which explains why all members of a family act in a way which increases the total family welfare and not the personal welfare of one member if one family head exists (BECKER 1974, p. 1080ff.). BECKER (1974, p. 1084f.) also explains the impact and meaning of charitable giving which increases if income of the giver increases and decreases when the income of the recipient increases. This thinking is completely different from the consumer choice theory which considers charitable giving to be a "good" which "enters the giver's utility function along with his other goods" (BECKER 1974, p. 1084f.). Critique of Becker's approach arose because Becker was not able to explain why people donate when they do not expect immediate or future return/reciprocity (MONROE 1994, p. 873).

Models of interdependent preferences suppose that whether individuals' preferences are altruistic or selfish depend on a second individual's preference and vice versa. Other disciplines, such as disaster research, confront the hypothesis of alliance with the hypotheses of utility interdependence (see DE ALESSI 1975) (FEHR and SCHMIDT 2006, p. 649ff.). The alliance hypothesis assumes society to be based on a social contract of maintaining the organisations of society which is understood as a collective good and to which individuals contribute by individual actions which can be donations (DE ALESSI 1975, p. 129). Others again like GOULDNER (1960) distinguished between the norm of reciprocity (I hope that somebody will help me) and complementarity.

The model of intention-based reciprocity assumes that an individual cares about his vis-à-vis intentions (FEHR and SCHMIDT 2006, p. 649ff.).

Pure and impure altruism

Definitions of altruism[90] differ throughout literature according to the disciplines defining it. But even within disciplines (e.g. psychology) various definitions are used (PILIAVIN and CHARNG 1990, p. 29). The general definition given by the DUDEN (2010) describes altruism as unselfish way of thinking and acting.

In microeconomics altruism is approached in two ways with regard to the theoretical framework and the utility function. First, altruism is integrated and measured in an

[90] For deeper insights into theory and research on altruism, see e.g. PILIAVIN and CHARNG (1990).

individual's utility function as the quantities which are consumed by others. An individual is called altruistic if he/she includes the utility of others in his/her own personal utility function and if the first partial derivatives of u ($x_1, \ldots, x_N$) with respect to $x_1,\ldots, x_N$ are strictly positive, i.e. if the utility increases with the well-being of other individuals. The assumption of utility maximisation is retained (ANTONIDES 1996, p. 39; FEHR and SCHMIDT 2005, p. 25). The result is that economics models philanthropy as a concern about the total supply arising from private gifts to a pure public good; it is irrelevant whether a person contributes because of so-called enlightened self-interest (hope that some day someone will help himself), or that the benefits for others are due to altruism included in an individual's utility function or that individuals get utility from the act of giving as such (a warm-glow feeling). ANDREONI and MILLER (2002) investigated whether altruistic choices are consistent with rationality axioms, especially with quasi-concave utility functions. They found that altruistic choices can be captured with quasi-concave utility functions which means, they were able to state that altruism can be seen as rational behaviour.

Second, dual utilities based on ethical and subjective preferences are assumed. Here the idea is that an individual consists of one altruistic, social oriented and one egoistic, selfish part in which sympathy enters (ANDREONI 2006, p. 1; MONROE 1994, p. 866, SEN 1977, p. 336). The origin of this nature and "the role of culture in its shaping" are assumed to be exogenous (MONROE 1994, p. 866). Nevertheless, ANDREONI (2006, p. 1) signifies philanthropy as "one of the greatest puzzles for economics" as behaviour which is unselfish is not easily reconciled with self-interest. According to MONROE (1994, p. 866), both ways fail to explain or give explanations as to why people have different affinity towards altruistic behaviour and why an individual's altruistic behaviour changes over time. MONROE (1994, p. 867) states furthermore that microeconomics often regards altruism as partly self-interest: people expect to get something back, i.e. a material good, kind behaviour, the cooperation of others or just feeling good about themselves. Altruism in this connotation can be considered to be an investment in the future.

The hypothesis that at least some individuals are altruistic has been used to explain charitable donations as well as the voluntary provision of public goods. Especially the public goods aspect is interesting for this work as environmental quality is in general a public good. Therefore altruism can be reflected in a purchase of an eco-labelled product (LOUREIRO et al. 2001, p. 401). Altruism is also defined as an action that is costly to oneself and beneficial to others (BOWLES and GINTIS 2003, p. 5) which means that people care about the payoffs of other individuals. Furthermore, it is defined as a favour that does not necessarily emerge as a response to a favour received (FEHR and SCHMIDT 2005, p. 4). MONROE (1994, p. 862) defines altruism in her review as behaviour aimed at benefiting others, "even when doing so may risk or entail some sacrifice to the welfare of the actor". The important points in this definition are that, on the one hand, altruism needs action and cannot just be well-meant thoughts or good intentions. On the other hand, the primary goal of the act must be the intention to increase the welfare of others which should not be just a by-product of the enhancement of one's own welfare. Impure altruism arises when individuals not only contribute to and care for the welfare of someone else or a public good, but also value the act of giving itself which means they derive additional utility by acting charitably and their gift per se. This kind of feeling good is called 'warm glow' (ANDREONI 1990, p. 465; ANTONIDES 1996, p. 40). To summarise, pure altruism is a preference for the well-being of others, warm glow is a good feeling arising from giving and impure altruism[91] is a combination of pure altruism and warm glow (KONOW 2006, p. 1).

A large part of research on warm glow and impure altruism is done in the framework of donations to charities and public goods. Especially the amount of reduction in private giving as a result of taxation[92], also called the crowding out effect, is often mentioned (see e.g. ANDREONI 1990; KONOW 2006; OFFERMAN et al. 1996; ECKEL and GROSSMAN 2008). Altruistic behaviour can be triggered by the desire for inequity aversion which can be expressed as the difference between payoffs to oneself and another person or preferences for social welfare maximisation (FEHR and SCHMIDT 2005, p. 4, 27).

WEBB et al. (2000, p. 301) state that researchers generally agree that internalised values and personal norms affect people's feeling about helping others.[93] WEBB et al. (2000, p. 301) found that empathy is the most frequently mentioned psychological mechanism motivating altruism. With the definition of empathy the borders of two paradigms schools become obvious: empathy can be defined as other-oriented behaviour or as egoistically motivated when the intention behind the help is the wish to avoid individual harm which is caused by observing suffering people. PILIAVIN and CHARNG (1990, p. 27) found that both altruistic and

[91] For a model of impure altruism, see ANDREONI (1990).

[92] PRILLER and SOMMERFELD (2005, p. 9) assume that in Germany donations to charity are influenced by the German fiscal framework. The question whether participants of the in chapter 6 described survey care for a contribution receipt originates from this deliberation.

[93] Ten psychographic variables which are consistent across 20 countries with different cultures are identified by SCHWARTZ (1992). Benevolence and universalism are the two variables of these ten which WEBB et al. (2000, p. 305) identify to "represent pro-social values of a self-transcending nature". The motivation behind benevolence is assumed to be that an individual wants to increase the welfare of people like friends or family. The welfare of all is the motivation behind universalism (WEBB et al. 2000, p. 305).

egoistic motives for helping behaviour exist and that personal norms and values are the basis for both.

4.3.1.2 Research areas of charitable giving

The following literature overview will, by necessity, address only a small subset of the hundreds of articles written since 1960 on philanthropy (ANDREONI 2006), charitable giving, helping behaviour, etc. and focus only on the most central themes. Nevertheless, a short insight into this broad field is given. First, work trying to arrive at comprehensive explanatory models of charitable giving is reviewed. Then, studies dealing with single determinants such as the importance of the donations of others, incentives, the role of disaster, gender and tax, attitudes towards charity organisations affecting personal contributions to charity as well as the effect of experimental settings on study results are mentioned.

Explanatory models and conceptual frameworks of helping behaviour

BENDAPUDI et al. (1996) present a conceptual framework of helping behaviour including antecedents, moderators and consequences to gain some understanding of factors affecting helping behaviour. Their starting point is that there is no consensus across disciplines as to what constitutes help but that there is consensus that the consequences for the helper and the recipient are of equal importance as the motives for providing support. BENDAPUDI et al. (1996) provide an extensive literature review on helping behaviour in marketing journals from 1971 to 1996. The interested reader is referred to this review.

MAYERL (2006) presents an explanatory model of monetary donations based on the Theory of Reasoned Action and models the willingness to donate (donation intention) as the only determinant of monetary donation behaviour. MAYERL (2008, p. 6ff.; 24) measures mediator and moderator effects and shows that the willingness to donate depends only on the intentions to donate which, in turn, depends on the behaviour attitude towards monetary donations and the individual and subjective perceived norm towards monetary donations.

Single determinants affecting charitable giving

BEKKERS and WIEPKING (2007, p. 20ff.) provide an extensive review of experiments in economics, biology, marketing, sociology and social psychology which provide insights in the determinants of philanthropy. BEKKERS and WIEPKING (2007, p. 20ff.) were able to identify eight key mechanisms influencing the likelihood of giving to charity. The first is the awareness of needs as a prerequisite for philanthropy, e.g. facilitated by media. The second finding is that a majority of charitable giving takes place in response to a solicitation. The more opportunities people have to donate the more likely they give. The third finding is that benefits for the donors related to the donations, e.g. exclusive concerts for those giving to an orchestra, are an important determinant of individual giving to charity. Altruism as well as an enhanced reputation (individuals giving to charity receive recognition and approval from their peers) are also found to be major determinants. Psychological benefits, such as the joy of giving and the resulting empathic self-image, can be mentioned as values and efficacy. This is based on the notion of donors that their giving makes a difference to the cause they are enhancing.

WEBB et al. (2000, p. 304) found that the likelihood of giving (which is measured in terms of the number of organisations people are giving to) and the level or value of giving (which is measured as the sum of financial donations in the last year) are the "two behavioural measures" most reported in literature on charitable giving. With regard to the main factor influencing the probability of donations to charity SMITH et al. (1995) found that the type of charity individuals have contributed to in earlier times (e.g. giving to religious organisations in contrast to giving to national charities) is of crucial importance. The influence of information on the contribution amount of others on charitable behaviour in general and individuals' donation amount in particular has been explored by CROSON and SHANG (2008). BÉNABOU and TIROLE (2006) determine the role of incentives for pro-social behaviour.

EAGLY and CROWLEY (1986) conducted a meta-analytic review of gender differences in helping behaviour especially with regard to giving of aid and found that in general women received more help than men which in contrast provided more help. But, gender differences in helping were very inconsistent across studies. AGUIAR et al. (2008) address the question as to how individuals perceive behavioural differences between men and women and which gender is expected to be more generous.

In addition, there are numerous studies by economists regarding the impact of the two policy-related issues of tax policy and marginal tax rates and government spending policy, in particular alterations in government spending and public subsidies on private giving (REECE 1979; ROSE-ACKERMAN 1996, p. 715; SMITH et al. 1995, p. 108; YOO and HARRISON 1989, p. 368). However, it is not possible to draw any clear conclusion regarding the effects of the above-mentioned changes on donations. CLOTFELTER (1985) found in his review that giving was price elastic and income inelastic while STEINBERG (1990, p. 70) found the opposite.

WEBB et al. (2000, p. 300) distinguish between "attitudes towards helping others and attitudes towards charitable organisations" both of which determine donation behaviour. The attitudes towards helping others are influenced by internalized personal norms and moral values and span a wide range of behaviour (PILIAVIN and CHARNG 1990, p. 32, WEBB et al. 2000, p. 300). Charitable organisations are one of many vehicles people can use to make donations. Three factors which are important for the donors' evaluation of the charitable organisations are identified by BENDAPUDI et al. (1996, p. 37): first, the familiarity of the donor with the charity; second, the efficiency of the organisation which is expressed in the amount of funds going to the charity purpose in relation to the total funds available; and third, the perceived effectiveness of the organisation in achieving its goal. That efficiency and effectiveness of charitable organisations influence donors' perception of the respective organisation was shown by HARVEY (1990) and SCHLEGELMILCH et al. (1992). [94]

As many experiments on altruistic behaviour using the game theory can be found (e.g. CARPENTER et al. 2008; GAUBE 2006; GNEEZY and RUSTICHINI 2000; KONOW 2006) BENZ and MEIER (2008) test whether the levels of pro-social behaviour differ in the laboratory experiments compared to field settings. They find that pro-social behavior in experiments is postitively correlated with individuals' behaviour in the field.

The above-mentioned studies reveal that the reasons for individual giving are quite different and that besides altruism many factors may influence individuals' decisions for philanthropy. Furthermore, people can be motivated by a wish to achieve respect, social acceptance, prestige, friendship, and other psychological and social objectives (BECKER 1974, p. 1083; OLSON 1965, p. 60). We can distinguish between individual financial deliberations such as the tax bracket and stimulating factors such as the desire to aid others or religious involvement (BIELEFELD et al. 2005, p. 129). VESTERLUND (2006, p. 568) mentions the public and private benefits donors recieve in return from transactions. Private benefits are exclusive to the person who has made the contribution and the benefits are similar to that of a purchase of another private good. Reputation and the 'warm glow' feeling are other private benefits (VESTERLUND 2006, p. 573). To sum up, personal donation behaviour depends on numerous factors, including attitudes towards helping others, along with social, economic and intrapersonal motives as well as the attitudes towards charitable organisations (WEBB et al. 2000, p. 301f.).

[94] In Germany, no general rules and standards exist for charitable organisations (PWC 2005) but an annual transparency prize, first awarded in 2005, is awarded to German charity organisations that provide information on their goals, achievements and their control mechanisms.

4.3.2 Characteristics of donors

Studies have indicated that different socio-economic characteristics such as income (e.g. PHAROAH and TANNER 1997) and education level (HARVEY 1990), demographic characteristics such as age (e.g. PHAROAH and TANNER 1997), gender (e.g. EAGLY and CROWLEY 1986), religious denomination (SCHEEPERS and Te GROTENHUIS 2005) and the neighbourhood/environment (rural or urban) in which someone lives (AMATO 1983; STEBLAY 1987), as well as the sibling's position of a person (DUNN and MUNN 1986) and psychographic characteristics (e.g. SCHLEGELMILCH and TYNAN 1989) affect the likelihood of charitable giving. Marital status (married), attitudes and personality traits (attitude towards self-orientation and group experiences, empathy, altruism and attitudes towards religion) and social norms are also found to have an influence (MAYERL 2006, p. 3). The socioeconomic variables mostly used to predict and explain donations are household income and education level (WEBB et al. 2000, p. 305). While age, education and income in most studies were found to have a positive effect on charitable giving (see e.g. the review in SCHLEGELMILCH et al. 1996, p. 550), the effects of employment status, marital status, the presence of children, gender and the meaning of religion tended to be inconsistent and differ from study to study (CARROLL et al. 2005, p. 230). For an extensive review of the numerous factors affecting donations to charity, see BEKKERS and WIEPKING (2007).

4.3.3 Charitable giving in Germany

Although we might think that there is a great interest in knowing more about the economics and motives for donations, data on charity is rare in Germany (PRILLER and SOMMERFELD 2005, p. 37) and, as WILHELM (2006, p. 27) or VESTERLUND (2006, p. 581) states, the same is the case in the US. Even the economics[95] (LANDRY et al. 2005, p. 1) and determinants (SMITH et al. 1995, p. 123) of charitable giving are not well known. One reason is that interviews on this topic have to deal with the problem of social desirability which leads to biased data (WILHELM 2006, p. 30). Research is furthermore hindered by the fact that findings from research concerning donation habits in the US are not entirely transferable to Germany because, unlike in the US where charitable giving is part of the daily political and social culture, this is not the case in Germany (HEIDBÜCHEL 2000, p. 3). In Germany philanthropic behaviour is more private than in the US, the church tax acts as a tax, etc.

---

[95] ANDREONI (2006) describes the economics of charity.

4.3.3.1 Development of donation volume

In the last 10 years, an increasing amount of information about donations has been published including figures about donation amounts and purposes as well as literature about donation behaviour in Germany. Regularly available figures regarding donations to non-profit organisations in Germany are provided by the Gesellschaft für Konsumforschung (GfK), TNS Infratest and the National Income Statistic (see Table 4). While the data of GfK and TNS Infratest are based on annual consumer surveys, the National Income Statistic is based on the income tax statistic. The first and only publication based on the national income statistic up to now is that of BUSCHLE (2006) which is based on the data of the income tax statistic of the year 2001. Recent evidence (see Table 4) suggests that individual donations to charities in Germany have remained stagnant around 2 billion € per annum according to GfK, around 3 billion € per annum according to TNS and the National Income Statistic.

The results of the three publications differ strongly with respect to the donation amounts and the donation purpose in Germany (PRILLER and SOMMERFELD 2005). For instance, TNS INFRATEST (2008a) reports that development projects recieve about 19 % of the 2.8 billion € which were donated in 2007 in Germany. GFK (2008a) reports different percentages on a different basis: in the first half of 2008 9.3 % of humanitarian aid, which is 80 % of the total donation volume, was given to long-term development projects and 18.7 % went to first aid. The differences might occur due to the different survey methods, sample composition (possibly more concerned respondents in the survey of the Deutscher Spendenmonitor) and social desirability provoking respondents to overestimate their donations. But the figures of the National Income Statistic can also overestimate the German donation volume as a donation of 50 € can be declared to be donated without proving this expenditure (LÄMMERZAHL 2008).

Although the available studies of the GfK, TNS, and the National Income Statistic regarding the volume and purpose of donations in Germany differ (see Table 4), it becomes obvious that Germans gave more money to charity than they pay for the purchase of Fair Trade products.

Table 4: Charitable giving survey data in Germany

Survey	Year	Billion €	Method
GfK Charity Scope	2005	2.4	Respondents at least 10 years old, 10.000 interviews, daily, monthly
	2006	2.0	
	2007	2.0	
	2008	2.2	
TNS Infratest Deutscher Spendenmonitor	2005	3.5	Respondents at least 14 years old, 4.000 interviews, face-to-face, yearly
	2006	3.4	
	2007	2.8	
	2008	2.9	
National Income Statistic	2001	2.9	Taxpayer, complete inventory count

Source: author's compilation based on SOMMERFELD (2008) for the data until 2006, data for 2007 from GFK (2008a) and TNS INFRATEST (2008b), data for 2008 from GFK and DEUTSCHER SPENDENRAT (2009) and TNS INFRATEST (2009), data for the national income statistic from BUSCHLE (2006).

4.3.3.2 Donation purposes

BUSCHLE's (2006) report is restricted to donation purposes supported by the German government through tax deductions. These are regulated in §10b and 34g EStG (BUSCHLE 2008, p. 1). Spontaneous donations without donation receipts, such as thise given in church's offertory box which are reported in GfK and TNS Infratest data, are not included. It is distinguished between benevolent, political and donations to foundations. Benevolent, church related, religious purposes as well as purposes of public utility, scientific and cultural purposes are summarized as benevolent purposes. In 2001, 44 million people, who represent 50 % of the German population, were covered. 66 % of all donations (2.8 billion €) went to ecclesiastical purposes and non-profit organisations, 23 % went to scientific and cultural aims and the remaining 10 % had different donation purposes, such as political parties, foundations, etc. (BUSCHLE 2006, p. 152). The church tax (8.2 billion € in 2001) is not included (GRÄB 2007). If we consider the church tax as being one form of donation, because people are free to leave church and then they do not have to pay church tax, the total amount of donations in 2001 would sum up to 11 billion €.

Legislative periods influence the amount of party donations; in years when the Bundestag elections take place, they are higher than in the other three years (BUSCHLE 2008, p. 1). Natural disasters, such as the Elb-flood in 2002 or the tsunami in 2004, increase the short-term donation volume.

GfK findings regarding the donation purpose might be biased to a certain extent as respondents are not asked to disclose the donation purpose for which they spent the money but the name of the organisation they gave it to. Then GfK assigns the charity organisations to the donation purpose, for example: Greenpeace: animal protection, BUND: environment protection, Deutsche Kriegsgräberfürsorge: preservation of monuments. Most of the donations are allocated to humanitarian aid such as Malteser and Johanniter. These organisations also support developmental projects. Attention should be paid to this issue because the charity organisations are not asked which percentage of their budget they spend on which purpose (LÄMMERZAHL 2007).

TNS INFRATEST (2005) found that most important objects of donations (each between 20 and 30 %) in Germany in 2003, 2004 and 2005 were care for disabled and sick persons, on-the-spot-aid and child welfare. The importance of development assistance increased in these years from a donation quota of 15 % to 19 %.

4.3.3.3 Profile of active donors

How restricted the current research regarding donations to charity in Germany is becomes clear when we look at the available studies and surveys. Besides the extensive surveys of GfK, TNS and National Income Statistic, little is available with respect to donation motives and motivations influencing personal giving (see, for instance, the program of the conference on motives, social context and influencing factors for charitable giving in Germany held in Berlin in 2008 organised by WZB and DZI (2008)). There it became obvious that for Germany research is still in its infancy and to some extent vague. WEST (2008) used a qualitative approach to find that socio- demographics are less important than the biographical embedding of motives. She identified five groups of motives: first, the moral obligation towards one's fellow human being with donations as compensation of engagement as variant; second, the compliance of social norms; third, one's own experience and concerns; fourth, political influence; and fifth, the pursuit of social acceptance. Altruistic and egoistic motives appear jointly and vary not only individual specific but also lifecycle specific and donation specific.

STEINER (2008) also assessed the motives driving personal donations to charity by means of a qualitative approach. He identified personal (system of motives, empathy, and identification with the donation purpose, social norms learned such as solidarity and social responsibility) and situational factors (actual mood, stimulus satisfaction controlled by me), as well as personal resources (money and time) which influence donations. As the most important motive, he identifies the pursuit of a better and fairer world.

More concrete findings are that the willingness to spend and the amount of donations depend of the age (younger people spent less and in 2008 more than 50 % of the monetary donations come, according to GFK (2008b, p. 13), from people older than 60 years, which are only 26 % of the panel, and more than 50 % of these are given by those people older than 70 years), the economic situation which often depends on the education level (wage earners spend more than trainees or unemployed people, and retirees and housewives spend the most), religious denomination (it raises the probability of contribution, while there is not much of a difference between Catholics or Protestants) and children in the household (the number of children and the probability of donations are positive correlated (PRILLER and SOMMERFELD 2005, p. 38f.; BUSCHLE 2006, p. 158)). Furthermore, church taxpayers spend more than non church taxpayers (BUSCHLE 2006, p. 153ff.). Related to the entity of taxpayers most of the donors can be found among the married couples with three or more children (BUSCHLE 2008, p. 4). No differences in terms of donation habits can be found regarding gender (GFK 2008b, p. 12).

Another remarkable discovery is that individual, honorary engagement (e.g. in sport associations) is positively correlated with donations (PRILLER and SOMMERFELD 2005, p. 38).

One interesting finding for Germany is that people in higher income classes spent in absolute figures more than the average but in percent of their net income this is much below the average. With respect to the fiscal data, the number of taxpayers who make donations rises when their income increases. In 2003, one fourth of the taxpayers with an income below 30,000 € donated while two-thirds of those with an income above 100,000 € made a contribution to charity. Up to an income of 10,000 € the percentage of income donated to charity is at 3.6 % the highest and decreases continuously with increasing income. Above 100,000 € income this changes and nearly 1.1 % of the income is given to charity (BUSCHLE 2008, p. 3). This shows that income alone is not able to explain charitable giving and that moral values might have an impact.

According to the National Income Statistic, each third individual liable to pay income tax in Germany is a donor (BUSCHLE 2008, p. 2). The fraction of donors has remained constant from 2001 to 2004. This group of donors (i.e. 33 % of the taxpayers) contributes 50 % of all income revenues and possesses an average income of 50,000 € which is 66 % above the average income of non-donors (30,000 €) (BUSCHLE 2008, p. 2). About 9 million donors made some 4 billion € donations which is 0.9 % of the income declared as tax-relevant donations. On average between 2001 and 2004, 107 € per taxpayer and respectively 325 € per donating taxpayer are accepted donations.

In Germany, regional differences become apparent. In Western Germany the willingness to donate is ten percent points higher than in Eastern Germany and the North spends less than

Bavaria. GfK (2008b, p. 16) figures also show that Bavaria (18.5 % of all donations in the first half of 2008 but only 14.9 % of the GfK Panel) and Baden-Württemberg (19.5 % but only 12.5 % of the GfK panel) contribute an over-proportional share to the national charity revenue.

Asked what has given rise to donate money one third of the people name mailings, and 13 % state the collection in church. Tips by friends are mentioned third most frequently (GfK 2008b, p. 21). Print runs of mailings for development aid increases by 52 % from 2007 to 2008 (GfK 2008b, p. 23). Highest donations amounts are generated by online banking (Deutscher Fundraisingverband 2007). In Germany half of all donations are done habitually and the other half can be described as spontaneous (Meulemann and Beckers 2003, p. 37).

4.4 Résumé

The review of ethical consumption, it's most important research areas and market relevance revealed that there are plenty of terms circulating in the field of ethical consumption, that ethical consumption is complex and hard to capture in a single definition, and that is has characteristics of altruism and other-related behaviour. Besides it became obvious that Fair Trade products are one prominent form of ethical products. The examination of the Fair Trade movement, its characteristis, rules and outcomes and the comparison to aid serves to create a greater awareness of the similarities as well as the differences of charitable giving and the purchase of ethical products, in particular Fair Trade products. The review of charitable giving focussed on the possible motivations stimulating people to give as well as the characteristics of these individuals. By this, a deeper understanding of the research subjects is provided and the foundation for the discussion of the empirical studies is laid. It becomes obvious that the forms of ethical behaviour considered in this thesis are similar but at the same time different and that down to the present day no assessment regarding consumers appraisal of these possibilities of ethical behaviour has been conducted.

4.5 References

Adams, M. and Raisborough, J. (2010): Making a difference: ethical consumption and the everyday. *The British Journal of Sociology*, 61 (2): 256-274.

Aguiar, F., Branas-Garza, P., Cobo-Reyes, R., Jimenez, N. and Miller, L. (2008): Are women expected to be more generous? *Experimental Economics*, 12 (1): 93-98.

Ahaus, B., Heidbrink, L. and Schmidt, I. (2009): Chancen und Grenzen der Konsumentenverantwortung: Eine Bestandsaufnahme. *Working Paper CRR*, 3 (5): 1-33.

AJZEN, I. (1991): The theory of planned behavior. *Organizational Behavior and Human Decision Processes*, 50 (1): 179-211.

AKERLOF, G. A. (1970): The market for "lemons": Quality Uncertainty and the Market Mechanism. *The Quarterly Journal of Economics,* 84 (3): 488-500.

AMATO, P. R. (1983): Helping behavior in urban and rural environments: Field studies based on taxonomic organization of helping episodes. *Journal of Personality and Social Psychology*, 45 (3):571-586.

ANDERSON, R. C. and HANSEN, E. N. (2004): Determining consumer preferences for ecolabelled forest products. *Journal of Forestry*, 102 (4): 28-32.

ANDREONI, J. (1990): Impure Altruism and Donations to Public Goods: A Theory of Warm-Glow Giving. *The Economic Journal*, 100 (401): 464-477.

ANDREONI, J. (2006): Philantrophy. In: Kolm, S. - C. and Ythier, J. M. (Eds.): *Handbook on the Economics of Giving, Reciprocity and Altruism*, 2. Amsterdam: North-Holland: 1201-1269.

ANDREONI, J. and MILLER. J. (2002): Giving According to GARP: An Experimental Test of the Consistency of Preferences for Altruism. *Econometrica*, 70 (2): 737-753.

ANTONIDES, G. (1996): Psy*chology in Economics and Business: An Introduction to Economic Psychology*. Dordrecht: Kluwer.

ARNOT, C., BOXALL, P.C. and CASH, S. B. (2006): Do Ethical Consumers Care About Price? A Revealed Preference Analysis of Fair Trade Coffee Purchases. *Canadian Journal of Agricultural Economics,* 54 (4): 555-565.

AUGER, P., DEVINNEY, T. M. and LOUVIERE, J. J. (2007): Measuring the importance of ethical consumerism: a multi-country empirical investigation. In: Hooker, J., Hulpke, J. F. and Madsen, P. (Eds.): *Controversies in International Corporate*. International Corporate Responsibility Series, 3: 207–221.

AWA (2008): *Der gesellschaftliche Wandel generiert neue Zielgruppen.* Available from: http://www.awa-online.de/praesentationen/awa08_Zielgruppen.pdf, [accessed 2008-07-13].

BABAKUS, E., CORNWELL, T. B., MITCHELL, V. and SCHLEGELMILCH, B. (2004): Reactions to unethical consumer behavior across six countries. *Journal of Consumer Marketing*, 21 (4): 254-263.

BACON, C. (2005): Confronting the Coffee Crisis: Can Fair Trade, Organic, and Specialty coffees Reduce Small-Scale Farmer Vulnerability in Northern Nicaragua? *World Development*, 33 (3): 497-511.

BAKER, S., THOMPSON, K. E., ENGELKEN, J. and HUNTLEY, K. (2004): Mapping the values driving organic food choice Germany vs the UK. *European Journal of Marketing,* 38 (8): 995-1012.

BARNETT, C., CLOKE, P., CLARKE, N. and MALPASS, A. (2005): Consuming Ethics: Articulating the Subjects and Spaces of Ethical Consumption. *Antipode*, 37 (1): 23-45.

BASU, A. K. and HICKS, R. L. (2008): Label performance and the willingness to pay for Fair Trade coffee: a cross national perspective. *International Journal of Consumer Studies,* 32: 470-478.

BECCHETTI, L. and ADRIANI, F. (2004): Fair Trade: A 'third generation' welfare mechanism to make globalisation sustainable. *CEIS Tor Vergata - Research Paper Series*, 21 (62).

BECCHETTI, L. and ROSATI, F.C. (2005): The demand for socially responsible products: empirical evidence from a pilot study on fair trade consumers. *Society for the study of economic Inequality - Ecineq, Working Paper Series, ECINEQ WP 2005 – 04.*

BECCHETTI, L. and ROSATI, F.C. (2007): Global social preferences and the demand for socially responsible products: empirical evidence from a pilot study on fair trade consumers. *The world economy*, 30 (5): 807-836.

BECCHETTI, L. and COSTANTINO, M. (2006): The effects of Fair Trade on marginalised producers: an impact analysis on Kenyan farmers. Society for the study of economic Inequality - Ecineq, *Working Paper Series, ECINEQ WP 2006*, 41.

BECCHETTI, L., PAGANETTO, L., and SOLFERINO, N. (2003): A Virtuous interaction between pressure groups, firms and institutions: subsidiarity principle in a horizontal differentiation model. *CEIS Working Paper*, 194.

BECK, U. (1999): *World Risk Society*. Cambridge: Polity Press.

BECKER, G. S. (1974): A Theory of Social Interactions. *The Journal of Political Economy*, 82 (6): 1063-1093.

BEKKERS, R. and WIEPKING, P. (2007): *Generosity and Philanthropy: A Literature Review*. Available from: http://papers.ssrn.com/sol3/papers.cfm?abstract_id=1015507, [accessed 2010-04-23].

BÉNABOU, R. and TIROLE, J. (2006): Incentives and Prosocial Behavior. *The American Economic Review*, 96 (5): 1652-1678.

BENDAPUDI, N., SINGH, S. N. and BENDAPUDI, V. (1996): Enhancing helping behaviour: An Integrative Framework for Promotion Planning. *The Journal of Marketing*, 60 (3): 33-49.

BENZ, M. and S. MEIER (2008): Do people behave in experiments as in the field? Evidence from donations. *Experimental Economics*, 11 (3): 268-281.

BIELEFELD, W., ROONEY, P. and STEINBERG, K. (2005): How do need, capacity, geography, and politics influence giving? In: Brooks, A. C. (Ed.): *Gift of money in American communities*. Lanham, MD: Rowman & Littlefield Pub Inc.: 127-158.

BITZER, V., FRANCKEN, M. and GLASBERGEN, P. (2008): Intersectoral partnerships for a sustainable coffee chain: Really addressing sustainability or just picking (coffee) cherries? *Global Environmental Change*, 18: 271-284.

BJØRNER, T. B., HANSEN, L. G. and RUSSELL, C. S. (2004): Environmental labeling and consumers' choice: An empirical analysis of the effect of the Nordic Swan. *Journal of Environmental Economics and Management*, 47 (3): 411-424.

BLEND, J. B. and VAN RAVENSWAAY, E. O. (1999): Measuring Consumer Demand for Ecolabeled Apples. *American Journal of Agricultural Economic*, 81 (5): 1072-1077.

BMU (2008): *Umweltbewusstsein in Deutschland 2008*. Available from: http://www.umweltdaten.de/publikationen/fpdf-l/3678.pdf, [accessed 2008-12-18].

BÖLW (2011): *Zahlen, Daten, Fakten: Die Bio-Branche 2011*.

BOONE, P. (1996): Politics and the effectiveness of foreign aid. *European Economic Review*, 40 (2): 289-329.

BOOTH, P. and WHETSTONE, L. (2007): Half a Cheer for Fair Trade. *26th IEA Current Controversies Paper*. Institute for Economic Affairs, London.

BOUGHERARA, D. and COMBRIS, P. (2009): Eco-labelled food products: what are consumers paying for? *European Review of Agricultural Economics*, 36 (3): 321-341.

BOULANGER, P. - M. (2007): What´s wrong with consumption for sustainable development. In: Zaccai, E. (Ed.): *Sustainable Consumption, Ecology and Fair Trade*. London: Routledge: 17-32.

BOURDIEU, P. (1984): *Distinction: A Social Critique of the Judgement of Taste*. London: Routledge.

BOWLES, S. and GINTIS, H. (2003): *Prosocial Emotions*. Available from: http://time.dufe.edu.cn/wencong/gintis/prosoc.pdf, [accessed 2009-07-15].

BROWNE, A. W., HARRIS, P. J. C., HOFNY-COLLINS, A. H., PASIECZNIK, N. and WALLACE, R. R. (2000): Organic production and ethical trade: definition, practice and links. *Food Policy*, 25 (1): 69-89.

BUSCHLE, N. (2006): Spenden in Deutschland. Ergebnisse der Einkommensteuerstatistik 2001. In: Statistisches Bundesamt (Ed.): *Auszug aus Wirtschaft und Statistik*. Wiesbaden: Statistisches Bundesamt: 151-159.

BUSCHLE, N. (2008): *Spenden - von wem und wofür?* Available from: http://www.destatis.de/jetspeed/portal/cms/Sites/destatis/Internet/DE/Navigation/Publikationen/STATmagazin/FinanzenSteuern2008__2,templateId=renderPrint.psml__nnn=true, [accessed 2011-06-21].

BUSSE, T. (2006): *Die Einkaufsrevolution. Konsumenten entdecken ihre Macht*. München: Karl Blessing Verlag.

BUXEL, H. and SCHULZ, S. (2010): *Akzeptanz und Nutzung von Güte- und Qualitätssiegeln auf Lebensmitteln*. Studienberich. Münster.

BYERS, A., GIOVANNUCCI, D. and LIU, P. (2008): Value-adding standards in the North American food market. Trade opportunities in certified products for developing countries. *FAO Commodities and Trade Technical Paper*, 11.

CARBONARO, S. (2009): *Zusammenfassung Simonetta Carbonaro*. 14. Deutscher Trendtag am 14.05.2009 in Hamburg 2009. Available from http://www.trendbuero.de/index.php?f_articleId=3542, [accessed 2011-06-06].

CARPENTER, J., CONNOLLY, C. and MYERS, C. (2008): Altruistic behavior in a representative dictator experiment. *Experimental Economics*, 11 (3): 282-298.

CARRIGAN, M. and ATTALLA, A. (2001): The myth of the ethical consumer – do ethics matter in purchase behaviour? *Journal of Consumer Marketing*, 18 (7): 560-576.

CARRIGAN, M., SZMIGIN, I. and WRIGHT, J. (2004): Shopping for a better world? An interpretive study of the potential for ethical consumption within the older market. *Journal of Consumer Marketing*, 21 (6): 401-417.

CARROLL, J., MCCARTHY, S. and NEWMAN, C. (2005): An econometric analysis of charitable donations in the Republic of Ireland. *The Economic and Social Review*, 36 (3): 229-249.

CCN (2010): *Consumer Citizenship Network*. Available from: http://www.hihm.no/Prosjektsider/CCN, [accessed 2010-01-20].

CHAMBOLLE, C. and PORET, S. (2007): *Fair Trade: in or out the Market?* Laboratoire d'économétrie, Cahier 2007-16.

CHATZIDAKIS, A., HIBBERT, S. and SMITH, A. P. (2007): Why People Don't Take their Concerns about Fair Trade to the Supermarket: The Role of Neutralisation. *Journal of Business Ethics*, 74 (1): 89-100.

CLARKE, N., BARNETT, C., CLOKE, P. and MALPASS, A. (2007): Globalising the consumer: Doing politics in an ethical register. *Political Geography*, 26: 231-249.

CLOTFELTER, C. T. (1985): *Federal tax policy and charitable giving*. Chicago: University of Chicago Press.

COLLIER, P. (1999): The political economy of ethnicity. *Annual Bank Conference on Development Economics 1998*, Washington D.C.: The World Bank.

COLLIER, P. (2000): Ethnicity, politics and economic performance. *Economics and Politics*, 12 (3): 225-245.

COLLIER, P. and DOLLAR, D. (2004): Development effectiveness: What have we learnt? *The economic journal*, 114: F244-271.

CONNER, D. S. and MABAYA, E. T. (2006): Consumer Preferences for Organic and Fair Trade Chocolate: Implications for Sustainable Agriculture in the Developing World. *Staff Paper SP 2006-02, Department of Applied Economics and Management, Cornell University*, Ithaca, New York, USA.

COSA (2007): *Information Brief on the COSA Project. A mult-criteria cost-benefit analysis of sustainable practices in coffee*. Available from: http://www.iisd.org/pdf/2007/cosa.pdf, [accessed 2008-06-26].

COWE, R. and WILLIAMS, S. (2000): *Who are the ethical consumers*? The Co-operative Bank.

CRANE, A. AND MATTEN, D. (2004): *Business Ethics: A European Perspective - Managing Corporate Citizenship and Sustainability in the Age of Globalisation*. New York: Oxford University Press.

CROSON, R. and SHANG, J. (2008): The impact of downward social information on contribution decisions. *Experimental Economics*, 11 (3): 221-233.

CSCP (2008): *Konzeptpapier: Nachhaltiger Konsum*. Konzeptpapier im Rahmen der Themenreihe „Nachhaltiger Konsum" für das Deutsche Global Compact Netzwerk (DGCN) in 2008. Available from: http://www.scp-centre.org/fileadmin/cscp/

Project_Files/DGCN_Files/Konzeptpapier_nachhaltiger_Konsum_DGCN_CSCP_2008.pdf, [accessed 2008-12-04].

DAC (2007a): *DAC Guidelines and Reference Series*. Available from: http://www.oecd.org/document/10/0,3343,en_2649_33721_1916746_1_1_1_1,00.html, [accessed 07-11-13].

DAC (2007b): Development Co-operation Directorate (DCD-DAC): About. Available from: http://www.oecd.org/about/0,3347,en_2649_33721_1_1_1_1_1,00.html, [accessed 07-11-13].

DAC (2007c): DAC1 Official and Private Flows. Available from: http://stats.oecd.org/wbos/default.aspx?DatasetCode=TABLE1, [accessed 07-11-13].

DALGAARD, C. J. and HANSEN, H. (2001): On Aid, Growth and good Policies. *Journal of development studies*, 37 (6): 17-41.

D'AUTON, M. and HILTON, M. (2001): *The Politics of Consumption. Material Culture and Citizenship in Europe and America.* Oxford: Berg.

DANKERS, C. (2003): *Environmental and Social Standards, Certification and Labelling for Cash Crops.* Rome: FAO.

DE ALESSI, L. (1975): Toward an Analysis of Postdisaster Cooperation. *The American Economic Review*, 65 (1): 127-138.

DE FERRAN, F. and GRUNERT, G. K. (2007): French fair trade coffee buyers' purchasing motives: An exploratory study using means-end chains analysis. *Food Quality and Preference*, 18 (2): 218-229.

DENEGRI-KNOTT, J., ZWICK, D. and SCHROEDER, J. E. (2006): Mapping consumer power: an integrative framework for marketing and consumer research. *European Journal of Marketing*, 40 (9/10): 950-971.

DE PELSMACKER, P. DRIESEN, L. and RAYP, G. (2003): Are fair trade labels good business? Ethics and coffee buying intentions. *Universiteit Gent Working Paper*, 2003/165.

DE PELSMACKER, P., DRIESEN, L. and RAYP, G. (2005a): Do consumers care about ethics? Willingness to pay for Fair-Trade Coffee. *The Journal of Consumer Affairs*, 39 (2): 363-385.

DE PELSMACKER, P., JANSSENS, W. and MIELANTS, C. (2005b): Consumer values and fair-trade beliefs, attitudes and buying behaviour. *International Review on Public and Nonprofit Marketing*, 2 (2): 50-69.

DE PELSMACKER, P., JANSSENS, W., MIELANTS, C. and STERCKX, E. (2007): Marketing ethical products: What can we learn from Fair Trade consumer behaviour in Belgium? In: Zaccaï, E. (Ed.): *Sustainable Consumption, Ecology and Fair Trade*. London: Routledge: 109-126.

DER SPIEGEL (2006): *Image-Politur: Lidl macht auf Bioladen*. 18.04.2006. http://www.spiegel.de/wirtschaft/0,1518,411838,00.html, [accessed 2006-04-18].

DEUTSCHER FUNDRAISINGVERBAND (2007): *Wieviel spenden die Deutschen*? Available from: http://fundraisingverband.de/Statistiken/Spendenaufkommen_insgesamt.html, [accessed 07-05-28].

DEUTSCHER KAFFEEVERBAND (2007): *Jahresbericht 2006*.

DEVINNEY, T. M., AUGER, P. and ECKHARDT, G. M. (2010): *The Myth of the Ethical Consumer*. Cambridge: Cambridge University Press.

DOHERTY, B. and TRANCHELL, S. (2008): *'Radical mainstreaming' of fair trade: the case of The Day Chocolate Company*. Paper presented at the CRRC Conference, Queen's University Belfast. Available from: http://www.crrconference.org/downloads/2006dohertytranchell.pdf, [accessed 2010-07-23].

DUDEN (2010): *Altruismus*. Available from: http://www.duden.de/definition/altruismus, [accessed 2010-10-20].

DUNN, J. and MUNN, P. (1986): Siblings and the Development of Prosocial Behaviour. *International Journal of Behavioral Development*, 9 (3): 265-284.

EAGLY, A. H. and CROWLEY, M. (1986): Gender and Helping Behavior: A Meta-Analytic Review of the Social Psychological Literature. *Psychological Bulletin*, 100 (3): 283-308.

ECKEL, C. and GROSSMANN, P. (2008): Subsidizing charitable contributions: a natural field experiment comparing matching and rebate subsidies. *Experimental Economics*, 11 (3): 234-252.

EFTA (2011): *What is Fair Trade*. Available from: http://www.european-fair-trade-association.org/observatory/index.php/en/fairtrade, [accessed 2011-04-14].

EPO (2008): *Globale Kaffee-Initiative präsentiert erste Ergebnisse*. Available from: http://www.epo.de/index.php?option=com_content&task=view&id=3073&Itemid=34, [accessed 2008-03-26].

ERNST AND YOUNG (2007): *LOHAS*. Available from: http://www.ey.com/Global/assets.nsf/Germany/Studie_RCP_LOHAS_2007/$file/Studie_RCP_LOHAS_2007.pdf, [accessed 07-11-05].

FEHR, E. and SCHMIDT, K. M. (1999): A theory of fairness, competition and cooperation. *Quarterly Journal of Economics*, 114 (3): 817-868.

FEHR, E. and SCHMIDT, K. M. (2005): The Economics of Fairness, Reciprocity and Altruism – Experimental Evidence and New Theories. Chapter written for the Handbook of Reciprocity, Gift-Giving and Altruism. *Munich Discussion Paper No. 2005-20.*

FEHR, E. and SCHMIDT, K. M. (2006): The Economics of Fairness, Reciprocity and Altruism – Experimental Evidence and New Theories. In: Kolm, S.-C. and Ythier, J. M. (Eds): *Handbook of the economics of giving, altruism and reciprocity.* Amsterdam: North-Holland: 615-691.

FELSER, G. (2007): *Werbe- und Konsumentenpsychologie.* 3rd ed. Heidelberg: Spektrum.

FLO (2007a): Annual Report 2007: An Inspiration for Change.

FLO (2007b): *Fairtrade Standards for Coffee for small farmers' organisations.* Available from: http://www.fairtrade.net/smfarmers.html, [accessed 07-07-02].

FLO (2007c): *Evolution of the Number of Licensees per Country.* Available from: http://www.fairtrade.net/figures.html, [accessed 07-11-12].

FLO (2009a): *About Fair Trade.* Available from: http://www.fairtrade.net/about_fairtrade.html, [accessed 09-01-20].

FLO (2009b): *Product standards.* Available from: http://www.fairtrade.net/standards.html, [accessed 09-01-20].

FLO (2009c): *Generic Fairtrade standards for small producers' organizations.* Current version: 15.08.2009. Available from: http://www.fairtrade.net/fileadmin /user_upload/content/SPO_Aug09_EN.pdf, [accessed 09-10-26].

FLO (2011): *About the mark.* Available from: http://www.fairtrade.net/about_the_markt.0.html, [accessed 2011-05-05].

FORUM FAIRER HANDEL (2006): *Zahlen & Fakten zum Fairen Handel in Deutschland 2005.* Available from: http://forum-fairer-handel.de/downloadc/23847_Zahlen%20des %20Fairen%20Handels%202005.pdf, [accessed 2009-02-20].

FORUM FAIRER HANDEL (2007): *Fairer Handel in Deutschland auch 2006 wieder auf Wachstumskurs.* Available from: http://forum-fairer-handel.de/downloadc/72151_2006%20Zahlen%20des%20Fairen%20Handels.pdf, [accessed 2009-02-20].

FORUM FAIRER HANDEL (2008a): *Fairer Handel in Deutschland 2007 – weiter auf Erfolgskurs!* Available from: http://forum-fairer-handel.de/downloadc/95885_Zahlen%20des%20Fairen%20Handels%202007.pdf, [accessed 2009-02-20].

FORUM FAIRER HANDEL (2009): *In Kürze: Zahlen des Fairen Handels 2008*. Available from: http://www.forum-fairer-handel.de/webelements/filepool/site/downloadc/Zahlen%20des%20Fairen%20Handels%202008-mit%20Factsheet.pdf, [accessed 2009-06-20].

FRAJ, E. and MARTINEZ, E. (2007): Ecological Consumer Behaviour: An Empirical Analysis. *International Journal of Consumer Studies*, 31 (1): 26-33.

FRIEDMAN, M. (1996): A positive approach to organized consumer action: the "boycott" as an alternative to the boycott. *Journal of Consumer Policy*, 19 (4): 439-451.

FRIEDMAN, M. (1999): *Consumer boycotts. Effecting change through the marketplace and the media.* New York: Routledge.

GABRIEL, Y. and LANG, T. (1995): *The unmanageable consumer: contemporary consumption and its fragmentation.* London: Sage.

GALTIER, F. and DIAZ PEDREGAL, V. (2010): Le développent du commerce équitable peut-il conduire à une réduction des injustices? Une réflexion à partir du cas du café. *Cahier Agricultures*, 19: 50-59.

GAUBE, T. (2006): Altruism and charitable giving in a fully replicated economy. *Journal of Public Economics*, 90 (8-9): 1649-1667.

GERT, B. (2011): The Definition of Morality. In: Zalta, E. N. (Ed.): *The Stanford Encyclopedia of Philosophy.* (Summer 2011 Edition). Forthcoming, Available from: http://plato.stanford.edu/archives/sum2011/entries/morality-definition/, [accessed 2011-05-25].

GFK (2008a): *GfK Charity Scope – Der Spendenmarkt 2007, Marktübersicht Januar bis März 2007,* April 2008. Available from: http://www.gfk.com/imperia/md/content/ps_de/chart_der_woche/2008/kw16_08_charity.pdf, [accessed 2008-04-28].

GFK (2008b): *Spendensituation und Spendenverhalten – Aktuelle Entwicklungen, Charity Scope 2008: Spendenmotivation – Eine soziostrukturelle Analyse.*

GFK (2008c): *Corporate Social Responsibility - GfK Consumer Tracking*. Available from: http://www.gfk.com/imperia/md/content/ps_de/chart_der_woche/2008/kw23_08_corporate_social_resonsibility.pdf, [accessed 2008-07-13].

GFK (2008d): *Globaler Klimaschutz birgt Chancen für Verbraucher und Handel*. Press Release. Available from: http://www.gfk.com/imperia/md/content/ps_de/chart_der_woche/2008/kw23_08_corporate_social_resonsibility.pdf, [accessed 2008-07-13].

GFK and DEUTSCHER SPENDENRAT E.V. (2009): *Bilanz des Helfens*. Available from: http://www.fundraiser-magazin.de/tl_files/bilder/Bundes_Pressekonferenz_8.10.2009_final.pdf, [accessed 2009-10-08].

GIBSON, C., OSTROM, E. and SHIVAKUMAR, S. (2001): *Institutions, Incentives, and Aid Sustainability: A workshop study for Sida*. Presented at a colloquium at the Workshop in Political Theory and Political Analysis, Indiana University, Bloomington, March 2, 2001. Available from: http://www.indiana.edu/~workshop/papers/sida030501_1.pdf, [accessed 07-11-10].

GIDDENS, A. (1990): *The Consequences of Modernity*. Stanford: Stanford University Press.

GIOVANNUCCI, D. and KOEKOEK, F. J. (2003): T*he state of sustainable coffee. A study of twelve major markets*. Washington, DC: World Bank.

GNEEZY, U. and RUSTICHINI, A. (2000): Pay enough or don't pay at all. *The Quarterly Journal of Economics*, 115: 791-810.

GOLAN, E., KUCHLER, F., MITCHELL, L., GREENE, C. and JESSUP, A. (2001): Economics of Food Labeling. *Journal of Consumer Policy*, 24: 117-184.

GOODMAN, M. K. (2004): Reading fair trade: political ecological imaginary and the moral economy of fair trade foods. *Political Geography*, 23: 891–915.

GRÄB, C. (2007): E-Mail Correspondence with C. Gräb, German Federal Statistical Office, 17.09.2007.

GRANKVIST, G., LEKEDAL, H. and MARMENDAL, M. (2007): Values and eco- and fair-trade labelled products. *British Food Journal*, 109 (2): 169-181.

GRIMES, K. M. (2005): Changing the Rules of Trade with Global partnerships: The Fair Trade Movement. In: Nash, J. C. (Ed.): *Social Movements: An Anthropological Reader*. Malden, Mass. [et al.]: Blackwell: 237-248.

GRIMM, F. (2006): *Shopping hilft die Welt verbessern: Der andere Einkaufsführer*. München: Mosaik bei Goldmann.

GUILLAUMONT, P. (2007): Assessing the Economic Vulnerability of Small Island Developing States and the Least Developed Countries. *Research Paper No. 2007/40.* Available from: http://www.wider.unu.edu/publications/rps/rps2007/rp2007-40.pdf, [accessed 07-10-27].

GUILLAUMONT, P. and LAAJAJA, R. (2006): When Instability increases the Effectiveness of Aid Projects. *World Bank Policy Working Paper* 4034, Washington, DC: World Bank. Available from: http://www-wds.worldbank.org/servlet/WDSContentServer/WDSP/IB/2006/10/12/000016406_20061012145457/Rendered/PDF/wps4034.pdf, [accessed 07-11-01].

HADFIELD, G. H. and THOMSON, D. (1998): An Information-Based Approach to Labeling Biotechnology Consumer Products. *Journal of Consumer Policy*, 21: 551-578.

HANSEN, U. and SCHRADER, U. (2001): Nachhaltiger Konsum – Leerformel oder Leitprinzip? In: Schrader, U. and Hansen, U. (Eds.): *Nachhaltiger Konsum – Forschung und Praxis im Dialog*. Frankfurt/New York: Campus Verlag: 17-48.

HARRIS, C. E. (1999): Towards a Theory of Moral Change. Presented at the OEC International Conference on Ethics in Engineering and Computer Science, March 1999. *Online Ethics Center for Engineering* 5/23/2006 National Academy of Engineering, Accessed: Wednesday, May 25, 2011. Available from: www.onlineethics.org/Topics/ProfPractice/PPEssays/moral_change.aspx, [accessed 2011-05-25].

HARRISON, R., NEWHOLM, T. and SHAW, D. (2005): Defining the Ethical Consumer. In: Harrison, R., Newholm, T. and Shaw, D. (Eds.): *The Ethical Consumer*, London: Sage: 1-10.

HARVEY, J. W. (1990): Benefit Segmentation for Fund Raisers. *Journal of the Academy of Marketing Science*, 18 (1): 77-86.

HAVAS MEDIA (2009): *Sustainable Future 09*: *German Factsheet.* Available from: http://www.havasmedia.com/staticfiles/Germany%20Factsheet.pdf, [accessed 2010-01-18].

HAYES, M. (2006): On the efficiency of fair trade. *Review of Social Economy*, 64 (4): 447-468.

HEIDBÜCHEL, A. (2000): Psychologie des Spenderverhaltens: Analyse eines theoriegeleiteten Prozeßmodells. In: Wiendieck, G. (Ed.): *Kölner Arbeiten zur Wirtschaftspsychologie*, 16. Frankfurt/Main: Peter Lang GmbH.

HILTON, M. (2003): *Consumerism in the 20th Century Britain.* Cambridge: Cambridge University Press.

HÖGE, H. (2008): *Konsumkritik.* Available from: http://blogs.taz.de/hausmeisterblog/2008/07/31/konsumkritik/, [accessed 2008-07-31].

HOLTHOFF-STENGER, M. (2008a): Wer sind die Lohas? *Fokus Online*. Available from: *http://www.focus.de/finanzen/news/studie-wer-sind-die-lohas_aid_305216.html,* [accessed 2008-05-30].

HOLTHOFF-STENGER, M. (2008b): Grün ist lecker. *Fokus*, 14/200: 120-122. Available from: https://umho.uni-hohenheim.de/fileadmin/einrichtungen/umho/Aktuelle_Berichte/Focus_Maerz_2008.tif.pdf, [accessed 2008-06-03].

HONKANEN, P., VERPLANKEN, B. and OLSEN, S. O. (2006): Ethical values and motives driving organic food choice. *Journal of Consumer Behaviour*, 5 (5): 420-430.

HUBERT BURDA MEDIA (2007): *Greenstyle Report: Die Zielgruppe der LOHAS verstehen.* Available from: http://www.hubert-burda-media.de/hps/upload/hxmedia/hbmi/HBMEUJIf.pdf, [accessed 2008-05-30].

IFAT (2011): *What is ... Fair Trade? IFAT? A Fair Trade Organization?* Available from: www.phytotradeafrica.com/downloads/whatisfairtrade.pdf, [accessed 2011-05-04].

IISD (2005): *Oslo Roundtable on Sustainable Production and Consumption*. Available from: http://www.iisd.ca/consume/oslo004.html, [accessed 2008-12-04].

ISEAL (2008a): *Monitoring and Evaluating Impacts*. Available from: http://www.isealalliance.org/index.cfm?fuseaction=Page.viewPage&pageId=493&parentID=490, [accessed 2008-06-17].

ISEAL (2008b): *What we do.* Available from: http://www.isealalliance.org/index.cfm?fuseaction=Page.viewPage&pageId=490, [accessed 2008-06-17].

IRI (2007): *Sustainability 2007: Consumer-focused CPG Growth Opportunities*. Available from: http://de1.infores.com/filelib/timestrends/TT_December_2007_Sustainability.pdf, [accessed 2008-05-05].

JACKSON, T. and MICHAELIS, L. (2003): *Policies for Sustainable Consumption: A report to the Sustainable Development Commission.* Available from: http://www.sd-commission.org.uk/publications/downloads/030917%20Policies%20for%20sustainable%20consumption%20_SDC%20report_.pdf, [accessed 2010-12-28].

JOLIBERT, A. and BAUMGARTNER, G. (1997): Values, motivations, and personal goals: Revisited. *Psychology and Marketing*, 14 (7): 675-688.

KAAS, K. P. and RUPRECHT, H. (2006): Are the Vickrey Auction and the BDM Mechanism really incentive compatible? – Empirical results and optimal bidding strategies in cases of uncertain willingness-to-pay. *Schmalenbachs Business Review*, 28: 37-55.

KALAFATIS, S. P., POLLARD, M., EAST, R. and TSOGAS, M. H. (1999): Green marketing and Ajzen's theory of planned behaviour: a cross-market examination. *Journal of Consumer Marketing*, 16 (5): 441-460.

KHARE, A. and INMAN, J. (2006): Habitual behaviour in American eating patterns: The role of meal occasions. *Journal of Consumer Research*, 32 (4): 567-575.

KIM, J.-O., FORSYTHE, S., GU, Q. and MOON, S. J. (2002): Cross-cultural consumer values, needs and purchase behaviour. *Journal of Consumer Marketing*, 19 (6): 481-502

KJARNES, U. (2007): Ethics and action: a relational perspective on food trends and consumer concerns. In: Zollitsch, W., Winckler, C., Waiblinger S. and Haslberger A. (Eds.): *Sustainable food production and ethics*. Wageningen: Wageningen Academic Publishers: 43-48.

KLEIN, J.G., SMITH, N.C. and JOHN, A. (2004): Why we boycott: consumer motivations for boycott participation. *The Journal of Marketing*, 68 (3): 92-109.

KLEINERT, U. (2000): Inlandswirkungen des Fairen Handels. In: Piepel, K. (Ed.): *Entwicklungspolitische Wirkungen des Fairen Handels - Beiträge zur Diskussion*. Aachen: Misereor: 19-110.

KOESTER, U. (1992): *Grundzüge der landwirtschaftlichen Marktlehre*. München: Vahlen.

KONOW, J. (2006): Mixed Feelings: Theories and Evidence of Warm Glow and Altruism. *Working Paper, MPRA* No. 2727.

KORT, K. (2010): Wir machen keine Geschäfte mit der Nachhaltigkeit. *Handelsblatt*, 27.02.2010.

KRIER, J. - M. (2005): *Fair Trade in Europe: Facts and Figures on Fair Trade in 25 European Countries*. Fair Trade Advocacy Office, Brussels. Available from: http://www.fairtrade.net/uploads/media/FairTradeinEurope2005.pdf, [accessed 07-04-13].

KRIER, J. - M. (2008): *Fair Trade 2007: new facts and figures from an ongoing success story: A report on Fair Trade in 33 consumer countries*. Available from: http://www.forum-fairer-handel.de/cms/lit_files/FairTrade2007newfacts+figures.pdf, [accessed 2009-02-20].

KUTSCH, T. (2001): Ethisch begründeter Konsum – Forderung, Wirklichkeit oder pragmatischer Kompromiss? *AID - Ernährung im Fokus*, 07/01: 170-1775

KUTSCH, T. (2002): Ethik und Moral – auch beim Essen? *Fundus*, 1: 10-11.

KUTSCH, T. (2005): Soziologische Aspekte – Lebenstile. In: Stehle, P. and Matissek, R. (Eds.): *Ernährung, Süßwaren und Lebensstil - Eine interdisziplinäre Betrachtung*. 1. Bonner Forum Ernährungswissenschaft. Berlin: Verlag Dr. Köster: 14-34.

LÄMMERZAHL, E. (2007): Memo regarding the publication ‚Bilanz des Helfens' by GfK, 27.11.07.

LÄMMERZAHL, E. (2008): *Spendensituation und Spendenverhalten – Aktuelle Entwicklungen. CharityScope 2008: Spendenmotivation. Eine soziostrukturelle Analyse.*

LANDRY, C., LANGE, A., LIST, J. A., PRICE, M. K. and RUPP, N. G. (2005): Toward an Understanding of the Economics of Charity: Evidence from a Field Experiment. *NBER Working Paper* no. 11611.

LANGEN, N. and HARTMANN, M. (2011): *New forms of consumer power – Implications from the first Cologne Carrotmob.* Paper presented at the 5th International European Forum on System Dynamics and Innovation in Food Networks, February 14-18, 2011, Innsbruck-Igls, Austria.

LECLAIR, M. S. (2002): Fighting the Tide: Alternative Trade Organizations in the Era of Global Free Trade. *World Development*, 30 (6): 949-958.

LECLAIR, M. S. (2003): Fighting Back: The growth of alternative trade. *Development*, 46 (1): 66-73.

LE MARE, A. (2008): The Impact of Fair Trade on Social and Economic Development. *Geography Compass*, 2 (6): 1922-1942.

LELAND, H. E. (1979): Quacks, Lemons, and Licensing: A Theory of Minimum Quality Standards. *The Journal of Political Economy*, 87 (6): 1328-1346.

LIEBIG, K. and SAUTTER, H. (2000): Politische Wirkungen des Fairen Handels. In: Piepel, K. (Ed.): *Entwicklungspolitische Wirkungen des Fairen Handels - Beiträge zur Diskussion.* Aachen: Misereor: 111-184.

LINDSEY, B. (2003): *Grounds for Complaint? Understanding the "Coffee Crisis".* Trade Briefing Paper, 16. Available from: http://www.cato.org/pub_display.php?pub_id=6807 [accessed 2011-04-28].

LINTON, A. (2005): Partnering for sustainability: business–NGO alliances in the coffee industry. *Development in Practice*, 15 (3/4): 600-615.

LITTRELL, M. A. and DICKSON, M. A. (1999): *Social Responsibility in the Global Market: Fair Trade of Cultural Products*. Thousand Oaks, California: Sage Publications.

LOUREIRO, M. L., MCCLUSKEY, J. J. and MITTELHAMMER, R. C. (2001): Assessing Consumer Preferences for Organic, Eco-labeled, and Regular Apples. *Journal of Agricultural and Resource Economics*, 26 (2): 404-416.

LOUREIRO, L. M., MCCLUSKEY, J. J. and MITTELHAMMER, R. C. (2002): Will Consumers Pay a Premium for Eco-Labeled Appeals? *Journal of Consumer Affairs*, 36: 203-219.

LOUREIRO, M. and LOTADE, J. (2005): Do fair trade and eco-labels in coffee wake up the consumer conscience? *Ecological Economics*, 53 (1): 129-138.

LUSK, J. L., NILSSON, T. and FOSTER, K. (2007): Public Preferences and Private Choices: Effect of Altruism and Free Riding on Demand for Environmentally Certified Pork. *Environmental & Resource Economics*, 36 (4): 499–521.

LYON, S. (2007): Maya Coffee Farmers and Fair Trade. *Culture and Agriculture*, 29 (2): 100-112.

LZ NET (2007): *Deutschland spielt bei fair gehandelten Produkten in der Top-Liga*. Available from: http://www.lz-net.de/archiv/lznet/mylznet/pages/show.prl?params=keyword%3D%26all%3D%26type%3D%26where%3D%26suchid%3D223139%26quelle%3D1%26laufzeit%3D&id=57839&currPage=1, [accessed 2007-03-27].

MAKOWSKY, A. (2007): *Nach der Bio-Bewegung kommt "Fairtrade" in Mode: Produkte aus fairem Handel werden bei Konsumenten immer beliebter*. Available from: http://www.sueddeutsche.de/,ra2m2/panorama/artikel/570/113457/, [accessed 2007-05-10].

MADDEN, T. J., SCHOLDER ELLEN, P. and AJZEN, I. (1992): A comparison of the theory of planned behavior and the theory of reasoned action. *Personality and Social Psychology Bulletin,* 18 (1): 3-9.

MAIETTA, O. W. (2003): *The Hedonic Price of Fair-Trade Coffee for the Italian Consumer*. In: Proceedings of the International Conference on Agricultural Policy Reform and the WTO: Where Are We Heading? Capri (Italy). Available from: http://www.ecostat.unical.it/2003agtradeconf/Contributed%20papers/Maietta.pdf, [accessed 2008-07-17].

MANN, S. (2003): Why organic food in Germany is a merit good. *Food Policy,* 28 (5-6): 459-469.

MARCUSE, H. (2008): *Der eindimensionale Mensch: Studien zur Ideologie der fortgeschrittenen Industriegesellschaft*. 6th ed. München: Deutscher Taschenbuch Verlag.

MASELAND, R. and DE VAAL, A. (2002): How fair is Fair Trade? *De Economist*, 150 (3): 251-272.

MAYERL, J. (2006): Zur soziologischen Erklärung individuellen Geldspendens: Eine Anwendung und Erweiterung der Theory of Reasoned Action unter Verwendung von Antwortlatenzzeiten in einem Mediator-Moderator-Design. In: *Schriftenreihe des Instituts für Sozialwissenschaften der Universität Stuttgart*. 2/2006.

MAYERL, J. (2008): *Kognitive Grundlagen sozialen Verhaltens. Theoretische und statistische Analysen zur Modellierung von Einstellungs-Verhaltens-Beziehungen*. Dissertation. University of Stuttgart.

MEULEMANN, H. and BECKERS, T. (2003): Hat die Flut vom August 2002 die Spendenaktivität gesteigert? Ein Vergleich der Häufigkeit und der Hintergründe habitueller und spontaner Spenden. *ZA-Information 52*, Zentralarchiv für Empirische Sozialforschung: 37-57.

MICHELETTI, M. (2003): *Political Virtue and Shopping: Individuals, Consumerism and Collective Action*. Basingstoke: Palgrave.

MICHELETTI, M. (2006): Political consumerism: Why the market is an arena for politics. In: Kaiser, M. and Lien, M. E. (Eds.): *Ethics and the politics of food*. Wageningen: Wageningen Academic Publishers: 23-27.

MICHELETTI, M., FOLLESDAL, A. and STOLLE, D. (2004): Introduction. In: Micheletti, M., Follesdal, A. and Stolle, D. (Eds.): *Politics, products, and markets: exploring political consumerism past and present*. New Brunswick: Transaction: ix-3.

MICHELSEN, J., HAMM, U., WYNEN, E. and ROTH, E. (1999): The European Market for Organic Products: Growth and Development. *Organic Farming in Europe: Economics and Policy*, 7, Universität Hohenheim - Stuttgart Hohenheim.

MISIK, R. (2007): *Das Kult-Buch: Glanz und Elend der Kommerzkultur*. Bonn: Bundeszentrale für politische Bildung.

MONROE, K. R. (1994): A Fat Lady in a Corset: Altruism and Social Theory. *American Journal of Political Science*, 38 (4): 861-893.

MOORE, G. (2004): The Fair Trade movement: parameters, issues and future research. *Journal of business ethics*, 53 (1-2): 73-86.

MOSLEY, P., HUDSON, J. and VERSCHOOR, A. (2004): Aid, Poverty reduction and the "new conditionality". *The Economic Journal*, 114: F 217-243.

MURADIAN, R. and PELUPESSY, W. (2005): Governing the coffee chain: the role of voluntary regulatory systems. *World Development*, 33 (12): 2029-2044.

MURRAY, D., RAYNOLDS, L. and TAYLOR P. (2006): The future of Fair Trade coffee: dilemmas facing Latin America's small-scale producers. *Development in Practice*, 16 (2): 179-192.

NEDERHOF, A. J. (1985): Methods of coping with social desirability bias: a review. *European Journal of Social Psychology*, 15: 263-280.

NEWHOLM, T. (2000): *Understanding the ethical consumer*: Employing a frame of bounded rationality. Unpublished doctoral thesis, Open University.

NEWHOLM T. and SHAW D. (2007): Studying the ethical consumer: a review of research. *Journal of Consumer Behaviour: an international research review*, 6: 253-270.

NICHOLLS, A. and OPAL, C. (2005): *Fair Trade: Market-Driven Ethical Consumption..*: London: Sage Publications Ltd.

NIELSEN (2008a): *LOHAS Imaginärer Gesellschaftstrend oder reale Differenzierung im (Einkaufs-)verhalten.* Eine Studie auf Basis des Nielsen Haushaltspanel & der Typologien von KarmaKonsum. Presented at KarmaKonsum Konferenz 2008, 30th, Mai 2008, Frankfurt /Main.

ÖBERSEDER, M. and SCHLEGELMILCH, B. B. (2010): Ethik im Marketing: Themen, Entwicklungen und Perspektiven. *Marketing*, 1: 53-64.

OECD (2007a): Where governments come together to make aid work. OECD publications, No. 88051 2007. Available from: http://www.oecd.org/dataoecd/39/58/39218438.pdf, [accessed 07-11-13].

OECD (2007b): Table 1: DAC Members' Net Official Development Assistance in 2005. In: *Statistical Annex of the 2006 Development Co-operation Report*. Available from: http:// www.oecd.org/document/9/0,3343,en_2649_34485_1893129_1_1_1_1,00.html, Tables updated on 19 January 2007, [accessed 07-11-13].

OECD (2007c): Table 19: Aid by Major Purposes in 2005. In: *Statistical Annex of the 2006 Development Co-operation Report.* Available from: http://www.oecd.org/document/9/0,3343,en_2649_34485_1893129_1_1_1_1,00.html, Tables updated on 19 January 2007, [accessed 07-11-13].

OECD (2007d): Table 2: Total Net Flows from DAC Countries by Type of Flow. In: *Statistical Annex of the 2006 Development Co-operation Report.* Available from: http://www.oecd.org/document/9/0,3343,en_2649_34485_1893129_1_1_1_1,00.html, Tables updated on 19 January 2007, [accessed 07-11-13].

OFFERMAN, T., SONNEMANS, J. and SCHRAM, A. (1996): Value Orientations, Expectations and Voluntary Contributions in Public Goods. *The Economic Journal*, 106 (437): 817-845.

ÖKOLANDBAU.DE (2006): *Bio-Markt kompakt: Kennzahlen zum Markt für Bio-Lebensmittel.* Stand 01.03.2006. Available from: http://www.oekolandbau.de/fileadmin/redaktion/dokumente/haendler/marktinformationen/biomarkt_kompakt.pdf, [accessed 2011-03-22].

OLSON, J. M. and ZANNA, M. P. (1993): Attitudes and Attitude Change. *Annual Review of Psychology*, 44: 117-154.

OLSON, M. (1965): *The Logic of Collective Action.* Harvard: Harvard University Press.

OSMUNDSVÅG, I. (2007): Fair-trade Max Havelaar Norway. In: Laloh, S. and Emmert, S. (Eds.): *Proceedings: Cases in Sustainable Consumption and Production: Workshop of the Sustainable Consumption Research Exchange (SCORE!) Network*, supported by the EU's 6th Framework Program, Paris, 4-5 June 2007: 167-182.

OZCAGLAR-TOULOUSE, N., SHIU, E. and SHAW, D. (2006): In search of fair trade: ethical consumer decision making in France. *International Journal of Consumer Studies*, 30 (5): 502-514.

PADEL, S. and MIDMORE, P. (2005): The development of the European market for organic products: insights from a Delphi study. *British Food Journal,* 107 (8): 626-646.

PADEL, S., RÖCKLINSBERG, H. and SCHMID, O. (2009): The implementation of organic principles and values in the European Regulation. *Food Policy*, 34: 245–251.

PARRISH, B. D., LUZADIS, V. A. and BENTLEY, W. R. (2005): What Tanzania's Coffee Farmers Can Teach the World: A Performance-Based Look at the Fair Trade-Free Trade Debate. *Sustainable Development*, 13 (3): 177-189.

PAUL, E. (2005): Evaluating Fair Trade as a development project: methodological considerations. *Development in Practice*, 15 (2): 134-150.

PHAROAH, C. and TANNER, S. (1997): Trends in Charitable Giving. *Fiscal Studies*, 18 (4): 427-443.

PIEPEL, K., MÖLLER, A. and SPIEGEL, K.-H. (2000): Fairer Handel, wohin? In: Piepel, K. (Ed.): *Entwicklungspolitische Wirkungen des Fairen Handels - Beiträge zur Diskussion*. Aachen: Misereor: 271-301.

PIEPER, A. (1994): *Einführung in die Ethik*. Tübingen, 3rd ed. Basel: Francke.

PILIAVIN, J. A. and CHARNG, H.-W. (1990): Altruism: A Review of Recent Theory and Research. *Annual Review of Sociology*, 16: 27-65.

PIROTTE, G. (2007): Consumption as a Solidarity-Based Commitment: The Case of Oxfam Worldshops' Customers. In: Zaccai, E. (Ed.): *Sustainable Consumption, Ecology and Fair Trade*. London: Routledge: 127-143.

PONTE, S. (2004): *Standards and Sustainability in the Coffee Sector: A Global Value Chain Approach*. International Institute for Sustainable Development, Winnipeg, Canada.

PRILLER, E. and SOMMERFELD, J. (2005): Wer spendet in Deutschland? Eine sozialstrukturelle Analyse. *WZB Discussion Paper*. Wissenschaftszentrum Berlin für Sozialforschung (WZB).

PWC (2005): *Transparenzpreis 2005: Deutsche Spendenorganisationen ausgezeichnet*. Available from: http://www.pwc.de/portal/pub/!ut/p/kcxml/04_Sj9SPykssy0xPLMnMz0vM0Y_QjzKLd4p3dg0CSZnFG8QbeXvrR0IYATAxR4RIkL63vq9Hfm6qfoB-QW5oRLmjoyIArJ-n3g!!?siteArea=49c234c4f2195056&content=e5fdfd4f8f078c1&topNavNode=49c4e4a420942bcb, [accessed 07-05-28].

RADELET, S., CLEMENS, M. AND BHAVNANI, R. (2005): Aid and Growth. *Finance and Development*, 42 (3). Available from: http://www.imf.org/external/pubs/ft/fandd/2005/09/radelet.htm, [accessed 07-11-14].

RANDALL, D. M. and FERNANDES, M. F. (1991): The Social Desirability Response Bias in Ethics Research. *Journal of Business Ethics*, 10: 805-817.

RANSOM, D. (2005): Fair trade for sale: David Ransom thinks not. New Internationalist, April 2005. Available from: http://findarticles.com/p/articles/mi_m0JQP/is_377/ai_n13801026/, [accessed 2008-06-20].

RAYNOLDS, L. T. (2002): *Poverty Alleviation Through Participation in Fair Trade Coffee Networks: Existing Research and Critical Issues*. Background Paper Prepared for Project Funded by the Community and Resource Development Program, The Ford Foundation, New York.

RAYNOLDS, L. T. (2009): Mainstreaming Fair Trade Coffee: From Partnership to Traceability. *World Development*, 37 (6): 1083-1093.

RAYNOLDS, L. T., MURRAY, D. and HELLER, A. (2007): Regulation sustainability in the coffee sector: a comparative analysis of third-party environmental and social certification initiatives. *Agriculture and Human Values*, 24 (2): 147-163.

REDFERN, A. and SNEDKER, P. (2002): Creating Market Opportunities for Small Enterprises: Experiences of the Fair Trade Movement. *SEED working paper*, 30. International Labour Office, Geneva.

REECE, W. S. (1979): Charitable contributions: new evidence on household behaviour. *The American Economic Review,* 69 (1): 142-151.

REGIL, DE A. J. (2007): *How Sustainable is Our Latte? An Assessment of Trends and Standards in Fair Trade from the Perspective of a New Truly Sustainable People and Planet-Centred Paradigm*. The Jus Semper Global Alliance. Available from: http://www.jussemper.org/Resources/Trade%20Activity/Resources/How_Sustainable_is_Latte.pdf, [accessed 2008-10-01].

RENARD, M. - C. (2003): Fair trade: quality, market and conventions. *Journal of Rural Studies*, 19: 87-96.

RENARD, M. - C. (2005): Quality certification, regulation and power in fair trade. *Journal of Rural Studies*, 21: 419-431.

REWE *(2008)*: *Tag der Nachhaltigkeit*. Press release. Available from: http://www.rewe-group.com/index.php?id=90&tx_ttnews[tt_news]=559&tx_ttnews[backPid]=45&cHash=eec744ff75, [accessed 2008-12-18].

RICE, J. (2010): Free Trade, Fair Trade and Gender Inequality in Less Developed Countries. *Sustainable Development*, 18 (1): 42-50.

RICE, R. A. (2001): Noble goals and challenging terrain: organic and Fair Trade coffee movements in the global marketplace. *Journal of Agricultural and Environmental Ethics*, 14, 39-66.

RIPPIN, M. (2009): *Organic market data for 2007/2008*. Presented at Biofach 20.02.2009. Available from: http://www.agromilagro.de/downloads/EUmarket2007_08.pdf, [accessed 2010-12-18].

ROBERTS, J. A. (1996): Will the real socially responsible consumer please step forward? *Business Horizons*, 39 (1): 79-83.

ROBINSON, R. and SMITH, C. (2002): Psychosocial and demographic variables associated with consumer intention to purchase sustainable produced foods as defined by the Midwest Food Alliance. *Journal of Nutrition Education and Behaviour*, 34 (6): 316-325.

RODRICK, D. (1999): Democracies pay higher wages. *Quarterly Journal of Economics*, 114: 707-738.

RONCHI, L. (2002b): The Impact of Fair Trade on Producers and their organisations: A case study with Coocafe in Costa Rica. *PRUS Working Paper*, No. 11, Poverty Research Unit at Sussex University of Sussex, Brighton.

RONCHI, L. (2006): "Fairtrade" and Market Failures in Agricultural Commodity Markets. *World Bank Policy Research Working Paper*, 4011.

ROSE-ACKERMAN, S. (1996): Altruism, Nonprofits, and Economic Theory. *Journal of Economic Literature*, 34 (2): 701-728.

RUSHTON, J. F. and SORRENTINO, R. M. (1981): *Altruism and helping behavior: social personality and developmental perspectives*. Hillsdale, N.J.: L. Erlbaum Associates.

RUWET, C. (2007): What justifications for a sustainable consumption? In: Zaccai, E. (Ed.): *Sustainable Consumption, Ecology and Fair Trade*. London: Routledge: 114-160.

SAGE, C. (2003): Social embeddedness and relations of regard: alternative 'good food' networks in south-west Ireland. *Journal of Rural Studies*, 19 (1): 47-60.

SCHEEPERS, P. and TE GROTENHUIS, M. (2005): Who Cares for the Poor in Europe? *European Sociological Review*, 21 (5): 453-465.

SCHLEGELMILCH, B. B. and TYNAN, A. C. (1989): The scope for market segmentation within the charity market: An empirical analysis. *Managerial and Decision Economics*, 10 (2): 127-134.

SCHLEGELMILCH, B. B., LOVE, A. and DIAMANTOPOULOS, A. (1996): Responses to different charity appeals: the impact of donor characteristics on the amount of donations. *European Journal of Marketing*, 31 (8): 548-560.

SCHLEGELMILCH, B.B., DIAMANTOPOULOS, A. and LOVE, A. (1992): Determinants of charity giving: an interdisciplinary review of the literature and suggestions for future research. In: Allen, T. et al. (Eds.): *AMA Winter Educators Conference Proceedings*, 3: 507-516.

SCHOENHEIT, I. (2007): Politischer Konsum: Ein Beitrag zum faustischen Konsumentenverhalten. In: Jäckel, M. (Ed.) *Ambivalenzen des Konsums und der werblichen Kommunikation.* Wiesbaden: Verlag für Sozialwissenschaften. Reihe: Konsumsoziologie und Massenkultur: 211-235.

SCHOENHEIT, I. (2009): Nachhaltiger Konsum. *Aus Politik und Zeitgeschichte*, 32-33: 19-26.

SCHULZ, I. and STIEß, I. (2008): Linking sustainable consumption to everyday life. A social-ecological approach to consumption research. In: Tukker, A., Charter, M. and Vezzoli, C. (Eds.): *System innovation for sustainability 1: Perspectives on radical changes to sustainable consumption and production.* Sheffield: Greenleaf Publishing: 288-300.

SCHULZ, W. F. (2008): *Megatrend Nachhaltigkeit - Marktpotenziale von LOHAS & Co.* Vortrag im Rahmen der Jahrestagung des Umweltausschusses des Vereins für Socialpolitik am 25. April 2008 an der Universität Hohenheim. Available from: https://umho.uni-hohenheim.de/fileadmin/einrichtungen/umho/Aktuelle_Berichte/Megatrend_Nachhaltigkeit_-_Marktpotenziale_von_LOHAS___Co._-_25._April_2008.pdf, [accessed 2008-06-03].

SCHWARTZ, S. H. (1992): Universals in the content and structure of values: Theory and empirical tests in 20 countries. In: Zanna, M. (Ed.): *Advances in experimental social psychology*, 25, New York: Academic Press: 1-65.

SEN, A. K. (1977): Rational Fools: A Critique of the Behavioral Foundations of Economic Theory. *Philosophy and Public Affairs*, 6 (4): 317-344.

SEVEN ONE MEDIA (2009): *TrendReport Grün.* Available from: http://www.sevenonemedia.de/imperia/md/content/content/Research/Marktanalyse/branchen/specials/TrendReport_Gruen.pdf, [accessed 2010-10-10].

SHAW, D. (2007): Consumer voters in imagined communities. *International Journal of Sociology and Social Policy*, 27 (3/4): 135-150.

SHAW, D. and CLARKE, I. (1999): Belief formation in ethical consumer groups: an exploratory study. *Marketing Intelligence & Planning*, 17 (2): 109–119.

SHAW, D. and SHIU, E. (2002): An assessment of ethical obligation and self-identity in ethical consumer decision-making: a structural equation modelling approach. *International Journal of Consumer Studies*, 26 (4): 286-293.

SHAW, D. and SHIU, E. (2003): Ethics in consumer choice: a multivariate modelling approach. *European Journal of Marketing*, 37 (10): 1485-1498.

SHAW, D., NEWHOLM, T. and DICKINSON, R. (2006): Consumption as voting: an exploration of consumer empowerment. *European Journal of Marketing*, 9/10: 1049-1067.

SHOGREN, J. F., CHO, S.; KOO, C.; LIST, J.; PARK, C.; POLO, P. and WILHELMI, R. (2001): Auction mechanisms and the measurement of WTP and WTA. *Resource and Energy Economics*, 23: 97-109.

SHOVE, E. and WARDE, A. (1997): Noticing Inconspicuous Consumption. Paper presented at the *ESF TERM Programme workshop on Consumption, Everyday Life and Sustainability. Lancaster University, April 1997.* Available from: http://www.lancs.ac.uk/fass/projects/esf/inconspicuous.htm, [accessed 2009-12-12].

SIDWELL, M. (2008): *Unfair Trade*. London: Adam Smith Institute.

SIKULA, A. and COSTA, A. (1994): Are Women More Ethical than Men? *Journal of Business Ethics*, 13: 859-871.

SMITH, S. and BARRIENTOS, S. (2005): Fair Trade and Ethical Trade: Are there moves towards convergence? *Sustainable Development*, 13 (3): 190-198.

SMITH, S. J. (2005): States, markets and an ethic of care. *Political Geography*, 24 (1): 1–20.

SMITH, V. H., KEHOE, M. R. and CREMER, M. E. (1995): The private provision of public goods: Altruism and voluntary giving. *Journal of Public Economics*, 58: 107-126.

SOLOMON, M. R. (2009): *Consumer Behavior - Buying, Having and Being.* New Jersey: Pearson Prentice Hall.

SOMMERFELD, J. (2008). Die Bedeutung des Spenden- und Gemeinnützigkeitsrechts in der Praxis - Eine Analyse von Experteninterviews. *Presented at WZB und DZI Tagung: „Motive, gesellschaftliche Rahmenbedingungen und Einflussfaktoren auf das Spendenverhalten"*, 13.10.2008, Berlin.

STATISTICAL INNOVATION (2005): *Tutorial #1*: Using Latent GOLD 4.0 to Estimate LC Cluster Models.

STEBLAY, N. M. (1987): Helping behavior in rural and urban environments: A meta-analysis. *Psychological Bulletin*, 102 (3): 346-356.

STEHR, N. (2007): *Die Moralisierung der Märkte*. Eine Gesellschaftstheorie. Frankfurt/Main: Suhrkamp.

STEINBERG, R. (1990): Taxes and Giving: New Findings. *International Journal of Voluntary and Nonprofit Organizations*, 1 (2): 61-79.

STEINER, A. (2008): Die Analyse der Spendenmotive anhand einer qualitativen psychologischen Studie. *Presented at WZB und DZI Tagung: Motive, gesellschaftliche Rahmenbedingungen und Einflussfaktoren auf das Spendenverhalten.* 13.10.2008. Available from: http://www.dzi.de/Spendenstatistik/tagung13102008/Steiner.pdf, [accessed 2008-10-20].

STEINKIRCHNER, P., BISKAMP, S., BUSCH, A., KLESSE, H. - J., RAMTHUN, C., SALZ, J., SCHNAAS, D., SCHUMACHER, H. and SCHUSTER, H. (2007): Die wirtschaftliche Macht des Guten. *Wirtschaftswoche,* 38/2007, 19.09.07. Available from: http://www.wiwo.de/pswiwo/fn/ww2/sfn/buildww/id/126/id/305789/fm/0/artpage/0/artprint/0/SH/0/depot/0/index.html, [accessed 07-09-19].

STEINRÜCKEN, T. (2002): Funktioniert fairer Handel? Ökonomische Überlegungen zum alternativen Handel mit Kaffee. *Discussion Paper TU Ilmenau.* Available from: http://www.tu-ilmenau.de/fakww/fileadmin/template/fakww/Institute_und_Fachgebiete/Volkswirtschaftslehre/Wirtschaftspolitik/Dokumente/Diskussionspapier_Nr_32.pdf, [accessed 2008-08-20].

STEINRÜCKEN, T. (2004): Fairer Handel durch Sozialsiegel? Ökonomische Analyse eines alternativen Handelskonzepts. *List Forum für Wirtschafts- und Finanzpolitik,* 30 (4): 339-356.

STOLLE, D. and MICHELETTI, M. (2003): The gender gap reversed: political consumerism as a women-friendly form of civic and political engagement. Paper prepared for the *Fender and Social Capital Conference May 2-3, 2003, St. John's College, University of Manitoba.*

STRATUM (2008): *Lohas - Mythos und Wirklichkeit.* Available from: http://www.stratum-consult.de/images/stories/download/stratum_lohas_mythos_wirklichkeit_leseprobe.pdf, [accessed 2008-11-13].

STRONG, C. (1996): Features contributing to the growth of ethical consumerism – a preliminary investigation. *Marketing Intelligence & Planning,* 14 (5): 5-13.

SUSTAINABLE AGRICULTURE INITIATIVE PLATFORM (2011): *What we do.* Available from: http://www.saiplatform.org/about-us/what-we-do, [accessed 2011-07-05].

SUWA-EISENMANN, A. and VERDIER, T. (2007): Aid and Trade. *Oxford Review of Economic Policy,* 23 (3): 481-507.

SYKES, G. M. and MATZA D. (1957): Techniques of Neutralization: A Theory of Delinquency. *American Sociological Review*, 6: 664-670.

TAGBATA, D. and SIRIEIX, L. (2008): Measuring consumer's willingness to pay for organic and Fair Trade products. *International Journal of Consumer Studies*, 32: 479-490.

TALLONTIRE, A. (2002): Challenges facing fair trade: which way now? *Small Enterprise Development*, 13 (3): 12-24.

TALLONTIRE, A., RENTSENDORJ, E. and BLOWFIELD, M. (2001): Ethical Consumers and Ethical Trade: A Review of Current Literature, *Policy Series*, 12. Chatham, UK: Natural Resources Institute.

TEISL, M. F. and ROE, B. (1998): The Economics of Labeling: An Overview of Issues for Health and Environmental Disclosure. *Agricultural and Resource Economics Review*, 27 (2): 140-150.

THE CO-OPERATIVE BANK (2010): *Ethical Consumerism Report 2010: Ethical shopping through the downturn.* Available from: http://www.goodwithmoney.co.uk/assets/Uploads/Documents/EthicalConsumerismReport2010.pdf?token=3b22ad06f250798d1441b6c0c2e54526fbcb8512|1298927960#PDFP, [accessed 2011-02-20].

THE ECONOMIST (2006): *Good Food? Why ethical shopping harms the world.* December 9th - 15th 2006: 70-73.

THØGERSEN, J. (2005): How may consumer policy empower consumers for sustainable lifestyles? *Journal of Consumer Policy* 28 (2): 143-177.

THOMPSON, P. B. (2007): Ethical bases of sustainability. In: Zollitsch, W., Winkler, C. Waiblinger, S. and Haslberger, A. (Eds.): *Sustainable food production and ethics.* Wageningen: Wageningen Academic Publishers: 63-68.

TNS INFRATEST (2005): *11 Jahre Deutscher Spendenmonitor - Fakten und Trends.*

TNS INFRATEST (2008a): 14 Jahre Deutscher Spendenmonitor: Fakten und Trends im Zeitverlauf.

TNS INFRATEST (2008b): *Bundesbürger spendeten in 2007 weniger.* Available from: http://www.tns-infratest.com/presse/pdf/Presse/20080116_TNS%20Infratest_Spendenmonitor2007.pdf, [accessed 2008-01-16].

TNS INFRATEST (2009): *15 Jahre Deutscher Spendenmonitor: Fakten und Trends im Zeitverlauf.*

TRANSFAIR (2007): *Vertragspartner*. Available from: http://www.transfair.org/ueber-transfair/ueber-uns/vertragspartner.html, [accessed 07-11-14].

TRANSFAIR (2010): *26 Prozent Plus für Fairtrade*. Press Release: 28.04.10. Available from: http://www.transfair.org/top/nachricht/browse/2/article/26-prozent-plus-fuer-fairtrade. html?tx_ttnews[backPid]=137&cHash=8ef6164167, [accessed 10-04-28].

TRANSFAIR (2011): *Absatz Fair Trade Produkte im Einzelnen*. Available from: http://www.transfair.org/produkte/absatz-fairtrade-produkte.html, [accessed 2011-03-09].

TRENDBÜRO (2007): *Otto Trendstudie Konsum-Ethik 2007: Die Zukunft des ethischen Konsums*. Available from: http://www.trendbuero.de/index.php?f_categoryId=166&f_page=1, [accessed 2007-03-14].

TRENDBÜRO (2009): *Otto Group Trendstudie 2009: Die Zukunft des ethischen Konsums*. Available from: http://www.ottogroup.com/uploads/media/Otto_Group_Trendstudie_2009_Ethischer_Konsum.pdf, [accessed 2010-12-20].

TRENTMANN, F. (2004): Beyond Consumerism: New Historical Perspectives on Consumption. *Journal of Contemporary History,* 39 (3): 373-401.

TRENTMANN, F. (2006): *The making of the consumer: knowledge, power and identity in the modern world.* Oxford: Berg.

TSALIKIS, J. and ORTIZ-BUONAFINA, M. (1990): Ethical Beliefs Differences of Males and Females. *Journal of Business Ethics*, 9 (6): 509-517.

UMBERGER, W.J., MCFADDEN, D. and SMITH, A. (2009): Does altruism play a role in determining U.S. consumer preferences and willingness to pay for natural and regionally produced beef? *Agribusiness*, 2: 268-285.

UN (1995): *World Summit for Social Development Copenhagen 1995 - Copenhagen Declaration on Social Development - Part A: Current social situation and reasons for convening the Summit*. Available from: http://www.un.org/esa/socdev/wssd/decl_parta.html, [accessed 2011-02-20].

UN (2011): *Goal 1: Eradicate extreme poverty & hunger*. Available from: http://www.un.org/millenniumgoals/poverty.shtml, [accessed 2011-05-09].

UNEP (2009): *Sustainable Consumption*. Available from: http://www.unep.fr/scp/sc/, [accessed 2009-08-25].

UNEP (2010): *About the Marrakech Process*. Available from: http://www.unep.fr/scp/marrakech/about.htm, [accessed 2010-12-20].

UNEP (n.d.): *Sustainable Consumption*. Available from: http://www.unep.fr/scp/sc/pdf/SCbrochure.pdf, [accessed 08-12-04].

UNESCO (n.d.): What is sustainable consumption? In: *Teaching and Learning for a Sustainable Future*. Available from: http://www.unesco.org/education/tlsf/TLSF/pdf/pdf_list.htm, [accessed 2011-02-20].

UTTING-CHAMORRO, K. (2005): Does fair trade make a difference? The case of small coffee producers in Nicaragua. *Development in Practice*, 15 (3-4): 584-599.

VALKILA, J. (2009): Fair Trade organic coffee production in Nicaragua - Sustainable development or a poverty trap. *Ecological Economics*, 68 (12): 3018-3025.

VANDERHOFF BOERSMA, F. (2002): *Poverty Alleviation through Participation in Fair Trade Coffee Networks: The Case of UCIRI, Oaxoca, Mexico*. Available from: http://welcome2.libarts.colostate.edu/centers/cfat/wp-content/uploads/2009/09/Case-Study-UCIRI-Oaxaca-Mexico.pdf, [accessed 2009-02-20].

VANTOMME, D., GEUENS, M., DE HOUWER, J. and DE PELSMACKER, P. (2006): Explicit and Implicit Determinants of Fair-Trade Buying Behavior. *Advances in Consumer Research*, 33: 699-703.

VERBRAUCHER INITIATIVE (2007): *Fairer Handel: Stetiges Wachstum*. Available from: http://www.fair-feels-good.de/pdf/86.pdf?title=Fairer_Handel:_Stetiges_Wachstum, [accessed 2008-05-30].

VERMEIR, I. and VERBEKE, W. (2006): Sustainable Food Consumption: Exploring the Consumer "Attitude – Behavioral Intention" Gap. *Journal of Agricultural and Environmental Ethics*, 19 (2): 169-194.

VESTERLUND, L. (2006): Why do people give? In: Powell, W. W. and Steinberg, R. (Eds.): *The non-profit sector: a research handbook*. 2. nd ed., New Haven, Conn.: Yale University Press: 568-587.

VICKERY, L. (2005): *The Ethical Consumerism Report 2005*. Manchester: The Co-operative Bank. Available from: http://www.co- operativebank.co.uk/images/pdf/coopEthical ConsumerismReport2005.pdf, [accessed 07-10-26].

VITELL, S. J., SINGHAPAKDI, A. and THOMAS, J. (2001): Consumer ethics: an application and empirical testing of the Hunt-Vitell theory of ethics. *Journal of Consumer Marketing*, 18 (2): 153-178.

VON ZIEHLBERG, R. and VON ALVENSLEBEN, R. (1998): Die Bedeutung ethischer Motive beim Kauf von Lebensmitteln am Beispiel fair gehandelten Kaffees. *Jahrbuch der Absatz- und Verbrauchsforschung*, 44 (2): 201-216.

WALLENBORN, G. (2007): How to attribute power to consumers? When epostemology and politics converge. In: Zaccai, E. (Ed.): *Sustainable Consumption, Ecology and Fair Trade*. Oxon: Routledge: 57-69.

WATHIEU, L., BRENNER, L., CARMON Z., CHATTOPADHYAY A., WERTENBROCH K., DROLET A., GOURVILLE J., MUTHUKRISHNAN A. V., NOVEMSKY N., RATNER R. K., and WU, G. (2002): Consumer Control and Empowerment: A Primer. *Marketing Letters*, 13 (3): 297-305.

WEATHERELL, C., TREGEAR, A. and ALLISON, J. (2003): In search of the concerned consumer: UK public perceptions of food, farming and buying local. *Journal of Rural Studies*, 19 (2): 233-244.

WEBB. D. J., GREEN, C. L. and BRASHEAR, T. G. (2000): Development and Validation of Scales to measure attitudes influencing monetary donations to charitable organisations. *Journal of the Academy of Marketing Science*, 28 (2): 299-309.

WEBER, M. and BUDDEMEIER, P. (2008): Philanthropie in Deutschland: Barrieren und Lösungsansätze. *Presented at WZB und DZI Tagung: Motive, gesellschaftliche Rahmenbedingungen und Einflussfaktoren auf das Spendenverhalten. 13.10.2008.*

WEDEL, M. and KAMAKURA, W. (2000): *Market Segmentation - Conceptual and Methodological Foundations*. Boston [et al.]: Kluwer.

WENZEL, E., KIRIG, A. and RAUCH, C. (2007): *Zielgruppe LOHAS: wie der grüne Lifestyle die Märkte erobert*. Kelkheim: Zukunfts-Institut.

WEST, C. (2008): *Jenseits von Altruismus und Egoismus*. Presented at WZB: Motive, gesellschaftliche Rahmenbedingungen und Einflussfaktoren auf das Spendenverhalten. 13.10.2008.

WILHELM, M. O. (2006): New data on charitable giving in the PSID. *Economics Letters*, 92: 26-31.

WISWEDE, G. (2000): Konsumsoziologie - Eine vergessene Disziplin. In: Rosenkranz, D. and Schneider, N. F. (Eds.): *Konsum: soziologische, ökonomische und psychologische Perspektiven*. Opladen: Leske und Budrich: 23-72.

WZB and DZI (2008): *Motive, gesellschaftliche Rahmenbedingungen und Einflussfaktoren auf das Spendenverhalten.* Tagung 13.10.2008. Available from: http://www.dzi.de/Spendenstatistik/tagung13102008/Programm13102008.pdf, [accessed 2008-10-20].

YOO, J. H. and HARRISON, W. B. (1989): Altruist in the "Market" for Giving and Receiving: A Case of Higher Education. *Economics of Education Review*, 8 (4): 367-376.

ZACCAI, E. (2007): Introduction: contradictions and studies. In: Zaccai, E. (Ed.): *Sustainable Consumption, Ecology and Fair Trade*. London: Routledge: 1-14.

ZANASI, C. and PALUAN, L. (2007): Relationship between ethics and Fair Trade supply chain organisation and performance: the case of Italian Alternative Trade Organisations (ATO's). Paper presented at *105th EAAE Seminar 'International Marketing and International Trade of Quality Food Products', Bologna, Italy, March 8-10, 2007.*

ZMP (2007): *Aufbau einer kontinuierlichen Berichterstattung zum Einkaufsverhalten bei ökologisch erzeugten Produkten in Deutschland unter Einbeziehung der Ergebnisse aus dem BÖL-Projekt 02OE367.* Available from: http://www.bundesprogramm-oekolandbau.de/fkz=02OE367/F, [accessed 2009-10-25].

C Empirical Studies based on the Example of Coffee

This part C presents the results of the three empirical studies carried out in 2008 and 2009 using the example of coffee. As described in the introduction, each of the studies focussed on different aspects of the central research question of the thesis. The results have been reported in five papers which were all presented at international conferences; two of them are already published in peer-revied journals. The respective journal or conference where the paper has been published/presented is indicated in footnotes related to the title of the study. A graphical overview of the overall research question of the dissertation, the specific questions addressed in the single papers, the methods applied, the sample, as well as the results of the papers is provided in Figure 1.

The common element of all papers is that the surveys presented and the analyses conducted in the five papers are carried out using coffee as an example. Coffee seems to be especially suitable for the analysis as (i) it was the first fair-traded product and thus German consumers associate it very well with the Fair Trade movement (SCHNEDLITZ and HALLER 2003, p. 19f.), (ii) it is the most important Fair Trade product regarding availability, volume of sales and variety in the German retail sector (RAYNOLDS 2002, p. 6), (iii) sustainability issues have been a significant factor in product development and marketing within coffee in general (IRI 2007, p. 7) and in particular 63 % of Fair Trade coffee is produced organically (FORUM FAIRER HANDEL 2008b, p. 10), (iv) it is the most established organic export crop (RAYNOLDS 2002, p. 302), (v) it is a commonly used fast moving consumer good (VANTOMME et al. 2006, p. 7), it is the most popular beverage of German consumers[96], (vi) as well as an outstanding export product for producers in the developing world, with over 90 % of the coffee production taking place in those countries (PONTE 2002, p. 1101). To summarise, coffee is crucial for the lifestyle of consumers in Germany while being at the same time a relevant export product for many producers in the developing world.

Another element present in the five studies is that information about the research objective is given to survey participants, i.e. regarding the charity organisation in the first paper, Fair Trade in the first and second paper, and CrM in the third, fourth and fifth paper. The reason is that according to PORST (2008, p. 96; 112), terms which the respondents might not understand at all or at least not in the same way need to be defined. A survey focussing on the recognition of environmental labels showed that 87 % know the German Biosiegel while only 30 % know

[96] The per capita consumption in 2008 was about 148 litres compared to 133 litre of potable water and increased by 4 litres since 2005 (DEUTSCHER KAFFEEVERBAND 2009).

the Fair Trade label (BMU 2008, p. 44). Due to the comparatively new appearance of CrM it can be assumed that consumers are even less familiar with CrM products (see chapter 7). The same holds true for the charity organisation 'Menschen für Menschen' whose label is used as a CrM label in the choice experiment. Therefore, information about the Fair Trade label, CrM and the charity organisation 'Menschen für Menschen' was provided to all respondents during the survey. In the survey described in paper no. 2 participants were additionally asked whether they know the Fair Trade logo and to define the meaning of Fair Trade and what they personally understand as Fair Trade before the information was given. The majority associated fair prices with Fair Trade (72 %). No exploitation of labour (30 %), no child labour (27 %), and support of marginalised producers (26 %) were mentioned by far fewer participants while issues such as gender equality (2 %) and long-term trading relationships (3 %) were almost not known. Results show furthermore that only 43 % know the Fair Trade label[97]. These results show that respondents have had different and vague associations concerning the term Fair Trade. Therefore, a clear and short definition by means of the main principles was appropriate to make sure that all respondents have the same level of information. Hence, the explanation of the research objectives was reasonable in the given cases.

Another common ground of all studies is that they were conducted in the Cologne/Bonn area and were targeted only at coffee drinkers to ensure the best possible involvement of participants.

[97] According to BMU (2008, p. 44) highly educated people are more familiar with environmental and ethical labels. The difference between the findings of BMZ regarding the awareness of the Fair Trade label and survey 2 can be explained as a result of the sample structure. The sample in survey 2 is characterised by a high educational level.

Figure 1: Overview of relevance, motivation, goal, surveys conducted, methods applied and results achieved

Ethics in Consumer Choice - An Empirical Analysis based on the Example of Coffee by Nina Langen

Relevance and Motivation

Individuals with a sense of responsibility towards ethical, ecological and sustainable concerns as well as society can give donations to charity and buy ethical products such as Fair Trade (FT) and organic food. Both are niche products with increasing sales volumes. Besides, so called Cause-related Marketing (CrM) products are offered. A purchase of a CrM product leads to a target oriented donation to a project / a good cause indicated on the product itself. Such products with ethical or sustainable additional value are increasingly offered in Germany while classical monetary donations to charity are stagnating on a comparatively high level. Budget constraint restricts consumers' financial resources to behave ethically.

Overall Research Question

Do consumers differentiate between different types of ethical behaviour?

Objectives

To give an answer to this question the importance of ethical and sustainable product and process attributes for consumers' product choice has to be assessed in the context of other products attributes such as price (paper 1; 2). Then, the question is whether consumer groups with preferences for the one or the other certification, marketing activity or donation can be differentiated (paper 2). Potential success factors for CrM products have to be investigated (paper 3) as well as whether consumers regard CrM as green-washing activity (paper 4). The importance of transparent communication (paper 5) and spending efficiency (paper 2; 5) are assessed.

Three consumer surveys (stratified samples) were conducted in Bonn, Germany. The study object was coffee. All respondents were coffee drinking adult consumers.

Paper 1

Relevance of Fair Trade, organic production and Cause-related Marketing for product choice: An analysis based on the Information Display Matrix

Methods: Two rounds of the Information Display Matrix (IDM) providing information on CrM and FT. Participants choose one coffee for daily use out of a choice set of three. Written questionnaires

Sample: n=214. Year: 2009

Data: Purchase behavior, attitudes towards Fair Trade, organic, CrM, search strategy, socio-demographics

Analysis: Relevance of ethical attributes versus brand, price, taste etc. Logit models regarding first attribute considered, to identify main determinants for information search. Stated versus revealed preferences. Information influences information search

Main Results

Price, brand, taste of central importance for choice

2nd Round: Information influences search towards ethical attributes

Stated and revealed preferences deviate

Paper 2

Are ethical consumption and charitable giving substitutes or not? Insights into consumers' coffee choice

Methods: Hypothetical choice experiments and face-to-face interviews. Participants had to chose six times 1 of 4 coffees

Sample: n=484. Year: 2008

Data: WTP, purchase behavior, donation habits, attitudes towards Fair Trade, organic, CrM, socio-demographics

Analysis: Choice data analyzed using latent class analysis. WTP measures are determined

Main Results

5 classes with statistically well defined preferences and different WTP for organic, FT and CrM donations

Product price, attitudes towards FT, organic production and donations to charity organizations determine class membership

Socio-demographics, except age, not relevant. Consumers liking FT and organic do not choose CrM products

Those preferring CrM dislike FT & organic but donate.

Consumers supporting FT clearly differentiate between FT and donations ➔ Cannibalism between CrM and FT/organic products unlikely

Donors regard FT to be comparable to charity, so it could be that those replace FT products by donations to charity or the purchase of CrM products

Paper 3

Acceptance and critical success factors of Cause-related Marketing in Germany – Evidence from a consumer survey

Methods: Written questionnaires

Sample: n=217. Year: 2009

Data: Purchase behavior, attitudes towards CrM

Analysis: Factor and cluster analysis, logit models

Main Results

Great potential for CrM: consumers hold a positive attitude towards CrM

52% willing to switch brands due to CrM

➔ Determined by consumption behavior, attitudes, product fit

Low share of consumers actually have switched brands due to CrM campaigns

➔ Possibly attributed to little information respondents obtain about CrM

Skepticism exists

➔ Marketing should address doubts regarding firms' underlying motives for applying CrM strategies

Paper 4

Is Cause-related Marketing green-washing?

Methods: Contingent valuation. Written questionnaires

Sample: n=112. Year: 2009

Data: Purchase behavior, attitudes towards CrM, Fair Trade and donations

Analysis: Cluster analysis, ordered logit models

Main Results

1/3 of consumers perceive CrM as form of corporate green-washing; 2/3 unsure

Young and urban consumers are more critical towards CrM, perceive this marketing strategy as green-washing

Participants distinguish CrM from FT and donations in general.

Purchase of a CrM product is able to replace a donation to the NGO involved in the CrM campaign

Paper 5

Is there need for more transparency and efficiency in Cause-related Marketing?

Methods: Written questionnaires

Sample: n=112. Year: 2009

Data: Purchase behavior, attitudes towards CrM and Fair Trade

Analysis: Ordered logit models

Main Results

Consumers have a great interest in being informed about the amount of money spent to the cause by the firm running the campaign

Gap between expected and requested efficiency of CrM donations

➔ Donation amount should be labeled, in order to create a successful CrM campaign and meet consumers' transparency needs

Overall Results

The studies reveal that even if ethical and sustainable issues are of minor importance for consumers' product choice in general most consumers differentiate between the researched forms of ethical behavior. Besides, five consumer groups with well distinguished preferences and willingness to pay measures are identified.

It succeeded to differentiate consumers buying Fair Trade products and giving to charity at the same time and others considering the purchase of CrM products as a substitute for charitable giving. The influencing characteristics were identified.

Furthermore, it becomes obvious that consumers want to be informed about spending efficiency and that a low donation amount (in relation to the sales price of the product) is disliked. Information about ethical labels given just before the choice for a good is made changes significantly consumers interest towards such product attributes. The studies with a focus on CrM reveal that consumers in general appreciate this kind of ethical purchase possibility. Nevertheless, a large share of consumers is skeptic and suspect CrM products to be green-washing of firms.

References

BMU (2008): *Umweltbewusstsein in Deutschland 2008: Ergebnisse einer repräsentativen Bevölkerungsumfrage*. Available from: http://www.umweltdaten.de/publikationen/fpdf-l/3678.pdf, [accessed 2008-12-18].

DEUTSCHER KAFFEEVERBAND (2009): *Lieblingsgetränke der Deutschen – Durchschnittskonsum pro Person 2008*. Available from: http://www.kaffeeverband.de/img/lieblingsgetraenke.jpg, [accessed 2009-07-23].

FORUM FAIRER HANDEL (2008b): *Doppelt gut - Bio im Fairen Handel*. Available from: http://www.transfair.org/presse/detailseite-presse/browse/4/article/45/doppelt-gut.html, [accessed 2008-02-20].

IRI (2007): *Sustainability 2007: Consumer-focused CPG Growth Opportunities*. Available from: http://de1.infores.com/filelib/timestrends/TT_December_2007_Sustainability.pdf, [accessed 2008-05-05].

PONTE, S. (2002): The 'Latte Revolution'? Regulation, Markets and Consumption in the Global Coffee Chain. *World Development*, 30 (7): 1099-1122.

PORST, R. (2008): *Fragebogen - Ein Arbeitsbuch*. Wiesbaden: Verlag für Sozialwissenschaften.

RAYNOLDS, L. T. (2002): *Poverty Alleviation Through Participation in Fair Trade Coffee Networks: Existing Research and Critical Issues*. Background Paper Prepared for Project Funded by the Community and Resource Development Program, The Ford Foundation, New York.

SCHNEDLITZ, P. and HALLER, T. (2003): Ethik im Handel - Empirische Befunde zu FairTrade. *Werbeforschung und Praxis*, 3: 18-20.

VANTOMME, D., GEUENS, M., DEHOUWER, J. and DE PELSMACKER, P. (2006): Explicit and Implicit Determinants of Fair-Trade Buying Behavior. *Advances in Consumer Research*, 33: 699-703.

5 Relevance of Fair Trade, organic production and Cause-related Marketing for product choice – An analysis based on the Information Display Matrix[98]

Abstract

This paper shows at the example of coffee that ethical and organic attributes are of minor importance in comparison to price, brand and taste in consumers' information search using the Information Display Matrix. The results of our study also indicate that stated preferences considerably deviate from revealed ones. Being asked directly consumers' exaggerate on average the relevance of those attributes for their purchase decision that are socially desirable (e.g. no child labour), while they understate those that might be seen of no or negative relevance from a social perspective (e.g. price, brand). The results can help to explain why the market shares of Fair Trade and organic products are still small in Germany though consumers stated preferences suggest different priorities. Nevertheless, despite those deviations, stated preferences prove to determine consumers' information search process as several logit models reveal. The results of our study also suggest that consumers consider only part of the available information and that background information on attributes referring to ethical production influences the amount and structure of the information search in favour of those attributes.

5.1 Introduction

Today consumers can choose among several labels indicating that a product is traded in a fair manner (Fair Trade certified products), produced in an organic way (organic certified) or that its purchase is linked to a donation (Cause-related Marketing products)[99]. Nevertheless, despite its growing importance (e.g. OLOKO 2008; TRANSFAIR 2010), the market share for organic products is still small and for 'ethical' products negligible (BLE, 2008, KRIER, 2008). This contradicts the results of many studies that indicate that 'ethical' and 'sustainable' attributes play an important role in consumers' purchase decision (e.g. ARNOT et al. 2006;

[98] This paper has been presented at the 11th Biennial ISEE Conference 'Advancing sustainability in a time of crisis', August 22-25, 2010, Oldenburg and Bremen, Germany. Co-authors are Vera Roidl and Monika Hartmann.

[99] In addition to the established certification schemes of Fair Trade and organic products, companies increasingly offer products whose purchases lead to target-oriented donations to charity organizations. The donation (indicated in form of the money spent or the things done for the good cause) is promoted on the product by label (ARORA and HENDERSON 2007). In the following, goods of this type will be called Cause-related Marketing (CrM) products.

BECCHETTI and ROSATI 2007; LANGEN et al. 2009; LOUREIRO and LOTADE 2005; TAGBATA and SIRIEIX 2008; TALLONTIRE et al. 2001). This inconsistency might be due to social desirability effects. If consumers are directly asked about the relevance of ethical labels in their purchase decision, socially desirable answers are likely to play a role (FISHER and KATZ 2000; GFK et al. 2009).

To elicit consumers' cognitive structures in consumer decision making processes while minimising socially desirable behaviour, the information display matrix (IDM) can be used (OTT and ROIDL 2008). The IDM is a computer-based information acquisition procedure mapping the information search of individuals. Results provide insights into e.g. the type of information considered and the order in which it is taken into account (PAYNE et al. 1993).

To assess the true importance of ethical labels (e.g. Fair Trade and Cause-related Marketing) and organic production for the decision making process and the choice of a product without gaining socially desirable answers, this paper analyses consumers' preferences for ethical and sustainable production in the context of eight different product attributes such as brand and taste using the IDM. In addition, the study examines whether supplementary information provided about ethical issues related to the product or its production process influences this process. In this study, coffee is used as the research object. Coffee is the Germans' favourite beverage and sales of several niches like Fair Trade[100] (FT) and organic[101] coffee have experienced high grow rates. In addition to single certified coffee, double certified coffee is a trend. In Germany e.g. 60% of the FT coffee is double certified (FORUM FAIRER HANDEL 2008). Cause-related Marketing (CrM) campaigns are also on the rise. Since 2008 one of the biggest German coffee roasters has promoted a special CrM coffee (DALLMAYR 2010). Thus, coffee seems to be especially suitable for analysing the information search (IS) process as this product is not only available on the market at different prices, brands and tastes but also promoted with labels indicating that sustainability and ethical considerations are taken into account. The empirical analysis is based on a consumer survey which was carried out in Bonn in 2009.

The paper is structured as follows: after providing the theoretical background of the study regarding consumers' decision making process (section 2), we introduce the methodology used to assess the relevance of ethical and ecological attributes in consumers' purchase

[100] From 2004 to 2006 FT labelled coffee showed a growth rate of 46 % worldwide. In Germany sales of FT labelled coffee increased from 2008 to 2009 by 26 % (BYERS et al. 2008; TRANSFAIR 2010)

[101] Organic labeled coffee has a market share of 3.5 % in Germany and sales show double digit growth rates (BLE 2008).

decision using the example of coffee (section 3). The design of the experimental study is described in section 4 while the results are presented and discussed in section 5. Section 6 concludes the paper.

5.2 Theoretical approaches to explain consumers' decision making

Consumers have to make thousands of decisions every day most of which are related to uncertainties and trade offs (BETTMAN et al. 1998). Several approaches have been developed to understand how consumers manage this multiple decision making process (BETTMAN et al. 1998). The rational choice approach assumes that consumers maximize their utility by considering and processing all available information, evaluating each choice option and selecting that which provides them with the highest value[102]. The information processing approach (IPA), in contrast, presumes that consumers have only a limited ability to perceive and process all information[103]. In addition, the IPA assumes that decision making behavior is shaped by the interrelation between the characteristics of the human information processing system itself and those of the task environment[104] (SIMON 1990). This implies that preferences for a choice option are constructed rather than revealed (BETTMAN et al. 1998). Thus, according to the IPA, consumers build their preferences in the moment they have to decide but do not necessarily have well-defined preferences until the particular choice situation occurs (BETTMAN et al. 1998). The decision making is thus assumed to be highly context dependant[105] and changes are influenced by e.g. the alternatives to choose from, the framing of the choices as gains or losses (see e.g. TVERSKY and KAHNEMAN 1981) as well as the information provided (learning effect) in the decision making process. As a consequence, preferences for one object compared to another can change if an additional object is included in the choice set. This contradicts the independence of irrelevant alternatives (IIA) assumption[106].

Two reasons for constructive preferences are discussed in the literature: one is the lack of cognitive resources to generate well-defined preferences for many different choice situations (MARCH 1978). Accordingly, it can be concluded that preferences may be more constructive

---

102 For some critics on this theory see SIMON (1959) who stated that "even in an extreme simple situation, subjects do not behave in the way predicted by a straightforward application of utility theory" (SIMON 1959, p. 261).

103 This human incapacity is known as bounded rationality, a concept tracing back to SIMON (1955).

104 The idea is that the relative (dis)advantage of a decision strategy depends on and varies between decision environments, e.g. a person may choose a different coffee brand when the visit of the mother-in-law is announced than for breakfast each morning.

105 The term 'adaptive decision maker' is used in this context (see e.g. MOORTHY et al. 1997; PAYNE et al. 1993).

106 With respect to the IIA and the similarity of alternatives, see PAYNE et al. (1993).

the higher the complexity of a problem is (BETTMAN et al. 1998). This is in accordance with the results of WRIGHT (1975) who showed that if people are familiar with the preference object, stable preferences exist and the decision making process can be explained according to the rational choice approach. The more complex choice decisions are, the higher the probability that the decision process becomes simple. In addition, the adaptive decision maker considers the trade-offs between the cost of the information search and the perceived benefits (MOORTHY et al. 1997). No clear relationship seems to exist regarding the influence product familiarity has on the search for information and how this again influences the decision process (see e.g. JOHNSON and RUSSO 1984; HONG and STERNTHAL 2010). Consumers who are very familiar with a product class might either seek more (enrichment hypotheses) or less information (inverted u hypothesis) (JOHNSON and RUSSO 1984).

The second reason for the existence of constructive preferences is that consumers want to meet several objectives with their choice (BETTMAN et al. 1998): the cognitive effort required to make the choice as well as negative emotions during the decision making have to be minimized, while the accuracy of the decision as well as the ease of justification have to be maximized. In this context, it has to be considered that decisions are not taken in a social vacuum, but that social factors influence decision making (TETLOCK 1985 in PAYNE et al. 1993). This, for example, is important for the goal of maximizing the ease of justification as the decision maker may have to defend his decision to others or him/herself (BETTMAN et al. 1998).

Consumers' decision strategies can be defined by four different characteristics (BETTMAN et al. 1998):

1. The **type and amount of information** which is **processed**. Information which is not considered cannot be processed and therefore is irrelevant for the heuristic applied by the respondent and for the decision. The type and amount of information requested indicates the relevance of the information for the product choice. It also provides an indication as to which product characteristic is important for respondents' decision making.

2. The **selectivity or consistency in information processing** i.e. whether the information processed differs from one attribute/alternative to another.

3. The **pattern of information request and processing**: if a person considers for each of the alternatives in the choice set first one single attribute before looking at a second attribute, this is defined as an attribute-based information strategy. In

contrast, an alternative-based strategy considers first all attributes of one alternative in a choice set before examining the second alternative.

4. The **degree to which a strategy is compensatory**. A compensatory strategy implies that a poor value of an attribute can be compensated by a good value of another attribute of the same alternative. This means explicit trade-offs between attributes are required for a compensatory strategy. Rational decision theory assumes that decisions are based on compensatory strategies (FRISCH and CLEMEN 1994). Accordingly, in a non-compensatory decision making strategy, poor attribute values cannot be compensated by good values of another attribute of the alternative.

According to those characteristics, strategies that are based on the rational choice approach are (1) extensive regarding the amount of information processed, (2) consistent regarding the information search and (3) compensatory. They can be either attribute or alternative based. IPA strategies are in general (4) non-compensatory or at least not consistently compensatory and are based on less extensive information.

5.3 Methods to assess consumers' information search: The IDM

There exists a large variety of process tracing techniques to determine the information search process and to assess how much (depth) of which information (content) is considered in which order (sequence) (JACOBY et al. 1977). Those methods include eye tracking or movement (see e.g. D'YDEWALLE and VAN RENSBERGEN 1993), verbal protocols (see e.g. GNEEZY et al. 2005), neuroeconomics (see e.g. CAMERER et al. 2004), the measurement of response time and the IDM, also called information display board (see e.g. PAYNE 1976).

The latter is a computer-based information acquisition procedure[107] (PAYNE et al. 1993) which maps the information search process of test persons (JUNKER and SEYFFERT 2007) via an alternative-by-attributes matrix. The results are not utility profiles that can be delivered by choice or willingness to pay measures as auctions may provide but insights into the kind and order of sequence in which product information is requested. The IDM enables researchers to make inferences about the information search and decision strategies individuals use to arrive at a certain decision (JASPER and SHAPIRO 2002). The underlying assumption of the IDM approach is that information search is strongly linked to information usage (JOHNSON et al. 2002). This implies information requested by participants is presumed to be processed at a

[107] In addition to computer adaptations of IDMs (mouse lab) there also exists a variety of other forms including mechanical information boards (for further information see JASPER and SHAPIRO 2002).

cognitive level. It is assumed that information (e.g. on price) is more relevant (the so-called cue information) the earlier and the more often it is considered (MUEHLBACHER and KIRCHLER 2003).

The IDM has been applied to e.g. reveal preferences (JOHNSON et al. 1988; SCHKADE and JOHNSON 1989), measure decision-makers' reactions to time pressure (Payne et al. 1988), and assess differences in risk attitudes across different response modes (JOHNSON and SCHKADE 1989; JOHNSON et al. 2002). Market researchers use this method to assess which product attributes are important for consumers. Based on these findings new product varieties and/or product labels can be created by enterprises (JASPER and SHAPIRO 2002). However, the results of this method can also provide interesting insights for policy makers, e.g. regarding the regulation of product labelling. The findings of the IDM relating to the relevance of product attributes can be used further to develop adequate choice sets for discrete choice analysis as well as for the assessment of individual utility measures by means of the analytic hierarchy process (see e.g. JUNKER and SEYFFERTH 2007).

The IDM delivers insights into the 'black box' of human decision making and thus fills the gap between stimulus (e.g. product label, advertisement) and response (the final product choice). It is a method that is quick and easy for participants to learn, the recording of information acquisition is automatic, errors are therefore reduced and the experiments can be run without intervention by the researcher, thereby reducing his/her influence. Thus, the reliability of this method is very high and consistent for different decision tasks. For our purpose, one important additional advantage of the IDM is that social desirability effects are minimised (OTT and ROIDL 2008). Finally, it is less expensive than other process tracing techniques such as e.g. eye tracking.[108] We used the IDM in our study to test the role and importance of ethical and sustainability characteristics on consumers' decision making.

5.4 Design of the study

The consumer experiment was conducted in Bonn in 2009. We drew a sample of adult consumers stratified by age, gender and education. It was required that participants were coffee drinkers. A total of 214 consumers took part in the experiment.

The design of the experiment was as follows: Participants were asked to choose one coffee for daily use from a choice set of three. The properties of the coffee were described on the eight

[108] For an insight into some limitations of IDM, see e.g. SUNDSTRÖM (1987); MUEHLBACHER and KIRCHLER (2003) and HELM and STEINER (2007).

dimensions - Price, Brand, Taste, Country of Origin (COO), Production Method, Helping People to Help Themselves, Donation to Coffee Producers and Health Issues – with each coffee having different values on each of those dimensions (see Table 1). Thus, the matrix consists of a total of 24 pieces of information. The choice was presented to each participant by means of a computerized version of an IDM developed by Nymphenburg. Thus, in the experiment respondents saw the 8x3 matrix of three coffees (each column is one coffee) with eight characteristics/attributes (in rows) which were all hidden behind blank cards at the start. At first, respondents had no information about any of the three coffees. The participants could uncover one attribute after another by moving the mouse pointer on the card. As a consequence, the hidden information behind the card was revealed. Once turned, cards remained open. The respondents were told that they could turn up to 11 of the 24 cards before they had to decide on one of the three coffees. Thereby, respondents were motivated to concentrate on those attributes most relevant for their purchase decision. Furthermore, this restriction mirrors to some extent the situation in a supermarket where due to e.g. time constraints the search for information is limited as well. The entire IS process including the response time was documented by the computer software. Two consecutive rounds were carried out. Each round started with an explanation of the task by the researcher. The first round was conducted without any additional information regarding any of the attributes. Prior to the second round, participants were provided with information on two levels of the "helping people to help themselves" attribute. These were FT (according to the Fairtrade Labelling Organizations International labelling scheme) and 'Menschen für Menschen'. The latter is a non-profit charity organisation working in Ethiopia. Its main focus lies in the promotion of gender equality, health and environmental issues.

Table 1: Attributes and attribute levels used in the decision lab

Attributes	Coffee 1	Coffee 2	Coffee 3
Brand	National Brand 1	Retail Brand 2	National Brand 2
Price	€2.99	€3.99	€4.99
Production Method	Organic	Rainforest Alliance Certified	Conventional
Helping People to Help Themselves	Fair Trade	Menschen für Menschen	./.
Donation	€0.50	€1	./.
Country of Origin	Ethiopia	Vietnam	Mexican Highland
Health issue	Decaffeinated	Natural source of antioxidant	./.
Taste	Mild	Strong	Aromatic

Note: ./.: no information provided.

Source: authors' calculations.

After conducting the experiment, consumers were asked to complete a questionnaire which consisted of two parts. The first part included questions about e.g. consumers' attitude and behaviour regarding ethical and sustainable production. In the second part of the questionnaire, the respondents were asked to provide information on their age, education, income and other socioeconomic characteristics.

5.5 Sample and experimental results

The following results are based on a sample of 214 observations. Some selected characteristics of the sample are summarized in Table 2.

Table 2: Participants' socioeconomic characteristics

Variable	*Specification*	% of the sample (n = 214)
Gender (n=206)	female	46.9
	male	53.1
Age (n=206)	18-24 years	10.7
	25-34 years	22.6
	35-44 years	19.3
	45-54 years	19.1
	55-64 years	16.6
	> 64 years	7.9
Income (n=196)	< €500	15.1
	€ 500 - < 1300	28.2
	€ 1300 - < 2000	17.2
	€ 2000 - < 3600	18.2
	€ 3600 - < 5000	6.1
	> € 5000	1.9
Education (n=206)	Volks-/ Hauptschulabschluss	19.2
	Mittlere Reife	25.9
	University entrance diploma	27.3
	University degree	24.1

Source: authors' calculations.

The gender split was 53.14 % females and 46.86 % males. Better-educated and high-income households were slightly over-represented in comparison to German census statistics.[109] 21.1 % of the respondents had already purchased a CrM product. For FT products this share was 40.5 %.

The results indicate that ethical considerations play an important role in consumers' purchase decision. 77.8 % of the respondents state that 'production without child labour' is of very strong or strong importance for their purchase decision of coffee (Top 2 Boxes of a 7 Likert Scale). Regarding the statements "adequate producer prices" this share at 54 % is also very high. The segment of consumers who indicated that 'organic production' plays a central role (Top 2 Boxes) in their purchase decision is at 28 % much lower. The 'low price' of the product (36 %), whether it is 'branded' (42 %) or not or a 'product on sale' (32 %) reach a higher relevance than 'organic production' but are compared to the ethical characteristics only of minor importance.

[109] See STATISTISCHES BUNDESAMT (2007) and (2008).

The results from the IDM are presented in Table 3. It is interesting to note that the average number of product attributes consumers inspected was 7.6 (Std. Dev. 2.76) in the first round, and 7.9 attributes (Std. Dev. 2.66) in the second round and thus considerably lower than the maximum possible number of 11 cards that consumers were allowed to turn.[110] In the first round only 21.5 % of the respondents requested the maximum possible number of pieces of information (11 cards), while the same share of respondents did not even request half of the maximum possible pieces of information and made their choice by the time they turned the 5th card at the latest. Providing additional information on the 'ethical' attribute 'helping-people-to-help-themselves' led to a significant change in the relevance of those who sought extensive information as well as those who sought little information in the total sample. The share of the former group rose from 21.5 % to 25.7 % while the latter segment declined from 21.5 % to 14.0 %. These results provide a first indication that additional information on attributes influences the IS intensity.

[110] The difference between the average number of pieces of information requested in the 1 and 2 round is statistically insignificant.

Table 3: Information search from the first to the last of eleven clicks

Attribute	Round	1. Click [%]	2. Click [%]	3. Click [%]	4. Click [%]	5. Click [%]	6. Click [%]	7. Click [%]	8. Click [%]	9. Click [%]	10. Click [%]	11. Click [%]	Total clicks on the attribute [absolute]	[%]
Price	1	28.0	25.7	23.4	19.6	22.4	22.0	12.1	9.3	10.7	2.8	1.4	380	16.1
	2	21.5	22.0	21.5	22.4	19.2	12.1	11.2	11.2	8.4	5.6	6.1	345	14.7
Taste	1	27.1	27.6	26.2	19.2	14.0	12.6	14.0	11.2	9.3	3.7	3.3	360	15.3
	2	21.5	23.8	17.3	16.8	15.0	18.7	9.8	8.4	5.1	2.3	1.4	300	12.7
Brand	1	18.7	19.2	20.6	25.2	17.3	15.0	13.1	11.7	7.0	3.3	1.4	326	13.8
	2	14.5	15.9	16.4	17.3	15.4	14.0	10.7	10.3	5.1	2.8	3.3	269	11.4
Country of Origin	1	7.0	7.0	7.0	7.5	5.6	7.5	7.9	4.7	7.0	7.5	3.3	154	6.5
	2	9.8	8.4	7.9	7.9	7.0	3.3	6.5	7.5	6.5	6.5	3.7	161	6.8
Production Method	1	7.5	9.8	7.9	2.8	5.1	4.7	7.0	7.9	3.3	1.9	2.3	129	5.5
	2	6.1	6.5	6.5	6.1	7.9	8.4	7.9	4.7	4.7	4.7	2.8	142	6.0
Donation	1	3.7	1.4	2.8	3.7	5.6	3.7	2.8	3.3	0.9	3.7	6.5	82	3.5
	2	9.3	8.9	7.0	6.5	9.8	9.8	7.9	5.1	6.5	5.1	4.7	173	7.3
Helping People to Help Themselves	1	3.3	1.9	2.3	3.3	1.9	1.9	2.8	0.9	1.4	1.4	0.5	46	2.0
	2	13.1	9.3	14.0	9.8	8.4	7.0	8.4	6.5	6.5	4.2	1.9	191	8.1
Health Issue	1	1.9	3.7	4.2	7.5	6.5	3.7	5.6	4.2	1.9	2.8	2.8	96	4.1
	2	1.9	2.8	4.2	42.0	3.3	2.8	2.8	3.3	2.8	1.9	1.9	68	2.9
Not Regarded	1	2.8	3.7	5.6	11.2	21.5	29.0	34.6	46.7	58.4	72.9	78.5	781	33.2
	2	2.3	2.3	5.1	8.9	14.0	23.8	34.6	43.0	54.2	66.8	74.3	705	29.9
Total Round 1 and 2 respectively		100	100	100	100	100	100	100	100	100	100	100	2354	100

Source: authors' calculations.

Table 3 also reveals that 'Price' and 'Taste' but also 'Brand' are by far the most important attributes in consumers' information search process. Together they account for 73.8 % of the first clicks and for 45.2 % of all eleven clicks in the first round (round without extra information). Thus, our results support the findings of MUEHLBACHER and KIRCHLER (2003) that these three attributes are the ones consumers most frequently search for and care about. About 7 % of all first clicks go to the attributes 'Production Method' and 'COO' respectively in this round which makes them the second most important group. Also regarding the total clicks (each about 6 %) they take a second rank. In contrast, 'Helping people to help themselves', 'Donation' and 'Health Issue' only attract 3.3 %, 3.7 % and 1.9 %, respectively of the first clicks and 2.0 %, 3.5 % and 4.1 %, respectively of all clicks and thus seem to be less important in consumers' decision making process regarding the purchase of coffee.

Furthermore, the results in Table 3 indicate that the additional information on the 'Helping people to help themselves' attribute does not only influence the overall intensity of the IS process in the direction towards a more extensive information process as discussed above, but also the relevance of the different attributes in this process in favour of those attributes closely linked to the information provided. While in the first round only 2 % of all the clicks were for the attribute 'Helping people to help themselves', this share significantly increased to 8.1 % in the second. This triplication of interest indicates that 'Helping people to help themselves', which ranks seventh before information is given, becomes more important in the search process and ranks fourth after information is given. In addition, the search for information regarding the related attribute 'Donation' also strongly and significantly increases (from 3.5 % to 7.3 %) after information is provided. The absolute importance of the other attributes in the IS process remains more or less stable or declines; the ranking order and therefore the relative importance remains with the exception of 'Helping people to help themselves' the same. The latter holds also for the most important attributes: 'Price', 'Taste' and 'Brand'. However, those three attributes remain the most relevant ones. At 60 % (49 %) a considerable majority of consumers request this combination of information before they chose a coffee in the first (second) round. Nevertheless, the results clearly demonstrate the extent to which the given information affects the interest in the product attributes and the search process.

To investigate the information search pattern that participants used, PAYNE's (1976) index of the relative degree of attribute-wise versus alternative-wise search was computed. The index can be used to identify the type of decision strategy that consumers use. More attribute-based decision strategies include the lexicographic and the majority of confirming dimensions strategy whereas weighted adding and satisficing are more alternative based decision strategies. For more information on this topic, see e.g. BETTMAN et al. (1998) and RIEDL et al. (2008). The Payne index is equal to the total number of alternative-wise transitions minus the total number of attribute-wise transitions divided by the sum of the attribute-wise and alternative-wise transitions. The index can range between -1 and +1 with negative Payne-scores indicating more attribute-wise while positive scores point to more alternative-wise search patterns. The mean Payne-score for the first round is at 0.2213 (SD= 0.56) positive but relatively low indicating that consumers follow to a slightly stronger degree alternative-wise compared to attribute-wise search strategies. With additional information the value of the Payne-index declines (0.1722, SD= 0.55), implying a small – but statistically significant – shift towards attribute-wise strategies in the second round.

For each of the eight attributes consumers could search for a maximum of three items/levels (e.g. price € 2.99; € 3.99 and € 4.99). Between the two rounds we notice a significant change in the number of items per attribute people look at (see 'mean' and the significance column in Table 4). This holds especially for the attributes 'Helping people to help themselves' and 'Donation' on the one hand and for 'Brand' and 'Taste' on the other. While in round 2 compared to round 1 on average significantly more items of the former attributes are looked at, the opposite holds for the latter group.

Table 4: Average number of attribute items per category looked at

Category	Round	N	Mean	Std. Dev.	Std. Err.	Sig. (two tailed)
Price	1	207	1.83	1.10	.08	.124
	2	208	1.66	1.18	.08	
Taste	1	207	1.73	1.16	.08	**.012**
	2	208	1.44	1.19	.08	
Brand	1	207	1.57	1.27	.09	**.022**
	2	208	1.29	1.17	.09	
COO	1	207	.74	1.00	.07	.769
	2	208	.77	1.08	.08	
Production Method	1	207	.62	.98	.07	.584
	2	208	.68	.105	.07	
Donation	1	207	.39	.74	.05	**.000**
	2	208	.83	1.09	.08	
Helping People to Help Themselves	1	207	.22	.57	.04	**.000**
	2	208	.92	1.18	.08	
Health Issue	1	207	.45	.83	.06	**.091**
	2	208	.32	.76	.05	

Source: authors' calculations.

To gain deeper insights into which factors determine the relevance of the different attributes in the search process, logit models are conducted for each of the three most important attributes in the IS process ('Price', 'Taste' and 'Brand') as well as for the sustainability ('Production Method') and for the ethical ('Helping people to help themselves') attribute. The variables used in the logit models are described in Table 5.

Table 5: Variable description

	Variable	Description	Mean [d]	Std. Dev. [d]
Dependant	Price	First regarded attribute: Price [a]	0.25	0.43
	Brand	First regarded attribute: Brand [a]	0.17	0.37
	Taste	First regarded attribute: Taste [a]	0.24	0.43
	Organic	First regarded attribute: Organic [a]	0.07	0.25
	Helping People to Help Themselves	First regarded attribute: Helping People to Help Themselves [a]	0.08	0.27
Independent Variable	CrM is meaningful	CrM is meaningful [b]	5.69	1.44
	CrM is not authentic	CrM is not authentic [b]	3.52	1.85
	CrM is green washing	CrM is green washing [b]	3.86	1.74
	Like CrM	"I like CrM" [b]	5.25	1.77
	Purchase CrM	Did purchase CrM previously [a]	0.21	0.41
	Organic	Important that coffee is produced organically [c]	4.24	1.83
	No child labour	Important that coffee is produced w/o child labour [c]	6.05	1.70
	Adequate Producer price	Important that coffee producers get an adequate price [c]	5.35	1.61
	Cheap	Important that coffee is cheap [c]	5.43	1.59
	On sale coffee	Important that coffee is on sale [c]	4.18	2.05
	Branded coffee	Important that coffee has a well-known brand [c]	4.52	2.19
	FT coffee tastes better	Opinion that FT coffee tastes better =3, 2=equally good, 1= worse than other coffee	1.92	0.37
	Fair Trade buyer	Did purchase Fair Trade products previously [a]	0.40	0.49
	Age	Categorical variable from 1 (< 25), 2 (25-29) to 11 (>70)	5.20	2.89
	Female	Gender (1=female, 0=male)	0.53	0.50
	Education: high	University degree and more [a]	0.25	0.43
	Education: middle	10 to 13 years of school [a]	0.55	0.50
	Income	Household Net-Income (EUR/month) Categorical variable from 1 (< 300 EUR) to 12 (>5000 EUR)	6.46	3.05
	Round_2	Round 2 with information given (1=round 2, 0= round 1)	0.50	0.50
	Search Pattern	Payne Score: ranges from +1: alternative-wise search to -1: attribute-wise search	0.21	0.56

[a] 1=yes, 0=no.
[b] 1=completely disagree to 7=completely agree.
[c] 1=very unimportant to 7=very important.
[d] round 1 and 2 together.

Source: authors' calculations.

Table 6: Results of the five logit models for the first regarded attribute

	Price		Brand		Taste		Prod. Method		Helping People to Help Themselves	
	Coef.	Std. Err.[a]	Coef.	Std. Err.	Coef.	Std. Err.	Coef.	Std. Err.	Coef.	Std. Err.
CrM is meaningful	-0.18	0.15	-0.22	0.19	0.07	0.16	0.22	0.55	0.42	0.31
CrM is not authentic	0.17	0.10 *	-0.13	0.13	-0.15	0.11	0.02	0.27	-0.23	0.17
CrM is green washing	-0.10	0.12	-0.01	0.13	-0.02	0.12	0.01	0.28	0.14	0.18
Like CrM	0.06	0.13	0.22	0.19	-0.28	0.14 *	0.09	0.48	-0.02	0.25
Purchase CrM	0.00	0.39	0.11	0.48	-0.36	0.40	2.26	1.02 **	0.38	0.68
Organic	0.19	0.11 *	-0.25	0.13 *	0.12	0.11	0.96	0.35 ***	-0.23	0.19
No child labour	0.03	0.11	0.04	0.13	-0.11	0.11	-0.29	0.30	0.13	0.24
Adequate producer price	-0.23	0.12 *	-0.17	0.15	0.06	0.13	-0.26	0.37	0.46	0.24 *
Cheap coffee	0.31	0.13 **	-0.17	0.13	-0.07	0.12	-0.34	0.34	0.16	0.21
On sale coffee	-0.12	0.09	-0.05	0.11	-0.04	0.10	0.87	0.33 **	0.06	0.17
Branded coffee	-0.05	0.08	0.22	0.10 **	-0.10	0.08	-0.37	0.21 *	0.18	0.13
FT coffee tastes better	-0.17	0.47	0.66	0.52	-0.92	0.50 *	3.26	1.05 ***	-1.46	0.86 *
Fair Trade buyer	-0.42	0.37	0.60	0.40	0.18	0.38	-2.76	1.41 *	0.84	0.61
Age	-0.11	0.07 *	0.09	0.07	-0.15	0.07 **	-0.07	0.17	0.11	0.10
Female	-0.13	0.32	0.23	0.40	0.01	0.34	0.31	0.93	-0.16	0.60
Education: high	-0.58	0.50	-1.42	0.63 **	-0.19	0.54	0.27	1.16	1.09	0.80
Education: middle	-0.58	0.45	-0.08	0.46	-0.14	0.47	-1.26	1.11	0.31	0.71
Income	0.03	0.05	0.02	0.06	0.08	0.05	0.18	0.15	-0.02	0.10
Round_2	-0.35	0.29	-0.55	0.34	-0.24	0.29	-0.29	0.67	1.29	0.53 **
Search Pattern	-0.21	0.29	-0.27	0.32	0.20	0.29	-73.00	-78.00	0.09	0.46
Constant	0.32	1.73	-0.96	2.03	3.61	1.84 *	-14.55	5.22 ***	-8.23	3.04 ***
LR chi2(24) (Prob> chi2)	34.92 (0.02)		37.51 (0.01)		23.52(0.26)		39.42 (0.01)		34.81 (0.02)	
Pseudo R2	0.11		0.14		0.08		0.37		0.22	

Note: [a] significance level *** p<0.01, ** p<0.05, * p<0.1; number of observations in each model: 281.

Source: authors' calculations.

Table 6 shows that all models, with the exception of the one with taste as the dependent variable, are highly significant. The IS pattern, as described by the Payne-score, has no influence in any of the models. The results indicate that respondents' stated preference for 'organic production', 'adequate producer price' and 'low price' positively influences their interest in 'Price' as the first attribute in their information search while the opposite holds for consumers' age. Consumers who choose brand as a first attribute to look at are characterised by a lower education level, little stated interest in organically produced coffee but a high declared interest in branded products. Factors with a significant positive influence on the choice of 'Production Method' as a first attribute include the declared importance of organic coffee and coffee on sale as well as past experiences with CrM products, little interest in brands and the opinion that FT coffee tastes better than non FT coffee. Surprisingly, the purchase of FT products has a negative influence on the probability that respondents are interested in the 'Production Method' as the first attribute. The model 'Helping people to help themselves' is the only one with a strong and significant positive influence with respect to the information provided in round 2. This shows that this attribute benefits from background information about Fair Trade and charity labels. The probability that consumers look at 'Helping people to help themselves' at the first click increases in round 2 after information is given. Furthermore, the interest in adequate payments for coffee producers has a positive significant influence. The belief that FT coffee tastes better has a negative influence on the possibility that 'Helping people to help themselves' is regarded as first attribute. As both the charity label as well as the Fair Trade label are items of the 'Helping people to help themselves' attribute, we cannot distinguish between those who click on the 'Helping people to help themselves' fields because they are interested in Fair Trade and those with an interest in the charity label. Therefore, one explanation for the finding might be that participants were searching for the charity label and not the Fair Trade label.

5.6 Conclusions

This paper examines the relevance of ethical and organic production in the context of different product and process attributes for consumers' information search using the IDM based on the example of coffee choice. In addition, consumers' information search pattern is analysed and the main determinants for active information search on specific attributes (e.g. price and ethical attributes) are identified based on several logit models.

The positive significant influence of the stated interest in cheap coffee in the 'Price' Model, of branded coffee in the 'Brand' model, of organic production in the 'Production Method' model and of fair producer prices in the 'Helping people to help themselves' model provides evidence that consumers' stated preferences are reflected in consumers' search process. But the results of our study also indicate that the validity and explanatory power of stated and revealed preferences deviates considerably. Whereas, for example, 78 % of the participants stated the characteristic 'production without child labour' to be of very great or great importance, only 36 % of the consumers indicate the same for the attribute 'low price'. But, nefore information was given 84.6 % regarded price while only 26% regarded the 'Helping people to help themselves' category. The results of the IDM reveal the overwhelming importance of price, brand and taste during the IS process. These findings support the results of OTT and ROIDL (2008), namely that the IDM is able to minimise social desirability effects; a problem which is likely to be of relevance in surveys on ethical product characteristics.

The results of our study also suggest that consumers consider only part of the available information package. In particular, labels referring to e.g. ethical and organic production only seem to be of minor importance. The results can help to explain why the market shares of FT and organic products are still small in Germany though consumers stated preferences suggest different priorities. This implies that ethical products have to be competitive in the most important product features. Then, there is a chance that consumer' stated and their revealed preferences are getting together.

Furthermore, our results reveal that consumer interest in attributes can be influenced by providing additional information at the point of sale. This shows that consumers' preferences for coffee are not stable, but context and information dependant although consumers are familiar with coffee as such. Our findings are therefore in line with the information processing approach described in section 2. In addition, it becomes obvious that information changes the search pattern from the hard fact attributes such as 'Price' and 'Brand' to other ones like 'Helping people to help themselves' as well as from alternative-wise to attribute-wise transition.

5.7 References

ARNOT, C., BOXALL, P.C. and CASH, S. B. (2006): Do Ethical Consumers Care About Price? A Revealed Preference Analysis of Fair Trade Coffee Purchases. *Canadian Journal of Agricultural Economics,* 54 (4): 555-565.

ARORA, N. and HENDERSON, T. (2007): Embedded Premium Promotion: Why it works and how to make it more effective. *Marketing Science*, 26 (4): 514-531.

BECCHETTI, L. and ROSATI, F.C. (2007): Global social preferences and the demand for socially responsible products: empirical evidence from a pilot study on fair trade consumers. *The world economy*, 30 (5): 807-836.

BETTMAN, J. R., LUCE, M. F. and PAYNE, J. W. (1998): Constructive Consumer Choice Processes. *The Journal of Consumer Research*, 25 (3): 187-217.

BLE (2008): *Kaffee - der Deutschen liebstes Heißgetränk*. Available from: http://www.oekolandbau.de/grossverbraucher/studien-und-info-materialien/marktdaten/wachstumsmarkt-kaffee-september-2008/ [accessed 2008-09-25].

BYERS, A., GIOVANNUCCI, D. and LIU, P. (2008): Value-adding standards in the North American food market - Trade opportunities in certified products for developing countries, *FAO Commodities and Trade Technical Paper*, 11.

CAMERER, C. F., LOEWENSTEIN, G. and PRELEC, D. (2004): Neuroeconomics: Why Economics Needs Brains. *The Scandinavian Journal of Economics*, 106 (3): 555-579.

DALLMAYR (2010): *Mit Kaffeegenuss Bäume in Äthiopien pflanzen*. Available from: www.dallmayr-ethiopia.de, [accessed 2010-07-30].

D'YDEWALLE, G. and VAN RENSBERGEN, J. (1993): *Perception and Cognition: Advances in Eye Movement Research,* Studies in Visual Information processing series 2. Amsterdam: New Holland Press.

FISHER, R. J. and KATZ, J. E. (2000): Social-desirability bias and the validity of self reported values. *Psychology and Marketing* 17: 105-120.

FORUM FAIRER HANDEL (2008): *Doppelt gut - Bio im Fairen Handel*. Available from: http://www.transfair.org/presse/detailseite-presse/browse/4/article/45/doppelt-gut.html, [accessed 2008-02-20].

FRISCH, D. and CLEMEN, R. T. (1994): Beyond Expected Utility: Rethinking Behavioral Decision Research. *Psychological Bulletin*, 116 (1): 46-54.

GFK, ROLAND BERGER and BVE (2009): *Consumers' Choice '09: Corporate Responsibility in der Ernährungsindustrie*. 3rd ed. Available from: www.bve-online.de/presseservice/veroeffentlichungen/consumers_choice2009, [accessed 2010-07-30].

GNEEZY, U., RUSTICHINI, A. and VOSTROKNUTOV, A. (2005): *Backward Induction as a Cognitive Process*. Working Paper, University of Chicago Graduate School of Business. Available from: www.econweb.tamu.edu/workshops/Theory%20and%20Experimental%20Economics/Aldo%20Rustichini.pdf, [accessed 2004-04-08].

HELM, R. and STEINER, M. (2007): *Präferenzmessung: Methodengestützte Entwicklung zielgruppenspezifischer Produktinnovationen*. Stuttgart: Kohlhammer.

HONG, J. and STERNTHAL, B. (2010): The Effects of Consumer Prior Knowledge and Processing Strategies on Judgments. *Journal of Marketing Research*, 47 (2): 301-311.

JACOBY, J., SZYBILLO, G. J. and BUSATO-SCHACH, J. (1977): Information Acquisition Behaviour in Brand Choice Situations. *Journal of Consumer Research*, 3 (4): 209-216.

JASPER, J. D. and SHAPIRO, J. (2002): A better mousetrap for catching decision processes. *Behavior Research Methods, Instruments, and Computers*, 34 (3): 364-374.

JOHNSON, E. J., PAYNE, J. W. and BETTMAN, J. R. (1988): Information displays and preference reversals. *Organizational Behavior and Human Decision Processes*, 42 (1): 1-21.

JOHNSON, E. J. and RUSSO, J. E. (1984): Product familiarity and learning new information. *Journal of Consumer Research*, 11 (1): 542-550.

JOHNSON, E. J. and SCHKADE, D. A. (1989): Heuristics and bias in utility assessment: Further evidence and explanations. *Management Science*, 35 (4): 406-424.

JOHNSON, E. J., CAMERER, C., SEN, S. and Rymon. T. (2002): Detecting Failures of Backward Induction: Monitoring Information Search in Sequential Bargaining. *Journal of Economic Theory*, 104 (1): 16-47.

JUNKER, H. AND SEYFFERT, C. (2007): Evaluation komplexer Produkte im Telekommunikationsmarkt. *Planung & Analyse*, 5: 66-70.

KRIER, J. - M. (2008): *Fair Trade 2007: new facts and figures from an ongoing success story: A report on Fair Trade in 33 consumer countries*. Available from: http://www.forum-fairer-handel.de/cms/lit_files/FairTrade2007newfacts+figures.pdf, [accessed 2009-02-20].

LANGEN, N., GREBITUS, C. AND HARTMANN, M. (2009): Fair Trade and Donations: two possibilities to contribute to poverty alleviation in daily purchase decisions – Do consumers care? In: Klein, A. and Thoresen, V. (Eds.): *Making a difference: Putting Consumer Citizenship into Action. Consumer Citizenship: Promoting New Response*, 5. Hedmark University College: 60-73.

LOUREIRO, M. and LOTADE, J. (2005): Do fair trade and eco-labels in coffee wake up the consumer conscience? *Ecological Economics*, 53 (1): 129-138.

MARCH, J. G. (1978): Bounded Rationality, Ambiguity, and the Engineering of Choice. *The Bell Journal of Econo*mics, 9 (2): 587-608.

MOORTHY, S., RATCHFORD, B. T. and TALUKDAR, D. (1997): Consumer Information Search Revisited: Theory and Empirical Analysis. *Journal of Consumer Research*, 23 (4): 263-277.

MUEHLBACHER, S. and KIRCHLER, E. (2003): Informations-Display-Matrix Einsatz- und Analysemöglichkeiten. *Der Markt*, 42 (3-4): 147-152.

OLOKO, S. (2008): *Cause related Marketing - Der Status Quo in Deutschland*. Berlin.

OTT, C. S. and ROIDL, V. (2008): Die Qual der (Aus)Wahl am POS. *Planung und Analyse*, 2: 28-31.

PAYNE, J. W., BETTMAN, J. R. and JOHNSON, E. J. (1988): Adaptive strategy selection in decision making. *Journal of Experimental Psychology: Learning, Memory, and Cognition*, 14 (3): 534–552.

PAYNE, J. W., BETTMAN, J. R. and JOHNSON, E. J. (1993): *The adaptive decision maker*. Cambridge: Cambridge University Press.

PAYNE, J. W. (1976): Task complexity and contingent processing in decision making: An informative search and protocol analysis. *Organizational Behavior and Human Performance*, 16 (2): 366-387.

RIEDL, R., BRANDSTÄTTER, E. and ROITHMAYR, F. (2008): Identifying decision strategies: A process- and outcome-based classification method. *Behavior Research Methods*, 40 (3): 795-807.

SCHKADE, D. A. and JOHNSON, E. J. (1989): Cognitive processes in preference reversals. *Organizational Behavior and Human Performance*, 44 (2): 203-231.

SIMON, H. A. (1955): A Behavioral Model of Rational Choice. *Quarterly Journal of Economics*, 69 (1): 99-118.

SIMON, H. A. (1959): Theories of Decision-Making in Economics and Behavioral Science. *The American Economic Review*, 49 (3): 253-283.

SIMON, H. A. (1990): Invariants of Human Behavior. *Annual Review of Psychology*, 41: 1-19.

STBA (Statistisches Bundesamt) (2007): *Statistisches Jahrbuch 2007*. Wiesbaden.

STBA (Statistisches Bundesamt) (2008): *Bevölkerung und Erwerbstätigkeit - Haushalte und Familien, Ergebnisse des Mikrozensus 2007*. Fachserie 1, Reihe 3, Wiesbaden.

SUNDSTRÖM, G. A. (1987): Information search and decision making: The effects of information displays. *Acta Psychologica*, 65: 165-179.

TAGBATA, D. and SIRIEIX, L. (2008): Measuring consumer's willingness to pay for organic and Fair Trade products. *International Journal of Consumer Studies*, 32: 479-490.

TALLONTIRE, A., RENTSENDORJ, E. and BLOWFIELD, M. (2001): Ethical Consumers and Ethical Trade: A Review of Current Literature, *Policy Series 12*. Chatham, UK: Natural Resources Institute.

TETLOCK, P. E. (1985): Accountability: The neglected social context of judgement and choice. *Research in Organizational Behavior*, 7: 297-332.

TRANSFAIR (2010): *26 Prozent Plus für Fairtrade*. Available from: http://www.transfair.org/top/nachricht/?tx_ttnews[tt_news]=275&tx_ttnews[backPid]=137 &cHash=9c1070f615, [accessed 2001-04-28].

TVERSKY, A. and KAHNEMAN, D. (1981): The framing of decisions and the psychology of choice. *Science*, 211 (4481): 453-458.

WRIGHT, P. L. (1975): Consumer Choice Strategies: Simplifying vs. Optimizing. *Journal of Marketing Research,* 12 (1): 60-67.

Appendix A1: Questionnaire

Fragebogen 1: Lebensmittelkauf und Konsum **NR ________**

Zu Beginn möchten wir Ihnen einige Fragen bezüglich Ihres Einkaufsverhaltens und Ihrer Person stellen. Es gibt keine ‚richtigen' oder ‚falschen' Antworten. Ihre Antworten werden vertraulich behandelt und stehen unter Verschluss. Sie sind nur den Wissenschaftlern zugänglich, die an dieser Studie beteiligt sind.

1. Sind Sie in Ihrem Haushalt **für den Einkauf zuständig**? *(Bitte ankreuzen)*

   Ja ______ Manchmal ______ Nein ______

2. **Wie häufig kaufen Sie** die folgenden Produkte? *(Bitte Zutreffendes ankreuzen)*

	Täglich	5-6 mal pro Woche	3-4 mal pro Woche	1-2 mal pro Woche	Alle zwei Wochen	1 mal im Monat	Seltener
Lebensmittel allgemein							
Kaffee							

3. **Wo kaufen Sie Kaffee** ein? *(Bitte Zutreffendes ankreuzen)*

	Sehr häufig	Häufig	Manchmal	Selten	Nie
Verbrauchermarkt, z.B. Real, Toom	5	4	3	2	1
Discounter, z.B. ALDI, Plus, Lidl	5	4	3	2	1
Supermarkt, z.B. Rewe, Edeka	5	4	3	2	1
Fachgeschäft, z.B. Tchibo	5	4	3	2	1
Biosupermarkt/ -laden	5	4	3	2	1
Im Internet	5	4	3	2	1

4. Wie viele **Tassen Kaffee** trinken Sie **pro Tag**? ______ Tassen
5. Wie viele **Packungen Kaffee kaufen** Sie **pro Monat**? ______ Packungen
6. **Wie** kaufen Sie Ihren Kaffee üblicherweise? *(Bitte ankreuzen)*

   Gemahlen ______ ganze Bohne ______ Pads ______ Instant Kaffee ______

7. **Lesen Sie** normalerweise allgemeine **Produktinformationen**? JA _______ NEIN _______

8. Was kommt Ihnen in den Sinn, wenn Sie **Fair Trade** hören? *(Bitte stichwortartig aufschreiben)*

9. **Wie gut** fühlen Sie sich über die folgenden Dinge **informiert**? *(Kreuzen Sie bitte Zutreffendes an: 1 = darüber weiß ich nichts und 5 = darüber weiß ich sehr viel)*

	Viel Wissen				Kein Wissen
Fair Trade	5	4	3	2	1
Spendenorganisationen	5	4	3	2	1
Menschen für Menschen	5	4	3	2	1
Effizienz von Spendenorganisationen	5	4	3	2	1
Effizienz von Fair Trade Organisationen	5	4	3	2	1
Spezielle Ziele von Fair Trade	5	4	3	2	1
Spezielle Ziele von Menschen für Menschen	5	4	3	2	1
Ökologisch erzeugte Lebensmittel	5	4	3	2	1

10. Stellen Sie sich vor, Sie erwarten Gäste und wollen einen **besonders guten Kaffee** anbieten. Wenn Sie einen solchen, guten Kaffee kaufen wollen, worauf achten Sie bei Ihrem Einkauf?

____

____

______

11. Stellen Sie sich nun bitte vor, es geht um den **Kaffee, den Sie jeden Tag trinken**. Worauf achten Sie beim Kauf dieses Kaffees?

____

____

______

12. Sind Sie **Mitglied** in einer oder mehrerer der folgenden Organisationen und/oder Bereiche?

_____ Kirche (zahle Kirchensteuer) _____Umweltschutz _____Sportverein _____ Partei _____Weltladen _____ Jugendarbeit _____Organisationen wie z.B. Greenpeace

13. Wie schätzen Sie Ihre eigene **Lebenssituation** (nicht nur die finanzielle) ein?
    Mir geht es sehr gut (5) (4) (3) (2) (1) Mir geht es sehr schlecht

14. Wie **alt** sind Sie? ____ Jahre

15. Wie viele Personen leben in Ihrem **Haushalt**? ________ Person(en)

16. Wie viele **Kinder unter 18** Jahren leben in Ihrem Haushalt? _________Anzahl

17. Wie viele **Kinder unter 12** Jahren leben in Ihrem Haushalt? _________Anzahl

18. Welches ist Ihr höchster **Bildungsabschluss**?

_____Ohne Schulabschluss _____ Fach-/ Hochschulreife (Abitur)

_____Volks-/Hauptschulabschluss _____ Fach-/ Hochschulabschluss

_____Mittlere Reife (Realschulabschluss) _____ Promotion

19. Wie hoch ist ihr monatliches **Haushaltsnettoeinkommen**? Ich meine damit die Geldsumme, die für Ihren Haushalt nach Abzug der Steuern und Sozialversicherung übrig bleibt. Eine WG gilt nur dann als Haushalt, wenn gemeinsam gewirtschaftet (eingekauft) wird.

____unter 300 € ____300 bis 500 € ____500 bis 700 € ____700 bis 900 €

____900 bis 1100 € ____1100 bis 1300 € ____1300 bis 1500 € ____1500 bis 2000 €

____2000 bis 2600 € ____2600 bis 3600 € ____3600 bis 5000 € ____5000 und mehr €

20. Welche **Postleitzahl** hat Ihr Wohnort? ___________

21. Ist die **Gegend**, in der Sie wohnen

____eher großstädtisch (ab 100.000 Einwohner, wie z.B. Bonn)

____eher kleinstädtisch (10.000 -100.000 Einwohner)

____eher ländlich

22. **Wie viele Geschwister** haben Sie? _____ Anzahl

23. Sind Ihre Geschwister: _____ Älter _____ Jünger _____ Beides

24. Sind Sie **weiblich** ______ oder **männlich** ______?

Fragebogen 3: Lebensmittelkauf und Konsum **NR ________**

In diesem Abschnitt der Befragung stellen wir überwiegend Fragen bezüglich Einstellungen und Meinungen. Wie bereits im ersten Fragebogen erwähnt, es gibt keine ‚richtigen' oder ‚falschen' Antworten. Bitte denken Sie sorgfältig über jede Frage nach. Das vollständige Ausfüllen des Fragebogens ist besonders wichtig für unsere Studie.

1. Was ist Ihnen beim **Kauf von Kaffee** wichtig?
   (Antworten Sie bitte mit Zahlen zwischen 1 (ist mir gar nicht wichtig) und 7 (ist mir sehr wichtig). Sie können Ihre Bewertungen zwischen 1 und 7 abstufen.)

Beim Kauf von Kaffee ist mir wichtig, dass....	(7) Sehr wichtig	(6)	(5)	(4)	(3)	(2)	(1) Gar nicht wichtig
er nachhaltig und ökologisch erzeugt wird							
er ohne Kinderarbeit hergestellt wird							
die Produzenten angemessene Preise erhalten							
er preiswert ist							
ich den Einkauf schnell erledigen kann							
er qualitativ hochwertig ist							
ein persönlicher Kontakt besteht und ich Beratung beim Einkauf erhalte							
er ein Sonderangebot ist							
er ein Markenkaffee ist							

2. Wie schmeckt **fair gehandelter Kaffee** im Vergleich zu normalem, nicht fair gehandelten, Kaffee? *(Bitte ankreuzen)*

   _____ besser _____ gleich gut _____ schlechter

3. **Kaufen Sie Fair Trade** Produkte? *(Bitte ankreuzen)*

   _____ JA _____ NEIN *(**Bitte bei Frage 6** weitermachen)*

4. **Wie oft verzehren Sie** die folgenden fair gehandelten Produkte? *(Bitte jeweils ankreuzen)*

	Mehrmals in der Woche	1 mal in der Woche	Alle 2 Wochen	1 mal im Monat	Seltener	Nie
Schokolade						
Bananen						
Kaffee						
Tee						
Orangensaft						
Gewürze						
Honig						
Kakao						
Wein						
Sonstiges:______						

5. **Wo kaufen Sie** fair gehandelte Produkte?

(Antworten Sie bitte mit Zahlen zwischen 1 (hier kaufe ich nie) und 7 (hier kaufe ich immer). Sie können Ihre Bewertungen zwischen 1 und 7 abstufen.)

Ich kaufe fair gehandelte Produkte im...	(7) Hier kaufe ich immer	(6)	(5)	(4)	(3)	(2)	(1) Hier kaufe ich nie
Supermarkt (Edeka, Rewe,...)							
Discounter (Aldi, Lidl, ...)							
Weltladen							
Bioladen							
Biosupermarkt							
Kirche							
Spezialitätengeschäft							
Verbrauchermarkt (Real, ...)							

6. Angenommen, ein **fair gehandeltes** Produkt kostet **1 €** mehr als ein nicht fair gehandeltes: wie viel muss von diesem Euro bei den Erzeugern **ankommen**, damit Sie nicht den Eindruck haben, dass irgendwo Geld versickert? *(Bitte eintragen)* ____ **Cent**

7. **Spenden können über Produktkäufe generiert werden,** indem Spenden-organisationen mit Markenartikelherstellern kooperieren, wie z.B. Dallmayr mit der Karl Heinz Böhm Stiftung Menschen für Menschen (bei dieser Kooperation werden von jedem verkauften Paket Dallmayr Ethiopia 5 Baumsetzlinge in Äthiopien gepflanzt). Inwieweit stimmen Sie den folgenden Aussagen auf einer Skala von 1 (trifft gar nicht zu) bis 7 (trifft voll zu) zu?
(Bitte ankreuzen. Sie können Ihre Bewertung zwischen 1 und 7 abstufen.)

Spenden in Verbindung mit Produktkäufen ...	(7) Trifft voll zu	(6)	(5)	(4)	(3)	(2)	(1) Trifft gar nicht zu
*sind **Sinnvoll***							
*sind ein **Marketinggag***							
*sind **Unglaubwürdig***							
*sind **Greenwashing (Deckmantel, Feigenblatt) der Unternehmen***							
ersetzen** eine **Spende an** die entsprechende **Nicht-Regierungs-Organisation							
***ersetzen** den **Kauf** von Fair Trade Produkten*							
ersetzen Spenden allgemein							
stärken** mein **Vertrauen in das Unternehmen							
beruhigen** mein **Gewissen							
finde ich gut							
*sollen als **prozentualer Anteil** am Kaufpreis genannt werden*							
*sollen als **absoluter Betrag** vom Kaufpreis genannt werden*							

8. Haben Sie schon einmal **an Hilfsorganisationen** mit Bezug zu Entwicklungsländern **gespendet**? Hierzu zählen auch spezielle Kollekten in der Kirche für Gemeinden oder Projekte in Entwicklungsländern. *(Bitte ankreuzen)* ______JA

______ NEIN

9. **Wie viel** haben Sie in den letzten 12 Monaten für Entwicklungshilfe **gespendet**? *(Bitte ankreuzen)*

______nichts ______unter 20 Euro ______20 bis unter 50 Euro

______50 bis unter 100 Euro ______100 bis unter 250 Euro______ mehr als 250 Euro

10. Wie viel muss von **1 € Spende an eine Entwicklungshilfeorganisation** bei den Empfängern ankommen, damit Sie nicht den Eindruck haben, dass irgendwo Geld versickert?

(Bitte eintragen) _____ Cent

***In Geschäften finden Sie vermehrt Produkte, deren Hersteller die Kooperation mit einer Spendenorganisation bewerben. Dabei wird damit geworben, dass der Verkauf der Produkte einen guten Zweck unterstützt. Diese Form der Spendengenerierung / Spenden-
erzeugung nennt sich*** *CrM.*

11. Welche **Produkte** würden Sie im Rahmen einer **CrM-Kampagne** kaufen? *(Antworten Sie bitte mit Zahlen zwischen 1 (trifft gar nicht zu) und 7 (trifft voll zu).)*

	(7) Trifft voll zu	(6)	(5)	(4)	(3)	(2)	(1) Trifft gar nicht zu
Kaffee							
Schokolade							
Wasser							
Cornflakes							
Zahnpasta							
Wandfarbe							
Tierfutter							

12. Wenn ein Unternehmen **CrM** durchführt, bin ich grundsätzlich bereit, deswegen die Marke zu **wechseln**. *(Bitte ankreuzen)* ______JA ______ NEIN

    Wenn ja, haben Sie dies schon mal gemacht? ______JA ______ NEIN

13. Haben Sie bereits **Produkte** im Rahmen einer CrM-Kampagne **gekauft**? __JA_NEIN

    Wenn ja, welche? ______________________________

14. Haben Sie sich **bewusst** für ein **CrM Produkt entschieden**? ___JA __ NEIN

15. Haben Sie, obwohl Sie nur ein Exemplar des Produktes benötigten, **mehrere Exemplare** gekauft, nur um die Kampagne zu unterstützen? _____JA _____ NEIN

16. Wie hoch schätzen Sie den **Anteil der Spende am Preis** des CrM Produktes ein? Mit Preis ist der Preis gemeint, den Sie im Laden für das Produkt bezahlen. *(Bitte ankreuzen)*

    ____0-2% ____>2-4% ____>4-6% ____>6-8% ____>8-10%
    ____>10-15% ____>15-20% ____>20-25% ____>25%

17. Ich finde es gut, wenn ich mit dem Kauf eines Produktes gleichzeitig etwas **Gutes für die Gesellschaft** tun kann. *(Bitte ankreuzen)* ______JA ______ NEIN

18. **Ich würde eine CrM-Kampagne für Kaffee unterstützen, wenn** von einem 5 €/Pfund teurem Kaffee...

    ____0,01 bis 0,50 € ____>0,50 bis 1,00 € ____>1,00 bis 1,50 €

    ____1,50 bis 2, 00 € ____>2,00 bis 2,50 € ____>2,50 € ... **an die wohltätige Organisation gespendet** werden. Kreuzen Sie bitte den **niedrigsten** Betrag an, den Sie bereit sind, zu akzeptieren.

19. Beenden Sie den folgenden Satz: „**Wenn ich anstatt eines herkömmlichen Produktes ein CrM Produktes kaufe, dann...**"

    ____

    ____

20. Angenommen Sie kaufen immer „Tchibo Kaffee". Nun **wechseln** Sie **wegen einer CrM-Kampagne** zu „Dallmayr Kaffee". Wie verhalten Sie sich, wenn die CrM-Kampagne von Dallmayr endet? *(Bitte ankreuzen)*

    Ich kaufe wieder „Tchibo Kaffe" _____ → *weiter mit Frage 22*

    Ich kaufe nun immer „Dallmayr Kaffee" _____

21. Sie kaufen nun „Dallmayr Kaffee". Kaufen Sie diesen Kaffee.... *(Bitte ankreuzen)*

......genauso oft wie im Rahmen der Kampagne? _____
......seltener als zur Zeit der Kampagne? _____

22. Wie wichtig ist es für Sie, dass die Aktivitäten des Unternehmens mit den Zielen der **CrM-Kampagne übereinstimmen**? Z.B. Volvic Wasser baut Brunnen in Afrika. *(Bitte ankreuzen)*

sehr wichtig (5) (4) (3) (2) (1) sehr unwichtig

23. Wo und in welchem Ausmaß haben Sie **von CrM-Kampagnen gehört**? *(Antworten Sie bitte mit Zahlen zwischen 1 (nichts gehört) und 7 (sehr viel gehört).)*

	(7) Sehr viel	(6)	(5)	(4)	(3)	(2)	(1) Nichts
TV							
Printmedien							
Internet							
Produktwerbung							
Einkaufsstätte							
Außenwerbung							
Radio							
Kino							
Auf dem Produkt							

Vielen Dank für Ihre Teilnahme!

Appendix A2: Example of the IDM

Verbleibende Klicks: 6

	Kaffee 3	Kaffee 1	Kaffee 2
Gesundheitswirkung	?	?	?
Geschmack	?	?	Kräftig
Spende an Kleinbauern	Keine Spende auf Packung beworben	?	?
Marke	?	?	?
Preis	?	2,99 €	3,99 €
Anbau- und Herstellungsweise	?	?	?
Herkunft	?	Äthiopien	?
Hilfe zur Selbsthilfe	?	?	?
Bitte wählen Sie ein Produkt:	• **Kaffee 3**	• **Kaffee 1**	• **Kaffee 2**

Weiter

6 Are ethical consumption and charitable giving substitutes or not? Insights into consumers coffee choice [111]

Abstract

While charitable giving stagnates, Fair Trade and organic labelling as well as Cause-related Marketing campaigns are on the rise in Germany. The question as to whether the efficiency of the different systems is of relevance for consumers has received little attention in the literature so far. A latent class model for discrete choice analysis reveals five consumer segments with well distinguished preferences and willingness to pay measures for the modes of ethical consumption as well as for different donation amounts. For 27 % of the 484 respondents ethical consumption occurs at the expense of other forms of ethical behaviour such as charitable giving.

Keywords: Fair Trade; Charitable Giving; Latent Class Analysis; Market Segmentation; Willingness to Pay

6.1 Introduction – Goal of the study

Over the last three decades ethical consumption has been increasing (HARRISON et al. 2005). Ethical consumption refers to a purchase based on an individual's sense of responsibility towards society and personal concerns for one or several ethical issues (DE PELSMACKER et al. 2005; HARRISON et al. 2005; TALLONTIRE et al. 2001). Ethical issues can be manifold, e.g. social and environmental concerns such as health issues, labour standards, social justice, animal welfare and sustainable production methods. They coexist with 'traditional' consumers' decision making criteria such as price and quality (HARRISON et al. 2005).

Classical 'ethical' products are Fair Trade (FT) and certified organic goods (DE PELSMACKER et al. 2005; SHAW and CLARKE 1999). FT products consider ethical issues as for instance working conditions, the absence of child labour as well as stable and higher prices for disadvantaged producers in developing countries all of which are guaranteed by labelling organisations such as Transfair in Germany (CARLSSON et al. 2007; OZCAGLAR-TOULOUSE et al. 2006). Organic certification focuses on environmental sustainability (soil degradation, no use of chemical fertilisers) and animal welfare issues.

In addition to those established areas that link consumers' purchase decision to personal concerns consumers increasingly have the opportunity to buy products whose purchases lead

[111] This paper has been published in Food Quality and Preferences (2011), 22: 412-421.

to target-oriented donations to classical charity organisations. The donation (indicated in form of the money spent or the things done for the good cause) is promoted on the product by label (ARORA and HENDERSON 2007). In the following, goods of this type will be called Cause-related Marketing (CrM) products. CrM food campaigns in Germany often support environmental issues (see 'Krombacher Regenwald Projekt' or 'Dallmayr Ethiopia' and its cooperation with 'Menschen für Menschen' which plant five trees in Ethiopia per sold coffee package of Dallmayr Ethiopia) or health issues (see Volvic's partnership with Unicef to provide clean drinking water in Ethiopia) and are similar to a regular donation to the respective charitable organisations. On one hand ROBERTS (1996) and others consider CrM to be similar to FT, i.e. a tool consumers use to express their social concerns; on the other hand e.g. EIKENBERRY (2009) distinguishes CrM from FT. While she regards the former primarily as a marketing tool she acknowledges the latter to indeed be aimed at promoting ethical consumption. Thus, unlike FT and organic production CrM is sometimes suspected to be a green-washing strategy of companies.

The growth of consumer expenditures for FT, organic certified and CrM products (OLOKO 2008; TRANSFAIR 2010) is, however, in contrast to another development: In nominal terms donations directly to charitable organisations have stagnated since 2005 (SOMMERFELD 2008; TNS-INFRATEST 2009).

In this respect three questions arise. First, is there a link between those two developments, i.e. does the rise in FT, organic and CrM products occur at the expense of donations? Second, are FT, organic and CrM perceived to be (almost) the same or do consumers distinguish between those 'labels'? Third, what determines the willingness to pay (WTP) for the different forms of support? To analyse these issues we have examined whether consumers who are engaged in ethical consumption are also the ones who have strong preferences for charitable giving to developmental organisations or whether these different forms of altruistic behaviour attract different consumer groups. In the latter case, we can assume that ethical consumption is to be seen complementary to donations. In the former case they might be substitutes which raises the question regarding the efficiency of the different forms of altruistic spending.

Though this latter aspect will not be subject of the present paper, our study will analyse whether consumers care at all about the donation amount reaching the producers which can be a first indicator and proxy for the efficiency of donation and FT systems and distinguish in their purchase decision between high and low donation amounts and therefore more and less efficient support systems. At present, there is no information provided on FT products regarding the amount of the price premium paid by consumers that actually reaches the producer. Though CrM campaigns frequently indicate the effect the purchase of one unit of a product has for the cause, the information is often provided only as project-specific donations in form of own currencies like e.g. hours of schooling provided, square meters of rainforest saved from destruction or trees which are planted. The monetary value of these actions is often not indicated which implies that also those labels lack transparency for the consumer as it is difficult to know the costs of e.g. a schooling hour (see OLOKO 2008).

In this study the product under investigation is coffee. Coffee seems to be especially suitable for the analysis as (i) it was the first fair-traded product and thus German consumers associate it very well with the FT movement (SCHNEDLITZ and HALLER 2003), (ii) it is still the most important FT product regarding availability, volume of sales and variety in the German retail sector (RAYNOLDS 2002), (iii) it is a commonly used fast moving consumer good (VANTOMME et al. 2006) and the most popular beverage of German consumers[112]. In addition, coffee is an outstanding export product for producers in the developing world, with over 90 % of the coffee production taking place in those countries (PONTE 2002). Thus, coffee is crucial for the lifestyle of consumers in Germany while being at the same time a relevant export product for many producers in the developing world.

As we attempt to estimate the willingness to pay (WTP) for coffee with various ethical attributes, we are confronted with the attitude behaviour gap. In our case this implies an overstatement of ethical motivation in purchase decisions of consumers as this behaviour is felt to be the socially desirable one. To mitigate this problem, which is described in several studies (see e.g. AUGER et al. 2007; DE FERRAN and GRUNERT 2007; DE PELSMACKER et al. 2005) we acknowledge in our analysis that purchase behaviour is based "on multi-attribute decision making in which the ethical attribute may or may not be important" (DE PELSMACKER et al. 2005, p. 365). Therefore we confront consumers with an as possible realistic multi-attribute purchasing situation applying choice modelling. Discrete choice analysis enables us to deal with the above mentioned challenges (AUGER et al. 2007) even though the hypothetical choice experiment conducted in this research can mitigate but not completely solve the problem of incentive compatibility. For data analysis, including market segmentation, latent class (LC) analysis is applied.

[112] The per capita consumption in 2008 was about 148 litres compared to 133 litre of potable water and increased by 4 litres since 2005 (DEUTSCHER KAFFEEVERBAND 2009).

6.2 Methodology: Choice modelling and latent class segmentation

Choice Experiments (CE) are a flexible approach to record preference data from individuals in artificial but at the same time realistic situations. Realistic in the sense that a situation is created where an individual is asked to compare alternatives on the basis of their attributes and come to a decision between the alternatives (ADAMOWICZ et al. 1998). Hypothetical because, as ALFNES and STEINE (2005) explain, the combination of the product attributes for which consumers' preferences are investigated may be new and accordingly the products are not available yet in the retail. This is the case in the present study. The combination of organic and FT labels on coffee is common. The cooperation of a coffee brand with a charity organisation, however, was new at the time the survey was carried out. In the meantime this has changed, e.g. in May 2008 Dallmayr launched a CrM campaign. Furthermore, the declaration of different absolute amounts of money going directly to the coffee producer in combination with a FT and CrM label on a coffee package has not yet been tested on the market yet.

Random utility models based on latent class or finite mixture modelling are applied to analyze the experimental consumer data and to model discrete choices (e.g. SCARPA and THIENE 2005). LC analysis assumes that within the basic population different groups or segments can be distinguished that have different needs and values[113] and hence may show different preference structures. The selection of attitudes and socio-demographic characteristics for the class membership model is based on findings of previous studies on charitable giving, Fair Trade and organic purchase decisions (see e.g. BUSCHLE 2006; DORAN 2009; GFK 2008; VERBRAUCHER INITIATIVE 2007). For example in the context of FT it is often stated that it enables consumers to make a difference (e.g. UTTING-CHAMORRO 2005). Accordingly, the item "With the purchase of Fair Trade products I can make a difference" was tested in the questionnaire and abbreviated "Fair Trade: do purchase because I can make a difference" in Table 1.

Thus, LC analysis allows for the simultaneous determination and description of both product choice and group membership as well as the separation of the sample in several internally homogenous subgroups mapping the heterogeneity in the population (BOXALL and

[113] It is widely accepted that consumption activities are influenced by a person's set of values. Many services and products are bought because consumers believe that the purchase of these goods help to reach a value-related goal. A value can be defined as "a belief that some condition is preferable to its opposite" (SOLOMON 2009, p. 173). Furthermore, values are identified to be more effective in profiling consumers and segmenting markets than demographics (DORAN 2009).

ADAMOWICZ 2002). Therefore LC models are a sophisticated way to account for preference heterogeneity among consumers on group level without requiring many hypotheses about the distribution of preferences (GREENE and HENSHER 2003; MILON and SCROGIN 2006). LC choice models assess individual choice behaviour as a function of observable attributes of the choices on one hand and of latent heterogeneity in the characteristics of the respondents on the other hand (BOXALL and ADAMOWICZ 2002; GREENE and HENSHER 2003). In a simultaneous process the LC choice model estimates utility parameters of the different attributes and the probability of the affiliation of the respondents to different segments. For the maximisation of both, the choice and the class membership probabilities a multinomial logit model (MNL) is applied (GREEN 2003).

One important feature of the LC choice model is that the LC choice model works without the assumption of independence from irrelevant alternatives (IIA). This is because membership in the segments is probabilistic (BOXALL and ADAMOWICZ 2002). For a more in-depth description the interested reader is referred the above literature as well as KAMAKURA and RUSSELL (1989), KAMAKURA et al. (1994), RUTO et al. (2008) and SWAIT (1994).

6.3 Empirical application – A choice experimental survey

To identify segments of consumers with different concerns, motives, characteristics and WTP for CrM, FT and organic products, respectively, a hypothetical choice experiment and LC choice modelling is applied. Based on the concept of BOXALL and ADAMOWICZ (2002) we developed a framework of coffee choice and segmentation as is revealed in Figure 1. BOXALL and ADAMOVICZ'S (2002) framework incorporates latent psychometric constructs, socio-demographic characteristics and observable product attributes to show how latent segmentation can model the interaction of the factors influencing individuals' choices. This means, the framework demonstrates the two lines of the LC model: the class membership model and the choice model. While in Figure 1 oval boxes refer to latent constructs, observable variables are indicated by square boxes.

Figure 1: Diagram outlining the application of the LC choice model for Fair Trade, organic and CrM coffee choice

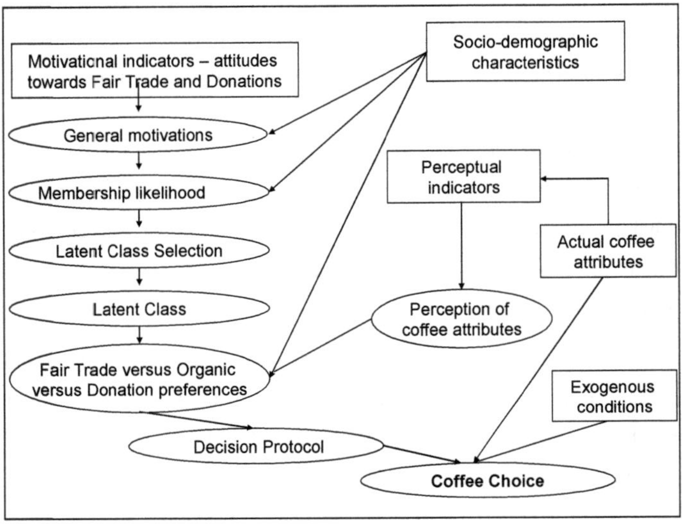

Source: modified based on BOXALL and ADAMOVICZ (2002, p. 427).

Based on this framework we analysed the choice as well as the WTP of coffee drinkers[114] in the Cologne-Bonn area, Germany. The survey was based on face-to-face interviews carried out by well trained students in January and February 2008. As the majority of the respondents (n = 484) were young (40 % < 34 years), highly educated (71 % holding a university-entrance diploma or a university degree), without children (72 %), and with a net family income between 1300 € and 3600 € / month the sample is not representative for the German population. A comparison with data for Germany (FEDERAL STATISTICAL OFFICE 2009a, b) shows that young and highly educated people without children are highly overrepresented. Since CE are cognitive demanding the overrepresentation of highly educated people is somehow desirable as one can assume that well educated people are better able to solve that task. Furthermore, the high share of young people may allow conclusions to be drawn concerning the allocation of private money to donations in form of CrM and FT in the future. Nevertheless the specific structure of the sample may influence the results in a way that conclusions cannot be easily transferred to the whole German population.

The interview consisted of questions regarding participants' purchase and consumption habits, their knowledge of FT, their donation habits, attitudes towards donations and FT, and

[114] Only coffee drinkers qualified for the study.

their socio-demographics as well as the CE. Regarding the latter, participants had to make six choices. This leads to multiple observations per respondent and to some dependence between observations. This dependence makes it possible to obtain stable estimates of the segment-specific regression parameters (VERMUNT and MAGIDSON 2005b). Each choice set consisted of four coffee packages characterised by attribute bundles with various attribute levels and an opt-out option. Four attributes, namely, PRICE (2.99 €, 3.99 €, 4.99 € and 5.9 €), ORGANIC (no, yes – indicated by the German Bio label), LABEL (no label, international FT label, CrM label[115]) and DONATION (no amount given, 0.2 €, 0.5 €, 1 € directly going to the producer) were tested. DONATION was indicated as money directly going to the producer. This attribute was included to test whether respondents care about the portion of the producers' sales revenue (in the case of FT) and the percentage of the CrM donation reaching people in need respectively. This is used as a proxy for the efficiency of the systems. In winter 2007/2008 diverse brands were available at prices between 2.9 € and 5.9 € while minimum prices for organic and FT coffees were 3.9 € in discount supermarkets. FT coffees in regular supermarkets were available between 4.5 € and 5.9 €. Thus, prices in our CE varied between 2.9 € and 5.9 €.

To control for the brand effect, a typical coffee package was chosen and instead of the brand's name 'Your favourite brand' appeared. The SAS macros described in Kuhfeld (2005) were used to generate an efficient fractional factorial design. 12 blocks with six profiles, each with four possible choices and the no-choice option, were generated resulting in a total of 2886 choice decisions.

6.4 Model specification and variable definition

Following previous studies that used LC choice analysis (e.g. BLEND and VAN RAVENSWAAY 1999; CHRISTOPH et al. 2006; MILON and SCROGIN 2006) or analysed ethical consumption (e.g. DORAN 2009), socio-demographic characteristics of the respondents, as well as his/her environmental, welfare and attitudinal concerns are included as explanatory variables in the model for defining the different classes. Respondents had to rate several attitudinal statements using a seven-point Likert scale ranging from strongly agree (1) to strongly disagree (7). We used the Bartlett's Test of Sphericity (0.000) and the Kaiser-Meyer-Olkin measure of sampling adequacy (0.859) to assess the adequacy of the correlation matrices of the obtained statements for factor analysis As the obtained values for both tests are very good, principal

[115] As CrM label the label of a well known German charity organisation working in Africa was used.

component analysis was used to develop psychometric measures of latent attitudes about FT and charitable giving as well as general altruistic attitudes. The survey statements and the factor loadings for each statement are presented in Table 1. Three attitudinal factor components were identified based on eigenvalues greater than or equal to 0.4 which explains 53.42 % of the variance.

The first factor reflects the respondent's opinion about charitable giving and is therefore labelled 'FA1_Donations'. The second factor includes all statements related to the respondent's opinion regarding FT products and was labelled 'FA2_FT'. The third factor reflects the respondent's opinion on general altruistic features and was labelled 'FA3_Altruism'. High values for factor 1 indicate a great interest in donations to charitable organisations; high values for the FT factor point to a strong pro-FT attitude. Finally, high values for the altruism factor are a sign of stronger concerns about other people that, however, are not necessarily linked to FT and/or donations.

Table 1: Principal component analysis of attitude statements about Fair Trade and donations

Response Item	Factor 1	Factor 2	Factor 3
Donation: as personal contribution for the well-being of others	0.812		
To be in line with religious conviction without giving to charity	-0.790		
Donation: organisation should be awarded with a checked label	0.752		
Donation: receipt = credibility	0.694		
Donation: with religious conviction	0.626		
Donation: receipt is an incentive	0.615		
Donation: have confidence in the organisation	0.543	0.443	
Donation: organisations known through friends	0.447		
Donation: do give because I can make a difference	0.420		
Fair Trade: do purchase because I can make a difference		0.735	
Fair Trade: higher price is ok		0.734	
Fair Trade: have confidence in the organisation		0.734	
Fair Trade: friends buy Fair trade products, too		0.578	
Fair Trade: I prefer giving to a Fair Trade purchase	0.495	-0.538	
Feel connected with people in developing countries			0.789
I want to help because I am fine			0.752
I have the responsibility to contribute to developmental aid			0.674

Source: own calculations.

6.5 Results: characterisation of the latent segments of coffee consumers

The determination of the optimal number of classes is not part of the maximisation procedure in Latent GOLD® Choice 4.5 which was used for estimation. In general, models are estimated for an increasing number of classes until an additional segment does not improve the model fit according to several information criteria. In this analysis, the optimal number of classes in the LC model (see Table 2) was identified by assessing the Akaike Information Criterion (AIC), its variant the modified AIC3, and the Bayesian Information Criterion (BIC) as well as the log likelihood statistic from the 1 to 6 class models (WEDEL and KAMAKURA 2000). Information criteria are used for latent class models because no statistical tests such as the likelihood ratio, the Wald Test or the Lagrange Multiplier Test are available for that model type. The reason is that these tests do not meet the prerequisite for a limiting chi-square distribution as they are not asymptotically chi-square distributed (KAMAKURA et al. 1994; WEDEL and KAMAKURA 2000).

Table 2: Criteria for selecting the optimal number of classes (n = 2886)

Number of Classes	LL	BIC(LL)	AIC(LL)	AIC3(LL)	$R^2(0)$	R^2
1-Class	-3681.2673	7411.9415	7378.5346	7386.5346	0.1771	0.1381
2-Class	-3462.4136	7147.1584	6996.8271	7032.8271	0.2693	0.2346
3-Class	-3318.9432	7033.1418	6765.8863	6829.8863	0.2962	0.2629
4-Class	-3210.7092	6989.5981	6605.4183	6697.4183	0.3340	0.3024
5-Class	-3134.5322	7010.1685	6509.0644	6629.0644	0.3737	0.3439
6-Class	-3080.7627	7075.5538	6457.5254	6605.5254	0.3922	0.3634

Source: authors' calculations.

Table 2 shows that with increasing the number of classes the log likelihood statistic as well as the AIC-, AIC3- and BIC-values (until the 4th class) considerably decline while at the same time the R^2 value strongly increases. To test whether the 5 class model provides a better model fit than the 4 class solution, a conditional bootstrap with 500 draws was conducted. The test statistic of the conditional bootstrap is defined as -2(LLH0-LLH1) with H0 being the more restricted model with s segments and H1 being a more general model with s+1 segments. The estimated bootstrap p-value is defined as the proportion of the bootstrap samples with a larger -2LL-difference value than the original sample (VERMUNT and MAGIDSON 2005a). The estimated p-value of 0.00 for the 5 class models shows that the 5 class model significantly increases the model fit compared to the 4 class model. The change in AIC- and AIC3-values from the 5- to 6-segment solution is noticeably smaller than for the 4- to the 5-segment solution. This suggests that adding an extra segment would not lead to much improvement (see e.g. BOXALL and ADAMOWICZ 2002). Furthermore, the significance of parameter estimates worsens as well as the model interpretability with the latter being as important as the statistical tests (SWAIT 1994). On the basis of these results and the characteristics and sizes of the classes, the five-class solution was selected.

Table 3 reports the results of the 5 class model for choices. The differences in the size, the significance, and the signs of the maximum likelihood parameter estimates[116] of the segment specific utility functions as well as the relative importance of the coffee attributes for the different classes demonstrate that there is considerable heterogeneity in preferences for coffee attributes across segments. The Wald statistic reveals that all coffee attributes significantly affect the choice over the classes while the Wald (=) statistic indicates that parameters differ significantly between groups, revealing preference heterogeneity for all attributes and the 'none' alternative. The model fit is with an $R^2 = 0.34$ very good for a discrete choice analysis (see LOUVIERE et al. 2000).

[116] In the model effect coding is applied as this provides estimates that are uncorrelated to the intercept of the model (LOUVIERE et al. 2000). This means that in the choice model the parameters for each attribute sum to zero over the levels of this indicator. For the model of classes the effect estimates sum to zero over the classes (STATISTICAL INNOVATION 2005). The interpretation is done with respect to the mean (COHEN et al. 2003).

Table 3: Parameter estimates of the 5 class model – model for choices and relative importance

	Class 1	Class 2	Class 3	Class 4	Class 5	Overall			
Class size	0.41	0.27	0.15	0.14	0.03				
R^2	0.39	0.04	0.46	0.39	0.29	0.34			
$R^2(0)$	0.43	0.09	0.50	0.42	0.53	0.37			
Relative Importance [%]									
Price	0.70	0.36	0.25	0.04	0.26				
Organic	0.05	0.11	0.32	0.18	0.14				
Label	0.10	0.15	0.18	0.55	0.20				
Donation	0.14	0.38	0.24	0.23	0.41				
Attribute	β_1	β_2	β_3	β_4	β_5	p-value (Wald)	p-value (Wald (=))	Mean	Std. Dev.
Price	-2.31*** (0.152)	-0.20*** (0.055)	-0.86*** (0.114)	-0.08 (0.106)	-1.45*** (0.356)	5E-63	5E-51	-1.17	0.99
Organic yes	0.27*** (0.046)	-0.09** (0.048)	1.64*** (0.202)	0.56*** (0.118)	-1.15*** (0.320)	1E-20	3E-18	0.37	0.60
Label									
no	-0.32***	-0.15**	-0.84***	-0.86***	1.40***	2E-58	0.00	-0.38	0.41
FT	0.66*** (0.078)	0.03 (0.078)	1.03*** (0.167)	2.16*** (0.177)	-1.95*** (0.607)			0.68	0.80
CrM	-0.34*** (0.069)	0.12* (0.068)	-0.19 (0.129)	-1.30*** (0.221)	0.54 (0.428)			-0.30	0.46
Donation									
no	-0.68*** (0.086)	-0.33*** (0.085)	-1.17*** (0.220)	-0.84*** (0.165)	2.38* (1.248)	4E-53	0.00	-0.59	0.57
0.20 €	-0.34*** (0.86)	-0.20** (0.090)	-0.71*** (0.203)	0.38** (0.186)	-4.57 (3.571)			-0.37	0.76
0.50 €	0.26*** (0.076)	0.35*** (0.069)	0.67*** (0.162)	0.62*** (0.154)	0.46 (1.273)			0.40	0.16
1 €	0.76*** (0.082)	0.18* (0.096)	1.21*** (0.214)	-0.16 (0.181)	1.72 (1.250)			0.56	0.48
None	-13.05*** (0.780)	-4.72*** (0.612)	-7.07*** (1.005)	-1.46** (0.638)	-1.30 (1.652)	3E-81	0.00	-7.89	4.56

Numbers in parentheses are standard errors
*, **, *** present significance at the 0.1, 0.05, 0.01 level.
Source: own calculations.

The most important findings are summarised in Table 3. As expected, the coefficient for the price variable is negative across all classes, indicating that it becomes less likely that interviewees choose the product the higher the price is. However, it should be noted that the price variable is not significant for class 4. While all estimates for class 1 are highly significant at the 1 % level as revealed by the z-values this is not the case for the other classes.

This implies, for example, that class 2 cannot be analysed with respect to FT because the respective z-value is insignificant. Interestingly, class 2 is the only class with a positive and significant CrM estimate. At the same time, the parameter value for organic production is both slightly negative and significant, indicating that this consumer segment dislikes organic production. The results also reveal that the attitude of the classes 3 and 4 are similar with respect to organic and FT production as for both classes the respective parameters are positive and highly significant. This suggests that organic as well as FT production increases groups 3 and 4's utility strongly. Whereas, for class 4 the opposite holds regarding CrM, for class 3 no statement can be made according to their valuation of CrM. Looking at the preferred level of donation Table 3 shows that classes 1, 2 and 3 assess donations of 0.5 € and 1 € positively while class 4 provides significant positive values for a donation amount of 0.2 €. Class 5 is special as only a few parameter estimates are significant. The results indicate that consumers in this class are very price conscious while, at the same time, they strongly dislike organic, FT and CrM products and prefer a coffee without any donation amount indicated.

To identify the sources of the differences between segments in the choice model, the class membership model is considered. For the class membership model several variables were selected which, according to previous studies (see e.g. BUSCHLE 2006; DORAN 2009; GFK 2008; SOMMERFELD 2008; VERBRAUCHER INITIATIVE 2007), are expected to have an influence on the classification. Table 4 presents maximum likelihood parameter estimates for the five class membership model. The results indicate that the following variables prove to be significant for class segmentation with regard to the food purchase decision: importance of organic production, relevance of adequate producer prices as well as the wish to buy cheap products (the coding for these items is based on a seven-point Likert Scale; 1: not important, 7: very important). Concerning socio-demographics age is the only significant variable. A positive attitude towards donations and FT represented by factor 1 and 2 influences the segmentation significantly.

Gender (here male), income and education (both high), even though identified as important influences on the purchase of FT products in other studies (see e.g. BLEND and VAN RAVENSWAAY 1999, CHATZIDAKIS et al. 2007; LOUREIRO et al. 2001) are not significant here. While other studies show that children in the household increase the likelihood of donations as well as the purchase of organic food (e.g. LOUREIRO et al. 2001), no significant effect on those variables on group membership can be found in this study. The same holds for social activities as well as church membership which increase preferences for FT and/or donations in other studies (e.g. BUSCHLE 2006; CHATZIDAKIS et al. 2007). The efficiency of a labelling system which we modelled by the indication of different DONATION levels is only important for group 4 and therewith the group which was willing to accept a small donation level of 0.2 €. Furthermore, we tested whether consumption frequency of coffee has an influence on group assignment but could not detect any. The same holds for the statement regarding production without child labour.

Table 4: Parameter estimates of the 5 class model - model for classes (n = 2886)

Covariates (coding in brackets)	Class 1		Class 2		Class 3		Class 4		Class 5		Overall
	β_1	s.e.[b]	β_2	s.e.	β_3	s.e.	β_4	s.e.	β_5	s.e.	p-value
Intercept	1.72	1.18	-0.40	1.28	-1.04	1.74	-3.59**	1.76	3.32	2.42	0.16
Organic (num.[a])	-0.15*	0.09	-0.02	0.09	0.37	0.14***	0.09	0.12	-0.29	0.19	0.05**
No child labour (num.)	-0.13	0.10	-0.05	0.12	-0.11	0.16	0,26	0.19	0.02	0.19	0.53
Adequate producer price (num.)	-0.13	0.09	0.14	0.10	0.09	0.13	0.20*	0.12	-0.31*	0.17	0.09*
Cheap (num.)	0.47***	0.11	0.18	0.11	-0.24	0.13*	-0.11	0.12	-0.29	0.23	0.00***
Gender: Male	0.10	0.12	0.18	0.13	-0.01	0.16	-0.10	0.16	-0.17	0.31	0.63
Age (11 classes)	-0.08	0.05	0.16***	0.05	-0.13	0.07*	-0.05	0.07	0.11	0.13	0.00***
Children < 18: Yes	0.12	0.16	-0.04	0.18	-0.51	0.24**	-0.19	0.21	0.63	0.41	0.20
Education (5 classes)	0.11	0.14	-0.09	0.14	0.20	0.20	0.10	0.19	-0.32	0.30	0.55
Income (12 classes)	-0.03	0.05	-0.07	0.06	0.09	0.07	0.08	0.07	-0.07	0.12	0.33
Church member: Yes	0.10	0.16	0.21	0.18	0.22	0.23	-0.44**	0.21	-0.09	0.39	0.13
Fair Trade = Donation (num.)	0.00	0.07	0.15**	0.07	0.01	0.09	0.10	0.08	-0.26	0.18	0.22
Efficiency of the labelling system											0.16
Top2 Boxes (6-7)	-0.19	0.14	-0.16	0.15	-0.03	0.19	0.40**	0.20	-0.03	0.35	
FA1_Donations	0.08	0.15	0.29*	0.15	0.20	0.19	0.68***	0.19	-1.25***	0.42	0.00***
FA2_FT	0.03	0.16	0.20	0.17	0.53	0.21**	0.70***	0.22	-1.47***	0.43	0.00***
FA3_Altrusim	-0.25*	0.14	-0.07	0.15	-0.09	0.18	-0.03	0.17	0.44	0.34	0.45
Coffeedrinker											0.70
few (up to 1 cup/day)	-0.10	0.24	0.17	0.25	-0.01	0.31	0.22	0.31	-0.28	0.63	
normal (2-3 cups/day	-0.01	0.18	-0.09	0.19	0.27	0.23	0.10	0.23	-0.27	0.48	
strong (> 3 cups/day)	0.11	0.18	-0.08	0.19	-0.27	0.25	-0.33	0.24	0.56	0.43	
Social Activities											0.46
no activity	-0.28	0.28	0.24	0.29	0.40	0.36	-0.08	0.32	-0.29	0.68	
1 activity	-0.11	0.17	-0.13	0.19	-0.13	0.23	-0.30	0.22	0.67	0.44	
2 and more	0.39	0.27	-0.11	0.27	-0.27	0.32	0.37	0.30	-0.38	0.77	

[a] denotes numeric; [b] denotes standard error.

*, **, *** presents significance at the 0.1, 0.05, 0.01 level.

Source: own calculations.

Members of classes 1 and 5 are significantly more price sensitive and less altruistic compared to the other groups. Class 2 includes significantly more elderly respondents with a positive attitude towards donations indicated by the significant positive donation factor 'FA1_Donations' in Table 4. They are the only group that regards FT as comparable to a charitable donation (statement to the question 'Fair Trade = donation' in Table 4). In class 3 we find significantly often younger people having no children with a concern for organic production and a positive attitude towards FT. Respondents of class 4 have a positive attitude towards donations and FT (see the respective factors in Table 4), they have no church membership and state that the share of money reaching the producer (and therefore the efficiency of a system) is an important issue. They are also concerned about fair producer wages, which is in line with their attitude towards FT. Therefore they are consistent in their answers to the FT issue. Class 5 includes respondents who neither have a positive attitude towards FT nor towards charity. Those respondents do not care about the producers' working conditions, which distinguishes them significantly from the other groups. Thus, the class membership model helps to understand the choice decisions reported in the choice model and reveals the sources of the differences in the choice model.

Based on the results (Table 3) obtained the classes can be named as follows: Class 1 consists of – *price conscious coffee shoppers* –, who are most price sensitive and for which the attribute PRICE is of outstanding relative importance (70 %). 41 % of all respondents belong to this group. Class 2 – *the donors* – are very supportive to DONATIONs (relative importance is 38 %) but are indifferent to ORGANIC production. With a share of 27 % of all respondents class 2 is considerable larger than class 3 which covers 15 % of the survey participants. Members of this latter class care about *organic production*. Though ORGANIC obtains a relative importance of 32 % respondents belonging into this group also emphasise DONATION and PRICE. Class 4 – *the supporters of FT* – encompass 14 % of all respondents. The FT LABEL is most important (55 %) for their preference formation. PRICE is with a relative importance of 4 % not at all relevant for group 4. The smallest class 5 (only 3 %) – *the denier* – dislikes any kind of label on coffee. Furthermore, any indicated amount of money reaching the producer decreases respondents' utility.

To summarise, LCA reveals five different market segments which can be easily distinguished. The choice model together with the model for classes allows a description of respondents' preferences and the identification of the influencing factors. In the choice model it becomes obvious that 70 % of the respondents (class 1, 3 and 4) have a strong preference for FT and organic production but dislike CrM. The model of classes reveals that only class 3 and 4 respondents pay attention to the organic and fair production process of goods whereas class 1 is more interested in cheap products. At the same time, 27 % (class 2) of the participants prefer CrM coffee to organic and FT coffee. Those people assigned to class 2 on average are older than those in the other classes. Furthermore the significant positive factor for donations in general and the insignificant factor for FT in the class model reveal that class 2 has a preference for donations in general but not for FT and can therefore easily be distinguished from the other respondents. Moreover, class 2 respondents do not differentiate between FT and donations as we can see in the model for classes. As class 2 with its preference for donations to charity and CrM differs strongly from the other classes, it is likely that the raise in FT and organic consumption does not occur at the expense of charitable giving in general and in form of CrM in particular. In fact, CrM on the one hand and the classical ethical consumption products – FT and organic products – on the other hand address different consumer types while FT supporters and organic production enthusiasts are similar in many respects. Thus, it is not surprising that for FT products double certification – organic and FT – is already widespread in Germany (60 % of the FT certified coffee is also certified organic (FORUM FAIRER HANDEL 2008b)). Therefore the answer to our principal research task is that the consumption of FT as well organic goods is seen as complementary to donating money to charity purposes in general as well as in form of CrM campaigns by more than 70 % of the respondents. Those 27 % who do not see a difference do not choose FT and organic products hence, it can be concluded that consumers are not substituting FT by CrM and vice versa. However, the question remains as to whether CrM possibly cannibalises traditional donations. As those consumers with a penchant for CrM products (class 2) have a strong preference for donations to charitable organisations, our findings indicate that cannibalism between CrM and traditional donations to charitable organisations might occur. Further research is needed to clarify this.

Table 5: Willingness to pay estimates of coffee attributes for the classes [€]

	Class 1		Class 2		Class 3		Class 4	Class 5		Mean
	WTP	s.e.[a]	WTP	s.e.	WTP	s.e.		WTP	s.e.	WTP
Organic	0.12***	0.02	-0.45**	0.23	1.91***	0.24	Price in-sig-nifi-cant	-0.79***	0.22	0.31
Label										
no	-0.14***	0.03	-0.71**	0.34	-0.98***	0.18		0.96***	0.28	-0.32
FT	0.29***	0.03	0.16	0.38	1.20***	0.20		-1.33***	0.42	0.58
CrM	-0.15***	0.03	0.55*	0.33	-0.22	0.15		0.37	0.29	-0.26
Donation										
no	-0.29***	0.04	-1.56***	0.41	-1.37***	0.26		1.63*	0.85	-0.50
0.20 €	-0.15***	0.04	-0.97**	0.43	-0.83***	0.24		-3.13	2.44	-0.31
0.50 €	0.11***	0.03	1.67***	0.33	0.78***	0.19		0.31	0.87	0.34
1 €	0.33***	0.04	0.85*	0.46	1.41***	0.25		1.18	0.86	0.47

[a] s.e. denotes standard error.
*, **, *** presents significance at the 0.1, 0.05, 0.01 level.
Source: own calculations.

As the coefficients presented in Table 3 represent the direct effects associated with each of the explanatory variables on the (unobservable) utility function, they can be used to calculate WTP estimates (presented in Table 5) for each of the attributes using equation (10). The WTP concept represents consumers' preferences which are "expressed in monetary terms" (Brent 2006, p. 72). Therefore, usually WTP estimates are of particular interest for marketing departments as well as policy makers. They can furthermore be used by FT organisations, producers and retailers to develop products with different attributes and prices to perfectly skim the market and to meet consumer preferences best. In addition, the WTP for an indicated amount of donation is important for policy makers and marketing experts as it represents consumers' preference for systems efficiency. We see that the estimates for each label differ strongly between the classes. As the price variable was insignificant for class 4 no WTP estimates can be estimated for consumers belonging into this group.

With regard to the attribute organic production the average WTP over the four considered classes is equal to 0.31 €. Between the classes WTP varies strongly. So have consumers belonging to the classes 2 and 5 a negative WTP[117] for this attribute (-0.45 € and -0.79 €, respectively). Thus, these groups are of little direct interest to economic agents. Respondents of class 1 are willing to pay a small (0.12 €) and of class 3 (1.91 €) a very high price premium. The results are similar with respect to the attribute FT for all four groups considered. Results indicate that class 1's WTP is with 0.29 € for a FT labelled coffee positive but obviously smaller than class 3's WTP (1.20 €). The average WTP for FT labelled coffee here again has little value for marketers as single classes WTP is either higher or lower. Given the significant positive but at the same time considerable different WTP of Class 1 and 3 for both attributes and the relevance of classes 1 and 3 in the total population (41 % and 15 %, respectively) suggests that a specialised pricing strategies with respect to those two consumers' segments would be adequate with regard to organic and FT coffee. This way it might be possible to increase the market share for organic and FT products, which is with 3 % and 1 %, respectively (2004) very low (KRIER 2005)[118]. Taking a closer look at FT, the price sensitive but major consumer segment of class 1 is willing to pay 0.29 € for a FT coffee. However, the price premium requested even in the German discount sector for FT coffee versus conventional one exceeds 1 € and thus might be one explanation for the low market share. The question is, whether it would be possible to offer FT coffee at a lower price. As it is an inherent characteristic of the FT certification that producers in the developing countries receive higher prices than those they would be able to obtain in conventional markets prices also in the German retail sector need to be higher for FT than for conventional coffee; e.g. the pricing scheme of the most important certification organisation, the Fairtrade Labelling Organizations International (FLO) fixed the minimum FT coffee price in the way that FT coffee producers receive at least 0.05 € / lb more than their colleagues who produce conventional coffee (FLO 2009). Additional costs of FT versus conventional coffee might occur during processing and distribution as due to smaller processing and trade volumes economies of scales cannot be realised to the same extent. Thus, the low sales volumes are due to high prices which are themselves due to high costs resulting from low sales volumes. A differentiated marketing and pricing strategy might be able to increase sales volumes. This might allow reducing prices in all segments if overall costs decline due to this differentiation strategy. One additional aspect, which further increases the differences in consumer prices between conventional and FT coffee is the German value added tax (VAT) system. Though

117 For the interpretation of negative WTP estimates which refer to the concept of willingness to accept see e.g. BRENT (2006) and PEARCE ET AL. (2006).

118 Besides, these results reveal once more the appropriateness of the application of the latent class approach for the analysis of discrete choice data.

the VAT level is equal for all coffee (19 %) higher base prices lead to a higher absolute tax consumers have to pay for FT coffee. Thus, if the promotion of FT products would be acknowledged as political strategy besides traditional development aid to support developing countries, exempting FT sales from VAT could be seen as an option.

Concerning the attribute CrM labelling, only class 2 (0.55 €) has a significant and positive WTP, while class 1 has a significant negative WTP. This means purchasing a CrM coffee decreases utility or wellbeing for those price sensitive respondents. For the other two classes (3 and 5) the coefficient is insignificant.

Finally, we estimated the WTP for the attribute DONATION, and thus, the amount of money directly going to the producer. The WTP is negative for small sums (0.2 €) for all considered classes except the fifth's. The findings suggest that 97 % of the consumers participating in the survey devalue small amounts, whereas a donation to the producer of 0.5 € or 1 € of the retail price (which was in our CE between 2.99 € and 5.99 €) results in a positive and significant WTP in the classes 1, 2 and 3. However, the WTP of respondents in class 1 is smaller than the indicated amount donated, while it is very high and exceeding this amount for consumers in class 3. The WTP estimate for Class 2, which is characterised by a strong preference for donations to a well known charity organisation, is somewhat inconsistent. For the medium donation of 0.5 € their WTP is with 1.67 € considerably higher but when a donation amount of 1 € is indicated on the package the WTP is with 0.85 € noticeably lower than the indicated donation. The finding that higher amounts of donations generate positive WTP estimates whereas missing labelling as well as a small donation amount decrease consumers' WTP is in line with the finding of Gneezy and Rustichini (2000) which stated: "pay enough or don't pay at all". Thus, enterprises are well advised to stay with their current practice and not claim the amount donated or to grant such a high amount that consumers appreciate that donation level. However, in the latter case we have to keep in mind that according to our analysis consumers belonging into class (1), and thus the largest class (41 %), are not willing to pay a price premium which covers the expenses.

6.6 Conclusions

Results from this paper provide valuable information on consumers' decision making with respect to FT, organic and charitable giving's also in form of CrM in Germany that can be used by policy makers as well as marketing departments and NGOs in the organic, FT and charity sector at national and regional level. Moreover this is the first empirical study that has been conducted to analyse and compare different forms of ethical consumption and/ or behaviour. The empirical results of the study show that German coffee consumers can be segregated into five classes with statistically well defined preferences. While variables such as product price and attitudes towards FT, organic production and donations to charity organisations determine class membership, socio-demographic characteristics with the exception of age proved not to be relevant. WTP for the attributes organic, FT and donations via CrM differ significantly between the groups as well as between the labelling schemes. Our results also indicate that those consumers that are inclined to buy FT products are the same that are in favour of organic products and vice versa. However, respondents with a preference for FT or organic production do not choose CrM promoted products. Those consumers with a preference for CrM products have an aversion to FT and organic (class 2) but give regular donations to charitable organisations. Furthermore those consumers with positive attitudes towards FT and donations (class 4) clearly differentiate between these two things. Thus findings indicate that cannibalism between CrM and FT / organic products is not very likely. However, as class 2 regards FT to be comparable to charitable giving it could be that those consumers substitute FT products by donations to charity or the purchase of CrM products. Therefore it seems more likely to assume that those consumers partly substitute traditional donations to charitable organisations by buying CrM promoted products. Further research is needed to clarify this.

Another important result is that, directly asked, information on the amount of money reaching the producer, which is a proxy for the efficiency of system supported through the purchase (FT or CrM), is only relevant for a small part of all consumers (segment 4). But if the absolute amount of money going to the producers is indicated on the product consumers perceive and value this information. In our case consumers benefit from a relatively high level (0.5 € and 1 € going directly to the producer) and devalue smaller donation amounts. This indicates that, if consumers have the possibility to judge supporting systems with respect to their efficiency they do it.

6.7 References

ADAMOWICZ, W. L., LOUVIERE, J. J. and SWAIT, J. (1998): *Introduction to Attribute-Based Stated Choice Methods, Final Report to Resource Valuation Branch*, Damage Assessment Center, NOAA, U.S. Department of Commerce.

ALFNES, F. and STEINE, G. (2005): None-of-these bias in stated choice experiments. Paper prepared for presentation at the *XIth International Congress of European Association of Agricultural Economists*, Copenhagen, Denmark, August 24-27, 2005.

ARORA, N. and HENDERSON, T. (2007): Embedded Premium Promotion: Why it works and how to make it more effective. *Marketing Science*, 26 (4): 514-531.

AUGER, P, DEVINNEY, T. M. and LOUVIERE, J. J. (2007): Measuring the importance of ethical consumerism: A multi-country empirical investigation. In Hooker, J., Hulpke, J. F. and Madsen, P. (Eds.): *Controversies in International Corporate Responsibility* International Corporate Responsibility Series, 3, Charlottesville. Virginia: Philosophy Documentation Center: pp. 207-221.

BLEND, J. R. and VAN RAVENSWAAY, E. O. (1999): Measuring Consumer Demand for Ecolabeled Apples. *American Journal Agricultural* Economics, 81 (5): 1072-1077.

BOXALL, P. C. and ADAMOWICZ, W. L. (2002): Understanding Heterogeneous Preferences in Random Utility Models: A Latent Class Approach. *Environmental and Resource Economics,* 23 (4): 421–446.

BRENT, R. J. (2006): *Applied Cost-Benefit Analysis*. Cheltenham: Edward Elgar.

BUSCHLE, N. (2006): Spenden in Deutschland, Ergebnisse der Einkommensteuerstatistik 2001. In Statistisches Bundesamt (Ed.): *Auszug aus Wirtschaft und Statistik (2).* Wiesbaden: pp.151-159.

CARLSSON, F., FRYKBLOM, P. and LAGERKVIST, C. J. (2007): Consumer willingness to pay for farm animal welfare: mobile abattoirs versus transportation to slaughter. *European Review of Agricultural Economics*, 34 (3): 321–344.

CHATZIDAKIS, A., HIBBERT, S. and SMITH, A. P. (2007): Why People Don't Take their Concerns about Fair Trade to the Supermarket: The Role of Neutralisation. *Journal of Business Ethics,* 74 (1): 89–100.

CHRISTOPH, I. B., ROOSEN, J. and BRUHN, M. (2006): Willingness to pay for genetically modified food and non-food products. *American Agricultural Economics Association Annual Meeting*, Long Beach, California, July 23-26, 2006.

COHEN, J., COHEN, P., WEST, S. G. and AIKEN, L. S. (2003): *Applied Multiple Regression/Correlation Analysis for the Behavioral Sciences.* Mahwah [et al.]: Erlbaum Associates.

DE FERRAN, F. and GRUNERT, K. G. (2007): French fair trade coffee buyers' purchasing motives: An exploratory study using means-end chain analysis. *Food Quality and Preferences*, 18: 218-229.

DE PELSMACKER, P., DRIESEN, L. and RAYP, G. (2005): Do Consumers Care about Ethics? Willingness to Pay for Fair-Trade Coffee. *The Journal of Consumer Affairs*, 39 (2): 363–385.

DEUTSCHER KAFFEEVERBAND (2009): *Lieblingsgetränke der Deutschen - Durchschnittskonsum pro Person 2008.* Available from: http://www.kaffeeverband.de/img/lieblingsgetraenke.jpg, [accessed 2009-07-23].

DORAN, C. J. (2009): The Role of Personal Values in Fair Trade Consumption. *Journal of Business Ethics, 84* (4): 549-563.

EIKENBERRY, A. M. (2009): The Hidden Cost of Cause Marketing. *Stanford Social Innovation Review*, Summer 2009: 51-55.

FEDERAL STATISTICAL OFFICE (2009a): *Statistisches Jahrbuch 2009*, Wiesbaden.

FEDERAL STATISTICAL OFFICE (2009b): *Bevölkerung und Erwerbstätigkeit – Haushalte und Familien*, Ergebnisse des Mikrozensus 2008, Fachserie 1, Reihe 3, Wiesbaden.

FLO (2009): *Fairtrade minimum price and fair-trade premium table.* Version 05.10.2009. Available from: www.fairtrade.net/standards.html, [accessed 2009-10-05].

FORUM FAIRER HANDEL (2008b): *Doppelt gut - Bio im Fairen Handel.* Available from: http://www.transfair.org/presse/detailseite-presse/browse/4/article/45/doppelt-gut.html, [accessed 2008-02-20].

GFK (2008): Spendensituation und Spendenverhalten - Aktuelle Entwicklung. Motive, gesellschaftliche Rahmenbedingungen und Einflussfaktoren auf das Spendenverhalten, 13. Oktober 2008, *Gemeinsame Tagung von WZB und DZI*, Berlin.

GNEEZY, U. and RUSTICHINI, A. (2000): Pay enough or don't pay at all. *The Quarterly Journal of Economics*, 115: 791-810.

GREENE, W. H. and HENSHER, D. A. (2003): A latent class model for discrete choice analysis: contrasts with mixed logit. *Transportation Research Part B*, 37: 681-698.

GREENE, W. H. (2003): *Econometric Analysis.* New Jersey: Upper Saddle River, Prentice Hall.

HARRISON, R., NEWHOLM, T. and SHAW, D. (2005): Defining the Ethical Consumer. In: Harrison, R., Newholm, T. and Shaw, D. (Eds.): *The Ethical Consumer*. London: Sage: 1-10.

KAMAKURA, W. A. and RUSSELL, G. J. (1989): A Probabilistic Choice Model for Market Segmentation and Elasticity Structuring. *Journal of Marketing Research*, 26 (4): 379-390.

KAMAKURA, W. A., WEDEL, M. and AGRAWAL, J. (1994): Concomitant variable latent class models for conjoint analysis. *International Journal of Research in Marketing*, 11 (5): 451-464.

KRIER, J.-M. (2005): *Fair Trade in Europe 2005.* Fair Trade Advocacy Office, Brussels.

KUHFELD, W. F. (2005). *Marketing Research Methods in SAS – Experimental Design, Choice, Conjoint, and Graphical Techniques*, SAS 9.1 Edition, TS-722.

LOUREIRO, M. L., MCCLUSKEY, J. J. and MITTELHAMMER, R. C. (2001): Assessing Consumer Preferences for Organic, Eco-labeled, and Regular Apples. *Journal of Agricultural and Resource Economics*, 26 (2): 404-416.

LOUVIERE, J. J., HENSHER, D. A. and SWAIT, J. D. (2000). *Stated Choice Methods: Analysis and Application*. Cambridge: Cambridge University Press.

MAGIDSON, J., EAGLE, T. and VERMUNT, J. (2003): New Developments in Latent Class Choice Models. *Sawtooth Software Conference Proceedings*: 89-112.

MILON, J. W. and SCROGIN, D. (2006): Latent preferences and valuation of wetland ecosystem restoration. *Ecological Economics*, 56: 162-175.

OLOKO, S. (2008): *Cause related Marketing - Der Status Quo in Deutschland*. Berlin.

OZCAGLAR-TOULOUSE, N., SHIU, E. and SHAW, D. (2006): In search of fair trade: ethical consumer decision making in France. *International Journal of Consumer Studies*, 30 (5): 502-514.

PEARCE, D., ATKINSON, G. and MOURATO, S. (2006): *Cost-Benefit Analysis and the Environment: Recent Development*. Paris: OECD.

PONTE, S. (2002): The 'Latte Revolution'? Regulation, Markets and Consumption in the Global Coffee Chain. *World Development*, 30 (7): 1099-1122.

RAYNOLDS, L. T. (2002): *Poverty Alleviation Through Participation in Fair Trade Coffee Networks: Existing Research and Critical Issues*. Background Paper Prepared for Project Funded by the Community and Resource Development Program, The Ford Foundation, New York.

ROBERTS, J. A. (1996): Will the real socially responsible consumer please step forward? *Business Horizons*, 39 (1): 79-83.

RUTO, E., GARROD, G. and SCARPA, R. (2008): Valuing animal genetic resources: a choice modeling application to indigenous cattle in Kenya. *Agricultural Economics*, 38 (1): 89-98.

SCARPA, R. and TIENE, M. (2005): Destination Choice Models for Rock Climbing in the Northeastern Alps: A Latent-Class Approach Based on Intensity of Preferences. *Land Economics*, 81 (3): 426-444.

SHAW, D. and CLARKE, I. (1999): Belief formation in ethical consumer groups: an exploratory study. *Marketing Intelligence & Planning*, 17 (2): 109-119.

SCHNEDLITZ, P. and HALLER, T. (2003): Ethik im Handel - Empirische Befunde zu FairTrade. *Werbeforschung und Praxis*, 3: 18-20.

SOLOMON, M. R. (2009): *Consumer Behavior - Buying, Having and Being*. New Jersey: Pearson Prentice Hall.

SOMMERFELD, J. (2008): Die Bedeutung des Spenden- und Gemeinnützigkeitsrechts in der Praxis - Eine Analyse von Experteninterviews. „Motive, gesellschaftliche Rahmenbedingungen und Einflussfaktoren auf das Spendenverhalten", 13. Oktober 2008, *gemeinsame Tagung von WZB und DZI*, Berlin.

STATISTICAL INNOVATION (2005): *Tutorial #1: Using Latent GOLD 4.0 to Estimate LC Cluster Models*.

SWAIT, J. (1994): A structural equation model of latent segmentation and product choice for cross-sectional revealed preference choice data. *Journal of Retailing and Consumer Services*, 1 (2): 77-89.

TALLONTIRE, A., RENTSENDORJ, E. and BLOWFIELD, M. (2001): Ethical Consumers and Ethical Trade: A Review of Current Literature, *Policy Series* 12. Chatham, UK: Natural Resources Institute.

TNS INFRATEST (2009): *15 Jahre Deutscher Spendenmonitor: Fakten und Trends im Zeitverlauf*.

TRANSFAIR (2010): *26 Prozent Plus für Fairtrade*. Press Release: 28.04.10. Available from: http://www.transfair.org/top/nachricht/browse/2/article/26-prozent-plus-fuer-fairtrade.html ?tx_ttnews[backPid]=137&cHash=8ef6164167, [accessed 2010-04-28].

UTTING-CHAMORRO, K. (2005): Does Fair Trade Make a Difference? The Case of Small Coffee Producers in Nicaragua. *Development in Practice*, 15 (3/4): 584-599.

VANTOMME, D., GEUENS, M., DE HOUWER, J. and DE PELSMACKER, P. (2006): Explicit and Implicit Determinants of Fair-Trade Buying Behavior. *Advances in Consumer Research*, 33: 699-703.

VERBRAUCHER INITIATIVE (2007): *Fairer Handel: Stetiges Wachstum*. Available from: http://www.fair-feels-good.de/pdf/86.pdf?title=Fairer_Handel:_Stetiges_Wachstum, [accessed 30.05.2008].

VERMUNT, J. K. and MAGIDSON, J. (2005a): *Latent GOLD® Choice 4.0 User's Manual*.

VERMUNT, J. K. and MAGIDSON, J. (2005b): *Technical Guide for Latent GOLD Choice 4.0: Basic and Advanced*. Belmont Massachusetts: Statistical Innovations Inc.

WEDEL, M. and KAMAKURA, W. (2000): *Market Segmentation - Conceptual and Methodological Foundations*. Boston [et al.]: Kluwer.

Appendix B1: Questionnaire

Institut für Lebensmittel- und Ressourcenökonomik
Rheinische Friedrich-Wilhelms-Universität Bonn

Marktforschung der Agrar- und Ernährungswirtschaft
Leitung: Prof. Dr. Monika Hartmann

universitätbonn

Vom Interviewer auszufüllen:
Interview geführt am:.......................... (Datum) **Ort: ....**

Fragebogennummer: ☐☐☐ **Version 1**

Name des Interviewers: ....Vorlage Block: ....

Interviewer: „Guten Tag, mein Name ist ______________, ich komme von der Universität Bonn. Wir führen eine Befragung zum allgemeinen Konsumverhalten und zu Kaffee im Besonderen durch. Ich würde mich freuen, wenn Sie unsere Fragen kurz beantworten.“

1. **Was ist Ihnen beim Kauf von Lebensmitteln wichtig?**
Antworten Sie bitte mit Zahlen zwischen 1 und 7 wobei 1 bedeutet: ist mir sehr wichtig und 7 bedeutet: ist mir überhaupt nicht wichtig. Mit den Werten zwischen 1 und 7 können Sie Ihre Bewertung abstufen.

	Achtung rotiert!	**(1)** **mir sehr wichtig**	**(2)**	**(3)**	**(4)**	**(5)**	**(6)**	**(7)** **überhaupt nicht wichtig**	*(98) weiß nicht*	*(99) keine Angabe*
Beim Kauf von Lebensmittel ist mir wichtig….										
F1.1	dass die Produkte nachhaltig und ökologisch erzeugt sind	☐	☐	☐	☐	☐	☐	☐	☐	☐
F1.2	dass die Produkte ohne Kinderarbeit hergestellt werden	☐	☐	☐	☐	☐	☐	☐	☐	☐
F1.3	dass die Produzenten angemessene Preise erhalten	☐	☐	☐	☐	☐	☐	☐	☐	☐
F1.4	dass die Produkte preiswert sind	☐	☐	☐	☐	☐	☐	☐	☐	☐
F1.5	dass ich den Einkauf schnell erledigen kann	☐	☐	☐	☐	☐	☐	☐	☐	☐
F1.6	dass die Produkte qualitativ und hochwertig sind	☐	☐	☐	☐	☐	☐	☐	☐	☐
F1.7	dass ein persönlicher Kontakt besteht und ich Beratung beim Einkauf erhalte	☐	☐	☐	☐	☐	☐	☐	☐	☐

2. **Trinken Sie Kaffee?**

☐ Ja → *weiter mit Frage 3*

☐ Nein → *Ausschluss von der Befragung*

3. **Wie viele Tassen Kaffee trinken Sie pro Tag?**

> *INTERVIEWER: Antwortmöglichkeiten nicht vorlesen; Espresso oder Cappuccino zählen ebenfalls dazu und gelten jeweils als eine Tasse. Ein Becher Kaffee/Cappuccino entspricht 2 Tassen.*

☐ *1 Tasse*	☐ *5 Tassen*	☐ *9 Tassen*
☐ *2 Tassen*	☐ *6 Tassen*	☐ *10 Tassen*
☐ *3 Tassen*	☐ *7 Tassen*	☐ ***Sonstiges:** ……………………*
☐ *4 Tassen*	☐ *8 Tassen*	

4. **Stellen Sie sich vor, Sie erwarten Gäste und wollen einen besonders guten Kaffee anbieten. Wenn Sie einen solchen, *guten* Kaffee kaufen wollen, worauf achten Sie bei Ihrem Einkauf?**

> *INTERVIEWER: ungestützte Antwortmöglichkeiten nicht vorlesen; Wenn der Befragte lediglich Geschmack oder Qualität nennt, muss gefragt werden, welche Dinge für ihn Geschmack und Qualität ausmachen. Bitte in einem solchen Fall INTENSIV nachfragen*

Marke	***milde Röstung***	***Herkunftsland***	***Koffeinfrei***
☐	☐	☐	☐
Preis	***Bio***	***Fair Trade***	***100% Arabica***
☐	☐	☐	☐

☐ ***Sonstiges:** ……………………*

5. **Stellen Sie sich nun bitte vor, es geht um den Kaffee, den Sie jeden Tag trinken. Worauf achten Sie beim Kauf dieses Kaffees?**

> *INTERVIEWER: Antwortmöglichkeiten nicht vorlesen. Wenn der Befragte lediglich Geschmack oder Qualität nennt, muss gefragt werden, welche Dinge für ihn Geschmack und Qualität ausmachen.*

Marke	***milde Röstung***	***Herkunftsland***	***Koffeinfrei***
☐	☐	☐	☐
Preis	***Bio***	***Fair Trade***	***100% Arabica***
☐	☐	☐	☐

☐ ***Sonstiges:** ……………………*

6. **Wie kaufen Sie den Kaffee normalerweise: gemahlen, als ganze Bohne, als Pads oder als Instant Kaffee?**

INTERVIEWER: Mehrfachnennungen sind möglich

Gemahlen ☐ *ganze Bohne* ☐ *Pads* ☐ *Instant Kaffee* ☐

7. **Kennen Sie dieses Zeichen?**

INTERVIEWER: Fair Trade Siegel zeigen

☐ Ja → *weiter mit Frage 8* ☐ Nein → *weiter mit Frage 9*

8. **Was bedeutet dieses Zeichen?**

INTERVIEWER: hier bitte Stichworte aufschreiben

………
………
………
………
………………………………………………………………………………………..

9. **Was verstehen Sie unter Fairem Handel**

INTERVIEWER: Antwortmöglichkeiten nicht vorlesen; *Gender Equality: Geschlechter Gerechtigkeit: Gleichbehandlung von Mann und Frau*

☐ *gerechte Preise* ☐ *Handel mit Entwicklungsländern* ☐ *Gender equality*
☐ *Dritte Welt Laden* ☐ *keine Kinderarbeit* ☐ *keine Ausbeutung*
☐ *Unterstützung benachteiligter Produzenten*

☐ *gute Arbeitsbedingungen* ☐ *Absatzsicherheit* ☐ *langfristige Verträge*

☐ *Sonstiges: ……………………………* ☐ *(98) weiß nicht*

Interviewer: „Ich möchte Ihnen nun kurz erläutern was Fair Trade nach Meinung der Fair Trade Organisationen leisten soll: Für fair gehandelte Produkte erhalten Erzeuger in Entwicklungsländern höhere Preise. Dafür müssen sie bestimmte Richtlinien erfüllen, die z.B. Kinderarbeit untersagen und Arbeitsschutz vorschreiben. Mit dem Kauf von fair gehandelten Produkten unterstützen Sie also Kleinbauern und Landarbeiter in Entwicklungsländern.“

10. **Kennen Sie Fair Trade Produkte? Welche?**

INTERVIEWER: Antwortmöglichkeiten nicht vorlesen

☐ *Schokolade* ☐ *Bananen* ☐ *Kaffee* ☐ *Spielzeug* ☐ *Handwerkskunst*
☐ *Schnittblumen* ☐ *Textilien* ☐ *Tee* ☐ *Fußbälle* ☐ *Zucker* ☐ *Kakao*
☐ *Honig* ☐ *Sonstiges:* ....
☐ *kein Produkt → weiter mit Frage 13*

11. **Welche der von Ihnen genannten, fair gehandelten Produkte kaufen Sie auch? Kaufen Sie die jeweiligen Produkte häufig, gelegentlich oder nie?**

INTERVIEWER: hier nur die Produkte abfragen, die auch in der vorhergehenden Frage 10 genannt wurden

		häufig	gelegentlich	nie	(98) weiß nicht	(99) keine Angabe
F11.1	Schokolade	☐	☐	☐	☐	☐
F11.2	Bananen	☐	☐	☐	☐	☐
F11.3	Kaffee	☐	☐	☐	☐	☐
F11.4	Spielzeug	☐	☐	☐	☐	☐
F11.5	Handwerkskunst	☐	☐	☐	☐	☐
F11.6	Schnittblumen	☐	☐	☐	☐	☐
F11.7	Textilien	☐	☐	☐	☐	☐
F11.8	Tee	☐	☐	☐	☐	☐
F11.9	Fußbälle	☐	☐	☐	☐	☐
F11.10	Zucker	☐	☐	☐	☐	☐
F11.11	Kakao	☐	☐	☐	☐	☐
F11.12	Honig	☐	☐	☐	☐	☐
F11.13	Sonstiges	☐	☐	☐	☐	☐

↓

INTERVIEWER: wer hier bei den nachgefragten Produkten immer nie sagt: weiter zu Frage 13

12. **Wo kaufen Sie Ihre fair gehandelten Produkte ein?**

INTERVIEWER: Mehrfachnennungen sind möglich

☐ Bioladen ☐ Biosupermarkt ☐ Edeka
☐ Weltladen ☐ Kirche ☐ Kaisers/Tengelmann
☐ Lidl ☐ Rewe ☐ Spezialitätengeschäft
☐ *Sonstiges: ……………………*

Interviewer: „Es muss auch kontrolliert werden, ob ein Fair Trade Siegel zu Recht verwendet wird. Sonst könnte ja jeder das Zeichen benutzen, ohne die Bedingungen einzuhalten. Solche Kontrollen kosten natürlich etwas. Deshalb kann das, was Sie im Geschäft für ein fair gehandeltes Produkt **mehr** zahlen, nicht zu 100% bei den Erzeugern in den Entwicklungsländern ankommen.

Bei der folgenden Frage geht es darum, wie viel Ihrer Meinung nach von dem gezahlten Aufpreis auf jedem Fall bei den Erzeugern ankommen sollte, damit Sie den Eindruck haben, dass nicht irgendwo zu viel Geld versickert."

13. **Angenommen, ein fair gehandeltes Produkt kostet einen Euro mehr als ein nicht fair gehandeltes: wie viel muss von diesem Euro bei den Erzeugern ankommen?**

☐☐ Cent ☐ *(98) weiß nicht*

14. **Was glauben Sie: wie schmeckt fair gehandelter Kaffee im Vergleich zu normalem, nicht fair gehandelten, Kaffee: besser, gleich gut oder schlechter?**

☐ ***besser***
☐ ***gleich gut***
☐ ***schlechter***
☐ ***(98) weiß nicht***

Interviewer: „Bis hierhin haben wir über Kaffee und Fair Trade gesprochen.

Spenden werden häufig als eine andere Möglichkeit gesehen, Menschen in Entwicklungsländern zu unterstützen.

Deshalb möchten wir Sie nun zu Ihrer Einschätzung zu **Spenden an Hilfsorganisationen mit einem Bezug zu Entwicklungsländern** befragen."

15. **Haben Sie schon einmal an entsprechende Hilfsorganisationen gespendet? Spezielle Kollekten in der Kirche für Gemeinden oder Projekte in Entwicklungsländern zählen beispielsweise ebenfalls hierzu.**

☐ **ja**
☐ **nein** → *weiter mit Frage 19*

16. **Darf ich Sie fragen, wie viel Sie in den letzten 12 Monaten für Entwicklungshilfe gespendet haben?**

- ☐ Unter 20 Euro
- ☐ 20 bis unter 50 Euro
- ☐ 50 bis unter 100 Euro
- ☐ 100 bis unter 250 Euro
- ☐ mehr als 250 Euro
- ☐ *Sonstiges: …………*

☐ *(98) weiß nicht*

☐ *(99) keine Angabe*

17. **Ich lese Ihnen nun einige Aussagen im Zusammenhang mit Spenden an Hilfsorganisationen vor. Sagen Sie mir bitte, inwieweit Sie diesen Aussagen zustimmen.**
Antworten Sie bitte mit Zahlen zwischen 1 und 7 wobei 1 bedeutet: trifft voll zu und 7 bedeutet: trifft überhaupt nicht zu. Mit den Werten zwischen 1 und 7 können Sie Ihre Bewertung abstufen.

	Achtung rotiert!	(1) trifft voll zu	(2)	(3)	(4)	(5)	(6)	(7) trifft überhaupt nicht zu	*(98) weiß nicht*	*(99) keine Angabe*
F17.1	Die Organisation an die ich spende, muss mit einem kontrollierten Siegel ausgezeichnet sein	☐	☐	☐	☐	☐	☐	☐	☐	☐
F17.2	Ich spende regelmäßig während des gesamten Jahres für Menschen in Entwicklungsländern	☐	☐	☐	☐	☐	☐	☐	☐	☐
F17.3	Ich spende besonders um Weihnachten herum	☐	☐	☐	☐	☐	☐	☐	☐	☐
F17.4	Ich spende besonders bei Katastrophen in Entwicklungsländern	☐	☐	☐	☐	☐	☐	☐	☐	☐
F17.5	Die Spendenquittung ist für mich ein Garant für die Glaubwürdigkeit der Spendenorganisation	☐	☐	☐	☐	☐	☐	☐	☐	☐
F17.6	Eine Spendenquittung ist für mich ein zusätzlicher Anreiz zu spenden	☐	☐	☐	☐	☐	☐	☐	☐	☐
F17.7	Durch Freunde bin ich auf die Organisation an die ich heute spende aufmerksam geworden	☐	☐	☐	☐	☐	☐	☐	☐	☐
F17.8	Ich fühle mich armen Menschen in Entwicklungsländern verbunden	☐	☐	☐	☐	☐	☐	☐	☐	☐
F17.9	Ich möchte anderen Menschen helfen, weil es mir gut geht	☐	☐	☐	☐	☐	☐	☐	☐	☐
F17.10	Ich leiste meinen Beitrag zum Wohl anderer Menschen durch Spenden	☐	☐	☐	☐	☐	☐	☐	☐	☐

18. **Schätzen Sie bitte ein, inwiefern die folgenden Aussagen auf Sie zutreffen. Antworten Sie bitte mit Zahlen zwischen 1 und 7 wobei 1 bedeutet: trifft voll zu und 7 bedeutet: trifft überhaupt nicht zu. Mit den Werten zwischen 1 und 7 können Sie Ihre Bewertung abstufen.**

	Achtung rotiert!	**(1) trifft voll zu**	**(2)**	**(3)**	**(4)**	**(5)**	**(6)**	**(7) trifft überhaupt nicht zu**	*(98) weiß nicht*	*(99) keine Angabe*
F18.1	Mit dem Kauf von Fair Trade Produkten kann ich etwas bewirken	☐	☐	☐	☐	☐	☐	☐	☐	☐
F18.2	Ich spende für Entwicklungs-hilfeorganisationen, weil ich mit meiner Spende etwas bewirken kann	☐	☐	☐	☐	☐	☐	☐	☐	☐
F18.3	Wenn ich spende, handle ich im Einklang mit meinen religiösen Überzeugungen	☐	☐	☐	☐	☐	☐	☐		
F18.4	Meine Bekannten kaufen Fair Trade Produkte	☐	☐	☐	☐	☐	☐	☐	☐	☐
F18.5	Ich bin bereit, für Fair Trade Produkte einen höheren Preis zu zahlen	☐	☐	☐	☐	☐	☐	☐		
F18.6	Es ist mir wichtig zu wissen, wie viel Geld beim Erzeuger ankommt	☐	☐	☐	☐	☐	☐	☐		
F18.7	Ich vertraue den Organisationen, an die ich Spenden für Entwicklungsländer gebe, dass sie das Geld gut verwenden	☐	☐	☐	☐	☐	☐	☐	☐	☐
F18.8	Ich spende lieber, als fair gehandelte Produkte zu kaufen	☐	☐	☐	☐	☐	☐	☐	☐	☐
F18.9	Ich vertraue den Fair Trade Organisationen, dass sie das Geld gut verwenden	☐	☐	☐	☐	☐	☐	☐		
F18.10	Der Kauf von Fair Trade Produkten ist eigentlich nichts anderes als eine Art von Spende	☐	☐	☐	☐	☐	☐	☐	☐	☐
F18.11	Fair Trade passt auch zu Lidl, Aldi oder Plus	☐	☐	☐	☐	☐	☐	☐	☐	☐
F18.12	Ich fühle mich verpflichtet, einen Beitrag zum Wohl der Menschen in Entwicklungsländern zu leisten	☐	☐	☐	☐	☐	☐	☐	☐	☐

INTERVIEWER: wenn Frage 18 beantwortet wurde: weiter mit Frage 20

INTERVIEWER: Frage 19 wird nur an die Teilnehmer gerichtet, die in Frage 15 geantwortet haben, dass sie noch nie an Entwicklungshilfeorganisationen gespendet haben

19. **Bitte schätzen Sie nun ein, inwiefern die folgenden Aussagen auf Sie zutreffen. Antworten Sie bitte mit Zahlen zwischen 1 und 7 wobei 1 bedeutet: trifft voll zu und 7 bedeutet: trifft überhaupt nicht zu. Mit den Werten zwischen 1 und 7 können Sie Ihre Bewertung abstufen.**

	Achtung rotiert!	**(1) trifft voll zu**	**(2)**	**(3)**	**(4)**	**(5)**	**(6)**	**(7) trifft überhaupt nicht zu**	*(98) weiß nicht*	*(99) keine Angabe*
F19.1	Meinen religiösen Überzeugungen werde ich auch gerecht, wenn ich nicht an Entwicklungshilfeorganisationen spende	☐	☐	☐	☐	☐	☐	☐	☐	☐
F19.2	Ich glaube nicht, dass die Organisationen, die Spenden für Entwicklungsländer sammeln, das Geld gut verwenden. Deshalb spende ich nicht	☐	☐	☐	☐	☐	☐	☐	☐	☐
F19.3	Ich würde lieber fair gehandelte Produkte kaufen, als zu spenden	☐	☐	☐	☐	☐	☐	☐	☐	☐
F19.4	Ich spende nicht für Entwicklungshilfeorganisationen, weil ich nicht glaube, dass ich mit meiner Spende etwas bewirken kann	☐	☐	☐	☐	☐	☐	☐	☐	☐
F19.5	Ich fühle mich verpflichtet, einen Beitrag zum Wohl der Menschen in Entwicklungsländern zu leisten	☐	☐	☐	☐	☐	☐	☐	☐	☐
F19.6	Ich fühle mich armen Menschen in Entwicklungsländern verbunden	☐	☐	☐	☐	☐	☐	☐	☐	☐
F19.7	Ich möchte anderen Menschen helfen, weil es mir gut geht	☐	☐	☐	☐	☐	☐	☐	☐	☐
F19.8	Mit dem Kauf von Fair Trade Produkten kann ich etwas bewirken	☐	☐	☐	☐	☐	☐	☐	☐	☐
F19.9	Meine Bekannten kaufen Fair Trade Produkte	☐	☐	☐	☐	☐	☐	☐	☐	☐
F19.10	Ich bin bereit, für Fair Trade Produkte einen höheren Preis zu zahlen	☐	☐	☐	☐	☐	☐	☐	☐	☐
F19.11	Es ist mir wichtig zu wissen, wie viel Geld beim Erzeuger ankommt	☐	☐	☐	☐	☐	☐	☐	☐	☐
F19.12	Ich vertraue den Fair Trade Organisationen, dass sie das Geld gut verwenden	☐	☐	☐	☐	☐	☐	☐	☐	☐
F19.13	Der Kauf von Fair Trade Produkten ist eigentlich nichts anderes als eine Art von Spende	☐	☐	☐	☐	☐	☐	☐	☐	☐
F19.14	Fair Trade passt auch zu Lidl, Aldi oder Plus	☐	☐	☐	☐	☐	☐	☐	☐	☐

20. **Stellen Sie sich vor, Sie befinden sich in einem Supermarkt und möchten eine 500g Packung Kaffee Ihrer Lieblingsmarke kaufen. Es stehen 4 verschiedene Kaffees zur Auswahl. Ich möchte das jetzt gerne mit Ihnen sechsmal durchspielen. In den sechs Wahlsituationen unterscheiden sich die Kaffees in Bezug auf den Preis, die Siegel und darin, ob es Bio-Kaffee ist oder nicht. Es handelt sich aber jedes Mal um Ihre Lieblingsmarke. Sehen Sie sich die verschiedenen Kaffees bitte in Ruhe an und sagen mir dann, welchen Sie kaufen würden. Es besteht auch die Möglichkeit, keinen der vier Kaffees zu kaufen.**

INTERVIEWER: Vorlage mit Kaffees zeigen. Vorlagen-Nr. bitte eintragen.

20a	Vorlage Set	**Kaffee 1**	**Kaffee 2**	**Kaffee 3**	**Kaffee 4**	**keinen dieser vier Kaffees**	*(98) weiß nicht*	*(99) keine Angabe*
	☐	☐	☐	☐	☐	☐	☐	☐

Wenn (4): keinen dieser vier Kaffees: Und warum nicht?..

20b	Vorlage Set ☐	Kaffee 1	Kaffee 2	Kaffee 3	Kaffee 4	keinen dieser vier Kaffees	*(98) weiß nicht*	*(99) keine Angabe*
		☐	☐	☐	☐	☐	☐	☐

Wenn (5): keinen dieser vier Kaffees: Und warum nicht?...

20c	Vorlage Set ☐	Kaffee 1	Kaffee 2	Kaffee 3	Kaffee 4	keinen dieser vier Kaffees	*(98) weiß nicht*	*(99) keine Angabe*
		☐	☐	☐	☐	☐	☐	☐

Wenn (5): keinen dieser vier Kaffees: Und warum nicht?...

20d	Vorlage Set ☐	Kaffee 1	Kaffee 2	Kaffee 3	Kaffee 4	keinen dieser vier Kaffees	*(98) weiß nicht*	*(99) keine Angabe*
		☐	☐	☐	☐	☐	☐	☐

Wenn (5): keinen dieser vier Kaffees: Und warum nicht?...

20e	Vorlage Set ☐	Kaffee 1	Kaffee 2	Kaffee 3	Kaffee 4	keinen dieser vier Kaffees	*(98) weiß nicht*	*(99) keine Angabe*
		☐	☐	☐	☐	☐	☐	☐

Wenn (5): keinen dieser vier Kaffees: Und warum nicht?...

20f	Vorlage Set ☐	Kaffee 1	Kaffee 2	Kaffee 3	Kaffee 4	keinen dieser vier Kaffees	*(98) weiß nicht*	*(99) keine Angabe*
		☐	☐	☐	☐	☐	☐	☐

Wenn (5): keinen dieser vier Kaffees: Und warum nicht?...

21. **Würden Sie mir verraten, welches Ihre Lieblingsmarke ist?**..

Interviewer: „Vielen Dank, dass Sie bis hierher die vielen verschiedenen Fragen beantwortet haben und sich die Zeit genommen haben, verschiedene Kaffeeverpackungen zu betrachten. Nun sind wir fast am Ende der Befragung angekommen.

Es fehlen nur noch die Angaben zu Ihrer Person, die wir selbstverständlich anonym auswerten und die dem Datenschutz unterliegen.

Möchten Sie die Fragen zur Person selbst ausfüllen?“

ANGABEN ZUR PERSON

22. Geschlecht:

☐ Weiblich ☐ Männlich

23. Wie alt sind Sie?

☐ < 20 Jahre	☐ 30-34 Jahre	☐ 45-49 Jahre	☐ 60-64 Jahre
☐ 20- 24 Jahre	☐ 35-39 Jahre	☐ 50-54 Jahre	☐ 65-70 Jahre
☐ 25- 29 Jahre	☐ 40-44 Jahre	☐ 55-59 Jahre	☐ älter als 70 Jahre

24. Sind Sie Mitglied in einer der folgenden Organisationen und/oder Bereiche? (Mehrfachnennungen sind möglich)

☐ Kirche (zahle Kirchensteuer) ☐ Umweltschutz ☐ Partei

☐ Weltladen ☐ Sportverein ☐ Jugendarbeit

☐ Nicht-Regierungs-Organisation wie z.B. Greenpeace

☐ Sonstiges: ………………………………………

25. Wie hoch ist das monatliche Nettoeinkommen Ihres <u>Haushalts</u>?

☐ Unter 300 Euro	☐ 1300 bis unter 1500 Euro
☐ 300 bis unter 500 Euro	☐ 1500 bis unter 2000 Euro
☐ 500 bis unter 700 Euro	☐ 2000 bis unter 2600 Euro
☐ 700 bis unter 900 Euro	☐ 2600 bis unter 3600 Euro
☐ 900 bis unter 1100 Euro	☐ 3600 bis unter 5000 Euro
☐ 1100 bis unter 1300 Euro	☐ 5000 und mehr Euro
	☐ *(98) weiß nicht*
	☐ *(99) keine Angabe*

26. Wie viele Personen leben von diesem Einkommen, Sie eingeschlossen? ☐☐

27. Wie viele Kinder (unter 18 Jahren) haben Sie? ☐

---

28. Welches ist Ihr höchster Bildungsabschluss?

☐ Ohne Schulabschluss	☐ Fach-/ Hochschulreife (Abitur)
☐ Volks-/Hauptschulabschluss	☐ Fach-/ Hochschulabschluss
☐ Mittlere Reife (Realschulabschluss)	☐ Anderer Abschluss

29. **Welchen Beruf üben Sie aus?**

- ☐ Schüler/in, Student/in, Azubi
- ☐ Hausmann/frau
- ☐ Arbeiter/in
- ☐ Angestellte/r
- ☐ Selbständige/r
- ☐ Rentner/in
- ☐ Pensionär
- ☐ Beamte/r
- ☐ Derzeit nicht erwerbstätig

---

30. **Wie würden Sie die Gegend, in der Sie wohnen einschätzen?**

- ☐ großstädtisch (ab 100.000 Einwohner, wie z.B. Bonn)
- ☐ kleinstädtisch (10.000 -100.000 Einwohner)
- ☐ ländlich

---

31. **Wie beurteilen Sie die Verfügbarkeit von Fair Trade Produkten in Geschäften in Ihrer Nähe (ca. 10 min Fußweg)?**

Sehr gut (1) (2) (3) (4) (5) Sehr schlecht

32. **Wie würden Sie Ihre eigene Lebenssituation (nicht nur die finanzielle) einschätzen?**

Mit geht es sehr gut (1) (2) (3) (4) (5) mir geht es sehr schlecht

---

Vielen Dank!

Appendix B2: Example of a choice set

1 2 3 4

Set 2 Block 4

7 Acceptance and critical success factors of Cause-related Marketing in Germany – Evidence from a consumer survey [119]

Abstract

Although Cause-related Marketing (CrM) is increasingly applied, little is known about consumers' attitudes, knowledge and perception of CrM campaigns and critical factors influencing consumers' purchase intention. Based on a consumer survey conducted in 2009, this paper focuses on the role of the cause-brand-fit and corporations' credibility for German consumers' willingness to switch to a CrM promoted product. Results provide evidence that consumers hold in general positive attitudes towards CrM but that these are not strongly reflected in actual or intended purchase behaviour. Based on a factor and a cluster analysis we have derived marketing recommendations for enterprises on how to effectively address different consumer segments regarding the CrM products. In this regard, we have identified four groups of consumers that differ in their attitudes towards CrM products. For example, one group of consumers appreciates CrM products while another group holds sceptical attitudes towards CrM.

Keywords: Cause-related Marketing; Market Segmentation; Cause-Brand-Fit; Willingness to Switch

7.1 Introduction

In the saturated and highly competitive food markets of the industrialized countries consumers can afford to be critical as to what they choose. Thus, differentiated products that satisfy consumers' needs and create 'customer value' for different consumer segments are vital for firms' success. One opportunity for companies to differentiate their products is by means of labelling, e.g. societal effects related to the production or consumption of the product or of the firms' whole strategy (GIOVANNUCCI and PONTE 2005; ZIMMERMANN and VAN DER LANS 2009). Studies have revealed that consumers value societal benefits such as environmental impact, ethics, and animal welfare supported by companies in addition to those attributes directly linked to the specific product under consideration (GFK, ROLAND BERGER and BVE 2009; SEVENONE MEDIA 2009; ZIMMERMANN and VAN DER LANS 2009). The Brands & Values Ethical Brand Monitor® (which uses the 'ethical brand value' to describe the

[119] This paper has been presented at the Corporate Responsibility Research Conference 2010 'Sustainability Management in a diverse world', September 15-17, 2010, Marseille, France. Co-authors are Dilani Saverimuthu, Carola Grebitus and Monika Hartmann.

impact ethical factors have on brand image and consumers' preferences for the brand) has recently demonstrated that consumers in Germany prefer brands they perceive to be sustainable (DRÖGE and BLUMBERG 2009). The results of this survey further indicate that social, ecological, and economical responsibility as well as the firms' code of conduct positively influence brand image and consumers' trust in the brand. The better trust results in increased purchase intentions for brands with a relatively higher perceived ethical brand value (DRÖGE and BLUMBERG 2009). The development of sales volumes for e.g. organic and Fair Trade (FT) products reveal that especially the growing environmental and social awareness increasingly motivates consumers in Germany to choose the environmental or ethical substitute of a regular good and that the increased awareness and respective consumer statements are sales relevant (TRANSFAIR 2010, BLE 2008). For instance, the enlarged number of Fair Trade products in Germany is evidence of corporations' efforts to meet consumers' 'new' requests. In addition, firms conduct diverse marketing activities – e.g. several studies have revealed that corporations in Germany are increasingly socially and environmentally engaged (KRÖHER 2009; POPPELREUTHER and STEIN 2008) – thereby trying to differentiate their brand from that of competitors. Such social commitment[120] can be perceived as an additional benefit of a brand or a company which might be purchase relevant for conscious consumers. Thus, supporting social or environmental causes account not only for satisfying consumers' demands or social or ecological issues but might also enhance brand awareness, create positive brand image and reputation all of which benefits the company.

Against this background, Cause-related Marketing (CrM) is a marketing strategy, whereby the product purchase leads to a target-oriented donation to a designated cause which is promoted on the product by label. This means that each time a consumer purchases a CrM product, money is donated to a charity organization or a good cause. Thus, CrM allows companies to advertise their social or environmental commitment via the product. In doing so, companies link their name or brand with a particularly good cause or a charitable organisation. Reasons for corporations to become involved with social causes via CrM range between the two poles of altruism and self-interest (WYMER and SAMU 2003). Altruism if the firm believes in the value of the cause. Self-interest as CrM enables firms to gain consumers' attention and at the same time to differentiate themselves from competitors (e.g. CADBURY 2000; BERGER et al.

[120] The commitment of companies for social causes is commonly known as Corporate Social Responsibility (CSR). As there is no consistent definition of CSR we refer to the one given by the European Commission (2001) which states that CSR is "a concept whereby companies integrate social and environmental concerns in their business operations and in their interaction with their stakeholders on a voluntary basis" (EUROPEAN COMMISSION 2010).

1996; BROWN and DACIN 1997). It also enables stakeholders to identify themselves with the corporation and its brands (ROY and GRAEFF 2003) and to increase sales volumes by encouraging consumers to switch brands or retailers (WEBB and MOHR 1998). Thus, it is not surprising that CrM is an increasingly applied marketing strategy.

Since 2002 more than 90 CrM promoted products have been launched in Germany (OLOKO 2008), but little is known about consumers' appreciation of CrM products and their motives for buying a CrM product instead of a comparable one without CrM (WEBB and MOHR 1998). For Germany up to now one study has shown that CrM is able to increase brand sympathy (BLUMBERG and CONRAD 2006). Nevertheless, manufacturers and retailers need to know the critical success factors of this strategy in order to apply it effectively. Therefore, our study investigates German consumers' purchase behaviour regarding CrM products and the sources they use to be informed about CrM, their attitudes, knowledge and perceptions of CrM campaigns and identifies critical factors that influence their purchase intention. Furthermore, we have examined whether CrM campaigns are able to change and influence brand preferences of consumers and the related role of the cause-brand-fit.

The paper continues with a brief literature review with respect to the motives for and the critical success factors of CrM. In section 3 we describe the design of the empirical study and the sample characteristics. The empirical results are presented in section 4. In section 5 a summary is given and conclusions are derived.

7.2 Theoretical background

In most cases, companies use CrM primarily to enhance their image, reputation and profile and, most importantly, to increase their sales volumes and consumers' loyalty. The support of a good cause is rather of secondary interest to them (CADBURY 2000). Several studies confirm that the economic objective of increasing sales volumes can be achieved by CrM as it encourages consumers to switch brands or retailers due to CrM (WEBB and MOHR 1998). Moreover, previous research revealed that consumers' perception of the corporate motivations of a company that claims to be socially responsible affects their responses towards the company itself (SEN and BHATTACHARYA 2001, DRUMWRIGHT 1996), the product (BROWN and DACIN 1997) and the cause (LICHTENSTEIN ET AL. 2004).

According to WEBB and MOHR (1998) empirical analyses show that consumers hold positive attitudes towards CrM campaigns and that they also express purchase intentions regarding CrM products. Nevertheless, research also reveals that elements of the promotion, such as type of product, can make a difference. Moreover, the success of CrM campaigns seems to depend on consumers' interest in the topic, i.e. the cause which is supported as well as the credibility of and the fit between the advertising profit organisation, the cause and the NGO.

In the following section, we will focus on the issues of cause-brand-fit, firms' credibility, and brand switching. Cause-brand-fit is discussed because it is considered to be important for consumers' positive evaluation of the campaign. The same holds for the credibility of the firm applying the CrM promotion. Finally, brand switching is likely to depend crucially on consumers' evaluation of CrM. From the companies' point of view, the more customers who purchase the CrM product, the more successful a CrM campaign is.

PORTER and KRAMER (2002) advise companies that are willing to take social responsibility to identify a social cause that relates to the company's business, on the grounds that the ability to compete depends on the area in which it operates. PRACEJUS and OLSEN (2004) agree with them and emphasise that companies that want to be authentic and gain a healthy margin from their competitors need to pay attention to the so-called 'cause-brand-fit'. They consider this fit to be the most important factor for the credibility of a CrM cooperation and thus for its success. In this context, it is important to identify social causes, which – from the consumers' point of view – appear related to the company's business or the brand itself. According to the brand-extension research, it is vital for a successful campaign to have at least one fit between the social cause and the brand or the company (LAFFERTY et al. 2004). The more the social cause and the brand/company relate to each other, the greater the credibility and consequently the consumer acceptance of the campaign. This directly influences purchase intention and willingness to switch brands. Studies from different countries have shown that the extent of compatibility and similarity that consumers perceive to exist between cause and brand leads to a positive effect on their attitudes (AAKER and KELLER 1990; BUCKLIN and SENGUPTA 1993; RIFON et al. 2004; SIMONIN and RUTH 1998). At the same time, DACIN and BROWN (2002) question whether the level of relatedness between a company and the supported charitable cause has an impact on consumer response at all. These two contrary positions reveal that the relevance of the cause-brand-fit for the success of CrM campaigns has not been answered yet.

Another critical success factor for effective CrM campaigns is, according to BLUMBERG and CONRAD (2006), the credibility of firms' social engagement promoted in the campaign. Also as stated by SINGH (2009) scepticism with respect to CrM arises primarily because customers question the companies' motivations for participating in such actions. Studies reveal that some consumers mistrust the altruistic motives of firms, firms' sustainability efforts and are sceptical with regard to the 'fair' amount of money spent on the 'cause' (OLOKO 2009; HAVAS MEDIA 2009). CrM is believed to be used primarily as a marketing tool and a fig leaf. This may be partly due to the fact that a great number of CrM promotions lack transparency with regard to the amount of donations as well as with respect to the success of the 'cause' the money is aimed at. Moreover, CrM campaigns seldom disclose details of the agreement between the NGO and the company (BERGLIND and NAKATA 2005).

The CONE CORPORATE CITIZENSHIP Study (2004) emphasizes that 86 % of consumers in the United States state they would switch brands from the one they normally purchase to one that supports a worthy cause, when price and quality are equal. The review of similar studies conducted by ENDACOTT (2004) reveals similar results for Australia, the UK, New Zealand and Mexico, although on a lower level. In Australia 54 % of consumers indicated they would switch brands due to CrM, in Mexico the respective share amounted to 76 %. The other countries show values in between. The higher willingness to switch brands articulated by respondents from the US might be explained by the long tradition of CrM in the US compared to the other countries. ADKINS (1999) concludes from this cross-national similarity, if CrM can influence consumer perceptions and their accepted customs, it can be considered a vital strategy in the marketing mix.

However, the change might be limited to a certain time or period and, therefore, needs to be differentiated from brand loyalty. Since the early 1960s researchers have studied the reasons and factors influencing brand switching behaviour. MAFFEI (1961) showed that marketing activities are able to influence brand preferences for at least a short time. GÖNÜL et al. (1996) found that purchase frequency influences the probability of brand switching. The more regularly a product is purchased the less likely it is that the brand is switched. SUN ET AL. (2003) came to the conclusion that most of the promotion-induced brand switching effect cannot be considered an actual brand switch by consumers but only a temporary change of purchases. This means brand loyal consumers adjust their purchase behaviour for a period of time due to promotions.

Therefore, we can conclude that the cause-brand fit as well as the credibility of CrM campaigns are critical for consumer acceptance and thus for the willingness to switch brands. Whether that holds true for Germany and which other determinants influence consumers' perception of CrM will be analysed based on a consumer survey in the next section.

7.3 Design of the study and sample characterisation

To answer our research questions we conducted a survey with n = 217 respondents in Germany in 2009. Table 1 describes participants' socioeconomic characteristics in comparison to the German population. It reveals that young and highly educated people are over-represented in the sample. Concerning consumers' social activities we can report that 50 % of the sample is affiliated to a church and pays church tax, 37 % are members in a sports club, 12 % in a NGO, 10 % are involved in youth work and 8 % are members of a political party. Only a small share of 5 % and 1 % are active in environmental organisations and world shops respectively.

Table 1: Socioeconomic characteristics of the sample and the German population

Variable	Specification	Percentage of the sample (n = 217)	Percentage of the German population (2007)
Gender	Female	53.6	51.0
	Male	46.4	49.0
Age[1]	18-24 years	11.5	9.9
	25-34 years	23.4	14.5
	35-44 years	20.1	20.4
	45-54 years	19.6	17.6
	55-64 years	17.2	14.0
	> 64 years	8.1	23.4
Income[1] (n=214)	< 500 €	16.0	3.3
	500 - < 1300 €	30.6	27.1
	1300 - < 2000 €	24.1	24.5
	2000 - < 3600 €	19.6	2000 to 4500 €: 33.8
	3600 - < 5000 €	7.0	
	> 5000 €	2.0	> 4500 €: 5.4
Education	Withour any graduation	0.0	2.9
	Volks-/ Hauptschulabschluss	19.4	42.9
	Mittlere Reife	26.3	26.4
	University entrance diploma	27.6	27.7
	University degree	23.0	n.p.

[1] Compared to German statistical office year 2005.
n. p.: not provided.

Source: authors' calculations; STBA 2007; STBA 2008, p. 29; 62.

7.4 Empirical results

7.4.1 Descriptive statistics

7.4.1.1 CrM purchase behaviour

To start with the analysis of consumers' acceptance of CrM we posed the question as to whether respondents had already purchased a CrM product. 22 % confirmed this and 16 % said they intentionally purchased the CrM product because of the CrM campaign. But on the downside only 4 % purchased several units of the product because of the CrM campaign. This suggests that consumers do not regard CrM to be comparable to a price promotion in which brand loyal consumers purchase more than one good and anticipate regular purchases to benefit from the reduced price.

7.4.1.2 Importance of product fit

According to WEBB and MOHR (1998) differences exist between products regarding their acceptability for a CrM campaign. To test whether the type of product is important for consumers' acceptance of a CrM campaign we focused on the perception of products' suitability regarding CrM campaigns. Hence, we investigated this issue by asking survey participants which products they would purchase in the context of a CrM campaign. Again, we applied a seven-point scale (1 = completely disagree to 7 = completely agree). Results are summarised in Table 2. The findings lead to the assumption that coffee seems to be most suitable to be promoted as a CrM product (mean 5). However, CrM was introduced to study participants using coffee as an example. This has most likely influenced responses. But, besides coffee, chocolate also seems to have a good fit with a CrM campaign. One possible explanation might be that the purchase of coffee and chocolate serves to satisfy hedonistic feelings and this might provide an additional motivation to do something good for someone else at the same time. Results also indicate that consumers do not distinguish between food and non-food as toothpaste ranks fourth before cereals. The results might be influenced by the frequency of purchasing specific products (e.g. wall paint versus water) and by the fact that some of the items are not needed by all consumers at the time of the campaign specifically or in general (e.g. pet food and wall paint). However, it seems noteworthy that CrM campaigns existed for all seven product categories in Germany.

Table 2: Products respondents would buy when subject of a CrM campaign

Variable*	Obs.	Mean	Std. Dev.
Coffee	210	5.00	1.98
Chocolate	208	4.59	2.11
Water	204	3.52	2.32
Tooth paste	202	2.99	2.07
Cereals	202	2.86	1.97
Pet food	199	2.58	2.08
Wall paint	199	2.54	1.87

*7 point scale from 7: completely agree to 1: completely disagree.

Source: authors' calculations.

7.4.1.3 Information sources

To assess whether the CrM promoting marketing strategy is effective to a degree that consumers remember it, we asked participants in which media they had heard about CrM and if so, to what extent. Table 3 reveals that consumers hardly heard anything about CrM campaigns. From all sources 'ads on the product', 'product advertisement' and 'TV commercials' had the greatest relevance. However, with a mean between 3 and 4 on a 7 point scale, their relevance is modest. All other information sources are of almost no relevance for consumer information regarding CrM campaigns (see Table 3).

Table 3: Consumers' previous sources of information about CrM

Variable*	Obs.	Mean	Std. Dev.
On-product info	205	3.97	2.17
Product advertisement	203	3.83	2.13
TV commercials	199	3.49	2.19
Retail outlet	203	2.90	1.88
Print media	197	2.85	1.81
Outdoor advertisement	199	2.51	1.80
Internet	195	2.42	1.78
Radio	204	2.22	1.70
Cinema	198	1.60	1.22

*7 point scale: 7: source of much information 1: not a source of information.

Source: authors' calculations.

7.4.1.4 Willingness to switch brands because of CrM

From the firms' point of view, the success of a CrM promotion depends on consumers' willingness to switch brands. As discussed in section 2, MAFFEI already discovered in 1961 that brand switching in general is influenced by marketing activities. And, as it is stated in literature, the additional benefits CrM products provide induce consumers to switch brands. Hence, we asked respondents whether they would be willing to switch from their regular brand to a brand which is promoted via CrM. 39 % answered they would. And 16% told us that they still did it.

In addition, participants were asked to hypothetically switch from their regular coffee brand A to a different coffee brand B that promotes its coffee within a CrM campaign. Participants were then asked to state what they would do once the CrM campaign of brand B ended. 75 % responded they would switch back to their regular brand A, the one they had purchased before the CrM campaign of brand B. 50 % of those 25 % who stated they would continue purchasing CrM brand B even after the end of the CrM campaign indicated they would purchase brand B as often as they did during the campaign. The other half stated they would purchase brand B less often.

7.4.1.5 Cause-Brand-Fit

In order to address the issue of brand-cause fit of companies with regard to CrM campaigns, participants were asked whether they think it is important that there is a 'good fit' between a company's general activities and the objectives of the promoted CrM campaign. 71 % of the respondents hold the opinion that this is important and very important respectively (Top-2-boxes; 5 point scale).

7.4.1.6 Attitudes towards CrM

To get a picture of consumers' opinions regarding CrM, we asked participants whether it is important to them that they are doing something good by purchasing a CrM product. Results show that this holds for 93 % of the respondents. While there is great consent on this question, detailed results show that there are indeed variations among consumers' perception of CrM as we will show in the following section.

In this regard, we assessed respondents' attitudes towards CrM. To this end, they had to evaluate a number of items on a scale ranging from 1 = 'completely disagree' to 7 = 'completely agree'. Items included, for example, whether participants agree that donations generated by product purchases through cooperation between a NGO and a brand are meaningful, not authentic, and the like (see Table 4). Table 4 reveals the degree of compliance with these statements and shows that it was highest for those items referring to labelling and thus for a greater transparency with respect to CrM campaigns. Consumers also agreed to a great extent with the positive statements regarding CrM (e.g. CrM is meaningful). In contrast, most of the rather sceptical and negative statements regarding CrM (e.g. CrM is a marketing gag) were on average not confirmed (a mean below 4, indicating that participants are either indifferent or do not agree).

Overall, the results lead to the conclusion that respondents hold rather positive attitudes towards CrM. Table 4 also shows that on average consumers perceive CrM products to be different from Fair Trade products, monetary donations in general and even monetary donations to the NGO cooperating with the brand in the CrM campaign. This is an interesting result as in both cases, the purchase is linked to an ethical (social or environmental or both) cause. It provides some evidence that CrM might be complementary and does not crowd out donations or Fair Trade purchases.

Table 4: Consumers' attitudes towards CrM

Variable*	Obs.	Mean	Std. Dev.
Donation amount labelled in %	213	5.87	1.51
Donation amount labelled in absolute figures	211	5.70	1.63
CrM is meaningful	215	5.69	1.44
Like CrM	212	5.23	1.79
CrM creates trust	212	4.08	1.90
CrM is a marketing 'gag'	210	3.92	1.97
CrM is green washing	208	3.87	1.74
CrM salve one's conscience	208	3.87	2.09
CrM is not authentic	207	3.54	1.85
CrM replaces donations to NGO	205	3.36	1.83
CrM replaces FT	208	3.00	1.89
CrM replaces donations in general	210	2.38	1.63

*7 point scale: 7: completely agree to 1: completely disagree.

Source: authors' calculations.

To describe these results more in detail, we consider first the share of consumers who completely or strongly agree (Top-2-boxes) and second, those who completely or mostly disagree (Bottom-2-boxes) (see Figure 1). This reveals a different picture for some of the above discussed statements especially for the negative statements regarding CrM where we find great heterogeneity among respondents, e.g. the responses to the statement 'CrM is a marketing gag' indicates that an almost equal share (28 %; 29 %) of survey participants exists who either completely/strongly agrees or completely/strongly disagrees. Furthermore, responses regarding the statement 'CrM creates trust' (in the company) are rather heterogeneous. These findings emphasize that we can differentiate between at least three groups of consumers who differ greatly in their perception of CrM. The first group has doubts about this form of marketing and social engagement, the second group appreciates it and the third group is indifferent as to whether they should like it or not.

Figure 1: Consumers' attitude towards CrM: Top-2-box and Bottom-2-box [%]

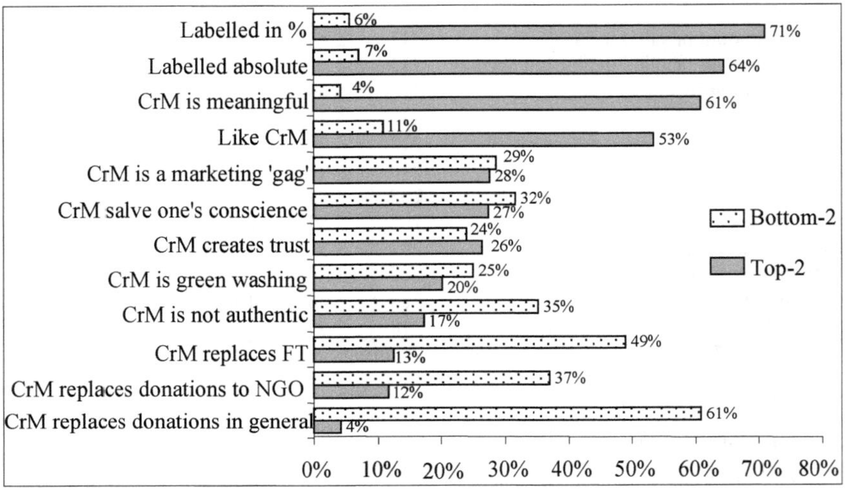

Source: authors' illustration.

7.4.2 Multivariate statistics

7.4.2.1 Factor analysis regarding consumers attitudes towards CrM

As Figure 1 suggests, different groups of consumers hold different opinions regarding CrM. To test this, we applied a factor analysis aiming at the identification of major dimensions of CrM attitudes. We used the Bartlett's Test of Sphericity (0.000) and the Kaiser-Meyer-Olkin measure of sampling adequacy (0.744) to assess the adequacy of the correlation matrices of the obtained items for factor analysis.

As the obtained values for both tests are good, principal component analysis was used to develop different components constituting the mental attitude about CrM. The survey statements and the rotated factor loadings for each item are presented in Table 5. Four attitudinal factor components were identified based on eigenvalues greater than or equal to 0.4 explaining 66 % of the variance.

The first factor ('FA1_Positive Perception') merges all positive statements towards CrM. Accordingly, respondents with a high score on this factor hold positive attitudes towards CrM. The second factor includes all negative items related to CrM. Participants with a high score on this second factor are sceptical and doubt the positive intentions of firms applying CrM. This factor was labelled 'FA2_Sceptics'. The third factor reflects the respondent's opinion on the nature of CrM compared to other forms of ethical behaviour, such as the purchase of Fair Trade products or giving to charity. High values for factor 3 indicate consumers do not differentiate between CrM and Fair Trade or donations to charity. They believe one is able to replace the other. Therefore, we call this factor 'FA3_Replacer'. The fourth factor combines the items 'Labelling the donation amount in percent' and 'labelling the donation amount in absolute figures'. High values for this factor point toward a strong pro-labelling attitude with regard to effects and amount of the CrM donation. This factor was labelled 'FA4_Effi Label less'.

Table 5: Rotated component matrix regarding consumers' attitudes towards CrM

Variable	FA1 Positive Perception	FA2 Sceptics	FA3 Replacer	FA4 Effi Label less
CrM is meaningful	.832			
Like CrM	.827			
CrM creates trust	.759			
CrM salves conscience	.654			
CrM is a marketing 'gag'		.836		
CrM is greenwashing		.813		
CrM is not authentic		.736		
CrM replaces donations in general			.828	
CrM replaces FT			.826	
CrM replaces donations to specific NGO			.533	
Donation amount labelled in %				.792
Donation amount labelled in absolute figures				.777

Extraction Method: Principal Component Analysis. Rotation Method: Varimax with Kaiser Normalization. Rotation converged in 6 iterations. Missing Values were excluded listwise.

Source: authors' calculations.

7.4.2.2 Segmenting consumers with regard to CrM

As Table 5 suggests, four different latent factors constituting the attitudes towards CrM can be identified. In this section, we group consumers based on these attitudinal factors identified previously in the principal component analysis (see Table 5) via a k-means cluster analysis. The aim is to answer the question as to which consumer characteristics influence positive, sceptical or other opinions concerning CrM. Therefore, we regard clusters' purchase behaviour, their use of information sources, their brand switching behaviour, their attitudes towards CrM, the social activities they perform, and their socioeconomic characteristics to identify factors influencing the different attitudes towards CrM. For a combined description of the determinants included in the analysis and presented in the individual tables, see Table C1 in the Appendix.

Tables 6, 7, 8 and 9 depict the differences in the clusters with regard to consumers' attitudes towards and purchase behaviour of CrM products, information sources they use with respect to CrM, their willingness for brand switching as well as consumers' social activities, and general socioeconomic characteristics. In each table the cluster specific means and the total sample means are given. If the variables are dummy variables, the data are shown in percent.

Clusters' attitudes towards CrM and the cause-brand-fit

Table 6 reveals that cluster 1 holds a positive attitude towards CrM as the lower than average scores regarding the negative statements ('CrM is a marketing gag', 'CrM not authentic' and 'CrM greenwashing') and the higher than average scores regarding the positive statements ('CrM meaningful', CrM creates trust', 'Like CrM' and 'do good for society') show. In contrast, cluster 2 is rather sceptical which is revealed by a higher than average score regarding the first set of items and a lower one for the second bundle. Members of the third cluster feel that the purchase of CrM promoted products is likely to replace the purchase of Fair Trade products or donations in general or to specific NGOs as the above average values for those items indicate. Finally, cluster 4 has little interest in the labelling of CrM (comparable low value for labelling items). The cause-brand-fit is especially important for clusters 1 and 2. However, it should be noted that all consumer segments are in favour of CrM. They perceive it as an opportunity to do something good.

Table 6: Attitudes towards CrM: Cluster means

Variable*	Cluster 1 *Positive Perception*	Cluster 2 *Sceptics*	Cluster 3 Replacer	Cluster 4 *Effi Label less important*	Total Sample
	n=43	n=35	n=27	n=35	n=213
CrM marketing ‚gag'[a]	2.26	5.34	4.37	3.77	3.92
CrM not authentic [a]	2.23	4.77	3.52	3.57	3.54
CrM greenwashing [a]	2.91	4.94	4.44	3.34	3.87
CrM meaningful [a]	5.84	5.80	5.85	5.83	5.69
CrM creates trust [a]	4.56	3.17	5.15	4.00	4.08
CrM salves conscience [a]	4.33	3.34	5.15	3.49	3.87
Like CrM [a]	5.70	4.94	5.70	5.23	5.23
CrM replaces [a] donations to specific NGO	2.56	3.14	5.30	3.06	3.36
CrM replaces FT [a]	2.40	2.09	4.78	3.71	3.00
CrM replaces donations in general [a]	2.02	1.49	4.15	2.51	2.38
Labelled in % [a]	6.60	6.54	6.44	4.03	5.87
Labelled absolute [a]	6.42	6.06	6.52	4.11	5.70
Do good for society	98%	88%	96%	97%	93%
Donation amount[b]	4.54	3.88	2.80	3.62	3.68
Cause Brand Fit[c]	4.30	4.24	3.65	3.76	3.97

*For a detailed variable description see Table C1 in the Annex.
[a] Attitude measured on scale from 1 (completely disagree) to 7 (completely agree)
[b] Categorical variable from 1 (0 - 2 %) to 9 (> 25 %)
[c] Measured on a scale from 1 (not important) to 5 (very important)
Note: each row depicts the mean of the variables of the particular cluster and total sample, respectively. If the variables are dummy variables, the data are shown in percent.

Source: authors' calculations.

Clusters' CrM purchase behaviour

However, so far only 22 % of the overall sample has experienced CrM products (see Table 7). Surprisingly, the share is lowest in cluster 1 which perceives CrM to be very positive. The sceptical consumers purchased more often CrM products than the survey participants grouped in the other clusters. Cluster 4 is composed of respondents indicating that the decision for a CrM product was a conscious one and not by pure chance. Moreover, cluster 4 participants stated they purchased several units of the CrM products even though they in fact needed just one to support the CrM campaign.

Table 7: Clusters' purchase behaviour of CrM products

Variable*	Cluster 1 *Positive Perception*	Cluster 2 *Sceptics*	Cluster 3 *Replacer*	Cluster 4 *Effi Label less important*	Total Sample
	n = 43	n = 35	n = 27	n = 35	n = 213
Did purchase CrM previously[a]	17 %	28 %	24 %	26 %	22 %
Conscious decision for a CrM product[a]	17 %	18 %	12 %	20 %	16 %
Did purchase several products because of CrM[a]	0 %	6 %	0 %	9 %	4 %

* For a detailed variable description see Table C1 in the Annex.

[a] Note: dummy variable equal to 1 if yes, 0 otherwise

Note: sample size of clusters is lower than the total sample size due to listwise exclusion of missing values in the factor analysis.

Source: authors' calculations.

Clusters' CrM information sources

As a marketing strategy, CrM depends on being communicated to consumers. In general, the results indicate that there is scope to improve communication to consumers. This holds for all clusters and sources of information. The findings also show that the different clusters use different information sources when it comes to CrM (see Table 8). The first cluster mainly refers to retail ads and on-product labels when seeking the information in question. The second consumer segment relies mainly on the product information, however, compared to the other clusters, results show an above average use of internet sources and information provided by retailers. The fourth cluster uses mainly product information but shows the least interest in information provided by retailers. The third cluster as well uses mainly product information. However, compared to the other segments, this cluster receives most information on CrM from the radio.

Table 8: CrM Information sources and social activities

Variable*	Cluster 1 *Positive Perception*	Cluster 2 *Sceptics*	Cluster 3 *Replacer*	Cluster 4 *Effi Label less important*	Total Sample
	n = 43	n = 35	n = 27	n = 35	n = 213
TV[a]	3.35	3.85	3.52	3.88	3.49
Print Media[a]	2.83	3.06	2.83	2.76	2.85
Internet info[a]	2.18	2.59	2.52	2.47	2.42
retail info[a]	3.10	3.38	3.21	2.63	2.90
outdoor ad[a]	3.03	2.76	2.33	2.31	2.51
Radio[a]	2.21	2.18	2.77	2.20	2.22
On-product info[a]	3.98	4.63	3.88	3.79	3.97

*For a detailed variable description see Table C1 in the Annex.
[a] The use of the information sources was measured on a scale from 1 (nothing) to 7 (a lot).
Note: each row depicts the mean of the variables of the particular cluster and total sample, respectively. If the variables are dummy variables, the data are shown in percent.

Source: authors' calculations.

Clusters' brand switching behaviour

52 % of the members in cluster 1 can imagine switching brands because of CrM (see Table 9). However, only 18 % of this cluster has already done so. The respective shares for cluster 2 are 47 % and 25 %. This shows that consumers might be sceptical but this is no barrier for CrM purchases. This suggests that effective marketing strategies are able to convince them to switch brands. Especially for the group of 'replacers' the share of respondents who can imagine switching a brand due to CrM is low (24 %) and so far they hardly have behaved accordingly (6 %).

One of the reasons for firms to introduce CrM is to increase their market share. However, the respondents indicate that once the CrM promotion ended, most of them (75 %) would switch back to their former brand. This means the success based on CrM campaigns could be rather temporary. Especially, the fourth cluster is prone towards switching back (91 %). Here it is important to remember that cluster 4 purchased CrM products comparatively often, indicated the CrM product was consciously chosen and that they bought several pieces of the CrM product to support the cause. This leads to the conclusion that cluster 4 is more a hybrid consumer[121] than a loyal one. In contrast, 35 % of members of the first consumer segment indicate that they would continue to purchase the new brand (product), even after the campaign ended.

[121] The term 'hybrid consumer' refers to a consumer type not fitting into any particular market segment as this consumer will sometimes buy cheap generic products and on another occasions expensive brands (MÜLLER 2001).

Table 9: Brand switching behaviour of the four clusters

Variable*	Cluster 1 *Positive Perception*	Cluster 2 *Sceptics*	Cluster 3 *Replacer*	Cluster 4 *Effi Label less important*	Total Sample
	n = 43	n = 35	n = 27	n = 35	n = 213
Brand switch imaginable	52 %	47 %	24 %	41 %	39 %
Brand switch done	18 %	25 %	6 %	15 %	16 %
After CrM promotion: Switch back to former brand 1	65 %	79 %	75 %	91 %	75 %

*For a detailed variable description see Table C1 in the Annex.

Note: each row depicts the mean of the variables of the particular cluster and total sample, respectively. If the variables are dummy variables, the data are shown in percent.

Source: authors' calculations.

Social activities and socioeconomic characteristics of the clusters

As CrM is a marketing strategy that targets the altruistic motives of consumers, it can be assumed that those consumers with altruistic traits in other parts of their lives might be more inclined to buy products promoted by a CrM campaign.

Table 10: Clusters' social activities and socioeconomic characteristics

Variable*	Cluster 1 *Positive Perception*	Cluster 2 *Sceptics*	Cluster 3 *Replacer*	Cluster 4 *Effi Label less important*	Total Sample
	n = 43	n = 35	n = 27	n = 35	n = 213
Donor[a]	72 %	71 %	70 %	51 %	67 %
Member: church[b]	0.44	0.53	0.44	0.51	0.5
Member: environmental organisation[b]	5 %	6 %	0 %	6 %	5 %
Member: sport[b]	30 %	29 %	48 %	29 %	37 %
Member: political party[b]	9 %	9 %	4 %	6 %	8 %
Member: world shop[b]	0 %	0 %	0 %	6 %	1 %
Member: youth work[b]	16 %	3 %	7 %	6 %	10 %
Member: NGO[b]	12 %	24 %	4 %	6 %	12 %
Age	47.47	39.97	42.93	39.69	42.71
Children < 18	19 %	15 %	37 %	34 %	29 %
Edu: 9	19 %	18 %	11 %	20 %	20 %
Edu: 10	38 %	15 %	26 %	31 %	27 %
Edu: University entrance diploma	21 %	32 %	41 %	31 %	29 %
Edu: University	21 %	35 %	19 %	14 %	23 %
Edu: PhD	0 %	0 %	4 %	3 %	1 %
Siblings: number	1.49	1.56	1.48	1.69	1.64
Siblings: older	53 %	44 %	11 %	37 %	34 %
Siblings: younger	23 %	24 %	44 %	29 %	30 %
Siblings: both	9 %	9 %	26 %	17 %	16 %
Female	60 %	44 %	46 %	57 %	54 %
Income[c]	6.51	6.43	6.67	5.8	6.02

*For a detailed variable description see Table A1 in the Annex.

[a] Gave to developmental charity organisations in the last 12 months. Dummy variable equal to 1 if yes, 0 otherwise

[b] Membership or voluntary engagement in the respective organisation. Dummy variable equal to 1 if yes, 0 otherwise

[c] Household net-income (EUR/month): Categorical variable from 1 (< 300 EUR) to 12 (> 5000 EUR).

Note: each row depicts the mean of the variables of the particular cluster and total sample, respectively. If the variables are dummy variables, the data are shown in percent.

Source: authors' calculations.

Results in Table 10 show that while members of cluster 1 and cluster 2 as well as to a lower degree cluster 4 support social causes such as youth work and/or NGOs or, in the case of cluster 4, world shops. This does not hold for members of cluster 3. Their involvement is highest in sport clubs, a membership which is in general more encouraged by egoistic than altruistic motives. This is in line with the results previously presented, e.g. only 24 % of this cluster could imagine switching brands for a cause and only 6 % had done this already. The respective shares were as twice as high for the other clusters. However, this might be explained as well by the fact that this cluster differentiates between donations and CrM. They believe these are substitutes. As 70 % of the members of this cluster have given to charity organisations in the last 12 months, their reluctance to buy CrM promoted products might be partly explained by their potential preference for direct donations. On average, cluster 4 donates considerably less than the other clusters.

With regard to socioeconomic characteristics, the results show that the first cluster is the oldest (47 years old on average. Only 19 % of the members of this cluster have children below the age of 18 years. Their education level is slightly below average, while they have the second highest income level. 60 % of this cluster are female and 53 % have older siblings. Members of the second cluster are on average rather young (almost 40 years old), have the lowest share of children and a higher than average education. 44 % of this cluster is female and the same share has older siblings. The third consumer segment is 43 years old on average. 37 % have children below 18 in their household. They have a rather high education level and income is highest in this consumer segment. 46 % are female and only 11 % have older siblings. Members of the fourth cluster are also about 40 years old, 34 % have children in the household and 51 % have low and medium education. Their income is the lowest compared to the other clusters. 57 % are female (see Table 10).

Thus, socio-demographics might explain differences in preferences when it comes to the purchase of CrM promoted products regarding the four consumer segments. Assuming that promoting the cause is somewhat reflected in higher prices, this is most difficult to bear for cluster 4 as a high share of members of this segment has children under 18 while the average income is lowest in this cluster. However, AMATO (1985) postulates that helping behaviour is correlated with everyday life characteristics and that involvement is higher at some stages in the life cycle than it is in others. Therefore, it is worth noting that those with the lowest percentage of children under 18 (cluster 1 and 2) either hold positive attitudes but have low purchase experience (cluster 1) or, as with cluster 2, are sceptical but purchase these products most often. Another interesting finding is that the sibling's position in the family plays a role in the respective consumer segments. Those with the highest share of older siblings (group 1) have a more positive attitude towards CrM products than those having e.g. the highest share of younger siblings (group 3). The explanation is difficult as on the one hand older siblings can be brought up to feel responsible towards others and on the other hand younger siblings can have learned to share things. As the role of the siblings' position has hardly been researched in the case of pro-social behaviour and charitable giving (HEIDBÜCHEL 2000), we cannot draw conclusions concerning the reasons here. Further research is needed with regard to this influencing factor.

Marketing recommendations based on the cluster analysis

The results indicate that there is a lack of information regarding CrM campaigns. Thus, given the overall positive attitude towards CrM, with respect to marketing recommendations these results suggest focusing especially on consumers with positive perceptions and sceptical consumers. Those respondents who are older than average and hold a positive attitude towards CrM promoted products typically demonstrate rather stable brand preferences. But if they are drawn to CrM and convinced to purchase the CrM product they have a lower probability to switch back than other consumer segments. As this cluster is so open towards CrM, marketers should try to convince this group to transform their positive attitudes into positive purchase decisions. The sceptics hold the highest share of participants who have already purchased CrM products and are willing to switch brands. This young segment has the highest education level. As results show, these consumers actively seek information. For example, their use of internet sources gives them an opportunity to access more detailed background information than is provided on the product itself or at the point of sale. Informational rather than emotional marketing strategies are recommended for these clusters. Cluster 3 and 4 are more difficult to address. Respondents grouped in cluster 3 do not differentiate between CrM and other kinds of ethical products or behaviour and are more interested in themselves than others (see their social activities). Addressing these more self-centred consumers would be more difficult compared to clusters 1 and 2. As the purchase and switching behaviour of cluster 4 reveals, these respondents seem to belong to the so-called hybrid consumers who are difficult to bond to a brand or company. The fact that this cluster sets no great store by efficiency labelling leads us to suspect that these respondents were less demanding than participants grouped in the other clusters. Moreover, the lowest share of donors and at the same time highest share of parents having children under the age of 18 leads to the assumption that income has an influence on these consumers' decision making. As CrM products are sometimes sold on a higher price level this could be an important purchase barrier for cluster 4.

7.4.2.3 Brand switching behaviour regarding CrM: A logit model

To finish our analyses with respect to CRM's potential for brand switching we applied a logit model to identify potential determinants of brand switching behaviour due to CrM (see Table

11). The dependent variable is the answer to the question 'If a company promotes products by means of a CrM campaign I am willing to switch brands'.

Table 11: Potential determinants of brand switching behaviour – a logit model

Variable*	Coef.	Std. Err.	z value [a]	
FA1_Positive Perception	0.565	0.278	2.03	**
FA2_Skeptics	-0.099	0.249	-0.4	n.s.
FA3_Replacer	-0.497	0.236	-2.1	**
FA4_Effi Label less important	-0.049	0.210	-0.23	n.s.
Cause Brand Fit	-0.066	0.237	-0.28	n.s.
CrM coffee thinkable [b]	0.372	0.165	2.26	**
Cups of coffee per day [c]	-0.389	0.142	-2.73	***
Income	0.018	0.068	0.26	n.s.
Female	-0.596	0.456	-1.31	n.s.
Age	0.002	0.018	0.09	n.s.
Education: Abitur and more	-0.917	0.543	-1.69	*
Constant	-0.053	1.634	-0.03	n.s.

*For a detailed variable description see Table A1 in the Annex.
[a] $p < 0.1$ = *, $p < 0.05$ = **, $p < 0.01$ = ***, n. s. = not significant.
Wald chi^2 (11) = 23.41, Prob > chi^2 = 0.01, Log Pseudolikelihood = -66.17, Pseudo R^2 = 0.22.
[b] Coffee as CrM product would be purchased (Scale: 7=fully agree; 1=do not agree).
[c] Cups of coffee the respondents drink per day.

Source: authors' calculations.

The results presented in Table 11 indicate that consumption behaviour and attitudes towards CrM are crucial for consumers' willingness to switch from their regular brand to the brand promoted via CrM. Respondents holding positive attitudes towards CrM, which were described in detail in section 4.1., are willing to switch to a brand promoted in a CrM campaign. Those who believe that the purchase of a CrM product replaces a donation to charity or the purchase of Fair Trade products are not willing to switch to a CrM brand. The same holds for participants who drink many cups of coffee per day. This is in line with the results of GÖNÜL et al. (1996) which indicate that intensive coffee drinkers are less likely to switch from their regular brand to one promoted via CrM. Furthermore, the results show that it is of great importance that consumers can imagine that the respective product is promoted in a CrM campaign. This supports the assumption of WEBB and MOHR (1998) that the type of product determines to some extent the success of a CrM campaign. The perceived fit between cause and brand has no influence on consumers' willingness to switch brands because of CrM. In addition, only education shows a significant effect out of all socioeconomic characteristics. Participants holding at least a university entrance diploma are less likely willing to switch a brand because another one is promoted in a CrM campaign. As we know from Table 10 and the clustering, those with the highest education level are the sceptical consumers.

7.5 Conclusions

The present study is one of the first to research German consumers' attitudes regarding CrM promoted products. Thus, our results provide insights to marketers on how to improve the effectiveness of CrM campaigns. Overall, there seems to be a great potential for CrM marketing campaigns as a large share of consumers holds a positive attitude towards CrM and 52 % of the respondents state that they are willing to switch brands due to CrM. Our findings indicate that the low share of consumers who have actually switched brands due to a CrM campaign might be attributed to the little information that respondents obtain about CrM. Thus, there seems to be a need for information not only on the products, but also in the retail stores and in the media.

Marketing strategies should address German consumers' scepticism regarding firms' underlying motives for applying CrM. Despite the positive attitude towards CrM this skepticism exists and is likely to be an impediment for the purchase of CrM products.

To gain deeper insights into consumers' perception of CrM, we clustered consumers according to their attitudes towards CrM. We identified factors influencing positive and negative attitudes towards CrM and derived critical success factors which allow companies to enhance the quality of their CrM activities. We showed that the cause-brand-fit is especially important for the positive thinking cluster 1 and the sceptical cluster 2. These two clusters form the consumer segments that are willing to purchase CrM products and to switch brands to do so. Therefore, marketers should focus their marketing activities on these two consumer groups. As the two groups differ explicitly in socioeconomic characteristics, social engagement, information utilisation, etc. targeted-marketing approaches would be appropriate.

Via a logit model we identified important factors influencing the brand switching behaviour. This analysis shows that attitudes and consumption behaviour as well as product fit are significantly influencing factors. Cause-brand-fit, over the whole sample considered, had no significant influence on brand switching.

Our findings are limited to the extent that consumers' willingness to purchase CrM was investigated via hypothetical questions instead of using incentive-compatible approaches, i.e. participants were not forced to actually buy CrM promoted products.

7.6 References

AAKER, D. A. and KELLER, L. K. (1990): Consumer Evaluations of Brand Extensions. *Journal of Marketing*, 54 (2): 27-41.

ADKINS, S. (1999): *Cause Related Marketing, Who cares wins*. Oxford: Butterworth-Heinemann.

ALEXANDER, T. (2005): Integrierte Markenkommunikation - Oder was hat „immer in die gleiche Kerbe hauen" mit Budget sparen zu tun? In: Gaiser, B.; Linxweiler, R. and Brucker, V. (Eds.): *Praxisorientierte Markenführung: Neue Strategien, innovative Instrumente und aktuelle Fallstudien*. Wiesbaden: Gabler: 325-347.

AMATO, P. R. (1985): An Investigation of Planned Helping Behavior. Journal of Research in Personality, 19: 232-252.

BERGER, I.E., CUNNIGHAM, P.H. and KOZINETS, R.V. (1996): The processing of cause-related Marketing claims: cues, biases or motivators? *American Marketing Association*, Summer 1996: 71-72.

BERGLIND, M. and NAKATA, C. (2005): Cause-related marketing: More buck than bang? *Business Horizons*, 48: 443-453.

BLE (2008): *Kaffee - der Deutschen liebstes Heißgetränk*. Available from: http://www.oekolandbau.de/grossverbraucher/studien-und-infomaterialien/marktdaten/wachstumsmarkt-kaffee-september-2008/ [accessed 2008-09-25].

BLUMBERG, M. and CONRAD, C. (2006): *Good Brand 2006: Gutes tun und davon profitieren?* Ethisches Verbraucherverhalten und Cause Related Marketing in Deutschland. Bremen: Brands & Values.

BROWN, T. J. and DACIN P. A. (1997): The Company and the Product: Corporate Associations and Consumer Product responses. *Journal of Marketing*, 61 (1): 68-84.

BUCKLIN, L. P. and SENGUPTA, S. (1993): Organizing Successful Co-Marketing Alliances. *Journal of Marketing*, 57: 32-46.

CADBURY, D. (2000): Foreword by Sir Dominic Cadbury. In: Adkins, S. (2000) (Ed.): *Cause Related Marketing – Who cares wins*. Oxford: Butterworth-Heinemann: vii-viii.

CONE (2004): *2004 Cone Corporate Citizenship Study Results*. December 8, 2004. Available from: http://www.causemarketingforum.com/page.asp?ID=330, [accessed 2010-02-14].

CRAWFORD, C. M. (1991): The Dual-Drive Concept of Product Innovation. *Business Horizons*, May-June: 32-38.

DACIN P. A. and BROWN, T. J. (2002): Corporate Identity and Corporate Associations: A framework for Future Research. *Corporate Reputation Review*, 5 (2/3): 254-263.

DRÖGE, A. and BLUMBERG, M. (2009): CSR zählt beim Kauf. *Markenartikel*, 6: 26-31.

DRUMWRIGHT, M. E. (1996): Company Advertising With a Social Dimension: The Role of Noneconomic Criteria. *Journal of Marketing*, 60: 71-87.

ENDACOTT, R. W. J. (2004): Consumer and CrM: A national and global perspective. *Journal of Consumer Marketing*, 21 (3): 183-189.

EUROPEAN COMMISSION (2010): *Enterprise and Industry: Sustainable and responsible business.* Available from: http://ec.europa.eu/enterprise/policies/sustainable-business/corporate-social-responsibility/index_en.htm, [accessed 2010-07-29].

GFK, ROLAND BERGER and BVE (2009): *Consumers' Choice '09: Corporate Responsibility in der Ernährungsindustrie*. 3rd ed. Available from: https://www.bve-online.de/presseservice/veroeffentlichungen/consumers_choice2009/, [accessed 2010-06-30].

GFK (2007): *Bio ist auf dem Vormarsch.* Available from: http://www.gfk.com/group/press_information/press_releases/001133/index.de.html [accessed 2010-07-05].

GIOVANNUCCI, D. and PONTE, S. (2005): Standards as a new form of social contract? Sustainability initiatives in the coffee industry. *Food Policy*, 30 (3): 284-301.

GÖNÜL, F. F., POPKOWSKI LESZCZYC, P.T.L. and SUGAWARA, T. (1996): Joint estimates of purchase timing and brand switch tendency: results from a scanner panel data set of frequently purchased products. *The Canadian Journal of Economics*, 29, Special Issue: Part 2: 501-S504.

HAVAS MEDIA (2009): *Sustainable Future 09: German Factsheet.* Available from: http://www.havasmedia.com/staticfiles/Germany%20Factsheet.pdf, [accessed 2010-01-18].

HEIDBÜCHEL, A. (2000): Psychology des Spendenverhaltens: Analyse eines theoriegeleiteten Prozessmodells. In: Wiendieck, G. (Ed.): *Kölner Arbeiten zur Wirtschaftspsychologie*, 16, Dissertation, Frankfurt/Main: Peter Lang.

HUBER, F., REGIER, S. and RININO, M. (2008): *Cause-Related-Marketing-Kampagnen erfolgreich konzipieren.* Wiesbaden: Gabler.

KRÖHER, M. O. R. (2009): Das Gute im Kapitalismus. *Manager Magazin*, 5: 92-95.

LAFFERTY, B., GOLDSMITH, R. E. and HULT, G. T. M. (2004): The Impact of the Alliance on the Partners: A Look at Cause-Brand Alliances. *Psychology & Marketing*, 7 (7): 509-531.

LICHTENSTEIN, D. R., DRUMWRIGHT, M. E. and BRAIG, B. M. (2004): The Effect of Corporate Social Responsibility on Consumer Donations to Corporate-Supported Nonprofits. *Journal of Marketing*, 68: 16-32.

MAFFEI, R. B. (1961): Advertising Effectiveness, Brand Switching and Market Dynamics. The *Journal of Industrial Economics*, 9 (2): 119-131.

MÜLLER, I. (2001): Der hybride Verbraucher: Ende der Segmentierungsmöglichkeit im Konsumgütermarketing? In: Diller, H. (Ed.): *Der moderne Verbraucher – Neue Befunde zum Einkaufsverhalten*. Nürnberg: 29-52.

OLOKO (2009): *Cause related Marketing – Ein neues Marketinginstrument im Überblick*. Available from: http://www.umc-potsdam.de/images/stories/wall-vl/vortraege/vortrag_cause_related_marketing_shamsey_oloko_140509.pdf, [accessed 2010-01-19].

POPPELREUTER, S. and STEIN, S. (2008): 1. *TrendScan Wirtschaft Studie 2009 – Vom guten Geschäft mit dem schlechten Gewissen, CSR und die deutsche Wirtschaft*. Bonn.

PORTER, M. E. and KRAMER, M. R. (2002): The Competitive Advantage of Corporate Philanthropy. *Harvard Business Review*, 80 (12): 56-69.

PRACEJUS, J. W. and OLSON, G. D. (2004): The role of brand/cause fit in the effectiveness of cause-related marketing campaigns. *Journal of Business Research*, 57 (6): 635-640.

RIFON, N. J., CHOI, S. M., TRIMBLE, C. S. and LI, H. (2004): Congruence Effects in Sponsorship - The Mediating Role of Sponsor Credibiity and Consumer Attributions of Sponsor Motive. *Journal of Advertising*, 33 (1): 29-42.

ROY, D. P. and GRAEFF, T. R. (2003): Consumer Attitudes Toward Cause-Related Marketing Activities in Professional Sports. *Sport Marketing*, 12 (3): 163-172.

SEN, S. and BHATTACHARYA, C. B. (2001): Does Doing Good Always Lead to Doing Better? Consumer Reactions to Corporate Social Responsibility. *Journal of Marketing Research*, 38 (2): 225-243.

SEVENONE MEDIA (2009): *Trendreport Grün*. Available from: http://www.sevenonemedia.de/imperia/md/content/content/Research/Marktanalyse/branchen/specials/TrendReport_Gruen.pdf, [accessed 2010-07-29].

SINGH, S. (2009): Overcoming scepticism towards cause related claims: the case of Norway. *International Marketing Review*, 26 (3): 312-326.

SIMONIN B. L. and RUTH J. A. (1998): Is a Company Known by the Company It Keeps? Assessing the Spillover Effects of Brand Attitudes. *Journal of Marketing Research*, 35 (1): 30-42.

StBa (Statistisches Bundesamt) (2007): *Statistisches Jahrbuch 2007*. Wiesbaden.

StBa (Statistisches Bundesamt) (2008): *Bevölkerung und Erwerbstätigkeit - Haushalte und Familien, Ergebnisse des Mikrozensus 2007*. Fachserie 1, Reihe 3, Wiesbaden.

Sun, B., Neslin, S. A. and Srinivasan, K. (2003): Measuring the Impact of Promotions on Brand Switching when consumers are forward looking. *Journal of Marketing Research*, 40 (4): 389-405.

Transfair (2010): *26 Prozent Plus für Fairtrade*. Available from: http://www.transfair.org/top/nachricht/?tx_ttnews[tt_news]=275&tx_ttnews[backPid]=137&cHash=9c1070f615, [accessed 2010-04-28].

Webb, D. J. and Mohr, L. A. (1998): A Typology of Consumer Responses to Cause-Related Marketing: From Skeptics to Socially Concerned. *Journal of Public Policy & Marketing*, 17 (2): 226-238.

Wymer, W. and Samu, S. (2003): *Nonprofit and Business Sector Collaboration: Social Enterprises, Cause-Related Marketing, Sponsorships, and Other Corporate-Nonprofit Dealings*. Binghamton, NY: Best Business Books.

Zimmermann, K. L. and van der Lans, I. (2009): The paradigm of consumer-driven and responsive supply chains: an integrated project approach. *Journal of Horticultural Science & Biotechnology*, ISAFRUIT Special Issue: 7-12.

Appendix C[122]

Table C1: Description of variables

Variable	Variable Description	Obs.	Mean	Std. Dev.
Attitudes towards CrM				
CrM marketing is a ‚gag'	CrM is a marketing ‚gag' [a]	210	3.92	1.97
CrM is not authentic	CrM is not authentic [a]	207	3.54	1.85
CrM is green-washing	CrM is green-washing of the firms[a]	208	3.87	1.74
CrM is meaningful	CrM is meaningful [a]	215	5.69	1.44
CrM creates trust	CrM creates trust in the company[a]	212	4.08	1.90
CrM salves one's conscience	CrM salves ones conscience [a]	208	3.87	2.09
Like CrM	I like CrM [a]	212	5.23	1.79
CrM replaces donations to NGO	CrM replaces donations to the specific NGO [a]	205	3.36	1.83
CrM replaces FT	CrM replaces the purchase of FT products[a]	208	3.00	1.89
CrM replaces donations in general	CrM replaces donations in general [a]	210	2.38	1.63
Donation amount labelled in %	CrM donation amount labelled in % [a]	213	5.87	1.51
Donation amount labelled in absolute figures	CrM donation amount labelled in absolute figures [a]	211	5.70	1.63
Do good for society	By purchasing CrM products I do something good for society [b]	211	0.93	0.26
Donation amount	Estimated donation amount of CrM relative to the product price [c]	197	3.52	2.13
Cause Brand Fit	Importance of the Cause Brand Fit [e]	199	3.97	1.16
Brand switching behaviour				
Switch imaginable	Brand switch due to CrM imaginable [b]	210	0.39	0.49
Switch done	Brand switch due to CrM done [b]	160	0.16	0.36
Switch back	After CrM promotion: switch back to former brand 1 [b]	198	0.75	0.43
Purchase behaviour CrM				
Purchase CrM	Did purchase CrM previously [b]	204	0.22	0.41
Conscious decision	Conscious decision for a CrM product [b]	205	0.16	0.37
Several products	Did purchase several products because of CrM [b]	204	0.04	0.19
Information sources				
TV commercials	Where and to which extent did you here about CrM campaigns [d]	199	3.49	2.19
Print media		197	2.85	1.81
Internet		195	2.42	1.78
Retail outlet		203	2.90	1.88
Outdoor ad		199	2.51	1.80
Radio		204	2.22	1.70
Product advertise		203	3.83	2.13
On-product info		205	3.97	2.17

[122] For the questionnaire, see Appendix A1 in chapter 5.

Table C1: Description of variables (continued)

Variable	Variable Description	Obs.	Mean	Std. Dev.
Social Activities				
Donor	Did give to developmental charity organisations in the last 12 month [b]	214	0.67	0.47
Member: church		210	0.50	0.50
Member: environmental organisation	Membership or voluntary engagement in the respective organisation [b]	210	0.05	0.22
Member: sport		210	0.37	0.48
Member: party		210	0.08	0.27
Member: world shop		210	0.01	0.12
Member: youth work		210	0.10	0.30
Member: NGO		210	0.12	0.32
Socioeconomic characteristics				
Age	Age in years	209	42.71	15.03
Children < 18	Number of children under the age of 18	210	0.29	0.70
Edu: 9	Education: 9 years	209	0.20	0.40
Edu: 10	Education: 10 years	209	0.27	0.44
Edu: University entrance diploma	Education: university entrance diploma (Abitur)	209	0.29	0.45
Edu: University	Education: university degree	209	0.23	0.42
Edu: PhD	Education: PhD	209	0.01	0.12
Siblings: number	Number of siblings	210		
Siblings: older	Older siblings	210	0.34	0.48
Siblings: younger	Younger siblings	210	0.30	0.46
Siblings: both	Siblings are younger and older	210	0.16	0.37
Female	Gender (1 = female, 0 = male).	209	0.54	0.50
Income	Household Net-Income (EUR/month) Categorical variable from 1 (< 300 EUR) to 12 (> 5000 EUR).	214	6.02	3.38

[a]: Attitude measured on scale from 1 (completely disagree) to 7 (completely agree).
[b]: Dummy variable equal to 1 if yes, 0 otherwise.
[c]: Categorical variable from 1 (0 -2 %) to 9 (> 25 %).
[d]: Measured on a scale from 1 (nothing) to 7 (a lot).
[e]: Measured on a scale from 1 (not important) to 5 (very important).

Source: authors' calculations.

8 Is Cause-related Marketing Green-Washing? [123]

Abstract

Cause-related marketing (CrM) is an increasingly applied marketing tool whereby the product purchase leads to a target-oriented donation to a designated cause promoted on the product by label. In a recent campaign Germany's coffee producer Dallmayr cooperated with the NGO 'Menschen für Menschen'. The campaign promotes that per sold package of coffee five trees are planted in Ethiopia. In this regard, the campaign is close to a regular target oriented donation and comparable to Fair Trade in terms of the prevention of soil degradation and therefore sustainable production methods. In order to maintain the success of CrM it is of great importance to avoid the impression that CrM is green-washing (see e.g. VARADARAJAN and MENON 1988). So far, only few studies examined the effect of CrM activities on consumers' attitudes and purchase behaviour.

Against this background, (i) we have investigated whether German consumers think CrM is green-washing and (ii) whether they differentiate between CrM and traditional donations or the purchase of Fair Trade products. To this end, we conducted a consumer survey (n = 112) in 2009 in Germany. Participants were asked about their overall evaluation of CrM. Results indicate that one third of the consumers perceive CrM as a form of corporate green-washing while the majority of 60 % is unsure about this. In addition, participants distinguish CrM from FT and donations in general but less from donations to such charity organisations involved in CrM promotions. An ordered logit model reveals that highly educated, young consumers living in urban areas are more sceptical towards CrM and perceive this marketing strategy as green-washing.

Key words: Cause-related marketing (CrM), green-washing, consumer behaviour, attitudes, Fair Trade (FT), donations

8.1 Introduction

A growing segment of conscious consumers[124] is not only attracted by environmental and social claims related to the products they purchase (FURLOW 2009, p. 22). Research reveals that the consumption choice can be influenced by a company's support of social causes e.g. via Cause-related Marketing (CrM) (BARONE et al. 2000, p. 248) or Fair Trade (FT) products

---

[123] This paper has been presented at the 11th Biennial ISEE Conference 'Advancing sustainability in a time of crisis', August 22-25, 2010, Oldenburg and Bremen, Germany. Co-authors are Carola Grebitus and Monika Hartmann.

[124] Conscious consumers take into consideration the consequences of their private consumption and attempt "to use his or her purchasing power to bring about social change" (WEBSTER 1975, p. 188).

(e.g. LANGEN et al. 2009). CrM is an increasingly applied marketing tool where the product purchase leads to a target-oriented donation regarding a designated cause promoted on the product by label. In a recent campaign Germany's coffee producer Dallmayr cooperates with the NGO 'Menschen für Menschen'. The campaign promotes that per sold package of coffee five trees are planted in Ethiopia. In this regard, the campaign is close to a regular target oriented donation and comparable to FT in terms of the prevention of soil degradation and therefore sustainable production methods.

A crucial **success factor** is consumers' trust in companies' altruistic motivation for engaging in the cause via CrM or FT. Sceptical consumers who question whether the support of the cause is designed to benefit the firm or the cause regard actions such as CrM as a form of green-washing[125]. The meaning of the term green-washing, the implication of accusing CrM to be green-washing and previous research on the issue is explained in the following sections. In this context the following research questions should be considered. First, do consumers think that CrM is green-washing? Second, do consumers distinguish between CrM and traditional donations as well as the purchase of FT products? To answer these questions we conducted a consumer survey in Germany in 2009.

The remainder of the paper is as follows. The relevance of CrM and its link to green-washing as well as previous research on the issue is discussed in section 2. In the third section we introduce the methodology used to assess consumers' attitude towards CrM and the factors that shape this attitude while the empirical results are presented in section 4. Some concluding remarks are provided in section 5.

8.2 Background on CrM and green-washing

8.2.1 Introduction into Cause-related Marketing

CrM works in the way that a consumer's product purchase leads to a target-oriented donation to a designated cause which is promoted on the product by label. Thus, each time a consumer purchases a CrM product, money is donated directly or via a charity organisation to a good cause. To distinguish CrM from other forms of corporate social responsibility (CSR) or purely altruistic behaviour, POLONSKY and WOOD (2001, p. 11) characterise CrM as post-purchase giving (which is made after the sale has been made), while e.g. sponsorship is pre-purchase giving (meaning that no sale is needed for giving to take place). Philanthropy is completely

[125] To the authors' knowledge there is no literature about accusing FT as such to be green-washing. The only context in which FT and green-washing are mixed is with respect to firms selling FT products, especially multinationals. These are criticized for selling some FT products to brighten the corporate image (see e.g. REIBER 2004).

unrelated to sales. Congruently ADKINS (1999, p. 12) notes "Whatever Cause Related Marketing is, it is certainly not philanthropy nor altruism: it's good business, and it's good business for charities and businesses". CrM allows firms to publicise their corporate social performance thereby enhancing its legitimacy in the eyes of its stakeholders (LIU et al. 2010, p. 195; DAWKINS 2004). It can help to enhance firms' corporate image, reputation and profile and thereby its sales volumes and consumers' loyalty (CADBURY 2000, p. vii).

WEBB and MOHR noted in 1998 (p. 226) for the Anglo-Saxon countries that despite an increasing relevance of CrM in practice little research has been undertaken. This holds for Germany even in 2010. So far, studies with a focus on the German market primarily looked at general issues of CrM such as consumers' knowledge (sources) of CrM campaigns and their general opinion towards CrM (see e.g. HUBER et al. 2008). OLOKO (2008), in addition, investigated consumers' assumption with respect to the firms' intentions for using CrM and to the share of money dedicated to the cause by the companies.

With respect to consumers' perception of CrM and the possible benefits CrM offers to consumers the review conducted by MOHR et al. (2001, p. 49ff.) shows that respondents evaluated CrM so positively that they stated the intention to try a new brand because of CrM or even to switch to the brand or the retailers who participate in CrM to support these corporations. A reason for the positive evaluation is the possible positive aspect of CrM for consumers. Consumers' utility consists of the direct product utility and an expected immaterial utility which e.g. can be represented by the warm glow a consumer of a CrM good feels (WEBB and MOHR 1998, p. 236). These results show that the degree of social responsibility (also known as ethical brand value) consumers associate with brands and corporations is decisive for the purchase decision (SEVENONE MEDIA 2009, p. 14f). The few studies with a focus on the German market reveal that CrM is able to increase the brand sympathy (BLUMBERG and CONRAD 2006), identified determinants of the intention to buy CrM products (HUBER et al. 2008) and investigated consumers' assumptions with respect to the firms' intentions for using CrM and to the share of money dedicated to the cause by the companies (OLOKO 2008). OLOKO's (2008, p. 6f.) findings reveal a positive attitude of German consumers towards CrM in general but also that German consumers are sceptical with regard to the "fair" amount of money spent on the "cause" as well as with regard to the altruistic motives of firms. Also DAWKINS (2004, p. 108f.) observes scepticism as well as public cynicism with respect to companies' messages whose credibility is sometimes called into question. Consumers may mistrust firms' motives to conduct CrM. As evidence for German consumers' cynicism concerning CrM the comments with regard to a CrM campaign by the brewery Krombacher and its rainforest campaign should be mentioned (e.g. "Guzzling for the rainforest") (MEFFERT and HOLZBERG 2009, p. 49). This leads to the situation that the correspondence between self-image of the corporation and the perceived public-image is weak and contributes to the impression of green-washing (MEFFERT and HOLZBERG 2009, p. 49). According to BARONE et al. (2000) consumers' perceptions about the company's driving forces to undertake CrM may affect the degree to which a CrM strategy is able to affect consumers' choice, therefore, this aspect is of crucial importance for the success of CrM. Also according to SINGH (2009, p. 314) and BARONE et al. (2000, p. 249) scepticism towards CrM arises primarily because customers question the company's motivations for participating in such actions. Consumers are challenging whether a company supports a certain good cause because of the cause or because of the company's benefits. This is in line with the results of HAVAS MEDIA (2009, p. 2; 4). Their findings indicate that consumers mistrust the sustainability efforts of companies in general. CrM is believed to be used primarily as a marketing tool and a fig leaf. This may be partly due to the fact that a great number of CrM promotions lack transparency with regard to the amount of donations as well as with respect to the success of the "cause" the money is aimed at. Furthermore, CrM campaigns seldom disclose details of the agreement between the NGO and the company (BERGLIND and NAKATA 2005, p. 450).[126] A transparency requirement, however, is not included e.g. in the German Act Against Unfair Practices (UWG) (ONLINE WERBERECHT 2010). The legal situation is slightly different in the US. There the Federal Trade Commission (FTC) established so-called Green Guides in 1992 to aid firms "in determining correct means for making claims about the environmental benefits of their products" (WOODS 2008, p. 75). These guides do not have the status of a law but violations of the recommendations may have negative effects as described in section 5 of the FTC Act (WOODS 2008, p. 77). WOODS (2008, p. 83f.) illustrates that these Guidelines can be criticised as e.g. too static for quickly changing consumer demands and marketing realities. For example, in the case of renewable energy certificates or carbon offsets, it is unclear which certificates companies should show to prove that advertising with these issues is legitimate. From WOODS' (2008, p. 91ff.) point of view the German Biosiegel as well as Blauer Engel are better tools of environmental labelling than the FTC Act. This shows that the Green Guides are not going further than these labelling schemes which are not able to deal with information problems arising from CSR and CrM campaigns.

---

[126] In Norway (see SINGH 2009, p. 314) the labelling and communication of the monetary amount donated to the cause is not allowed. This, however, does not hold for Germany.

Since the early 1990s NGOs and lobby groups have criticised corporations that describe themselves as green and caring although the reality is otherwise (SEELE 2007, p. 5). This problem of being accused of green-washing is inherent in the concept of CrM. As CrM is a marketing tool[127] companies have at least one special reason for conducting CrM campaigns besides supporting social causes: to achieve marketing objectives, e.g. increase brand sales and create durable differentiation from competitors (LAFFERTY et al. 2004). This leads, on the one hand, to a situation of mutual benefits for all stakeholders involved (firms, NGOs, consumers)[128] but, on the other hand, this may lead to consumer distrust. Consumers might think that CrM promotions are meant to primarily serve companies' interests and that the good cause is only put in front to hide the real intentions behind it. Furthermore, consumers might get the impression that firms use environmental as well as social claims and causes to attract a growing segment of conscious consumers. The claims are felt to be vague and are sometimes proved to be false. False claims are the reason why some NGOs and consumers consider certain advertisements or corporate action to be green-washing. Therefore, CrM is sometime regarded as green-washing.

8.2.2 What is meant by calling actions and promotions green-washing?

Both the media and researchers use the term green-washing when discussing delusive and misleading green advertising. Hence, if companies try to give a semblance of accountability, socially responsible or environmentally sustainable behaviour and business activities by conducting marketing activities with delusive information this is referred to as green-washing (LOBBY CONTROL 2007, p. 1). Mainstream media, activists and even the 10th edition of the CONCISE OXFORD ENGLISH DICTIONARY take a harsher tone, which describes green-wash(ing) as "disinformation disseminated by an organization so as to present an environmentally responsible public image". The US NGO CORPWATCH (2001) defines green-washing as first "phenomenon of socially and environmentally destructive corporations attempting to preserve and expand their markets by posing as friends of the environment and leaders in the struggle to eradicate poverty", second "Environmental whitewash" and third "any attempt to brainwash consumers or policy makers into believing polluting mega-corporations are the key to environmentally sound sustainable development". Or as the GREENWASHING INDEX (2010) explains: "What is Green-washing? It's Whitewashing, But With a Green Brush". To be more

[127] From sales promotion over advertising to public relation etc. (ADKINS 1999, p. 10).

[128] For a deeper insight into the benefits for nonprofits, companies and consumers, see e.g. LANGEN et al. (2010), ADKINS (1999), WEBB and MOHR (1999), POLONSKY and WOOD (2001, p. 12). For insights into the drivers for environmental management in general see (RAMUS and MONTIEL 2005, p. 379).

precise, "It's green-washing when a company or organisation spends more time and money claiming to be 'green' through advertising and marketing than actually implementing business practices that minimise environmental impact." This means, promoting a product or feature as environmentally responsible when it has little to no effect at all or communicating misleading environmentally friendly claims to consumers can be called green-washing[129]. With respect to CrM, if the money spent on advertising to inform consumers about a special CrM promotion is more than the money afterwards collected for the promoted good cause, this can be called disproportionate and green-washing or the greening of business. Other scenarios are also possible. According to LOBBY CONTROL (2007, p. 24) typical characteristics of green-washing are selectivity in the description of reality, the adoption of typical ecological terms, green and positive picture language, the accentuation of the one's own responsibility to minimise the influence of third parties like Greenpeace, the emphasis on technical solutions as well as the fading out of current political debates. From LOBBY CONTROL's (2007, p. 2) point of view, green-washing is to a lesser extent aimed at increasing sales rather than influencing politicians, decision makers and opinion leaders of critical consumers. It used to cloud environmentally harmful business practices or to build up acceptance for such business (see e.g. the advertisement of electricity corporations such as RWE indicating that RWE is supporting Galapagos Island by financing wind energy to reduce CO2 emissions per year in a size of which CO2 is emitted in the biggest power station Niederaussem, Germany per hour (RWE 2005, STAUDT 2008).[130] Interestingly, the impression that "green-washing is continuing to become a bigger problem as companies try to meet an ever-increasing consumer demand for sustainable products" (CELSIAS 2010) cannot be found in a comparable size in academic research as it can be found in many blogs worldwide in 2010 (e.g. CELSIAS 2010; GREEN ECO COMMUNITIES 2010, THE CHIC ECOLOGIST 2010) This means, the blogger community has embraced this problem field which is still not to the same extent covered in academics (see also WHELLAMS and MACDONALD 2008; SEELE 2007, p. 4). SEELE (2007, p. 5) had this impression that most of the green-washing literature originates from activists still in 2007.

As a consequence of the proliferation of environmental and social claims by firms, EnviroMedia and the University of Oregon developed the green-washing index (GREENWASHING INDEX 2010). It is a critical review of advertisements by interested

[129] SEELE (2007, p. 5) gives a short review of the term green-washing and points out that the nature of green-washing has changed since the first definitions in 1992 were made.

[130] Other examples of campaigns which are criticised as green-washing can be found in LOBBY CONTROL (2007) and up to date at www.greenwashingindex.com.

consumers who post and rate 'green' claims used by companies. In Germany, LOBBY CONTROL (2007, p. 1), a transparency initiative in Germany, regards the new wave of green image advertisements and promotions as a consequence of increased consumers' power and their pressure on firms to behave in a socially responsible and environmentally sustainable manner.

While in the 1990s companies described themselves as green and caring and thus provoked the protest of NGOs, since 2000 these companies have started a dialogue with the opposition, i.e. the NGOs and activists criticising them, which has resulted in cooperation such as CrM[131]. For MONBIOT (2002) this development follows the fact that for companies "one of their simplest and most successful strategies is to buy their critics". This is a another reason why some consumers consider CrM to be green-washing.

8.2.3 What are the risks in general if consumers question corporate honesty and regard a company as a green-washer?

CREYER and ROSS (1996) review studies dealing with the question as to whether CSR activities of firms such as CrM is correlated with corporate performance. Most studies did not find positive impacts. This means consumers are not willing to reward companies for doing good and acting ethically, but just the opposite can be observed: unethical behaviour is punished, e.g. in the form of a consumer boycott[132] which became popular in the 1990s. And even if firms' unethical behaviour is not directly punished in form of a consumer boycott, CREYER and ROSS (1996, p. 182f.) show that consumers are very aware of the ethical performance of firms and show in the long run a decreasing willingness to purchase the products of such companies. This weakens the firms' capability to effectively compete on the market.

FURLOW (2009, p. 23f.) lists several implications of consumer loss of trust resulting from the accusation that firms are green-washing. An overuse or misuse of ecological and social claims can lead to consumer saturation and that 'green' aspects become meaningless and unimpressive to them. Moreover, consumers might become confused about which products are actually environmentally, socially and animal friendly and which are not. If this confusion results in lower willingness to purchase those products which are really 'green', companies offering those products lose competitive advantage. Furthermore, engagement in pro-social

[131] This development is also known as bluewashing (see SEELE 2007, p. 5; 9).

[132] As the boycott of Shell in conjunction with the oil platform Brentspar in 1995 has shown, NGOs may attempt to punish such companies by denunciating them in the media and encouraging consumers to boycott them (see e.g. KINTZINGER 1995).

and pro-environmental action might decrease to the harm of these issues so that in the end all actors (company, consumer, and environment) lose.

It is important to keep in mind that environmental policy statements are voluntary and not required by law (RAMUS and MONTIEL 2005, p. 377). Therefore, no mechanism such as a third party certification controls whether advertising companies behave as they claim to do. Because environmental and social policy statements are easy to make but hard to verify whether they are implemented or not (RAMUS and MONTIEL 2005, p. 409), the accusation of green-washing as a result of scepticism and confusion can be seen as a result of market failure. STOLL (2002, p. 122) names one reason for market failure: consumers do not trust companies because of asymmetric information and consumer confusion which is caused by the increase in variety of environmental claims (Newell et al. 1998). In addition, academics like STOLL (2002) and WULFSON (2001) have queried "the ethics of marketing good corporate conducts" as STOLL (2002) entitled her respective paper.

8.2.4 Relevance for the food sector

During the past 20 years company support of good causes has grown significantly. For example, the expenditures for CrM by firms in the US increased from almost zero in 1983 to around $1.57 billion in 2009 (CHONG 2009, p. 1). In contrast to most of the Anglo-Saxon countries, CrM has only been applied in Germany for a short time (HUBER et al. 2008, p. 6), hence, the number of CrM campaigns is relatively low there. However, in recent years the trend has been comparable to the one in the US. Since the legal practice changed in 2004[133] the number of CrM campaigns in Germany has increased steadily. Overall more than 90 firms have offered CrM products in Germany since 2002 (OLOKO 2008, p. 3). OLOKO (2008, p. 34) reveals in his review of CrM campaigns in Germany that this marketing tool is most often applied by the food industry. 35 % of all CrM promotions in Germany OLOKO (2008, p. 34) reviewed were undertaken by the food and beverage sector.

8.2.5 Similarities between CrM and Fair Trade

We increasingly observe that positive purchasing is more attractive for so-called conscious consumers than boycotting. Not only CrM products, but also FT products attract consumer attention by dealing with ethical issues and appealing to the consumers' conscience. Assuming that consumers are convinced about the good intentions and results of a CrM

[133] Since the amendment of the Act Against Unfair Practices (UWG) in 2004 CrM is no longer seen as an unfair advertising practice. Emotional advertising like CrM can fall in the category of §4 Nr. 1 UWG and the prohibition of mislead of §5 UWG has to be considered (ONLINE WERBERECHT 2010).

promotion and purchase a CrM good, this purchase might compete with the purchase of FT products or monetary donations to charity organisations and NGOs. Therefore, the question arises as to whether German consumers distinguish between CrM, donations and FT. If they do not trust CrM, the reason might be that they consider the company to be green-washing. Therefore, we have investigated two important questions with respect to CrM, namely whether German consumers think CrM is green-washing and secondly, whether they prefer CrM over traditional donations or the purchase of FT products.

8.3 Methodological background

To analyse determinants towards the attitude that CrM campaigns are green-washing we have applied an ordered logit model. As we are measuring the attitude towards green-washing on 7-point Likert scale, we need a model for ordered categorical response such as the ordered logit model. Because ordered categorical response is a natural extension of a binary response, such data can be analysed using a generalisation of the logistic regression model (COLLET 2003, p. 325). In this model the probabilities of each outcome (strongly agree, moderately agree, strongly disagree), conditional on the independent variables (such as income, education) are modeled using the Weibull distribution (STOCK and WATSON 2004, p. 330). In the following section, the ordered logit model will be explained.

Suppose U_i^m is the utility that consumer i derives from holding the attitude m and U_{ij} can be expressed as follows:

$$U_i^m = X_i\beta^m + \varepsilon_i^m;\quad i = 1,\cdots,n; m = 1,\cdots \qquad (1)$$

where X_i is the design matrix which is a row vector of the ith consumer's characteristics. These characteristics include socio-demographics and attitudes. β^m is the coefficient associated with X_i. And ε_i^m is the residual error term that is not captured by design matrix X_i. There are n consumers and M attitudes.

In a survey that asks the respondents' opinion, the respondents' intensity of feelings is dependent on the measurable factors X and unobservables. In many situations, the respondents are not asked to respond to U directly. Instead, they are given only a set number of possible answers, say seven, to the question of y. Consumers choose the cell that most closely represents the intensity of response to the question. For example, for attitude m (here CrM is green-washing), consumer i is asked to choose among the seven choices: agree very strongly $(y_i^m = 7)$, agree strongly $(y_i^m = 6)$, agree $(y_i^m = 5)$, neither agree nor disagree $(y_i^m = 4)$, disagree $(y_i^m = 3)$, disagree strongly $(y_i^m = 2)$, and disagree very strongly $(y_i^m = 1)$.

The ordered logit model is based on the idea of the cumulative logit which relies on the idea of the cumulative probability. Let C_{ij}^{m} denote the probability that the *i*th individual is in the *j*th or higher category for attitude *m*:

$$C_{ij}^{m} = \Pr ob(y_i^m \leq j) = \sum_{k=1}^{j} \Pr ob(y_i^m = k) \qquad (2)$$

Then we turn the cumulative probability into cumulative logit for product *m*:

$$\text{logit}(C_{ij}^{m}) = \log\left(\frac{C_{ij}^{m}}{1 - C_{ij}^{m}}\right) = \alpha_j^m - \beta^m X_i. \qquad (3)$$

With regard to this paper the consumers' attitude is expressed in degree of agreement such as agree very strongly and so on to measure the corresponding latent utilities.

8.4 Empirical results

To answer the research questions, we conducted a consumer survey (n = 112) in 2009 in Germany. The sample (for participants socioeconomic characteristics see also Table 1) consists of an equal share of female and male participants. It is slightly underrepresented by older consumers (16.2 % are 55 years and older whereas 15.5 % are below the age of 25, 19.1 % are between 25 and 34, 20.9 % between 35 and 44 years and 28.2 % are between 45 and 54 years old) and interviewees with a higher income level (14.3 % indicated their household has a net income below 500 € per month, 34.9 % stated this income is between 500 and 1300 €, 16.1 % have an monthly net income between 1300 and 2000 €, 22.3 % have an available net income between 2000 and 2600 € and 9 % have more than 3600 € per month). Moreover, highly educated consumers are overrepresented (23.2 % hold an university entrance diploma and 34.8 % an university degree).

8.4.1 Consumers' attitudes towards CrM and green-washing

To start with the analysis some descriptive statistics are presented. First of all, we want to assess participants' general attitudes towards CrM. Therefore we asked them whether they perceive CrM e.g. as meaningful or green-washing of profit organisations, as being able to provide confidence and trust in the brand or just being a marketing 'gag', as being able to replace donations in general and to the involved NGOs in the CrM campaign in particular, or as a substitute of the purchase of FT products (for all questions asked see Figure 1).

Figure 1: Attitudes towards CrM and the role of green-washing

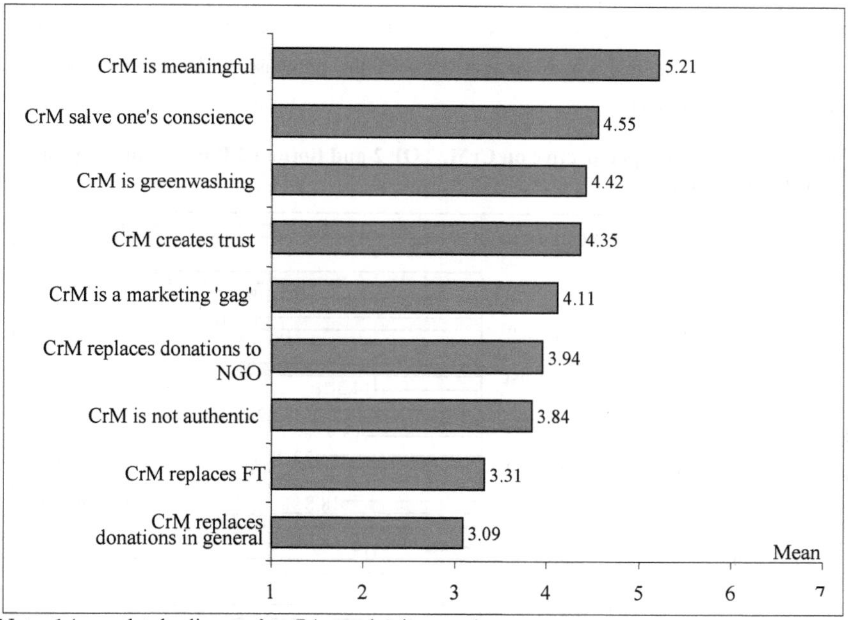

Note: 1 'completely disagree' to 7 'completely agree'.

Source: authors' calculations.

Figure 1 illustrates the mean of the answers given to the statement battery applying Likert-scales (1 = completely disagree to 7 = completely agree). It becomes obvious that participants to a great extent agree that CrM is a meaningful tool and able to salve consumers' consciences. At the same time, the statement that CrM is a form of green-washing experiences with a mean of 4.42 a slightly more than average compliance on the 7 point scale. This indicates that participants are either indifferent or agree that CrM is a form of company green-washing. With regard to the possible substitution of FT, regular donations to charity or a donation to the charity organisation cooperating in a CrM campaign through the purchase of a

CrM product, participants strongly distinguish, on the one hand, between CrM and charity in general as well as FT and, on the other hand, between giving to charity in general and to an NGO participating in a CrM cooperation. While consumers agree that the purchase of a CrM product is not able to replace the purchase of FT products (mean 3.31) and donations to charity organisations in general (mean 3.09) they are less sure with respect to giving to the NGO participating in a CrM campaign (mean 3.94). A paired t-test reveals the difference in the means between 'CrM replaces FT' and 'CrM replaces donations to NGOs' as well as between 'CrM replaces donations in general' and 'CrM replaces donations to NGO' is highly significant at $p<0.01$. This finding indicates that consumers differentiate between charity organisations engaging in CrM promotions and those not engaged in such activities. Moreover, consumers make a distinction between the purchase of FT products and the purchase of CrM products.

Figure 2: Consumers' perspective on CrM: TOP 2 and Bottom 2 Boxes indicate groups differ in their opinion

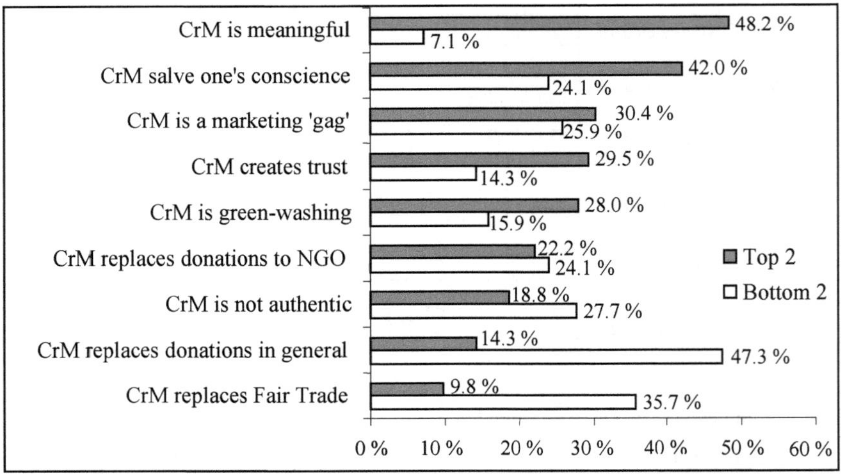

Source: authors' calculations.

To assess differences between consumers' assessment of CrM, we further analysed the compliance with these statements by using TOP 2 and Bottom 2 boxes. Figure 2 reveals well distinguished preferences regarding the issues of CrM's substitution potential (35.7 % and 47.3 % strongly disagree that CrM is able to replace FT and donations in general respectively) and some positive characteristics of CrM.

More than 40 % of the respondents state that the purchase of a CrM product is both able to salve one's conscience and meaningful. This response leads to the conclusion that consumers on average assess CrM rather positively. But, the deeper view via Top 2 and Bottom 2 Boxes reveals that consumers are to some extent disunited. Even though, for instance, 28 % agree and strongly agree that CrM is green-washing, a smaller group of 16 % strongly disagrees. But the majority of 56 % of the survey participants is unsure with respect to the question. This picture is similar regarding the questions 'CrM is a marketing 'gag'' and 'CrM replaces donations to NGO'. The majority of consumers are not able to formulate clear and well distinguished assessments of these CrM questions. An explanation might be that CrM is a rather unfamiliar topic to them and that therefore they are undecided when asked such detailed questions.

The special focus of the paper is to investigate whether consumers perceive CrM to be a form of green-washing of companies. Based on the findings in Figure 2, we clustered consumers according to their attitude towards the green-washing question and examine in which characteristics (important features of a coffee purchase in the first block of the table, attitudes towards CrM (second block of the Table 1), purchase behaviour, socioeconomic characteristics and knowledge) consumers differ regarding this question. Table 1 presents three clusters: one cluster thinking CrM is not green-washing with 26 respondents grouped into this cluster named 'No', a second cluster formed by 30 participants agreeing that CrM is green-washing and accordingly termed 'Yes' and the largest cluster including all other respondents being not sure and therefore 'Indifferent' to this green-washing question. The results demonstrate that those who do not regard CrM as green-washing indicate that it is important that the coffee they purchase is organic. This cluster shows in general a positive attitude towards CrM (the mean is above that of the other two cluster means regarding the statements positively describing CrM in the second block), a higher percentage of the respondents purchase FT products and give to charity with a focus on developmental aid. The respondents grouped in the 'No' cluster are older and less educated than those in the other two clusters. The 'Yes' cluster indicates these respondents care a lot about FT issues such as an adequate producer price (mean 5.72) and production without child labour (mean: 5.97). The high means on the statements 'CrM is a marketing gag' and 'CrM is not authentic' as well as the lower means (compared to the other clusters) on 'CrM is meaningful' and 'CrM creates trust' reveals that the 30 respondents grouped in the 'Yes' cluster are more sceptical about CrM than the other respondents. They are considerably higher educated and more knowledgeable about FT which is interestingly not reflected in a higher share of FT purchasers.

Table 1: Cluster agreeing and disagreeing in CrM to be green-washing

CrM is green-washing	No		Yes		Indifferent	
	Obs.	Mean	Obs.	Mean	Obs.	Mean
Organic: Coffee [a]	25	5.04	30	4.73	49	4.78
No child labour: Coffee [a]	26	5.73	30	5.97	51	6.16
Adequate producer price: Coffee [a]	26	5.12	29	5.72	50	5.40
Cheap: Coffee [a]	24	5.71	29	5.72	50	5.12
CrM is meaningful [b]	26	6.12	30	4.13	51	5.31
CrM creates trust [b]	24	4.92	30	3.47	51	4.51
CrM salves one's conscience [b]	26	3.92	30	4.33	51	4.96
CrM replaces donation to NGO [b]	26	4.27	27	3.70	51	3.84
CrM replaces FT [b]	26	3.15	30	3.23	51	3.31
CrM is a marketing gag [b]	26	2.38	30	5.67	51	4.16
CrM is not authentic [b]	24	2.33	30	5.00	51	3.88
FT purchaser [c]	24	0.71	29	0.41	50	0.50
Donor [d]	26	0.69	30	0.57	51	0.43
Donation amount [e]	18	1.83	17	1.94	22	2.00
Education: min. university entrance diploma [f]	25	0.44	30	0.80	51	0.55
Age < 40 [g]	26	0.23	29	0.55	50	0.54
Fair Trade Knowledge [h]	25	2.84	0	3.06	50	2.36
Donation Knowledge [h]	25	2.84	30	2.63	50	2.50

Note: [a]: for the variable description, see Table 2.
[b]: Attitude measured on Likert-Scale from 1 (completely disagree) to 7 (completely agree).
[c]: Dummy variable equal to 1 if consumption is given, 0 if otherwise.
[d]: Gave to developmental charity organisations in the last 12 months: dummy variable equal to 1 if yes, 0 otherwise
[e]: Donation amount given to developmental purposes in the last 12 months in €: categorical variable from 1 (< 20 €) to 5 (> €).
[f]: Dummy variable equal to 1 if education minimum university entrance diploma, 0 if otherwise.
[g]: Dummy variable equal to 1 if respondent's age is below 40 years, 0 if otherwise.
[e]: Knowledge about Fair Trade/ donations: categorical variable from 1 (no knowledge) to 5 (very knowledgeable).

Source: authors' calculations.

In addition, we investigated whether intensive FT shoppers (minimum of two FT products at least once a week) and donors (donated in the last 12 months to developmental aid) have different attitudes regarding the issue of green-washing compared to occasionally and no FT shoppers as well as non donors. The results reveal no significant differences between both FT shoppers versus FT non and occasional shoppers and donors versus non donors regarding the issue of green-washing.

8.4.2 Determinants of consumers' green-washing attitude

To gain deeper insights into the determinants influencing the attitude that CrM campaigns are green-washing we have applied in the following an ordered probit model (robust), as explained in section 3 of the paper, for the econometric analysis. Table 2 displays the dependent and independent variables used in the analysis. We included socio-demographics, consumption of coffee (the CrM product that was used as an example in the statement battery towards CrM attitudes) as well as consumption of FT products. Results in Table 3 show that the model fit is satisfying compared with other cross-sectional consumption studies. The model is highly significant and has a Pseudo R^2 of 0.08. We can report that age is the only socio-demographic characteristic that influences the attitude towards green-washing. The direction is negative. This means that the younger participants are more likely to be convinced that CrM is green-washing. The region in which participants live also significantly influences the green-washing attitude. Those living in rural areas are less sceptical and those living in urban areas are more sceptical. With regard to consumption patterns the results lead to the conclusion that a moderate consumption level of FT products (at minimum 2 products at least once in a month) influences consumers, i.e. they do not regard CrM as green-washing. Consumers stating that an adequate producer price of coffee is important for them when choosing and purchasing a coffee mistrust CrM. This variable significantly influences the green-washing attitude positively. Via a contingent valuation task we measured consumers' willingness to pay for CrM coffee. We asked consumers whether they are willing to pay 4.99 € and 5.99 € for a CrM coffee if the coffee without a CrM promotion costs 2.99 €. Those consumers who are willing to pay 5.99 € for the CrM coffee do not agree that CrM is green-washing. This is plausible as consumers having doubts about CrM would not be willing to pay more for such a product than for a non-CrM product.

Table 2: Variable description

Dependent Variable	Variable description	Obs.	Mean	Std. Dev.	Min	Max
CrM is green-washing	Attitude measured on Likert-Scale from 1 (completely disagree) to 7 (completely agree)	107	4.42	1.67	1	7
Independent Variables	**Variable description**	**Obs.**	**Mean**	**Std. Dev.**	**Min**	**Max**
Gender (male)	Dummy variable equal to 1 if gender male, 0 if female.	112	0.49	0.50	0	1
Age	Categorical variable from 1 (< 25 yrs.) to 10 (>65 yrs.) (categories in between in 5 year steps).	110	4.80	2.70	1	10
Income	Household Net-Income (EUR/month) Categorical variable from 1 (< 300 EUR) to 12 (>5000 EUR).	109	6.54	3.12	0	12
Education	Categorical variable from 1 (no graduation) to 6 (PhD).	111	3.80	1.12	2	6
Children under the age of 18	Dummy variable equal to 1 if children under the age of 18 are living in the household, 0 if otherwise.	112	0.21	0.41	0	1
Living in rural area	Categorical variable. 3= rural, 2=sub-urban area, 1=urban area.	111	1.46	0.66	1	3
Consumes FT (min. of 2 products) at least once a month	Dummy variable equal to 1 if consumption is given, 0 if otherwise.	112	0.21	0.41	0	1
Consumes FT (min. of 2 products) at least once a week		112	0.29	0.45	0	1
Donor	Did give to developmental charity organisations in the last 12 month	112	0.52	0.50	0	1
Life situation	Attitude measured on Likert-Scale from 1 (completely disagree) to 5 (completely agree).	112	3.54	0.77	1	5
Organic: Coffee	Important that coffee is produced organically [a]	109	4.83	1.61	1	7
No child labour: Coffee	Important that coffee is produced without child labour [a]	112	6.00	1.38	2	7
Adequate producer price: Coffee	Important that coffee producers get an adequate price [a]	110	5.40	1.53	1	7
Cheap: Coffee	Important that coffee is cheap [a]	108	5.38	1.42	1	7
Intensive coffee drinker	More than 3 cups of coffee daily	112	0.41	0.49	0	1
Higher WTP for CrM	Dummy variable equal to 1 if consumer is willing to pay 5.99 € for a pound of CrM coffee, 0 if he is willing to pay less	110	0.12	0.32	0	1

[a]: Measured on a scale from 1 (not important) to 7 (very important).

Table 3: Determinants of the attitude that CrM is green-washing

Determinants of CrM being Green-washing	Coefficient	Std. Err.[1]	
Gender (male)	-0.09	0.22	
Age	-0.15	0.05	***
Income	-0.07	0.05	
Education	0.10	0.11	
Children under the age of 18	-0.16	0.34	
Living in rural area	-0.30	0.17	*
Consumes FT (minimum of 2 products) at least once a week	0.00	0.30	
Consumes FT (minimum of 2 products) at least once a month	-0.68	0.29	**
Donor	0.05	0.25	
Life situation	-0.04	0.17	
Organic: Coffee	-0.05	0.11	
No child labour: Coffee	-0.12	0.11	
Adequate producer price: Coffee	0.24	0.11	*
Cheap: Coffee	-0.04	0.08	
Intensive coffee drinker	0.03	0.26	
Higher willingness to pay for CrM	-0.74	0.33	**
Wald chi2 (17)	30.31		
Prob>chi2			0.0123
Pseudolikelihood	-156.15067		
Pseudo R2	0.0837		
Number of observations	94		

[1] Level of significance: *** <0.01, ** < 0.05, *** < 0.1.

Source: authors' calculations.

8.5 Discussion and conclusions

Nowadays, CrM is an increasingly applied marketing tool. In order for CrM to be successful it is of great importance for companies to avoid the impression that CrM is green-washing. But research on the effects of CrM activities regarding consumers' attitudes and purchase behaviour is rare. Our study contributes to the literature by analysing whether consumers consider CrM to be green-washing and if they make a distinction between CrM and traditional donations as well as purchasing FT products. In this regard, we implemented a consumer survey with 112 respondents in Germany in 2009. First, we displayed consumers' compliance to different CrM statements to get a feeling as to whether consumers are in general sceptical or supporting of CrM. It became obvious that the compliance to the statement that CrM is a form of green-washing is with a mean of 4.42 slightly more than average on the 7 point scale. This indicates that participants are either indifferent or agree that CrM is a form of company green-washing. Regarding CrM's potential to replace FT purchases or donations in general the results show respondents are persuaded that CrM is not a substitute of these. This shows that CrM is distinguished from FT and donations in general. But respondents significantly more agree that the purchase of a CrM product is able to replace a donation to the NGO involved in the CrM campaign. This finding is important for NGOs that are considering participating in a CrM campaign. They should assess whether the earnings resulting from such a CrM campaign are higher than the potential losses they could face in regular donations if consumers replace their donation to the NGO by a CrM product purchase. A cluster analysis revealed that consumers assessing CrM as green-washing are higher educated and more familiar with FT than the two other identified groups. In addition, they mistrust CrM in general. Respondents who do not regard CrM as a form of green-washing of the companies conducting CrM campaigns are older, less educated, and more interested in organic production than the other groups. Their attitude towards CrM in general is more positive. An ordered logit model illustrates the role of socio-demographics and consumption patterns in influencing the belief that CrM is green-washing. The younger and urban consumers as well as those caring more than average about adequate producer prices are more critical with respect to CrM. In contrast, those purchasing FT products from time to time and at least 2 products once in a month and those showing a higher willingness to pay for CrM coffee do not agree that CrM is green-washing. Overall the results reveal that around one third of the participants assume CrM to be a form of green-washing. These consumers are in general more critical towards CrM, live in urban areas and have a higher education level than those consumers not assessing CrM to be a form of corporate green-washing. The majority of the participants are unsure as to whether CrM is green-washing or not but definitely distinguish between CrM and Fair Trade products and donations in general. Only a minority of around 26 % of the sample do not regard CrM as a form of corporate green-washing.

8.6 References

ADKINS, S. (1999): *Cause Related Marketing: Who Cares Wins*. Boston: Butterworth Heinemann.

BARONE, M. J., MIYAZAKI, A. D. and TAYLOR, K. A. (2000): The influence of cause-related mar-keting on consumer choice: does one good turn deserve another? *Journal of the Academy in Marketing Science* 28 (2): 248-262.

BERGLIND, M. and NAKATA, C. (2005): Cause-related marketing: More buck than bang? *Business Horizons*, 48: 443-453.

BLUMBERG, M. and CONRAD, C. (2006): *Good Brand 2006: Gutes tun und davon profitieren? Ethisches Verbraucherverhalten und Cause Related Marketing in Deutschland*. Bremen: Brands & Values.

CADBURY, D. (2000): Foreword by Sir Dominic Cadbury, In: Adkins, S. (2000): *Cause Related Marketing – Who cares wins*. Boston: Butterworth Heinemann: vii-viii.

CELSIAS (2010): *Peeling back the green paint: Getting rid of greenwash*. Available from: http://www.celsias.com/article/peeling-back-green-paint-getting-rid-greenwash/, [accessed 2010-06-30].

CHONG, R. (2009): Cause-Related Marketing: Just Plain Ol' Marketing? *Huffington Post*, 13.01.2010.

COLLETT, D. (2003): *Modeling Binary Data*. 2nd ed. Boca Raton: Chapman and Hall/CRC.

CONCISE OXFORD ENGLISH DICTIONARY (2011): 10th ed. Oxford: Oxford University Press.

CORPWATCH (2001): *Greenwash Fact Sheet*. Available from: http://www.corpwatch.org/article.php?id=242, [accessed 2010-06-15].

CREYER, E. H. and ROSS, W. T. JUNIOR (1996): The Impact of Corporate Behavior on Percieved Product Value. *Marketing Letters* 7 (2): 173-185.

DAWKINS, J. (2004): Corporate responsibility: The communication challenge. *Journal of Communication Management*, 9 (2): 108-119.

FURLOW, N. E. (2009): Green-washing in the New Millennium. *Journal of Applied Business and Economics*, 10 (6): 22-25.

GREEN ECO COMMUNITIES (2010): *What is greenwashing*. Available from: http://www.greenecocommunities.com/News/What-is-green-washing.html, [accessed 2010-30-06].

GREENWASHING INDEX (2010): *About Greenwashing*. Available from: http://www.greenwashingindex.com/ [accessed 2010-06-18].

HAVAS MEDIA (2009): *Sustainable Future 09: German Factsheet*. Available from: http://www.havasmedia.com/staticfiles/Germany%20Factsheet.pdf, [accessed 2010-01-18].

HUBER, F., REGIER, S. and RININO, M. (2008): *Cause-Related-Marketing-Kapmpagnen erfolgreich konzipieren – Eine empirische Studie*. Wiesbaden: Gabler.

KINTZINGER, A. (1995): Shell-Boykott: Wer ist der nächste? *Fokus Magazin*, 26: 20-24, Available from: http://www.focus.de/politik/deutschland/shell-boykott-wer-ist-der-naechste_aid_153027.html, [accessed 2010-08-29].

LAFFERTY, B. A., GOLDSMITH, R. E. and HULT, G. T. (2004): The impact of the alliance on the partners: A look at cause-brand alliances. *Psychology of Marketing*, 21 (7): 509-531.

LANGEN, N., GREBITUS, C. and HARTMANN, M. (2009): Fair Trade and Donations: two possibilities to contribute to poverty alleviation in daily purchase decisions – Do consumers care? In: Klein, A. and Thoresen, V. (Eds.): *Making a Difference: Putting Consumer Citizenship into Action, Consumer Citizenship: Promoting New Responses*, 5: 60-73.

LANGEN, N., GREBITUS, C. and HARTMANN, M. (2010): Is there need for more transparency and efficiency in cause-related marketing? *International Journal on Food System Dynamics*, 1 (4): 366-381.

LIU, G., LISTON-HEYES, C. and KO, W.-W. (2010): Employee Participation in Cause-Related Marketing Strategies: A Study of Management Perceptions from British Consumer Service Industries. *Journal of Business Ethics*, 92: 195-210.

LOBBY CONTROL (2007): *Greenwash in Zeiten des Klimawandels: Wie Unternehmen ihr Image grün färben*. Available from: http://www.lobbycontrol.de/download/greenwash-studie.pdf, [accessed 2010-06-29].

MEFFERT, H. and HOLZBERG, M. (2009): Cause-related Marketing: Ein scheinheiliges Kooperationskonzept? *Marketing Review St. Gallen*, 26 (2): 47-53.

MOHR, L.A., WEBB, D. and HARRIS, K. (2001): Do Consumers Expect Companies to be Socially Responsible? The impact of Corporate Social Responsibility on Buying Behavior. *Journal of Consumer Affairs*, 35 (1): 45-72.

MONBIOT, G. (2002): Greens Get Eaten. *The Guardian*, 15th January 2002. Available from: http://www.monbiot.com/archives/2002/01/15/greens-get-eaten/, [accessed 2010-06-15].

NEWELL, S. J., GOLDSMITH, R. E. and BANZHAF, E. J. (1998): The effects of misleading environmental claims on consumer perceptions of advertising. *Journal of Marketing Theory and Practice*, 6 (2): 48-60.

OLOKO, S. (2008): *Cause related Marketing: Der Status Quo in Deutschland*. Available from: http://www.makingsense.de/dokumente/Studie_CauserelatedMarketing_Deutschland_Bericht_Juli2008.pdf, [accessed 2010-06-26].

ONLINE WERBERECHT (2010): *Cause Related Marketing*. Available from: http://www.online-werberecht.de/causerelatedmarketing.html, [accessed 2010-01-08].

POLONSKY, M. J. and WOOD, G. (2001): Can the Overcommercialization of Cause-related Marketing Harm Society? *Journal of Macromarketing*, 21 (1): 8-22.

RAMUS, C. A. and MONTIEL, I. (2005): When Are Corporate Environmental Policies a Form of Greenwashing? *Business and Society*, 44 (4): 377-414.

REIBER, D. (2004): *Brewing a Better Cup*. Available from: http://www.organicconsumers.org/starbucks/greenwash_fairtrade.cfm, [accessed 2010-06-28].

RWE (2005): *Von Galapagos nach Niederaußem und zurück*. Press Release, 18.10.2005, Available from: http://www.rwe.com/web/cms/de/37110/rwe/presse-news/presse mitteilung/?pmid=4000833, [accessed 2010-06-15].

SEELE, P. (2007): Is Blue the new Green? Colors of the Earth in Corporate PR and Advertisement to communicate Ethical Commitment and Responsibility. W*orking Paper, Center for Responsibility Research,* 1 (3): 1-20.

SEVENONE MEDIA (2009): *TrendReport Grün*, Available from: http://www.sevenone media.de/imperia/md/content/content/Research/Marktanalyse/branchen/specials/ TrendReport_Gruen.pdf, [accessed 2010-06-28].

SINGH, S. (2009): Overcoming scepticism towards cause related claims: the case of Norway. *International Marketing Review*, 26 (3): 312-326.

STAUDT, T. (2008): *RWE: Vorweg gehen im Schildkrötentempo*. Available from: http://www. klima-luegendetektor.de/2008/09/12/rwe-vorweg-gehen-im-schildkrotentempo/, [accessed 2008-09-12].

STOCK, J. H. and WATSON, M. W. (2004): *Introduction to Econometrics*. Addison-Wesley, Boston: Pearson Education.

STOLL, M. L. (2002): The Ethics of Marketing Good Corporate Conduct. *Journal of Business Ethics*, 41 (1/2): 121-129.

THE CHIC ECOLOGIST (2010): *What is Greenwashing – The Spin of Environmentally Friendly Marketing*. Available from: http://www.thechicecologist.com/2009/02/what-is-green-washing-the-spin-of-environmentally-friendly-marketing/, [accessed 2010-06-30].

WEBB, D. J. and MOHR, L. A. (1998): A Typology of Consumer Responses to Cause-Related Marketing: From Skeptics to Socially Concerned. *Journal of Public Policy & Marketing*, 17 (2): 226-238.

WEBSTER, F. (1975): Determining the characteristics of the socially conscious consumer. *Journal of Consumer Research*, 2: 188-96.

WHELLAMS, M. and MACDONALD, C. (2008): *Greenwashing*. Available from: http://www.businessethics.ca/greenwashing/, [accessed 2010-06-30].

WOODS, J. (2008): Of Selling the Environment – Buyer Beware? An Evaluation of the proposed F.T.C. Green Guides Revisions. *Loyola Consumer Law Review*, 21 (1): 75-95.

WULFSON, M. (2001): The Ethics of Corporate Social Responsibility and Philanthropic Ventures. *Journal of Business Ethics*, 29: 135-145.

Appendix D: Questionnaire

<u>Abschnitt I:</u> Lebensmitteleinkauf und Konsumverhalten **NR** ________

1. Lesen Sie normalerweise allgemeine Produktinformationen?

   JA __________ NEIN __________

2. Wie gut fühlen Sie sich über die folgenden Dinge informiert? (Kreisen Sie bitte die Antwort ein: 1 = darüber weiß ich nichts and 5 = darüber weiß ich sehr viel)

	Kein Wissen			Viel Wissen	
Fair Trade	1	2	3	4	5
Spendenorganisationen	1	2	3	4	5
Menschen für Menschen	1	2	3	4	5
Effizienz von Spendenorganisationen	1	2	3	4	5
Effizienz von Fair Trade Organisationen	1	2	3	4	5
Spezielle Ziele von Fair Trade	1	2	3	4	5
Spezielle Ziele von Menschen für Menschen	1	2	3	4	5
Das DZI Spendensiegel	1	2	3	4	5

3. Wie viele Tassen Kaffee trinken Sie pro Tag? ______

4. Wie kaufen Sie Ihren Kaffee normalerweise?

   Gemahlen ______ ganze Bohne ______

   Pads ______ Instant Kaffee ______

Abschnitt II:

In diesem Abschnitt der Befragung stellen wir überwiegend Fragen bezüglich Einstellungen und Meinungen. Wie bereits im ersten Fragebogen erwähnt, es gibt keine ‚richtigen' oder ‚falschen' Antworten. Bitte denken Sie sorgfältig über jede Frage nach. Das vollständige Ausfüllen des Fragebogens ist besonders wichtig für unsere Studie.

1. Was ist Ihnen beim **Kauf von Kaffee** wichtig?

   Antworten Sie bitte mit Zahlen zwischen 1 (ist mir sehr wichtig) und 7 (ist mir überhaupt nicht wichtig). Sie können Ihre Bewertung zwischen 1 und 7 abstufen.

	(1) sehr wichtig	(2)	(3)	(4)	(5)	(6)	(7) gar nicht wichtig
Beim Kauf von Kaffee ist mir wichtig, dass....							
die Produkte nachhaltig und ökologisch erzeugt sind							
die Produkte ohne Kinderarbeit hergestellt werden							
die Produzenten angemessene Preise erhalten							
die Produkte preiswert sind							
ich den Einkauf schnell erledigen kann							
die Produkte qualitativ hochwertig sind							
ein persönlicher Kontakt besteht und ich Beratung beim Einkauf erhalte							

2. Wie schmeckt **fair gehandelter Kaffee** im Vergleich zu normalem, nicht fair gehandelten, Kaffee? (bitte ankreuzen)

_____ besser _____ gleich gut _____ schlechter

3. Kaufen Sie **Fair Trade Produkte**? (bitte ankreuzen)

_____ JA _____ NEIN (Bitte bei Frage 6 weitermachen)

4. **Wie oft verzehren Sie** die folgenden fair gehandelten Produkte? (bitte ankreuzen)

	Mehrmals in der Woche	1 mal in der Woche	alle 2 Wochen	1 mal im Monat	Seltener	Nie
Schokolade						
Bananen						
Kaffee						
Tee						
Orangensaft						
Gewürze						
Honig						
Kakao						
Sonstiges:______						

5. **Wo kaufen Sie** fair gehandelte Produkte?

Antworten Sie bitte mit Zahlen zwischen 1 (hier kaufe ich immer) und 7 (hier kaufe ich nie). Sie können Ihre Bewertung zwischen 1 und 7 abstufen.

Ich kaufe fair gehandelte Produkte im...	(1) Hier kaufe ich immer	(2)	(3)	(4)	(5)	(6)	(7) Hier kaufe ich nie
Bioladen							
Supermarkt (Edeka, Rewe,...)							
Discounter (Aldi, Lidl, ...)							
Weltladen							
Biosupermarkt							
Kirche							
Spezialitätengeschäft							
Verbrauchermarkt (Real, ...)							

6. Angenommen, ein fair gehandeltes Produkt kostet **1 €** mehr als ein nicht fair gehandeltes: **wie viel muss** von diesem Euro bei den Erzeugern **ankommen**, damit Sie nicht den Eindruck haben, dass irgendwo Geld versickert? ______ Cent

7. Worin liegen Ihrer Meinung nach die Unterschiede zwischen einer Spende und fair gehandelten Produkten?

____

____

8. Spenden können über Produktkäufe generiert werden, indem Spendenorganisationen mit Markenartikelherstellern kooperieren, wie z.B. Dallmayr mit der Karl Heinz Böhm Stiftung Menschen für Menschen (bei dieser Kooperation werden von jedem verkauften Paket Dallmayr Ethiopia 5 Baumsetzlinge in Äthiopien gepflanzt). In wie weit stimmen Sie den folgenden Aussagen auf einer Skala von 1 (trifft voll zu) bis 7 (trifft gar nicht zu) zu? Sie können Ihre Bewertung zwischen 1 und 7 abstufen.

Spenden über Produktkäufe zu generieren, ist:	(1) trifft voll zu	(2)	(3)	(4)	(5)	(6)	(7) trifft gar nicht zu
Sinnvoll							
Marketinggag							
Unglaubwürdig							
Greenwashing der Unternehmen							
Ersetzt eine Spende an die entsprechende Nicht-Regierungs-Organisation (NGO)							
Ersetzt den Kauf von Fair Trade Produkten							
Ersetzt Spenden allgemein							
Eine solche Maßnahme des Corporate Social Responsibility (CSR) schafft Vertrauen in das Unternehmen							
Beruhigt das eigene Gewissen							

9. Haben Sie schon einmal an Hilfsorganisationen mit Bezug zu Entwicklungsländern gespendet? Spezielle Kollekten in der Kirche für Gemeinden oder Projekte in Entwicklungsländern zählen hierzu. ______JA ______NEIN

10. An welche Organisation(en) spenden Sie?

____

11. Wie viel haben Sie in den letzten 12 Monaten für Entwicklungshilfe gespendet?

____nichts ______unter 20 Euro ______20 bis unter 50 Euro

____50 bis unter 100 Euro ______100 bis unter 250 Euro ____mehr als 250 Euro

12. Wie viel muss von **1 €** Spende an eine Entwicklungshilfeorganisation bei den Empfängern ankommen, damit Sie nicht den Eindruck haben, dass irgendwo Geld versickert?

_____ Cent

13. Ein normaler Kaffee kostet 2,99 €. Ein Fair Trade Kaffee kostet 4,99 €.

Sind Sie bereit diesen Preis zu zahlen?
Fair Trade Kaffee: 4,99 € ____ JA ____ NEIN
Wären Sie auch bereit 5,99 € zu zahlen?
Fair Trade Kaffee: 5,99 € ____ JA ____ NEIN
Welchen Preis wären Sie ansonsten zu zahlen bereit?
Fair Trade Kaffee ____________________

14. Ein normaler Kaffee kostet 2,99 €. Ein Fair Trade Kaffee der zusätzlich Bio zertifiziert ist kostet 4,99 €. Sind Sie bereit diesen Preis zu zahlen?

BIO Fair Trade Kaffee: 4,99 € ____ JA ____ NEIN
Wären Sie auch bereit 5,99 € zu zahlen?
BIO Fair Trade Kaffee: 5,99 € ____ JA ____ NEIN
Welchen Preis wären Sie ansonsten zu zahlen bereit?
BIO Fair Trade Kaffee ____________________

15. Ein normaler Kaffee kostet 2,99 €. Ein normaler Kaffee von dem ein Teil der Verkaufserlöse an Menschen für Menschen (MFM) gespendet wird kostet 4,99 €. Sind Sie bereit diesen Preis zu zahlen?

MFM Kaffee: 4,99 € ____ JA ____ NEIN
Wären Sie auch bereit 5,99 € zu zahlen?
MFM Kaffee: 5,99 € ____ JA ____ NEIN
Welchen Preis wären Sie ansonsten zu zahlen bereit?
MFM Kaffee ____________________

16. Ein normaler Kaffee kostet 2,99 €. Ein biologisch erzeugter Kaffee kostet 3,99 €. Sind Sie bereit diesen Preis zu zahlen?

Bio Kaffee: 3,99 € ____ JA ____ NEIN
Wären Sie auch bereit 4,99 € zu zahlen?
Bio Kaffee: 4,99 € ____ JA ____ NEIN
Welchen Preis wären Sie ansonsten zu zahlen bereit?
Bio Kaffee ____________________

17. Inwieweit stimmen Sie den folgenden Aussagen zu? Kreuzen Sie bitte die Zahlen zwischen 1 (trifft voll zu) und 7 (trifft überhaupt nicht zu) an. Sie können Ihre Bewertung zwischen 1 und 7 abstufen.

	(1) trifft voll zu	(2)	(3)	(4)	(5)	(6)	(7) trifft gar nicht zu
Die Organisation an die ich spende, muss mit einem kontrollierten Siegel ausgezeichnet sein							
Ich spende regelmäßig während des gesamten Jahres für Menschen in Entwicklungsländern							
Ich spende besonders um Weihnachten herum							
Ich spende besonders bei Katastrophen in Entwicklungsländern							
Die Spendenquittung ist für mich ein Garant für die Glaubwürdigkeit der Spendenorganisation							
Eine Spendenquittung ist für mich ein zusätzlicher Anreiz zu spenden							
Ich bin durch Freunde auf die Organisation aufmerksam geworden an die ich heute spende							
Ich fühle mich armen Menschen in Entwicklungsländern verbunden							
Ich möchte anderen Menschen helfen, weil es mir gut geht							
Durch Spenden leiste ich meinen Beitrag zum Wohl anderer Menschen							
Ich leiste meinen Beitrag zum Wohl anderer Menschen, indem ich Fair Trade Produkte kaufe							
Ich spende für Entwicklungshilfeorganisationen, weil ich mit meiner Spende etwas bewirken kann							
Wenn ich Fair Trade Produkte kaufe handle ich im Einklang mit meinen religiösen Überzeugungen							
Wenn ich spende, handle ich im Einklang mit meinen religiösen Überzeugungen							
Ich bin bereit, für Fair Trade Produkte einen höheren Preis zu zahlen							
Es ist mir wichtig zu wissen, wie viel Geld von FT Produkten beim Erzeuger ankommt							
Ich habe Mitgefühl für arme Menschen in Entwicklungsländern							

	(1) trifft voll zu	(2)	(3)	(4)	(5)	(6)	(7) trifft gar nicht zu
Es ist mir wichtig zu wissen, wie viel % der Spenden beim Empfänger ankommt							
Die Organisationen, an die ich Spenden für Entwicklungsländer gebe, verwenden das Geld gut							
Ich spende lieber, als fair gehandelte Produkte zu kaufen							
Der Kauf von Fair Trade Produkten ist eigentlich nichts anderes als eine Art von Spende							
Meinen religiösen Überzeugungen werde ich auch gerecht, wenn ich nicht an Entwicklungshilfeorganisationen spende							
Ich spende nicht, weil die Organisationen, die Spenden für Entwicklungsländer sammeln, das Geld nicht gut verwenden							
Ich kaufe lieber FT Produkte als zu spenden							
Ich spende nicht für Entwicklungshilfe-organisationen, weil ich mit meiner Spende sowieso nichts bewirken kann							
Ich fühle mich verpflichtet, einen Beitrag zum Wohl der Menschen in Entwicklungsländern zu leisten							
Mit dem Kauf von Fair Trade Produkten kann ich etwas bewirken							
Meine Bekannten kaufen FT Produkte							
Fair Trade Organisationen verwenden das Geld gut							
Fair Trade passt auch zu Lidl, Aldi oder Plus							
Meinen religiösen Überzeugungen werde ich auch gerecht, wenn ich keine FT Produkte kaufe							
Fair Trade Organisationen verwenden das Geld nicht gut. Deshalb kaufe ich keine FT Produkte							
Ich habe Mitleid mit armen Menschen in Entwicklungsländern							
Ich vertraue Fair Trade Organisationen							
Ich vertraue Entwicklungshilfeorganisationen							

18. **Welches ist Ihre Lieblingsmarke bei Kaffee?**

____

ANGABEN ZUR PERSON

19. **Geschlecht**: _____Weiblich _____Männlich

20. **Wie alt** sind Sie? _____ Jahre

21. Sind Sie **Mitglied** in einer oder mehrerer der folgenden Organisationen und/oder Bereiche?

_____ Kirche (zahle Kirchensteuer) _____Umweltschutz _____ Partei _____Sportverein

_____Weltladen _____ Jugendarbeit _____Organisationen wie z.B. Greenpeace

22. Wie hoch ist ihr monatliches **Haushaltsnettoeinkommen**? Ich meine damit die Geldsumme, die für Ihren Haushalt nach Abzug der Steuern und Sozialversicherung übrig bleibt. Eine WG gilt nur dann als Haushalt, wenn gemeinsam gewirtschaftet (eingekauft) wird.

___unter 300 € ____300 bis 500 € ___500 bis 700 € ____700 bis 900 €

___900 bis 1100 € ____1100 bis 1300 € ____1300 bis 1500 € _____1500 bis 2000 €

___2000 bis 2600 € ____2600 bis 3600 € ____3600 bis 5000 € _____5000 und mehr €

23. **Wie viele Personen** leben in Ihrem Haushalt, Sie selbst eingeschlossen? _____

24. **Wie viele Kinder** (unter 18 Jahren) haben Sie? _____

25. **Wie viele Geschwister** haben Sie? _____

26. Welches ist Ihr höchster **Bildungsabschluss?**

_____Ohne Schulabschluss _____ Fach-/ Hochschulreife (Abitur)

_____Volks-/Hauptschulabschluss _____ Fach-/ Hochschulabschluss

_____Mittlere Reife (Realschulabschluss) _____Anderer Abschluss: welcher? _______

27. Welchen **Beruf** üben Sie aus?

_____ Schüler/in, Student/in, Azubi _____ Selbständige/r_____Pensionär

_____ Hausmann/frau _____ Rentner/in _____ Arbeiter/in

_____ Angestellte/r _____Beamte/r ____Derzeit nicht erwerbstätig

28. Ist die **Gegend, in der Sie wohnen**

_____ eher großstädtisch (ab 100.000 Einwohner, wie z.B. Bonn)
_____ eher kleinstädtisch (10.000 -100.000 Einwohner)
_____ eher ländlich

29. Wie beurteilen Sie die **Verfügbarkeit von Fair Trade Produkten** in Geschäften in Ihrer Nähe (ca. 10 min Fußweg)?

Sehr gut (1) (2) (3) (4) (5) Sehr schlecht

30. Wie schätzen Sie Ihre eigene **Lebenssituation** (nicht nur die finanzielle) ein?

Mir geht es sehr gut (1) (2) (3) (4) (5) Mir geht es sehr schlecht

Vielen Dank für Ihre Teilnahme!

9 Is there need for more transparency and efficiency in cause-related marketing [134]

Abstract

The popularity of ethical consumption is increasing. This has motivated firms to increasingly implement Cause-related Marketing (CrM) campaigns in Germany. But research reveals that especially German consumers are sceptical with regard to the amount of money donated to the good 'cause' by the enterprises. This can be explained by the limited information provided by CrM campaigns to consumers. In consequence, this can reduce consumers' willingness to purchase CrM products. Therefore, this study analyses whether the efficiency and transparency of a CrM campaign are important for consumers. The share of money reaching the cause relative to the product price consumers pay is taken as a proxy for efficiency while transparency is understood as the open communication of donated amounts on the product by label.

A consumer survey conducted in Germany in 2009 reveals that consumers have a great interest in the transparency of a CrM campaign. Furthermore, the study provides evidence that there is a gap between the levels of expected and requested efficiency of CrM donations. Consequently, firms should label the donation amount to meet consumers' transparency needs. Furthermore, to create a successful CrM campaign companies also have to consider that the amount of money earmarked for the good cause is of relevance for consumers.

Keywords: Cause-related Marketing, transparent labelling, donations efficiency

9.1 Introduction

Awareness regarding ethical issues[135] and sustainable development[136], such as fair wages for workers and recycling is growing. This is shaping consumption and purchase patterns in Germany regarding ethical consumption[137] (PARTOS 2009). Conscious consumers are concerned about the impact of their individual consumption. They strive to act in accordance

---

[134] This paper has been published in the International Journal on Food System Dynamics (2010), 1 (4): 366-381. Co-authors are Carola Grebitus and Monika Hartmann.

[135] Ethical issues can be manifold, e.g. social and environmental concerns such as health issues, labour standards, social justice, animal welfare and sustainable production methods. They coexist with 'traditional' consumers' decision making criteria such as price and quality (HARRISON et al. 2005).

[136] The Brundtland Report defines sustainable development as meeting the needs of today "without compromising the ability of future generations to meet their own needs" (UNITED NATIONS GENERAL ASSEMBLY 1987, chapter 2).

[137] Ethical consumption refers to a purchase based on an individual's sense of responsibility towards society and personal concerns for one or several ethical issues (HARRISON et al. 2005; DE PELSMACKER et al. 2005; TALLONTIRE et al. 2001).

with their moral code and consequentially place substantial value on ethical and sustainable issues (NIELSEN 2008). This is shown, for instance, by increasing sales volumes of Fair Trade (FT)[138] products in Germany[139] and consumers asking for sustainable production processes (e.g. organic farming) (HAVAS MEDIA 2009). For similar reasons, the application of Cause-related Marketing (CrM) campaigns has met with increasing interest.

CrM is a marketing tool, where the product purchase leads to a target-oriented donation regarding a designated cause which is promoted on the product by label. This means that each time a consumer purchases a CrM labelled product, money is donated to a charity organisation or a good cause. For example, in one campaign Germany's coffee producer Dallmayr is cooperating with the non-profit organization (NPO) 'Menschen für Menschen'. The campaign promotes that per coffee package sold five trees are planted in Ethiopia. In this regard, the campaign is close to Fair Trade in terms of the prevention of soil degradation and therefore sustainable production methods.

Hence, CrM products allow consumers to express their concerns about environmental and social issues, such as poverty in developing countries, fair producer prices and schooling for poor children, via daily shopping in a supermarket without the additional (transaction) costs of donating to charity. One can hypothesize that the level of spending efficiency would be relevant for consumers. But, for the average consumer an evaluation is only possible if the respective organisations and firms communicate the donated amount in a transparent manner.

Against this background, we aim to answer two questions. First: What is the amount of money consumers expect to be contributing to the 'cause' by purchasing the respective product? Second: Is this information of relevance to consumers? This issue – the share of money reaching the cause relative to the product price consumers pay – is in the following used as a proxy for efficiency of the CrM donation. Furthermore, we investigate whether transparency with respect to CrM is of importance to consumers.

The remainder of the paper is structured as follows. Section 2 provides background information on CrM. In the third section, we introduce the methodological background. In

[138] Fair Trade is an approach aiming to alleviate poverty and improving the livelihoods of small producers by the payment of so-called fair and sustainable, guaranteed minimum contract prices, by implementing social and environmental standards in all areas related to the production process of the traded goods, by improving market access and providing stability in trading relationships (GIOVANNUCCI and KOEKOEK 2003). Therefore, Fair Trade certified products are products guaranteeing a so-called fair price to producers of raw material such as coffee beans. Fair Trade certified products are considered as the typical ethical product.

[139] The sales volume of Fair Trade products were 213 Mio. € in 2008, which is an increase in sales of 50 % compared to 2007 (TRANSFAIR 2009).

section 4, the sample of the study is described and section 5 presents and discusses estimation results from the econometric analysis. The final section of the paper concludes and derives implications for further research needs.

9.2 Background on Cause-related Marketing

Expenditures for CrM by firms in the US increased from almost zero US$ in 1983[140] to around 1.57 billion US$ in 2009 (CHONG 2009). In Germany, CrM was only recently introduced as a marketing instrument (HUBER et al. 2008) and since the legal praxis changed[141] in 2004, the number of CrM campaigns has increased steadily (see Table 1) leading to a trend that is comparable to the US. Overall, more than 90 firms have offered CrM products in Germany since 2002. 35 % of these CrM promotions in Germany were undertaken by the food and beverage sector (OLOKO 2008).

Table 1: Number of CrM campaigns in Germany

Year	1998	2001	2002	2003	2004	2005	2006	2007	2008
Number	1	3	1	5	5	18	31	33	39

Source: Oloko (2009, p. 5).

9.2.1 Theoretical background regarding Cause-related Marketing

Definition of Cause-related Marketing

Manifold definitions for CrM are provided by the literature. There is general agreement that the one proposed by VARADARAJAN and MENON in 1988 is the most widely used and accepted in science (HUBER et al. 2008): “Cause-related marketing is the process of formulating and implementing marketing activities that are characterized by an offer from the firm to contribute a specified amount to a designated cause when customers engage in revenue-providing exchanges that satisfy organizational and individual objectives” (VARADARAJAN and MENON 1988, p. 60).[142]

[140] In 1983, the first promotion entitled as a CrM campaign was initiated by the credit card institute ‘American Express’ (ADKINS 1999). American Express announced it would spend 1 cent of each credit card transaction to the restoration of the Statue of Liberty. The card usage (plus 28 %) as well as the number of new customers (plus 45 %) increased considerably compared to the respective period in the previous year (WALL 1984 in VARADARAJAN and MENON 1988).

[141] See the novel of the German Act Against Unfair Competition (UWG) §4 in 2004 and BGH AZ. I ZR 55/02 from 22.09.2005 which allows advertising with social motives (ONLINE WERBERECHT 2010).

[142] Other definitions are e.g.: “commercial activities by which businesses and charities or causes form a partnership with each other to market an image, product or service for mutual benefit” (ADKINS 1999, p. 11) and the definition by EIKENBERRY (2009, p. 61) serving as a critique of the construct, CrM “adroitly serves two masters, earning profits for corporations while raising funds for charities”.

Firms' profits as well as the donation amount depend on the sales volumes of the CrM product under consideration which in turn is linked to consumers' willingness to buy these products. In this regard, a CrM campaign is linked to firm and brand, non-profit organisation (NPO) and consumers, respectively. Accordingly, the success of a CrM strategy depends on the interaction of these three actors, illustrated in Figure 1. The relationship exists only for the length of the CrM campaign and is in most cases limited to one specific product and one specific cause (e.g. Dallmayr Ethipia) (KOTLER and LEE 2005). The depicted triadic relationship can only be successful if it is a win-win-win situation for all involved groups leading to mutual benefits (ADKINS 1999). Nevertheless, the three actors have different motivations to take part in the CrM campaign.

Figure 1: The triadic relationship of actors of a CrM-campaign

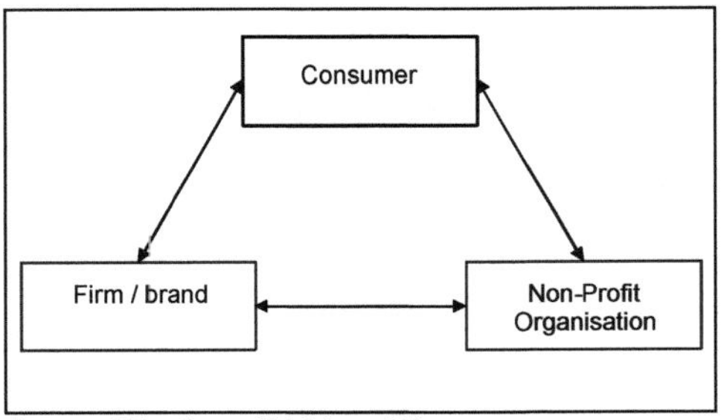

Source: Westberg (2004, p. 41).

Motivation of firms to launch CrM campaigns

WYMER and SAMU (2009) differentiate between two key motivations for firms to support causes by means of CrM promotions: altruism and self interest. The former implies that a business implements a CrM campaign because of its belief in the value of the cause. The latter motivation holds if a cause is supported with the aim to increase firms' profits in the short or long term. WYMER and SAMU (2009) assume that in reality both motivations play a role in most cases. Firms use CrM as a tool which allows the core business activities of trading to be integrated with the needs of a particular charity cause (MASON 2000). VARADARAJAN and MENON (1988) are less optimistic: for them CrM is an innovative form of corporate philanthropy which is exclusively profit-oriented.

From a marketing perspective successful CrM campaigns allow companies to perform well by doing well (VARADARAJAN and MENON 1988). CrM is a means to gain consumers' attention (CADBURY 2000), a precondition for selling products especially in saturated markets. An increasing share of consumers asks for and places considerable value on sustainability issues

(HAVAS MEDIA 2009). Firms take into account this development being aware of the power of consumers: the power of knowledge, purchase, protest and boycott (ADKINS 2004). Thus, they search for opportunities to effectively demonstrate their social commitment and social responsibility, e.g. by CrM campaigns, thereby differentiating their brand from those of competitors (BERGER et al. 1996; BROWN and DACIN 1997; WEBB and MOHR 1998). With such campaigns firms enable not only consumers but also other stakeholders to identify themselves with the corporation and its brands (ROY and GRAEFF 2003). In addition, employees' attitudes towards their company change for the better due to a CrM promotion as they feel proud of their company (ADKINS 2004). Thus, CrM allows companies to make their values meaningful to stakeholders and to take their consumer relationship well beyond a simple transaction-based relationship which only relies on price and functionality of the product (ADKINS 2006). To conclude, from firm's perspective CrM is a marketing tool that can be used to achieve many objectives (SINGH 2009). While some have been discussed here, additional ones are summarized in e.g. VARADARAJAN and MENON (1988).

Motivation of charity organisations to become involved in CrM activities

Non-profit organisations (NPOs) face declining funds from government agencies (BERGLIND and NAKATA 2005). CrM allows charity organisations to raise additional resources that permit NPOs to maintain or even increase their activities. Furthermore, CrM leads to non-monetary benefits as it helps to inform consumers (EIKENBERRY 2009). NPOs enjoy and gain far greater awareness for their projects through the media attention, as their logo can be found on the CrM products and the marketing material. This potentially increases the number of supporters, advocates and volunteers for the causes (BERGLIND and NAKATA 2005). The CrM promotion by a well-known and esteemed business partner increases not just the publicity but potentially also the profile of the NPO. Thus, NPOs lend credibility not only to firms but benefit from the (high) reputation of the company they collaborate with. In addition, the cooperation between companies and NPOs leads to knowledge transfer from the former to the latter, for example with respect to conducting efficient marketing campaigns.

Motivation of consumers to purchase CrM products

The literature on consumers' perception and motivation to purchase CrM products is still scarce (WYMER and SAMU 2009). According to WEBB and MOHR (1998), consumers evaluate CrM campaigns in general with mostly positive attitudes and express purchase intentions. However, the authors do not provide any reasons. One explanation for consumers' willingness to purchase CrM products is that the pairing of cause and brand creates additional benefits to consumers. Purchasing CrM products provides them with the feeling 'to make a difference in the world'. In addition it "makes philanthropy simple and convenient" (EIKENBERRY 2009, p. 53).[143] Nevertheless, research reveals that elements of the promotion, such as type of product, sum of donation and the fit between product and cause, can make a difference.

The expositions above reveal that there are specific reasons for all three stakeholders to become involved in CrM activities. In the following the focus will be on the perspective of consumers to better understand the determinants that motivate them to purchase CrM products.

9.2.2 Transparency as a critical success factor for effective CrM

According to BLUMBERG and CONRAD (2006), success factors for CrM are relevance, commitment, integrity and credibility. In this context, relevance means that the target group is addressed specifically – emotionally and rationally. Commitment considers that the additional utility consumers gain through the purchase of a CrM product will be transferred and added to the CrM brand only in a long-term perspective. Thus, investments in CrM most likely will not lead to returns in the short term and firms have to be patient. First, integrity concerns the fit of the brand and the charity organisation. Second, it implies that CrM activities have to be fully integrated in the overall marketing mix (MASON 2000). Credibility is vital for the success of a CrM campaign. If consumers mistrust the altruistic motives of the firm, such a campaign can have a negative influence on the firm's and brand's reputation and might lead to a decline in sales. Especially, if the gap between the sum consumers expect to be contributed and the amount actually donated by the companies is too large this could lead to mistrust among consumers once they become aware of this. In the long run, this might decrease their willingness to pay for those products in general. Also, firms' reputation could be harmed (see e.g. WEBB and MOHR 1998). The more familiar consumers are with CrM the lower their scepticism (WEBB and MOHR 1998; SINGH 2009). Thus, if consumers believe they have sufficient knowledge about the CrM activity, the campaign becomes more trustworthy (SINGH 2009). Open communication, i.e. transparency, about the donation amount creates knowledge. Hence, transparency is the identified crucial element to secure credibility (WEBB and MOHR 1998; SINGH 2009). According to OLSEN et al. (2003), consumers are often confused about the donation amounts in CrM programs. Two general options to communicate CrM measures

[143] Note that several authors such as EIKENBERRY (2009) and SMITH and HIGGINS (2000) argue that this type of consumption is not philanthropy. Accordingly, this tool to achieve philanthropic efforts in tandem with business objectives and commercial interests can be considered strategic philanthropy.

exist: providing information as 1) project-specific donations (project-oriented donations) and 2) exclusive monetary terms e.g. in euros or dollars – regarding the money donated in absolute terms or percent of retail price or profit. The use of project-specific donations implies that own currencies like e.g. 'schooling hours provided', 'wells built' or 'trees planted' are defined and reported. In this case, the actual amount donated is generally not known to the consumer as it is difficult for a consumer to assess the cost of 'providing a schooling hour', 'building a well' or 'planting a tree'. Thus, this information does not lead to transparency. This can be illustrated with the example of the Dallmayr Ethiopia CrM campaign: the campaign promotes that per coffee package sold five trees are planted in Ethiopia. If German consumers assume that a tree in Ethiopia is as expensive as in Germany, this type of labelling is misleading[144] and intransparent. For the consumer it is difficult to know the costs of e.g. five trees and how those costs relate to the sales volume the firm earned by the CrM promotion. In contrast, a very transparent form of labelling is indicating a donation amount in absolute units. This was done e.g. by the furniture company IKEA in a CrM promotion in 2007. The company informed consumers that from each soft toy sold 1 € would be donated (UNICEF 2010). Other formats used by businesses are percentage-of-the-profit (e.g. the product red initiative (JOINRED 2010)) and percentage-of-the-sales-price. According to OLSEN et al. (2003), the former is problematic because consumers have to calculate two steps to arrive at the final amount of money donated: first estimate the profit as a percentage of the price and then calculate the amount donated as a percentage of the profit. But usually people take computational shortcuts and fail to take into account that profit is only a small fraction of price. This leads to overestimation in the case of percentage-of-the-profit formats. Furthermore, consumers often do not know the actual profit level of a firm or brand and overestimate profit in general. In addition, in most cases it remains unclear whether net or gross profit is meant (OLSEN et al. 2003).

9.2.3 Previous studies on Cause-related Marketing

So far, studies with a focus on the German market have primarily looked at general issues of CrM such as consumers' knowledge (sources) of CrM campaigns and their general opinion towards CrM (see e.g. HUBER et al. 2008). OLOKO (2008) also investigated consumers' assumption with respect to the firm's intentions using CrM and to the share of money dedicated to the cause by the companies. The findings reveal that German consumers are

[144] According to MENSCHEN FÜR MENSCHEN (2009), five trees have a value of € 0.12. No further costs incur, because coffee farmers plant the trees without being paid.

sceptical with regard to the "fair" amount of money spent on the "cause" as well as with regard to the altruistic motives of firms (see OLOKO 2008). Also, according to SINGH (2009), scepticism with respect to CrM arises primarily because customers question the company's motivations for participating in such actions, they have doubts concerning unselfish motives of firms. This is in line with results of HAVAS MEDIA (2009), which indicate that consumers mistrust the sustainability efforts of companies in general. Consumers believe that CrM is primarily used as a marketing tool and a fig leaf. This may be partly because little information is provided in CrM campaigns on how much of the sales price is spent on the 'cause' by the respective organization or on the success of the campaign. Moreover, CrM campaigns rarely disclose details of the agreement between the NPO and the company (BERGLIND and NAKATA 2005).[145] Hence, a great number of CrM promotions lack transparency.

While such a transparency requirement is not included in the German Act Against Unfair Competition (UWG) (ONLINE WERBERECHT 2010), ADKINS (2004) identifies transparency in general to be crucial for a firm's credibility. This is an important finding, considering that credibility is identified as one of the four critical success factors for effective CrM (BLUMBERG and CONRAD 2006). In this respect, one key aspect of successful CrM is the way the donation is communicated. OLOKO (2008) shows that providing information on **project-specific donations** in form of own currencies lacks transparency (see also discussion above). But also if information is provided in percent of the retail price and thus as exclusive monetary terms, most consumers are confused as OLSEN et al. (2003) show based on a series of five studies. Though highly educated people are in general able to convert information provided in percent into the respective absolute numbers and vice versa, this does not hold for the population at large. Other studies (see e.g. DALY 1976; ESTELAM 1999; SCHAPIRA et al. 1990) also reveal that for many consumers e.g. 10 % of 5 Euro and 50 cents is not the same. Based on a content analysis, OLSEN et al. (2003) found that percentage-of-the-profit formats are used five times more often than percentage-of-the-sales-price formats. Up to now, there is no study available that has researched the dominant reporting format for CrM campaigns in Germany. However, as has been shown above, examples for several kinds of donation formats exist.

Several studies investigated the impact of the donation volume on consumers' attitude and purchase intention of CrM products. DAHL and LAVACK (1995 in HAJJAT 2003) show that

---

[145] In Norway (see SINGH 2009) the labelling and communication of the monetary amount donated to the cause is not allowed. This does not hold for Germany.

CrM is more effective with larger donations to the NPO or the charity cause than with smaller ones. In the case of small contributions, consumers are more likely to believe that the company exploits the NPO and is primarily driven by egoistic rather than altruistic motives. Consumers' disappointment will likely be negatively reflected in their attitudes and purchase intentions of the product/brand (HAIJAT 2003). In contrast, HOLMES and KILBANE (1993 in HAJJAT 2003) find no significant differences in consumer responses to different levels of charitable giving or price levels. In their study, consumers' attitudes towards the product as well as their purchase intentions were not influenced in a negative way, even if the increases in price relative to the donation being made to the NPO were disproportionate.

Some studies indicate that consumers' interpretation of CrM depends on their level of scepticism towards the CrM claim (WEBB and MOHR 1998) which differs from individual to individual. Scepticism in WEBB and MOHR's (1998) study was formed through four issues: First, consumers distrust the company's claim to donate the promised amount of money to the NPO. Second, consumers perceive the donated amount of money as small. Third, the relation between firms' gains by increased sales versus the money collected for the charity is perceived to be unfair. And fourth, consumers fear they will be forced to buy products that are of low quality or overpriced. This reveals that the money dedicated to the cause as well as the transparent communication of this is of importance for sceptical consumers.

Against this background, this study will investigate whether the efficiency and transparency of promotions are important issues for consumers with regard to CrM. In addition, we will also examine whether consumers with a high risk perception are more sceptic towards CrM products.

9.3 Methodological background

We investigate (i) whether consumers want products to carry a label indicating the percentage and/or absolute amount of money being donated to the 'cause', (ii) how much money consumers think should be contributed to the 'cause' in the case of CrM, and (iii) how much money consumers assume companies actually spend on the 'cause'. To analyse determinants that shape those attitudes, we apply ordered logit models. As we are measuring the attitude towards CrM on a 7-point Likert scale, we need a model for ordered categorical response such as the ordered logit model. Because ordered categorical response is a natural extension of a binary response, such data can be analysed using a generalization of the logistic regression model (COLLET 2003). In this model the probabilities of each outcome (e.g. strongly agree, moderately agree, strongly disagree), conditional on the independent variables (such as income, education) are modeled using the Weibull distribution (STOCK and WATSON 2004). In the following the ordered logit model will be explained.

Suppose U_i^m is the utility that consumer i derives from holding the attitude m which can be expressed as follows:

$$U_i^m = X_i\beta^m + \varepsilon_i^m \,;\; i = 1,\cdots,n\,; m = 1,\cdots \qquad (1)$$

where X_i is the design matrix which is a row vector of the ith consumer's characteristics. These characteristics include socio-demographics and attitudes. β^m is the coefficient associated with X_i. And ε_i^m is the residual error term that is not captured by design matrix X_i. There are n consumers and M attitudes.

In many situations, the respondents are not asked to respond to U directly. Instead, they are given a set of possible answers. Consumers choose the option that most closely corresponds to their response to the question. For example, for attitude m (here e.g. donation amount should be labelled), consumer i is asked to choose among the seven categories: agree very strongly ($y_i^m = 7$), agree strongly ($y_i^m = 6$), agree ($y_i^m = 5$), neither agree nor disagree ($y_i^m = 4$), disagree ($y_i^m = 3$), disagree strongly ($y_i^m = 2$), and disagree very strongly ($y_i^m = 1$).

The ordered logit model is based on the idea of the cumulative logit which relies on the concept of the cumulative probability. Let C_{ij}^m denote the probability that the ith individual is in the jth or higher category for attitude m:

$$C_{ij}^m = \Pr ob(y_i^m \le j) = \sum_{k=1}^{j} \Pr ob(y_i^m = k) \qquad (2)$$

Equation 2 can be transferred into the cumulative logit for attitude m:

$$\text{logit}(C_{ij}^m) = \log\left(\frac{C_{ij}^m}{1 - C_{ij}^m}\right) = \alpha_j^m - \beta^m X_i. \qquad (3)$$

In this paper consumers' attitude is expressed in degree of agreement (from agree very strongly to disagree very strongly) to measure the corresponding latent utilities.

9.4 The sample

Data were collected via a written survey with n = 217 consumers in Germany in 2009. Participants were recruited from the general public according to quotas on gender, age, and education level. Table 2 describes participants' socioeconomic characteristics. Compared to the German population young and highly educated people are overrepresented in the sample.

Table 2: Sample characteristics

Variable	*Specification*	*% of the sample (N=217)*	*% of the population (Year 2007)*
Gender	Female	53.6	51.0
	Male	46.4	49.0
Age[1]	18-24 years	11.5	9.9
	25-34 years	23.4	14.5
	35-44 years	20.1	20.4
	45-54 years	19.6	17.6
	55-64 years	17.2	14.0
	older than 64 years	8.1	23.4
Income[1] (N=214)	less than 500 €	16.0	3.3
	500 to 1299 €	30.6	27.1
	1300 to 1999 €	24.1	24.5
	2000 to 3599 €	19.6	2000 to 4500 €: 33.8
	3600 to 4999 €	7.0	
	greater than 5000 €	2.0	> 4500 €: 5.4
Education	Without any graduation	0.0	2.9
	Low school education	19.4	42.9
	Medium school education	26.3	26.4
	University entrance diploma	27.6	27.7
	University degree	23.0	

[1] Compared to German statistical office year 2005.

Source: authors' calculations; StBA 2007; StBA 2008.

9.5 Empirical results

Consumers' desire for transparent CrM labelling

To start with the empirical analysis, we investigate whether German consumers want CrM products to carry a label that indicates the amount of money being spent on the CrM cause – in percent and/or as the absolute amount. [146] A seven-point scale with 1: I strongly agree to 7: I strongly disagree was applied. Results show that in general respondents are very interested in having the information labelled. 71 % agree or strongly agree (Top 2 answers) that such a label should provide the information in percent (M = 2.1; SD = 1.5) and 64 % agree or strongly agree that absolute figures are appropriate (M = 2.3; SD = 1.6). Both answers are weakly correlated with 0.3 at a significance level of 0.001. The difference between the means is not significant. 60 % agreed or strongly agreed on both questions. Thus, we conclude that most consumers would like to be informed about the amount of money spent on the cause by the firm but that they are indifferent regarding the way the information is provided.

[146] The German questionnaire will be provided by the authors upon request.

Determinants of interest in transparency of CrM labelling

To gain deeper insight into the characteristics of those consumers who are interested in the information, we performed a k-means cluster analysis to group respondents according to these two questions. 149 persons are classified in cluster 1 and 61 in cluster 2. In the first cluster all respondents indicated that the donation amount should be labelled in percent of the retail price (Top-2-boxes 100 %). The compliance to labelling this share in absolute figures is less strong (80 % Top-2-boxes). Respondents attached to cluster 2 are not interested in labelling as a percentage share (0 % Top-2-boxes) and only a small share of them is interested in the absolute figures (Top-2-boxes 28 %). This reveals that those who attach less importance to transparency are grouped in cluster 2. A Kruskal Wallis test indicates that there is a statistically significant difference among the two clusters.

To analyse whether the socioeconomic characteristics age, gender, household size, presence of children under the age of 18 in the household, respondents' education level and income determine consumer segmentation with regard to the type of labeling a logistic regression model is applied. Results reveal that none of the socioeconomic characteristics significantly influence participants' affiliation to one of the two segments. Therefore, we assumed that other behavioural factors and attributes[147] may be able to explain preference for labels regarding donations and might allow a characterisation of the two clusters. We tested this assumption and incorporated additional items – "paying attention to product information", "buying CrM" and "requesting donation of a 5 € CrM coffee" – in the analysis. But again, no significant differences regarding the two clusters could be identified. Finally, we applied a risk perception scale from the domain-specific risk taking scale by Weber (2003). For a series of statements the risk perception of consumers was measured on a scale from 5 (high risk) to 1 (low risk). A risk perception index was then calculated as an unweighted average of the obtained scores over all statements. We expected that people who perceive a greater number of events as highly risky would request information on CrM's efficiency rather than others. However, the item "Risk Perception" did not show a significant influence on differences regarding the two clusters.

In the next step, we calculate a labelling index as the sum of the answers to the labelling in percent and in the absolute figures statement. This index ranges from 2 (very strong agreement on labelling in percent and in absolute figures) to 14 (both labelling methods are

[147] For a variable description, see Table A1 in the Appendix.

not of interest for the participant who gave two times a seven as answer). We use an ordered logit model to analyse whether socioeconomic factors and risk perception influence the interest in a labelling scheme using the labelling index as the dependent variable. As Table 3 reveals, age, gender and university degree significantly influence interest in labelling. Female and elderly consumers are more interested in the provision of information than men and younger consumers. Also, the better educated shoppers are, the more they desire the labelling. This is in line with previous findings in the literature where education showed a positive impact on the interest in using labels (e.g. NAYGA et al. 1998). Furthermore, we included respondents' attitude towards the efficiency of Fair Trade (*Effi_FT*) and donations (*Effi_Donation*) as dummy variables (equal to 1 if respondent requests a higher than average efficiency of FT, i.e. if respondent requests a higher than average efficiency of donations, 0 otherwise). We assume that consumers interested in a high efficiency of Fair Trade and donations to charity organisations are also more interested in the efficiency of CrM and thus ask for information about this on the product itself. However, both variables have no significant influence in this model.

Table 3: Influence of socioeconomic factors and risk perception on interest in labelling on CrM products – an ordered logit model

	Coef.	Std. Err.	z value [a]	
Effi_Donation	-0.37	0.48	-0,76	
Effi_FT	0.02	0.48	0.04	
Risk Personality	-0.18	0.30	-0.61	
Age class	-0.11	0.06	-2.01	**
Female	-0.54	0.33	-1.66	*
Children < 18	0.32	0.29	1.10	
HH size	-0.06	0.16	-0.37	
Low edu	-1.36	0.1	-1.38	
Medium edu	-0.84	0.89	-0.95	
High edu	-1.27	0.92	-1.38	
University degree	-1.66	0.92	-1.79	*
Income	0.03	0.08	0.38	

[a] p<0.1 =*, p<0.05 =*, p<0.01 =***, n.s. = not significant.
Number of observations: 151, Wald chi^2 (12) = 19.88, Prob>chi^2 = 0.07, Log pseudo likelihood = -286.13, Pseudo R^2 = 0.03.

Source: authors' calculations.

Consumers' expected efficiency of CrM

We are interested in consumers' general expectation regarding the share of the price of a CrM product donated to the cause. Results are illustrated in figure 4.

Figure 2: Consumers' expectations regarding the efficiency of CrM promotions

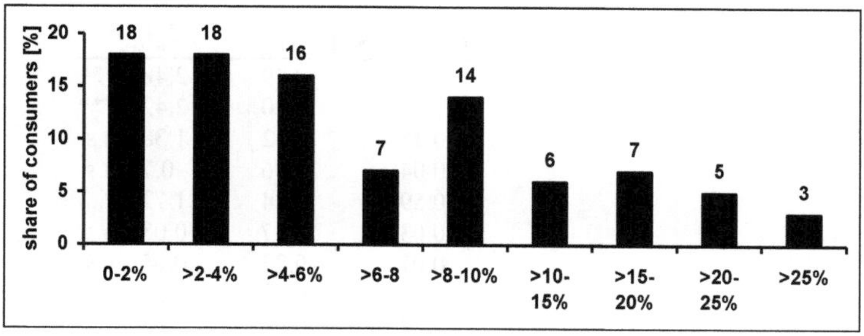

Source: authors' calculations.

The results reveal that 73 % of the respondents expect that less than 10 % of the price of the CrM product is donated to the cause (see Figure 2).

Determinants of expected efficiency of CrM

An ordered logit model shows which factors influence consumers' expectations regarding the efficiency of CrM (Table 4). Factors significantly influencing consumers' expectations are whether consumers desire a high efficiency for FT (more than the on average mentioned 0.74 € should reach the FT producer if the FT products costs 1 € more than a non FT product) and a high efficiency of monetary donations to charity.[148] While the first has a positive influence the latter has a negative one. This means that consumers requesting an above average efficiency of FT expect CrM to be more efficient as well. Those respondents expecting donations to be efficient expect CrM to have a low efficiency. This shows that the reputation of charity organisations can be harmed by participation in a CrM campaign. Furthermore, female respondents as well as respondents with low, medium and very high education levels expect a significantly higher CrM efficiency level. Other socioeconomic characteristics, such as age and income as well as whether consumers are characterised by a high risk personality or a high desire for transparency of CrM campaigns, proved not to significantly influence the expected efficiency level.

[148] Requested efficiency of FT and donations was introduced in the ordered logit model as a dummy variable with 0 for those respondents that request, compared to all survey participants, a below average efficiency level and 1 for those that expect an above average efficiency level for FT and donations, respectively.

Table 4: Factors influencing consumers' expectation of CrM efficiency – an ordered logit model

	Coeff.	Std. Err.	z-value [a]	
Effi_ Donation	-1.21	0.49	-2.48	***
Effi_ FT	1.20	0.50	2.42	***
Risk Personality	0.45	0.32	1.38	n.s.
Age class	0.04	0.06	0.7	n.s.
Female	0.59	0.34	1.72	*
Children < 18	-0.03	0.37	0.08	n.s.
HH size	0.01	0.22	0.05	n.s.
Low edu	1.74	0.69	2.51	***
Medium edu	1.22	0.63	1.92	**
High edu	0.83	0.66	1.25	n.s.
University degree	1.58	0.68	2.32	**
Income	-0.03	0.10	-0.28	n.s.
Labelling Index	-0.02	0.06	-0.44	n.s.

Note: for the variable description see Table A1 in the Appendix.
[a] p<0.1 =*, p<0.05 =*, p<0.01 =***, n.s. = not significant.
Number of observations: 149, Wald $chi^2(13) = 26.27$, Prob > $chi^2 = 0.0$, Log-pseudolikelihood = -294.77 Pseudo $R^2 = 0.04$.

Source: authors' calculations.

Consumers' requested efficiency of CrM

While the previous analysis focused on the CrM donation amount *expected* by consumers we were also interested in the share of money consumers *request* to reach the indicated cause. This issue is addressed posing a question using the example of coffee. Respondents were asked how much from a 5 € coffee should be spent on the CrM cause so that consumers would be willing to support such a campaign by buying the coffee. The results, illustrated in Figure 3, show that about 50 % of the respondents would support a CrM campaign if at least 1 € is given to the cause. Only 12 % are willing to buy the product if the donation is below 50 cents.

The results of Figure 3 are to be interpreted in the framework of market prices for coffee at the time of the survey. The only available CrM coffee in Germany in 2009 was Dallmayr Ethiopia with a minimum price of 5.29 €. However, coffee prices were in general rather low that year. Aggressive promotions were common that year: even coffee from companies like Dallmayr or Mövenpick had been available at times for a price below 3 €. Thus, 5 € was likely to be considered to be a high price for coffee in 2009 by most consumers. From this point of view, the request that 1 € or more has to be devoted to the 'cause' seems reasonable. Nevertheless, as mentioned above in the case of Dallmayr Ethiopia, it was indicated that per pack of coffee sold, five trees would be planted in Ethiopia. As discussed before, the NPO

Menschen für Menschen participating in the CrM promotion informed the authors that the value of five trees is € 0.12. This is much lower than the donation amount consumers think is appropriate if a coffee is sold at a price of 5 €. Hence, it seems reasonable to assume that consumers knowledgeable about the price of the five trees would have some doubt regarding the fair price of the Dallmayr coffee.

Figure 3: Consumers' requested efficiency for a CrM labelled coffee of 5 €

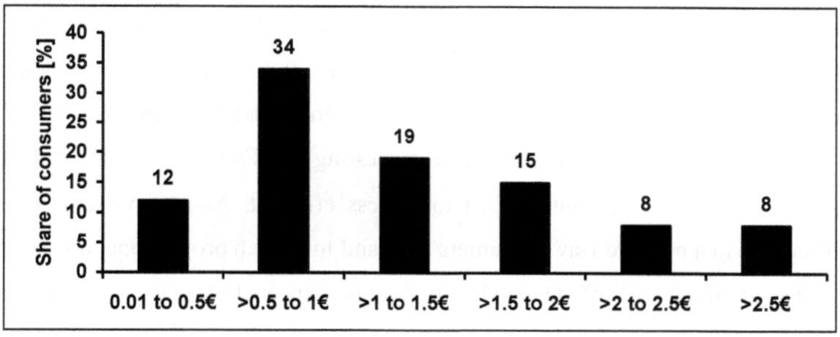

Source: authors' calculations.

As coffee prices are especially low at discounters, it can be assumed that price conscious consumers who primarily buy their coffee at those stores require a higher amount to be donated from a 5 € coffee than those consumers who are used to paying more for their coffee. However, a chi-square test revealed no significant differences between the donation requested between those 50 % of respondents who shop for coffee very often and often at the discounter and those survey participants who primarily buy their coffee in e.g. speciality stores and supermarkets.

Because the question regarding the expected efficiency was not framed for an example of a specific food product the results between the *requested* level (targeting the example of coffee) and the *expected* share are not directly comparable. Nevertheless, the results are striking as 73 % of the respondents expect that less than 10 % of the price of the CrM product is donated to the cause (see Figure 2) but in the case of coffee only 12 % would have been willing to buy a 5 € coffee if the donated amount was less than 0.5 € and thus 10 % of the price (compare Figure 3). This reveals a strong gap between requested and expected efficiency and might be one explanation for the rather low share of only 20 % of respondents who so far have bought CrM products. It seems that consumers simply do not trust CrM to use the money efficiently. The difference between the 'required' and 'expected' level of donation is likely to cause problems with regard to the acceptance of CrM in the future as well.

Determinants of requested efficiency of CrM

Based on an ordered logit model potential determinants of the requested CrM efficiency level are analysed (see Table 5). With the exception of the presence of children under 18 in the household (which influences the request positively) none of the socioeconomic characteristics nor the higher than average risk perception included in the model proved to be significant. Furthermore, we included respondents' attitudes towards the efficiency of Fair Trade and donations. Both variables significantly influence the requested CrM donation level: those expecting that from every euro they donate to charity more than 0.76 € (this was the average requested share; see also Table A1 in the appendix) reaches the cause also request a higher share of a 5 € CrM coffee to reach the cause. Those requesting that Fair Trade be more than average efficient at the same time request CrM to be less efficient. Another variable that significantly influences in a positive way consumers' demand for a high proportional donation is consumers' expectation of CrM efficiency. The higher the expected efficiency, the higher the requested efficiency.

Table 5: Potential determinants of requested CrM efficiency level – an ordered logit model

	Coef.	Std. Err.	z value [a]	
Dummy_Effi_Donation	1.05	0.42	2.51	***
Dummy_Effi_FT	-0.74	0.41	-1.82	**
Risk Personality	0.29	0.32	0.91	n.s.
Age class	-0.04	0.06	-0.65	n.s.
Female	0.29	0.37	0.79	n.s.
Children < 18	0.56	0.30	1.88	**
HH size	-0.28	0.19	-1.44	n.s.
Low edu	1.37	2.04	0.67	n.s.
Medium edu	1.79	1.99	0.90	n.s.
High edu	2.07	2.03	1.02	n.s.
University degree	1.19	2.02	0.55	n.s.
Income	0.01	0.11	0.08	n.s.
Labelling Index	-0.04	0.06	-0.65	n.s.
Expected efficiency of CrM	0.23	0.08	2.94	***

Note: for the variable description, see Table E in the Appendix.
[a] $p<0.1$ =*, $p<0.05$ =**, $p<0.01$ =***, n.s. = not significant.
Number of observations: 147, Wald chi^2 (14) = 25.16, Prob>chi^2 = 0.03, Log pseudo likelihood = -229.81, Pseudo R^2 = 0.05.

Source: authors' calculations.

Gender differences in expected and requested CrM efficiency

Women are considered to be more compassionate and emphatic than men. Furthermore, they are regarded to be more willing to help others (Wymer and Samu 2009). Thus, it can be assumed that they attach more importance to a high amount of the 5 € coffee being donated to the 'cause'. Our results show that differences exist between male and female participants (see Table 6). Females expect the share of the CrM donation relative to the retail price to be higher (mean 4.11) than men (mean 3.33) as table 6 illustrates (part A). A Levene Test reveals that the variances differ significantly and according to the t-test the difference between the means is significant. Also with respect to the requested efficiency, which is measured as the amount a company has to donate to the cause in order for the respondent to be willing to purchase a coffee for 5 €, significant differences between females and males can be reported (see table 6 part B). Female respondents request a significantly higher amount of donation if the coffee costs 5 € (mean 3.20) than men (mean 2.77).

Table 6: Gender differences with respect to expected and requested CrM efficiency

	Gender	N	Mean	Std. Dev.	Std. Error Mean	Levene's Test for Equality of Variances	F [a]	t [a]
A) Expected efficiency of CrM								
	female	102	4.11	2.4	.241	equal var. assumed	3.71*	
	male	95	3.33	2.1	.216	equal var. not assumed		2.418**
B) Requested donation of a 5 € CrM coffee								
	female	107	3.20	1.4	.138	equal var. assumed	.089	2.106**
	male	94	2.77	1.5	.151			

[a] p<0.1 =*, p<0.05 =*, p<0.01 =***.
A) 7 point scale from 1 = I fully agree to 7 = I do not agree at al.
B) Ordinal scale (6 levels from 1: 0.01 to 0.5 €, 2: >.5 to 1 €, 3: >1 to 1.5 €, 4: >1.5 to 2 €, 5: >2 to2.5 and 6: >2.5 €).

Source: authors' calculations.

9.6 Conclusions

CrM campaigns, though still of marginal relevance in Germany, reveal strong growth rates. This study provides insights into recent developments and key motives for companies, NPOs and consumers for supporting those activities. So far, most firms have provided only little information on their CrM campaigns. Therefore, in the empirical part of the paper we first investigate whether consumers have a preference for transparency and identify factors influencing those preferences. As information on CrM campaigns, e.g. amount of money donated to the cause, is a precondition for consumers to be able to evaluate the efficiency of CrM campaigns we secondly analyse consumers' expectations and requests regarding CrM efficiency and the respective determinants.

Our results reveal that though differences exists among consumers regarding the preferred labelling format, the overwhelming share of consumers is interested in obtaining information on the donation provided by the firm to the NPO/cause. Using an ordered logit model to examine determinants of the interest in more transparency regarding CrM campaigns leads to the conclusion that women, elderly and highly educated people are significantly more interested compared to other shoppers. However, the explanatory power of the model is restricted by a poor model fit.

The study also reveals that the majority of consumers (73 %) expect firms to donate less than 10 percent of the retail price to the good cause, while given the example of a CrM labelled coffee of 5 € only 12 percent of the respondents would be willing to buy this coffee if 10 % of the price is dedicated to the good cause. Though both results are not strictly comparable they lead to the conclusion that a strong gap between requested and expected efficiency exists. This might explain the very low share of only 20 % of respondents who purchased CrM products in the past. Analysing the determinants of consumers' expectation and requests regarding efficiency does not provide a clear picture. Socioeconomic factors prove to be of limited influence. Gender and education significantly influence consumers' expectation and children under 18 significantly impact consumers' request regarding CrM efficiency. The only variables significantly influencing both models, though neither in a consistent nor in a plausible way, are consumers' request for charity and Fair Trade donations to be efficient. Overall those models also suffer from a low explanatory power and insufficient model fit. The comparison of expected and requested efficiency of CrM donations gives evidence that there is a gap between the share of money consumers desire to reach the cause and the share of money they believe is reaching the cause in reality. This might decrease the acceptance of CrM promotions and therefore the success of CrM campaigns. Overall, as stated by 60 % of the respondents; the amount of money donated by means of CrM products should be indicated on the product either in absolute figures or relative to the retail price.

In summary, the study provides evidence that in order to meet consumers' transparency needs labelling of the donation amount is needed. This will increase the success of CrM campaigns. However, companies also have to consider that the level of money devoted to the good cause is of relevance for consumers.

9.7 References

ADKINS, S. (1999): *Cause Related Marketing, Who cares wins*. Oxford: Butterworth-Heinemann.

ADKINS, S. (2004): Cause Related Marketing: Who Cares Wins. In: *CSR: the business case*: 50-55. Available from: http://www.iccuk.net/csrpdf/CSR%20the%20business%20case/Cause%20Related %20Marketing%20who%20cares%20wins.pdf, [accessed 2010-01-08].

ADKINS, S. (2006): Cause Related Marketing: Putting your marketing where your values are. *Market Leader*, 1-6.

BARONE, M. J., MIYAZAKI, A. D. and TAYLOR, K. A. (2000): The influence of cause-related marketing on consumer choice: does one good turn deserve another? *Journal of the Academy in Marketing Science*, 28 (2): 248-262.

BERGER, I. E., CUNNIGHAM, P. H. and KOZINETS, R. V. (1996): The processing of cause-related Marketing claims: cues, biases or motivators? *American Marketing Association*, Summer 1996: 71-72.

BERGLIND, M. and NAKATA, C. (2005): Cause-related marketing: More buck than bang? *Business Horizons*, 48: 443-453.

BLUMBERG, M. and CONRAD, C. (2006): *Good Brand 2006: Gutes tun und davon profitieren? Ethisches Verbraucherverhalten und Cause Related Marketing in Deutschland.* Bremen: Brands & Values.

BROWN, T. J. and DACIN, P. A. (1997): The company and the product: corporate associations and consumer product responses. *Journal of Marketing*, 61 (1): 68-84.

CADBURY, D. (2000): Foreword by Sir Dominic Cadbury. In: Adkins, S. (Ed.): *Cause Related Marketing – Who cares wins.* Oxford: Butterworth-Heinemann: vii-viii.

CHONG, R. (2009): Cause-Related Marketing: Just Plain Ol' Marketing? *Huffington Post*, 13.01.2010.

COLLETT, D. (2003): *Modeling Binary Data.* 2nd ed. Boca Raton: Chapman and Hall/CRC.

CREYER, E. and ROSS, W. JR. (1996): The Impact of Corporate Behavior on Perceived Product Value. *Marketing Letters*, 7 (2): 173-185.

DAHL, D. and LAVACK, A. (1995): Cause-Related Marketing: Impact of Size of Corporate Donation and Size of Cause-Related Promotion on Consumer Perceptions and Participation. In: Stewart, D. and Vilcassim, N. (Eds): *1995 AMA Winter Educators' Conference: Marketing Theory and Applications*, 6: 476-481.

DALY, P. A. (1976): The Response of Consumers to Nutrition Labeling. *Journal of Consumer Affairs*, 10 (2): 170-191.

DE PELSMACKER, P., DRIESEN, L. and RAYP, G. (2005): Do Consumers Care about Ethics? Willingness to Pay for Fair-Trade Coffee. *The Journal of Consumer Affairs*, 39 (2): 363-385.

EIKENBERRY, A. (2009): The Hidden Cost of Cause Marketing. *Stanford Social Innovation Review*, Summer 2009, 51-55.

ESTELAM, H. (1999): The computational effect of price endings in multi-dimensional price advertising. *Journal of Product and Brand Management*, 8 (3): 244-256.

GIOVANNUCCI, D. and KOEKOEK, F. J. (2003): *The State of Sustainable Coffee: A study of twelve major markets*. International Institute of Sustainable Development, Winnipeg and International Coffee Organization, London. Available online: http://ssrn.com/abstract=996763, [accessed 2008-05-20].

GURIN, M. (1987): Cause-Related Marketing in Question, *Advertising Age*, July 27, 16.

HARRISON, R., NEWHOLM, T. and SHAW, D. (2005): Defining the Ethical Consumer. In: Harrison, R., Newholm, T. and Shaw, D. (Eds.): *The Ethical Consumer*. London: Sage: 1-10.

HAVAS MEDIA (2009): *Sustainable Future 09: German Factsheet*. Available from: http://www.havasmedia.com/staticfiles/Germany%20Factsheet.pdf, [accessed 18.01.2010].

HAJJAT, M. M. (2003): Effect of Cause-Related Marketing on Attitudes and Purchase Intentions: The Moderating Role of Cause Involvement and Donation Size. *Journal of Nonprofit & Public Sector Marketing*, 11 (1): 93-109.

HOLMES, J. H. and KILBANE, C. J. (1993): Cause-related marketing: selected effects of price and charitable donations. *Journal of Nonprofit and Public Sector Marketing*, 1 (4): 67-83.

HUBER, F., REGIER, S. and RININO, M. (2008): *Cause-Related-Marketing-Kampagnen erfolgreich konzipieren*. Wiesbaden: Gabler.

JOINRED (2010): *(Red)® designed to help eliminate aids in Africa*. Available from: http://www.joinred.com/FAQ, [accessed 2010-08-04].

KOTLER, P. AND LEE, N. (2005): *Corporate social responsibility: Doing the most good for your company and your cause*. Hoboken: Wiley.

MASON. T. (2000): Foreword by Tim Mason. In: Adkins, S. (2000) (Ed.): *Cause Related Marketing – Who cares wins*. Oxford: Butterworth-Heinemann: ix-xii.

MENSCHEN FÜR MENSCHEN (2009): Telephone Interview with Anne Dreyer, Head of Press and PR Department: 09.03.2009.

NAYGA, R., LIPINSKI, D. and SAVUR, N. (1998): Consumers' use of nutritional labels while food shopping and at home. *Journal of Consumer Affairs*, 32 (1): 106-120.

NIELSEN (2008): *Corporate Ethics and Fair Trading: A Nielsen Global Consumer Report*. Available from: http://www.nielsen.com/solutions/CSR_Fairtrade_global_report October08.pdf, [accessed 2009-01-02].

OLOKO, S. (2008): *Cause related Marketing - Der Status Quo in Deutschland.* Berlin.

OLOKO, S. (2009): *Cause related Marketing - Ein neues Marketinginstrument im Überblick.* Berlin.

OLSEN, D, PRACEJUS, J. and BROWN, N. (2003): When profit equals price: consumer confusion about donation amounts in Cause-related Marketing. *Journal of Public Policy and Marketing*, 22 (2): 170-180.

ONLINE WERBERECHT (2010): *Cause Related Marketing.* Available from: http://www.online-werberecht.de/causerelatedmarketing.html, [accessed 2010-01-08].

PARTOS, L. (2009): Ethical economic model spells opportunity for food firms. *FoodQualityNews.com*, 19 Nov 2009. Available from: http://www.foodqualitynews.com/Innovation/Ethical-economic-model-spells-opportunity-for-food-firms, [accessed 2009-11-19].

ROY, D. P. and GRAEFF, T. R. (2003): Consumer Attitudes Toward Cause-Related Marketing Activities in Professional Sports. *Sport Marketing*, 12 (3): 163-172.

SCHAPIRA, D. V., KUMAR, N. B., LYMAN, G. H, and MCMILLAN, S. C. (1990): The Value of Current Nutrition Information. *Preventive Medicine*, 19: 45-53.

SINGH, S. (2009): Overcoming scepticism towards cause related claims: the case of Norway. *International Marketing Review*, 26 (3): 312-326.

SMITH, W. and HIGGINS, M. (2000): Cause-related marketing: Ethics and the ecstatic. *Business and Society*, 39 (3): 304-322.

STBA (Statistisches Bundesamt) (2007): *Statistisches Jahrbuch 2007.* Wiesbaden.

STBA (Statistisches Bundesamt) (2008): *Bevölkerung und Erwerbstätigkeit - Haushalte und Familien, Ergebnisse des Mikrozensus 2007.* Fachserie 1, Reihe 3, Wiesbaden.

STOCK, J. H. and WATSON, M. W. (2004): *Introduction to Econometrics.* Boston: Pearson Education.

TALLONTIRE, A., RENTSENDORJ, E. and BLOWFIELD, M. (2001): Ethical Consumers and Ethical Trade: A Review of Current Literature, *Policy Series 12.* Chatham, UK: Natural Resources Institute.

TRANSFAIR (2009): *50 % Plus für Fairtrade.* Available from: http://www.transfair.org/presse/detailseite-presse/browse/4/article/45/50-prozent-p.html, [accessed 2009-04-23].

UNICEF (2010): *Aktionen: IKEA weitet Engagement aus.* Available from: http://www.unicef.de/aktionen.html, [accessed 2010-08-04].

UNITED NATIONS GENERAL ASSEMBLY (1987): Re*port of the World Commission on Environment and Development: Our Common Future*. Transmitted to the General Assembly as an Annex to document A/42/427 - Development and International Co-operation: Environment. Available from: http://www.un-documents.net/ocf-02.htm, [accessed 2010-08-04].

VARADARAJAN, P.R. and MENON, A. (1988): Cause-related Marketing: A Coalignment of Marketing Strategy and Corporate Philanthropy. *Journal of Marketing*, 52: 58-74.

WALL, W. L. (1984): Companies Change the Ways They Make Charitable Donations. *Wall Street Journal*, June 21, 1: 19.

WEBB, D. J. and MOHR, L. A. (1998): A Typology of Consumer Responses to Cause-Related Marketing: From Skeptics to Socially Concerned. *Journal of Public Policy & Marketing*, 17 (2): 226-238.

WEBER, E. U. (2003): *Domain-Specific Risk Taking*. Updated version of Weber, Blais, Betz (2002): Journal of Behavioral Decision Making. Available from: http:// decisionsciences.columbia.edu/uploads/File/Articles/DospertEnglish.doc, [accessed 2010-01-15].

WESTBERG, K. J. (2004): *The Impact of Cause-Related Marketing on Consumer Attitude to the Brand and Purchase Intention: A Comparison with Sponsorship and Sales Promotion. Dissertation*. Griffith University. Available from: http://www4.gu.edu.au:8080/adt-root/uploads/approved/adt-QGU20050211.124210/public/02Whole.pdf, [accessed 2010-01-18].

WYMER, W. and SAMU, S. (2003): *Nonprofit and Business Sector Collaboration: Social Enterprises, Cause-Related Marketing, Sponsorships, and Other Corporate-Nonprofit Dealings*, New York: Haworth Press.

WYMER, W. AND SAMU, S. (2009): The influence of cause marketing associations on product and cause brand value. *International Journal of Nonprofit and Voluntary Sector Marketing*, 14: 1-20.

Appendix E: Variable description[149]

Variable	Variable Description	Obs.	Mean	Std. Dev.
Labelling Index	Sum of the answers to the statement "labelling in percent" and the statement "labelling in absolute figures" on a scale from 1: fully agree to 7: do not agree. Categorical variable = 2 (very strong agreement on labelling in percent and in absolute figures) to 14 (both labelling methods are not of interest for the participant who checked twice seven as their answer)	210	4.41	2.59
Requested efficiency of FT	Statement "Assumed a FT product cost 1 € more than a non FT product: how much of this € should reach the producer so that you have not the impression that money trickles away"	192	74.01	20.90
Effi_FT	Dummy variable = 1 if respondent requests a higher than average efficiency of FT, 0 otherwise	192	0.57	0.50
Requested efficiency of donations	Statement "How much from a donation of 1 € should reach the cause so that you have not the impression that money trickles away"	204	76.06	21.36
Effi_Donation	Dummy variable = 1 if respondent requests a higher than average efficiency of donations, 0 otherwise	204	0.63	0.48
Expected efficiency of CrM	Statement: "What do you think is the share of donation going to the CrM cause relative to the retail price you pay for the CrM product". Categorical variable from 1 (0-2 %) to 9 (>25 %); see also Figure 4	203	3.68	2.30
Requested donation of a 5 € CrM coffee	Statement: "I would support a CrM campaign if from a 5 € coffee at least ... € are spent to the cause".	206	3.00	1.46
Buy CrM	Dummy variable = 1 if respondent purchased CrM products before, 0 otherwise	204	0.22	0.41
Buy FT	Dummy variable = 1 if respondent purchased FT products before, 0 otherwise	207	0.41	0.49
Donor	Dummy variable = 1 if respondent donated to charity in the last 12 month, 0 otherwise	214	0.67	0.47
Paying attention to product information	Dummy variable = 1 if respondent states to pay attention to information provided on a product, 0 otherwise	206	0.72	0.45
Age	Age in years	209	42.71	15.03
Age class	Age in categories. Categorical variable from 1 (<25), 2 (25 to 29) to 11 (>70)	209	5.18	2.90
Children < 18	Number of children under the age of 18	210	0.29	0.70
Children < 12	Number of children under the age of 12	210	0.16	0.49
Low edu	Education: Volks-/ Hauptschulabschluss	209	0.20	0.40
Medium edu	Education: Mittlere Reife	209	0.27	0.44
High edu	Education: university entrance diploma (Abitur)	209	0.29	0.45
University degree	Education: university degree	209	0.23	0.42
Female	Gender (1=female, 0=male)	209	0.54	0.50
Income	Household Net-Income (EUR/month); Categorical variable from 1 (< 1100 EUR) to 6 (>3600 EUR)	214	2.45	1.77
Risk Personality	Risk perception index. Dummy variable = 1 if the respondent is more than average risk averse, 0 otherwise	179	0.56	0.50

[149] For the questionnaire, see Appendix A1 in chapter 5.

D Synthesis: Ethics in Consumer Choice and Empirical Analysis based on the Example of Coffee

This chapter provides a synthesis of part B and part C of the dissertation. It brings together the findings of the more theoretical analysis of ethical behaviour with the empirical findings from face-to-face interviews and experiments with consumers in Germany. In a short summary the major issues of this thesis, such as the question as to whether consumers distinguish between different forms of ethical behaviour, are brought together with the findings of chapter 4 and conclusions and implications are drawn accordingly. Limitations of the thesis are discussed and suggestions are made for researchers as well as consumer policy, business and NGOs concerned about the ethics of consumer choices.

10 Summary, conclusions and implications

This dissertation deals with ethics in consumer choice. It contributes to and deepens the general understanding of consumers' attitudes towards and perception of different forms of ethical behaviour. The considered forms of individuals' choice for and within ethical behaviour are the consumption of ethical products and charitable giving. As explained in chapter 4.1.1, up to five forms of ethical consumption can be distinguished. In the context of this research ethical consumption is operationalised as positive ethical purchase behaviour especially regarding Fair Trade, organic and CrM products. The central research question addressed is "Do consumers differentiate between different types of ethical behaviour?". For this purpose the thesis has been divided into four parts: The first part A introduces the topic, disucsses the relevance as well as the research questions and the approaches chosen to address the questions appropriately. By means of an overview of models explaining and illustrating consumers decision making with particular emphasis on preferences and approaches of preference measurement as well as a literature review on selected forms of ethical behaviour Part B deals with ethics and consumer choice. Part B provides background information on the issues and topics which are under consideration in the three experimental studies conducted using the example of coffee choice in Germany in 2008 and 2009 and described in five papers in the third part C. The fourth section D merges part B and part C, draws conclusions and recommandations for those concerned with the ethics of consumers' choice.

The conclusions drawn can be distinguished between those providing insights into consumers' preferences for the assessed forms of ethical behaviour and which are accordingly directly related to the central research question and those giving insights into more theoretical and methodological issues such as the comparison of stated and revealed preferences and the consideration of socially desirable answers.

This research is, to the authors' knowledge, the first to assess, analyse and compare consumers' preferences for different kinds of ethical consumption and/or behaviour. In particular, the comparison of consumers' appraisal of the complementarity and substitutionality of Fair Trade and charitable giving is unique. Detailed insight into the valuation of different kinds of ethical labelling (Fair Trade, organic, CrM) is also provided for the first time. It is furthermore the first research that investigates consumers' preferences for transparent labelling of donation amounts as well as for different types of transparency labelling (whether survey participants want products to carry a label indicating the amount of money being spent on the CrM cause in percent and/or as an absolute value) in the context of ethical products. In addition, this research is one of the few that reveal German consumers' attitudes towards CrM promoted products. Critical success factors for CrM can be accordingly identified. One specific characteristic of this dissertation is the use of different methods (CE, IDM, logit models, contingent valuation) as well as a combination of methods (latent class analysis of the choice experimental data) to overcome the shortcomings of the applied techniques due to the respective underlying assumptions. In this way, the unavoidable (because the product attributes tested are not on the market yet) hypothetical bias of the single surveys can be minimised to a certain extent. In particular, the effect of social desirability can be identified by the comparison of revealed and stated preferences in paper 1 (chapter 5) as well as the comparison of the results of the single papers presented in chapters 5 to 9.

To sum up, the thesis provides a first glance at the complex decision making process regarding the purchase of ethical products by investigating important influencing factors. Based on the models of consumer choice described in chapter 2 the experimental studies and the questionnaires were designed. It succeeded to indentify individual characteristics in the empirical studies such as a generally altruistic character, positive attitudes towards organic production, Fair Trade and monetary donations to charity organisations, perceptions of the relationship between Fair Trade and donations, and of the green-washing character of CrM, as significant influences on consumers' choices for ethical products and charitable giving.

The most important findings arising from parts B and C are mentioned in the following section.

Consumers distinguish between different forms of ethical behaviour

Differences between ethical consumption and charitable giving as well as between the various forms of ethical consumption, in particular the question as to whether Fair Trade and sustainable consumption are to a certain extent identical or not, were discussed in chapter 4. Furthermore, the differences between Fair Trade and charitable giving have been evaluated with respect to the consequences for the recipients of the support; in particular, the economics of the systems were analysed. Market shares of ethical products are small but increasing whereas monetary donations are stagnating in Germany. Therefore, three surveys were conducted to assess whether consumers distinguish between the different forms of ethical behaviour. No previous study is available that focusses on this question.

The studies reported in part C of this thesis show that most consumers clearly distinguish between the regarded possibilities of ethical behaviour. In addition, consumers have clear and strong preferences for the different kinds of ethical product labels. This means, on the one hand, consumers value ethical product characteristics. On the other hand, consumers differentiate between different kinds of credence attributes and the respective labels communicating these. In contrast to the feeling described in chapter 4.1.4 that ethical, sustainable and Fair Trade consumption are merging, the conducted consumer surveys reveal that most of the interviewed consumers do not in general relate sustainability issues connected with organic production to aspects linked to Fair Trade certification, i.e. working conditions or fair wages which allow people to make a living over a longer period of time. In particular, paper 2 (chapter 6) reveals that consumers have diverse preferences and distinguish between the labels indicating different forms of ethical engagement and perceive Fair Trade, organic, and donations not to be the same. However, as paper 4 (chapter 8) shows, while consumers are convinced that CrM is not a substitute of Fair Trade and donations in general, they significantly more agree that the purchase of a CrM product is able to replace a donation to the NGO engaged in the CrM promotion. This finding is of particular interest to NGOs involved in CrM campaigns. The results also indicate that those consumers who are inclined to buy Fair Trade products are the same that are also in favour of organic products and vice versa. However, respondents with a preference for Fair Trade or organic production do not choose CrM promoted products. Those 27 % of consumers with a preference for CrM products have an aversion to Fair Trade and organic but give regular donations to charitable organisations. Furthermore, those consumers with positive attitudes towards Fair Trade and donations clearly differentiate between these two concepts. These findings indicate that cannibalism between CrM and Fair Trade/organic products is not very likely. However, as a fraction of the respondents regards Fair Trade to be comparable to charitable giving, it is possible that those consumers substitute Fair Trade products by donations to charity or the purchase of CrM products as the results of the choice model (see paper 2) for those respondents indicate. Therefore it seems more likely to assume that those consumers partly substitute traditional donations to charitable organisations by buying CrM promoted products. This assumption has been confirmed by the consumer opinion detected in paper 4, presented in chapter 8, that the purchase of a CrM product is able to replace a donation to the NGO engaged in the CrM promotion. Moreover, the group identified in chapter 6 that does not differentiate between Fair Trade and donations consists of elderly people; interestingly, elderly and less educated people are less sceptical with regard to CrM than younger people and those with a fairly high level of education, as the study described in chapter 8 reveals. Therefore, it can be concluded that the consumption of Fair Trade as well organic goods is seen as complementary to donating money to charity purposes in general as well as in form of CrM campaigns by more than 70 % of the respondents. Those who do not see a difference do not choose Fair Trade and organic products, hence, it can be concluded that consumers are not substituting Fair Trade by CrM and vice versa. However, it seems to be that CrM cannibalises traditional donations to the NGO engaged in CrM promotions.

To sum up, this thesis succeeded in elaborate the similarities as well as the differences between the regarded forms of ethical behaviour and in identifying and distinguishing groups of consumers that, on the one hand, purchase ethical products and, on the other hand, give to charitable organisations. Furthermore, the results indicate that there are groups of consumers that regard the purchase of CrM products as substitute to monetary donations.

Socially desirable answers occur

In chapter 4 it was highlighted that, due to respondents' tendency to give socially desirable answers, there is a considerable gap between market shares for ethical products and the results of stated preference studies. In addition, studies showed that Fair Trade and organic labels increase the attractiveness of a product but not automatically its purchase probability. In particular, price mark-ups were identified as a barrier. The IDM experiment, reported in the first paper of part C was intended to identify and minimise socially desirable answers, which are, as described in chapter 4.1.1.2, expected with respect to stated preferences for ethical product attributes in particular and ethical behaviour in general. The first striking outcome of the IDM experiment is that consumers' stated preferences are on the one hand reflected in consumers' search process, but on the other hand the validity of stated and revealed preferences deviates considerably. In all three conducted surveys consumers state that ethical product features, operationalised through the questions as to whether they prefer and place emphasis on organic products, production without child labour, fair prices for producers, etc.are of great importance for their purchase decision. However, in the IDM task social and ecological aspects were considered only by a small share of consumers during the information search process. This reveals that for most German consumers Fair Trade and other ethical product features are in reality of minor importance compared to other product attributes such as price, brand and taste. These findings help to explain the small market share of ethical products in Germany. Furthermore, these findings signify that the IDM is able to minimise social desirability effects, a problem that is of relevance in surveys on ethical product characteristics. In addition, they are in line with CARRIGAN and ATTALA (2001) as well as WEATHERELL et al. (2003), who assume that market shares of Fair Trade and organic products are small because price, quality, convenience and brand familiarity are the most important purchase criteria while ethical factors are only relevant and considered by a minority of consumers characterised by a specific profile. The CE study described in chapter 6 of this thesis also confirmed that interested consumers are characterised by a particular preference structure. Accordingly, it can be concluded that ethics comes in consumers' choice decision if it does not imply a compromise between ethical product features and other important purchase criteria such as taste, price and convenience.

The applied methods are appropriate

Chapter 2 and 3 in part B of the dissertation describe the foundations, assumptions, advantages and limitations of the concepts of consumers' decision making and preference measurement. The sub-chapter on consumers' decision making strategies provides information about consumers' search strategie that are distinguishable by e.g. the degree to which a strategy is compensatory (see chapter 2.3). One important issue highlighted in chapter 2 were the assumptions of compensatory decision making underlying CE. In the second paper (chapter 6) a CE was applied to investigate consumers' preferences for the above-mentioned possibilities of ethical behaviour in detail. Consumers were asked to choose a pack of coffee for their daily use at home. In the CE only four coffee attributes were tested whereas in the IDM experiment eight different coffee attributes were presented. As the IDM experiment described in chapter 5 revealed that consumers' search strategy has no significant influence on the estimated models for the first attribute click, it can be assumed that the type of consumers' search strategy for a choice task, which is as simple as the one described in the survey presented in chapter 6, does not significantly influence the results. Furthermore, according to BETTMAN et al. (1998), less complex decision making strategies are applied in simple choice sets. Therefore, it can be assumed that rational choice theory, the assumption of utility maximisation and compensatory decision making, which are underlying the CE, are in this context appropriate to model consumers' decision making. The analysis of the CE data furthermore employs a latent class approach to characterise heterogeneity in valuations for Fair Trade, organic and charitable giving also in form of CrM. Empirical results show that German coffee consumers can be separated into five classes with statistically well-defined preferences. While variables such as product price and attitudes towards Fair Trade, organic production and donations to charity organisations determine class membership, socio-demographic characteristics with the exception of age proved not to be relevant. WTP for the attributes organic, Fair Trade and donations via CrM differ significantly between the groups as well as between the labelling schemes.

Information influences consumers

The survey reported in chapter 5 tested the influence of additional background information about Fair Trade and charitable organisation. This was provided just before respondents conducted the experiment a second time. As the relevance of Fair Trade and CrM changed significantly in the second IDM round, it becomes apparent that consumers' interest for product attributes can be influenced by the provision of additional information right prior to consumers' product choice. This indicates that even though consumers are familiar with the product as such (here coffee) consumers' preferences are not stable but context and information dependant. This relates to the discussion of the nature of consumers' preferences in chapter 2.2.

Another important result of the IDM experiment is that consumers consider only part of the available package information. A brand's leeway to communicate ethical product features is accordingly limited, a finding relevant for policy makers as well as marketers.

Nevertheless, as the papers in chapter 6 and 9 reveal, consumers want to be informed about the amount of the donation reaching the cause promoted on ethical products.

Critical factors for success regarding CrM are identified

As CrM in study 2 (chapter 6) was positively assessed only by a small group of consumers, paper 3 concentrated on potential success factors for and of CrM. In this study participants were asked under which circumstances they are willing to switch from their favoured brand to a brand advertising a CrM product. By means of multivariate statistics it was possible to identify groups of consumers having positive attitudes towards CrM and willing to switch to a CrM brand. Especially cause-brand fit and product fit are important for consumers' evaluation of CrM promotions. Consumers' scepticism is a further critical success factor especially of CrM in Germany identified in each of the papers in chapter 7, 8, and 9. Accordingly, CrM campaigns can only be successful if consumers' scepticism regarding the underlying motives of the companies for launching CrM products is addressed appropriately.

The in chapter 8 presented paper 4 concentrates on the reproach of green-washing which is discussed in connection with CrM but not in conjunction with Fair Trade. This study reveals that only few consumers suspect CrM to be a means designed to improve companies' image. These consumers are highly educated, young and live in urban areas. Most of the respondents regard CrM as an opportunity to do something good in a quick and easy way. This paper also reveals that respondents differentiate between CrM, monetary donations to charity organisations in general and the purchase of Fair Trade products. But, for the NGO engaged in a CrM campaign, the commitment might lead to a decrease in general monetary contributions as people consider a donation going to a particular NGO via a CrM promotion as a substitute to general monetary contributions to this NGO.

Efficiency and transparent labelling is important

As demonstrated in the introduction, organic, Fair Trade and CrM products are to some extent similar but might vary in the level of spending efficiency, i.e. what percentage of one euro that is paid additionally for organic, Fair Trade or CrM products actually reaches the cause it was meant to support. As shown in chapter 4.2.4, there are some studies posing the question as to who benefits from higher retail prices of Fair Trade products: the producer or the retailer. To answer this question for Germany, a market analysis was conducted and the percentage of the retail price reaching the producer as well as the percentage of the price premium paid by the consumer for Fair Trade coffee was calculated. However, for consumers, a comparison of the level of efficiency of the different forms of ethical behaviour is only possible if the respective organisations and firms communicate this issue in a transparent manner. The transparency issue with respect to Fair Trade, charitable giving and CrM is also a crucial topic of this thesis. The role of standards and labelling, especially with regard to credence attributes, was explained in chapter 4.2.3. Accordingly, survey participants were asked how much of one euro paid additionally for Fair Trade products or given to a charity organisation should reach the marginalised people. These requested efficiencies of Fair Trade and donations were integrated as independent variables in the analysis conducted in the papers presented in chapter 6 and 9. A striking result of the choice experiment as well as the study reported in chapter 9 is that consumers place emphasis on the amount of money reaching the good cause promoted on CrM products or the Fair Trade producer and wish to be informed about it. Remarkably, here again stated and revealed preferences diverge. When directly asked whether the information on the amount of money reaching the producer, which can be considered as a proxy for the efficiency of the system supported through the purchase of a Fair Trade or a CrM product, is important for consumers, results show that this is only relevant for a small part of all consumers (see also the class 4 of Fair Trade supporters described in the paper presented in chapter 6). But the CE reveals that if consumers have the possibility to evaluate supporting systems with respect to their efficiency, they do so. This has implications both for Fair Trade organisations and Fair Trade brands as well as for companies and NGOs launching CrM campaigns. Furthermore, consumers can be differentiated with regard to their WTP for different donation amounts. As chapter 6 and 9 also show, there are certain minimum levels of donation amounts consumers require. If these are not assured, consumers' WTP is below the donation amount indicated on the product (see the 0.2 € going directly to the producer in chapter 6). In this case, the transparent labelling would decrease consumers' WTP for ethical products. If the level of donation is considered appropriate, consumers' WTP even exceeds the indicated donation amount (see classes 2 and 3 WTP for an amount of 0.5 € and 1 € to coffee producers in chapter 6).

A further important result of the paper presented in chapter 9 is that consumers' expecations regarding the efficiency of CrM promotions differ from consumers' requested efficiency. This gap between the share of money consumers want to reach the cause and the share of money they believe actually reaches the cause might be, in addition to the lack of information regarding the spending efficiency, an important obstacle for the success of CrM products, which only a small share of survey participants had experiences with.

The survey presented in chapter 9 demonstrated that consumers advocate the transparent labelling of the donation amount that reaches the indicated cause (in the case of CrM) and, in the case of Fair Trade products, the higher wages of farmers achieved by the participation in the Fair Trade network. Results indicate that the majority of consumers are interested in obtaining information on the donation amount provided by the firm to the NGO or the cause. Whether the information is provided in percent or in absolute figures, is not relevant for consumers. It is only important that the information is given at all. This shows that chapter 9 also discusses a solution to overcome the purchase barriers with respect to CrM products. However, the results raise the question as to whether transparent communication with regard to CrM efficiency can be recommended to firms and brands as long as consumers have unrealistic assumptions of possible levels of spendings efficiency, the brands share of profits compared to the retail price, etc.

10.1 Limitations

There are three major limitations to this study which are common to most empirical research. First, there is the question of sample representation. Can accurate conclusions be drawn from studies where the education level of the participants compared to the German population as a whole is rather high? This might to a certain extent reduce the transferability of the findings to the mass market. At the same time, it could be that especially the CE task benefited from the cognitive capability of respondents and that the results mirror very well at least the preferences of people with a fairly high level of education.

Secondly, in all five studies the research object was coffee and in particular respondents were asked to make their decisions and evaluations with respect to a coffee for their daily use at home. On the one hand, this reduces the potential of transferring the findings to other products. On the other hand, as coffee is the most important German beverage and only coffee drinkers qualified for the surveys, it can be assumed that results benefit from a very high involvement of consumers. In addition, there is a wide variety of coffee specialities available on the German coffee market. They differ with respect to the production and trade process, such as organic, conventional, and Fair Trade, and with regard to health issues such as decaffeinated. Furthermore, a variety of tastes such as mild and strong as well as different countries of origin and coffee species such as 100 % Arabica or Robusta or blends are sold in the market under different brands and pricing schemes. And last but not least because of the diversity especially in the out-of-home consumption/coffee-to-go market where consumers can e.g. add a wide variety of flavours to their coffee, it can be assumed that consumers are accustomed to innovations and new product characteristics regarding coffee. Therefore, it can be assumed that consumers quite easily accept new variants of coffee as they were tested in the two experiments (see papers 5 and 6). From this point of view, adding the characteristics 'Helping people to help themselves' in the IDM experiment as well as the 'Donation' amount in the CE will not influence the search process and the choice of consumers towards misleading results.

Thirdly, the incentive compatibility of the CE, here the hypothetical nature, and the IDM, here that the costs for search duration are not considered, can be questioned. To minimise these limitations in the case of the CE the interviewer were instructed to clearly explain to the respondents that they are asked to only choose a product of the choice set that fits their demands and to choose the opt-out option when no such product was available in the choice set. In the case of the IDM, respondents were asked by the interviewees to look at a maximum of 11 out of 24 possible product attributes and, if possible, even fewer than 11, which most of the sample did. These are both instruments to make the experiments as incentive compatible as possible so that respondents disclose their true preferences. Both experiments could not be constructed as real-world experiments because a product consisting of those attributes for which preferences were assessed in this thesis is not available in the retail so far. Therefore, neither the CE nor the IDM could be conducted as non-hypothetical CE or non-hypothetical IDM and, accordingly, there was no possibility to force consumers to reveal their true preferences by telling them that at the end of the study they would have to purchase the chosen products. This procedure, to force respondents to pay for the product they choose in a choice set, is also hardly – if at all – realisable in a consumer survey where consumers are not recruited in advance and interviewed in a special room at an appointed day but are just interviewed spontaneously on the street and at the place where they do their shopping. The question arising in this context is whether a sample recruited for an in-house experiment is comparable to a sample recruited on the streets and in the store, and which bias is the preferred one. The triangulation of methods used in this thesis helps to overcome the limitations of the single surveys and, to a certain extent, the hypothetical bias, hence, the described possible objections and limitations can be regarded as largely mitigated.

10.2 Outlook and implications

Suggestions for future research and theoretical contribution

The results of this thesis reveal very well that triangulation, here in the way of combining different methods is appropriate for assessing consumers' preferences and providing a picture which is very close to reality. Especially with regard to ethical products, the combination of different methods to reveal preferences and the comparison with consumers' stated preferences has proved to be suitable.

RYAN et al. (2008) come to the conclusion that consumers' information search process should be taken into account when designing CE. Based on the findings of papers 1 and 2, presented in chapter 5 and 6 respectively, it seems likely that the combination of the IDM in a first stage and the CE in a second stage would enhance the results of the choice analysis. The IDM can be used to assess how much and which type of information consumers assess before they make a decision. This knowledge can be then used in the design stage of the CE so that for each respondent choice sets are created that fit their information search revealed in the IDM task. In addition, the appropriateness of CE for the assessment of consumer preferences can be tested in more detail if the search strategy of participants in the relevant choice context is revealed by the IDM and not just assumed to meet the assumptions of compensatory decision making.

The application of non-hypothetical incentive-compatible methods would be prefereable if combinations of product attributes are tested that are available in the market at the time of the study. Otherwise the methods chosen in this thesis, the combination of hypothetical CE and the application of IDM, seem to be suitable. The combination of CE and latent class analysis is also adequate to analyse consumers' heterogeneous preferences. Even though preferences can be assumed to vary from individual to individual, results derived by the assessment of individual preferences, e.g. through conjoint analysis, would not be useful for marketing purposes and market segmentation and therefore not transferable to actual market action. The assumption that groups of consumers with homogenous preferences can be distinguished and that this assumption is appropriate for marketing and other applied purposes, e.g. in the context of product design, is self-evident because market segmentation is successfully applied not only in the retail sector. The identification of well distinguishable market segments via latent class discrete choice analysis makes the results of the study not only informative for researchers and interested people but especially relevant for decision makers in governmental agencies as well as marketing departments of NGOs and companies.

Suggestions for consumer policy, business and NGOs

The findings of the thesis provide public policy and marketing recommendations for stimulating ethical food consumption. It has been shown that for a successful positioning of ethical products in the market it is necessary to identify the existing divergent consumer preferences, segment consumers accordingly and offer segment specific, customised products. This finding is in line with FRANKE et al. (2009, p. 116) who found that "products customized on the basis of measured customer preferences deliver clear benefits to the customer". The research shows that demographic characteristics are good proxies for some attitudes, such as the assessment as to whether CrM is a form of company green-washing (see chapter 8) but are on the other hand poor proxies of preferences for ethical behaviour in a broader sense (see chapter 6).

A very prominent result of the IDM survey presented in chapter 5 is that consumers consider only part of the available product information and that their search process prior to making a choice for a product is very much influenced by the product price, taste and brand. This leads to the conclusion, as stated by ROOSEN et al. (2007, p. 767f.), that strong preferences for certain product attributes might not directly result in a purchase. But as a high WTP for a product attribute serves as an indicator that the preference is also transferred to a purchase of products holding the respective attributes (DE PELSMACKER et al. 2005, p. 368), the following conclusions that can be drawn from the findings in chapters 5 and 6: Only if consumers' requirements regarding a product's pricing, taste and brand (which were faded out in the CE) are fulfilled, consumers will also base their choice on the ethical attributes related to the product. As shown by the CE in chapter 6, consumers' pronounced preferences differ so that market segmentation is feasible and would increase both the sales of ethical products as well as the retailers' and brands' scope for price setting. The size of the five consumer groups distinguished in chapter 6 can therefore be assumed to resemble market shares if all of consumers' favoured brands would offer the tested different types of ethical product characteristics at different price levels.

If governments, NGOs or firms want to create an increased awareness for ethical aspects related to the production and trading of goods, irrespective of the reasons, they could use these results as a starting point. As mentioned in the chapter on ethical consumption, THØGERSEN (2005) discusses how consumer policy and business may empower consumers for sustainable lifestyles. The empowerment should help to overcome individuals' personal limitations in time, financial resources, cognitive capacity and knowledge. Hence, the reduction of the German value added tax proposed in chapter 6 could be one possibility to make Fair Trade products cheaper. This would enable a larger consumer group to purchase Fair Trade products as the market segmentation in chapter 6 shows. Transparent labelling of donation volumes with regard to CrM products as described in chapter 9 would give businesses/companies the opportunity to reduce consumers' doubts, increase their trust in ethical products and make them more informed. It can be assumed that not only CrM campaigns would benefit from this and that enlarged market shares might be an outcome. Consumers' relative WTP measures for an indicated amount of donation calculated in chapter 6 can be used for policy makers, marketing experts and NGOs as it represents consumers' preference for the systems' efficiency.

To conclude, the synthesis of the theoretical and the empirical analysis of this study of the ethics in consumer choice, the empirical part of which was conducted based on the example of consumers' coffee choice, it can be maintained that valuable insights into consumers' preferences for different kinds of ethical behaviour were given. Motives, attitudes and other consumer preferences influencing factors were elaborated in the first part of the dissertation and tested in the empirical studies. The triangulation of methods applied in the empirical studies enabled the author to arrive at answers to the research questions regarding preferences for the different forms of ethical behaviour, consumers' transparency needs as well as critical factors constraining ethical behaviour. A very prominent result of the empirical studies is that consumers have strong preferences for different types of ethical behaviour and can be distinguished accordingly. These findings provide a basis for the actors involved in the promotion of ethical behaviour and enables researchers to further investigate aspects of the ethics of consumer choice.

10.3 References

BETTMAN, J. R., LUCE, M. F. and PAYNE, J. W. (1998): Constructive Consumer Choice Processes. *The Journal of Consumer Research*, 25 (3): 187-217.

CARRIGAN, M. and ATTALLA, A. (2001): The myth of the ethical consumer – Do ethics matter in purchase behaviour? *Journal of Consumer Marketing*, 18 (7): 560-576.

DE PELSMACKER, P., DRIESEN, L. and RAYP, G. (2005): Do consumers care about ethics? Willingness to pay for Fair-Trade Coffee. *The Journal of Consumer Affairs*, 39 (2): 363-385.

FRANKE, N., KEINZ, P. and STEGER, C. J. (2009): Testing the Value of Customization: When Do Customers Really Prefer Products Tailored to Their Preferences? *Journal of Marketing*, 73: 103-121.

ROOSEN, J., MARETTE, S., BLANCHEMANCHE, S. and VERGER, P. (2007): The effect of product health information on liking and choice. *Food Quality and Preference*, 18 (5): 759-770.

RYAN, M., GERARD, K. and AMAYA-AMAYA, M. (2008): *Using Discrete Choice Experiments to Value Health and Health Care*. Dordrecht: Springer.

THØGERSEN, J. (2005): How may consumer policy empower consumers for sustainable lifestyles? *Journal of Consumer Policy*, 28 (2): 143-177.

WEATHERELL, C., TREGEAR, A. and ALLISON, J. (2003): In search of the concerned consumer: UK public perceptions of food, farming and buying local. *Journal of Rural Studies*, 19 (2): 233-244.

MIX
Papier aus verantwortungsvollen Quellen
Paper from responsible sources
FSC® C105338

If you have any concerns about our products,
you can contact us on
ProductSafety@springernature.com

In case Publisher is established outside the EU,
the EU authorized representative is:
Springer Nature Customer Service Center GmbH
Europaplatz 3, 69115 Heidelberg, Germany

Printed by Libri Plureos GmbH
in Hamburg, Germany